BRIAN COWEN

IN HIS OWN WORDS

BRIAN COWEN

IN HIS OWN WORDS

JOHNNY FALLON

MERCIER PRESS
Irish Publisher – Irish Story

MERCIER PRESS
Cork
www.mercierpress.ie

Trade enquiries to CMD,
55a Spruce Avenue, Stillorgan Industrial Park,
Blackrock, County Dublin

© Johnny Fallon, 2009

ISBN: 978 1 85635 647 3

A CIP record for this title is available from the British Library

10 9 8 7 6 5 4 3 2 1

TO OUR SON MICHAEL
Fortiter et Fideliter

Printed and bound in the EU.

CONTENTS

FOREWORD

The expression on his face.

The way he stands.

The colour of his tie.

The files he holds.

The documents he reads.

Who is sitting beside him and why?

More importantly, who isn't sitting beside him and why?

What is being whispered to him?

Before he even utters a word, each aspect of Brian Cowen's demeanour is parsed whenever he takes his place, the taoiseach's seat, in Dáil Éireann.

The enigma that is Brian Cowen takes to his feet two days a week with the eyes of the country upon him. Frequently casting an uncomfortable figure, Mr Cowen is struggling in what he himself describes as 'a defining moment in our nation's history' to communicate effectively with the people he leads. At times, he appears incapable of breaking free from the shackles of civil service jargon. The uncertainty over whether or not he would give a clearly defined State of the Nation address to set out the country's economic position betrays a lack of confidence in his ability to connect. The paradox of what he actually produces now and what he is known to be capable of is apparent from some of his speeches in this book.

His predecessor, Bertie Ahern, used statistics to great effect as he endeavoured to kill off debate and stifle his opponents. But Mr Ahern was more noted for his mangling of ordinary language than any great oratory. His was a different type of leadership and speaking style.

Brian Cowen places a greater emphasis on the primacy of the national parliament and its elected representatives. Yet he too has gone down the same road as his predecessor, who put the social partners and the so-called 'doorstep' interview ahead of responding to probing questions in the Chamber. When Mr Cowen delivered a crucial speech in February 2009 outlining the government's plans to save €2 billion for the exchequer, including a public sector pension levy, the verdict was negative. The delivery was dull, and he barely lifted his head through an uninspiring ten minute statement. The reason behind the low key performance was an apparent desire to save his best product for a live slot on the RTÉ Six One News.

Later that same week, he cast the script aside to deliver probably his most passionate display to date as taoiseach at the now celebrated Dublin Chamber of Commerce annual dinner. The question then arose: why can't he do it before a larger audience and the nation at large?

When taking over as taoiseach, Cowen started out as it was presumed he intended to continue. In a series of thoughtful and emotional speeches, from his election as President of Fianna Fáil in the Royal College of Physicians of Ireland, to the back of a lorry in Clara, County Offaly, Mr Cowen invoked the memory of Seán Lemass to invoke a rallying call for national spirit. However, the honeymoon was soon over, with an ill-fated Lisbon Treaty campaign and the rhetoric dried up as the economic downturn took hold.

Fianna Fáil's Ard Fheiseanna, with a partisan audience present, are regarded as his favourite forum and the general election campaign trail his chosen battleground.

Despite having twenty-four years of experience under his belt, he has made few memorable speeches in the Dáil since taking over, leading to questions over whether he is up to the job and doubts about his consistency.

Johnny Fallon does not claim to be a dispassionate observer. Similar to Mr Cowen, Fianna Fáil blood courses through his veins. His first book, *Party Time*, is a candid and often amusing account of growing up in a Fianna Fáil family in Longford, aspects of which resonated with people from a political background, regardless of their own persuasion.

In His Own Words does not claim to be a critical appraisal of Brian Cowen's career in Leinster House. That's not to say it doesn't generate food for thought on the taoiseach's record. Moreover, the book is a worthwhile anthology of Brian Cowen's speeches in the Oireachtas, providing a valuable resource to anybody interested in learning about how the taoiseach's views were shaped. The author's opinion on Mr Cowen is not hidden, but he does not seek to make a definitive judgement. Painstakingly put together, the book allows the reader ample scope to draw their own conclusions. Some historians believe it is too early to assess a figure's contribution until they are gone from the scene for at least 100 years. Brian Cowen is still in the early days of his Premiership (although given current trends, the opposite might also be said) so it will be some time before his legacy can be truly evaluated.

Certain themes emerge quite strongly from this book, none more so than animosity towards Fine Gael which pops up again and again. The very first spat on record is traced by the author to 23 January 1985, with then junior minister Seán Barrett dismissing the still newly-elected TD with the remark: 'Give that young fellow five minutes and let him talk …' The young Brian Cowen takes umbrage: 'I will not be patronised by him or anyone else.'

Almost a quarter of a century on and the battle still rages, with shots being fired across the House on a daily basis. Fine Gael's latest tactic is to turn Mr Cowen's disdain for them to their advantage by deliberately waving the red rag in anticipation of him charging. Notably, what the author says was 'arguably one of Cowen's finest and most well-structured arguments', occurred when the taoiseach was on the opposition benches facing Fine Gael's Michael Noonan as an under fire Minister for Health in the wake of Brigid McCole controversy.

Loyalty to Fianna Fáil and its leadership is also, unsurprisingly, heavily evidenced, such as his visceral attack on Des O'Malley during the fall of the Fianna Fáil/Progressive Democrats government in 1992. 'When this election is over I hope we will get rid of moral indignation in politics, the attempt to put oneself above the rest. I will not concede my integrity to Deputy O'Malley or anybody else,' the then Minister for Labour opined.

From these exchanges, it is clear that Mr Cowen excels in attack, but now his record in defence is under scrutiny. Throughout his ministerial career, it is enlightening to see how Mr Cowen handles issues, from the threat to Aer Lingus as minister for transport, energy and communication to the tricky diplomacy of the stance on the war in Iraq as minister for foreign affairs. In the current climate, his record on the economy and the public finances will be of most interest. It is truly ironic to see Mr Cowen criticise the Rainbow government as he stated that the coalition's 'public expenditure increases are too high'. Once in government and later as minister for finance, Mr Cowen clearly forgot his own words of warning as Fine Gael's Richard Bruton consistently called for an emphasis on value for money and competitiveness, along with cautions about the benchmarking process.

But Mr Cowen's ongoing commitment to social partnership is also established from an early stage. And his time in charge of the public purse is also marked by measures to 'ensure that all those on the minimum wage are fully outside the tax net' and significant increases in social welfare payments and pensions in particular. The obsession with the property market and Mr Cowen's taxation policies in this area do not go unmentioned. The lack of action to prepare for a rainy day – as far back as March 2006 – is also noted by the author: 'Cowen could be criticised for not being alert to the fact that international factors were changing.'

At the time of writing, the enormous and intertwined challenges facing Brian Cowen include navigating the country through the worst economic crisis in living memory, securing a Yes vote for the Lisbon Treaty and maintaining a united party in the face of an angry public waiting at the ballot box. *In His Own Words* is a timely resource providing an insight into the character formation and policy perspective of the man who now leads the country through these troubled times.

Perhaps it would be no harm if the taoiseach himself read the book to remind him of his obvious, yet now rarely seen, oratorical capabilities.

Fionnán Sheahan
March 2009

INTRODUCTION

In *De Oratore* Cicero quoted Lucius Licinus Crassus as saying that 'oratory is the greatest achievement of a nation', and his assertion is certainly a reasonable one. For instance we know more about that period of Roman history than any other, mainly because of the writings of Cicero himself. Therefore, long after many of the other Roman achievements lay in ruins, the records of what they said still live on.

In modern Ireland the record of our state, our government and in some ways the views and opinions of our society, are reflected in most depth through the Dáil record. Politics is full of opinion. In fact it is entirely based upon opinion. Getting a fair picture is often clouded by personal beliefs, arguments, agendas and plain personality. Therefore I have decided not to try to assess Brian Cowen in terms of the media, or comments of friends or detractors. Instead this book represents the archaeology of a piece of Irish political history. By being based upon the Dáil record it gives an assessment of what Cowen's views are, an insight into how he sees himself and perhaps, most importantly, how he relates to his colleagues in the Dáil and how they, his peers, rate him.

Obviously, the full Dáil record runs to many volumes, but here I have tried to take the most relevant points and assess them. It is always difficult to decide what to keep and what to leave out, but I believe this book represents a fair reflection of Cowen's views. It is even more difficult to decide how much of the contributions made by his opponents should be included, but I think what is here will give a fair idea of the flavour of criticism he faced. Obviously the subject matter is Brian Cowen himself; however, I would encourage readers to read more of the Dáil record to inform themselves further if they are interested. So much debate takes place that is never covered or mentioned by the media and yet in an age when we often complain about lack of information on issues, the Dáil record is more accessible than ever and can provide more information than will possibly ever be needed.

On 7 May 2008, Dáil Éireann elected Brian Cowen as taoiseach. He had served twenty-four years as a public representative, having been elected in 1984 via a by-election caused by the death of his father. He was the unanimous choice as leader of Fianna Fáil following the departure of Bertie Ahern. Yet despite being an experienced minister and under much public scrutiny, not much is known about the ideals, aims or vision of Brian Cowen. Without doubt, in his role as taoiseach he will impact, in some way, upon the lives of every person in the state, so what is the record that has brought him to this point? And more importantly what does it signal for the future?

This book gives an insight into the strengths, weaknesses and indeed wit of Brian Cowen. It covers his major positions on public policy and illustrates how this has changed and grown over the years. But in the Dáil record we can see how opponents have tangled and locked horns with Cowen on various subjects.

In the modern age we are often sidetracked by small issues. There is a desire to know more about people and their lives as evidenced by the sheer volume of celebrity-related and gossip magazines. Politicians are, however, different creatures. Their private lives, experiences and hobbies do not tell us much about the policies they will implement or the way they will act in public. The reason for this is very simple. What is crucial to understanding a politician is to try and understand how they see themselves. The public image is carefully crafted, structured and presented. This is not to say it is artificial, but the politician who acts as a legislator may often be quite different from the man or woman we know as an individual.

As Brian Cowen forges a path as taoiseach it is an opportune time to assess his record up to this point and in doing so to try and evaluate what can be expected from 'Cowen's Ireland'.

THE EARLY YEARS

On 14 June 1984 the people of Laois-Offaly constituency went to the polls in a by-election caused by the death of Fianna Fáil TD, Ber Cowen. His son Brian contested the election at the age of twenty-four, younger than any TD then sitting in the Dáil chamber. The result was unequivocal. Brian Cowen attained nearly 55 per cent of the first preference vote, with a total of 26,022 votes. He was elected on the first count and his long political career had begun.

There is no doubt but that Brian Cowen owes much to his strong support base in Laois-Offaly. His ability to draw a vote and to ensure that it transfers to others on the party ticket has made the constituency the political envy of many other regions. However, politics is not all glamour and accolades. For the most part it involves long hours of thankless work to establish a base. The first mention of Brian Cowen in the Dáil records comes in the form of written parliamentary questions and points to a young man keenly aware of how fragile a support base can be, and his dealing with the hard task of constituency politics with some gusto.

For constituency work these questions are the bread and butter of politicians, in particular backbenchers. They allow swift access to information on behalf of a constituent and provide the details necessary for the TD to revert to the constituent with some authority. They most certainly do not make for exciting business or reading. To illustrate the type of business Brian Cowen was dealing with, the following are the first two queries that appear under his name on 6 November 1984, with the reply of the minister for social welfare, in this case Barry

Desmond, included. Brian Cowen asked Desmond when free telephone rental would be given to a person in County Offaly. Desmond replied: 'In order to qualify for a free telephone rental allowance a person in receipt of a qualifying payment must be living entirely alone or only with children under fifteen years of age or other persons who are so permanently incapacitated as to be unable to summon aid in an emergency. An application for a free telephone rental allowance was received from the husband of the person concerned. The application was refused as his wife, who is living with him, is not, from the information furnished, permanently incapacitated as required by the scheme. He was notified accordingly on 10 April 1984. His wife is not in receipt of a qualifying payment in her own right and cannot, therefore, qualify for this allowance.'

Cowen then asked Desmond if arrears of disability benefit had been paid to a person in County Offaly and if payment of this benefit was continuing. According to Desmond: 'The person concerned claimed disability benefit from 26 May 1980 to 12 July 1983, after which date she was certified fit to resume work. During the course of that claim she was requested to attend for medical referee examination on 2 February 1983 but failed to do so. Regulations provide that a person who fails to attend for such an examination may be disqualified from receiving further benefit for a period of six weeks unless good cause can be shown for the failure to attend. No explanation was received and accordingly no benefit was paid for the period from 7 February 1983 to 19 March 1983. The person concerned made a further claim to benefit from 15 March 1984 and payments have been issued as medical evidence is received. Payment of benefit will continue while she remains incapable of work and satisfies the contribution conditions for receipt of disability benefit.'

Further questions go on to ask about such items as unemployment benefit, widows' pensions and even on when the minister would make arrangements to allow residents of Pollagh in County Offaly to sign on at the local post office.

It is clear that Brian Cowen had learned from his father. He was under no illusions about what politics involved and was quickly fitting into the system. His constituency base was obviously important to him. We also find him trying to address not just personal issues for constituents, but also trying to raise issues with regard to developments in his home patch. On 6 November 1984 Brian Cowen raises a matter under the order of business when he asked about 'the proposal for a detention centre at Kinnitty Castle, County Offaly'.

There is certainly nothing in the written questions that sets Brian Cowen apart from any number of backbench TDs. Throughout 1984 it's a picture of just another rural TD doing the same tasks that have become their stock in trade.

In 1985 Brian Cowen began to establish himself both as an orator and a man capable of reasoned and fair argument. He also, however, established himself as a bulwark of Fianna Fáil, a man who would defend his party in any circumstance and would be merciless when the need arose to score political points; he was undoubtedly partisan in approach.

Cowen's first speech of substance to the Dáil came on 22 January 1985. Fianna Fáil had tabled a private members' motion on the unemployment problem, the biggest ill facing Irish society at the time. He started his contribution with an attempt to show his fairness, but also showing his disdain for certain members of the government benches: 'I trust that my contribution will not be interrupted unduly, as I respect the sincerity of the views held by the minister and his attempts to redress the problems we face ... the points raised by the minister sound good and there are some good ideas in the White Paper on Industrial Policy. I seek to obtain from this debate – and there can be a reply at its conclusion tomorrow night – the implementation of some of those ideas. I would like to put that White Paper in perspective. It refers simply to the creation of a maximum of 5,000 jobs per year, which is not going to redress the unemployment problem and is of no benefit to the vast population of young people who are coming on to the jobs market. One in six of the workforce is at present out of work and one in twelve is on unemployment assistance ... if we are to try to address ourselves properly to this problem we need fresh thinking and a radical approach.'

Brian Cowen was very comfortable when speaking on economic issues, and even though only twenty-five years of age, his ability to set the scene and summarise such a huge problem was clear to see. But one of his main reasons for speaking in the debate was once again his own local roots; he devoted a significant amount of time to discussing the problems of the peat industry in the midlands and in County Offaly in particular: 'I come from a constituency, County Offaly, where 43 per cent of those unemployed are involved in the public sector. I was delighted to hear the minister tonight applauding the achievements of Bord na Móna and the ESB (Electricity Supply Board) in providing not just social employment but also profitable employment which has involved great benefit and was in the national interest and the development of this country. However, we know from the recent report on electricity prices that those 2,500 jobs are once again being placed at risk.'

The case was being made in no uncertain terms that the jobs of the Bord na Móna workers were of paramount importance. As he developed this argument he made clear his understanding that bogs cannot last forever and put forward a very interesting and innovative proposal for the time: 'I, as a backbench TD, was able to get in touch with the European Commission on this matter with the help of my constituency colleague, Mr Paddy Lalor, MEP. I asked about the possibility of getting funding for a midland research project and pilot scheme in relation to the food-processing area in my constituency, and we got a very favourable reply from the director general of the regional policy directors in the Commission to the effect that the future development of a food-processing industry in the midland area may well be eligible for fund aid, and as such a feasibility study of establishing this type of industry might also be eligible for fund assistance. I do not know whether there is a unit within government buildings which tries to monitor the many regulations and directives that come out of the Commission and the council of ministers. A regulation of 1984 amends the European Regional Development Fund to allow for a large amount of funds to be available for research in various programmes which could possibly come under grant assistance from that fund.'

With hindsight we know that this proposal never came to anything, but it does illustrate that as a young politician he was eager to be involved in solution-based politics and in working to create alternatives. We see him adapt this constructive approach but not without letting the government know their own inadequacies. He then turned his attention to the small industry clinics that the government had introduced to try to encourage entrepreneurship: 'There have recently been clinics on small industries in my constituency which I can guarantee not more than twenty people attended. How can one get any reaction from people who might have an entrepreneurial spirit faced with the hopeless approach pursued by this government? Nothing great can be achieved in government or any area of life unless it is done with enthusiasm.'

In the circumstances his criticism was being levelled at a very easy target. The government of the day was very much strapped for cash and was struggling to keep some handle on the problem of national debt. The government simply lacked the resources to bring greater effort to these areas. However, Cowen was very pointed in his belief that the government was abandoning the workers of Bord na Móna in the midlands in favour of newer technologies: 'The minister for energy visited the Moneypoint plant recently and applauded the great work being done there. It should be remembered that, after fifty years of Laois-Offaly people working hard to build an industry, lauded by anybody who knows about it, thousands of cutaway bog will revert to the moorlands of the 1920s. At that stage probably it will revert to the natives only being able to use that area to hunt out snipe for the gentry in the shooting season ... as a representative of Laois-Offaly I have a duty to let people in the ivory towers of government buildings know that we will not accept a run-down of that industry. If the recent by-election results were insufficient to get the message across to the government, I can assure them that when the next general election takes place if they do not nail their colours to the mast on this issue they will have no hope of receiving any decent government representation in my constituency. If they allow the present industry to be run down they must provide an alternative. Our constituency has been denied, generation after generation since the 1950s, any indigenous or indeed foreign-based industry, because we had Bord na Móna and the ESB.'

Cowen was stating the very real concerns of his constituency and a large section of his own vote was employed in this sector. There was a belief at the time that as the new coal-burning Moneypoint station could provide enough electricity for the entire island, there would be no more need of the power stations in the midlands. This was one of the most crucial issues of Cowen's early political life. Now, many years later, as Ireland struggles to produce sufficient energy to meet its modern demands and new power stations open, it is difficult to appreciate how real a problem this was. In typical style he finished his contribution with a flourish of rhetoric and a thinly veiled warning to the government: 'This government will be remembered for the production of glossy reports, the contents of some of which carried good ideas. I do not question the sincerity of any member of the government benches. But until such time as these proposals are implemented on the ground, through the necessary heavy investment – because we have a growing population different from any other in Europe – and unless such investment is done over the next decade, there will be no hope whatever for the country, and the government will receive their answer when they face the people. Until then we shall continue to be as constructive as possible despite the continued portrayal by the national handlers that the people on these benches are being destructive.'

However, if he expected things to go all his own way he would have been disappointed. He was still a relatively new deputy and was dismissed as such. The following day when the debate resumed, there was much heckling and shouting in the chamber, the ceann comhairle struggled to keep order and while the record does not tell us what Brian Cowen may have said amid all the other comments, we do find Seán Barrett, the Fine Gael junior minister, dismissively shouting across: 'Give that young fellow five minutes and let him talk …'

Cowen replied: 'I would ask the deputy to withdraw that remark. I will not be patronised by him or anyone else.'

The request for a withdrawal was ignored and Cowen had to resume his seat. He may have felt that he had made his point, but it does show that the Dáil chamber is no respecter of persons and while Cowen himself may have been busy trying to build a reputation, his opponents certainly saw him as little more than another promising TD.

Clearly, however, if Cowen did not impress his opponents, he was certainly making his mark within Fianna Fáil. His next major contribution came in the form of an assessment of a social welfare amendment bill. Unlike his previous contribution, Cowen was systematic in his approach to this national issue and there was no mention of local politics or problems. The debate was notable from the point of view that it shows Cowen's ability to widen an issue and how he engaged in the often tricky business of making your point while remaining within parliamentary rules. His interaction with the ceann comhairle is interesting in that he treads a fine line between going outside of the debate's remit, yet managing to keep going and avoid being stopped by the ceann comhairle.

In his speech Cowen moved from the content of the bill itself to questioning at some length how it was to be funded. It was Cowen's contention that other areas of social welfare would be cut to pay for new measures; as this is not strictly part of the bill, but rather the budgetary and estimates process, he ran foul of the ceann comhairle: 'I accept that it is not the minister's fault that that is the case, but these people are not being looked after properly under our social security system. While that point is possibly outside the ambit of this debate, it is a passing reference which should be made at every opportunity when social welfare bills or estimates are discussed in this House. There are very many people, widows and widowers, who have no proper family income supplement or recognition of the difficulties they have to overcome in trying to rear a family.'

An ceann comhairle: 'This is more suited to an estimates speech.'

Mr Cowen: 'I do not care whether it is an estimates speech or not.'

An ceann comhairle: 'The chair does.'

Mr Cowen: 'The chair is the boss and I respect the chair's ruling. I will continue to make that point until such time as it is rectified. Unfortunately during the past twelve months there have been various references to the great achievement of this minister in bringing in social legislation which puts us on a par with our colleagues in Europe and western democracies with their modernistic approach to life. People who are finding it very difficult to rear a family are not being properly looked after. We have more concern for people who do not have the responsibility of rearing a family than for those who have that responsibility. I will continue to make that point to a minister for social welfare at every opportunity.

'Many other aspects of this legislation are slightly misleading. The minister spoke of the great achievement in allowing women to apply for unemployment assistance. It subsequently became clear that very few women living at home but available for work will have any chance of getting unemployment assistance because the income of their spouse will be taken into consideration. Also, social welfare officers may not feel they are available for work simply because no jobs are available in the area. While a woman will now be able to apply for unemployment assistance, there is no more hope of gaining unemployment assistance then under the existing system …

'The department of social welfare simply do not have the necessary money. The delays in processing claims for unemployment assistance are actually criminal.'

An ceann comhairle: 'The deputy is making an estimates speech …'

Mr Cowen: 'The minister provides in the bill that women can apply for unemployment assistance. I would make the point that they are no better off under this bill than under the existing system because they will not get unemployment assistance on these terms. If they are foolish enough to apply they will wait at least fourteen weeks before being told they will not get it. If we cannot say that in the House, we should not be here at all … These points have to be made. They are facts of life and we are talking about a category of people who have no voice. It is my business as a public representative to state it and I think the ceann comhairle respects that.

'While I have pointed out the various aspects of this bill which I welcome, the minister has not properly explained to me where the extra money is to come from. If there is to be a transfer of resources within the department of social welfare, who loses out? That should be made clear to the opposition so that they can be constructive and responsible. Surely we are entitled to the information which is available to the department. We should not have to put down parliamentary questions over the next three weeks to find out how many people are on disability benefit. This sort of information is available to the minister on second stage. It would help the debate if we were given the proper information at the outset.

'The family income supplement was the great novel idea of the new Fine Gael Party, but it has proved a lamentable failure since so few people have applied or qualified for it. This is another example of an inadequate response to what is becoming a crisis.'

An ceann comhairle: 'The deputy is now taking up another topic which does not come within the bill ...'

Mr Cowen: 'There are many inequities in the social welfare system and many injustices as between men and women, and between the old and the young ... I should like to know precisely what resources are being transferred from what category of social welfare recipients and the cost of implementing this legislation. We had a bill here the week before last under the guise of social legislation whereby the midland health board will have to fund changes, but as they are underfunded at present that will never become a reality. I should like to be told how this legislation will be effective and where the money will come from to implement these changes.'

The tactic used by Cowen is an example of pushing the parliamentary rules as far as one can without breaking them – he succeeded in making several points which were outside the remit of the debate itself and avoided being ruled out of order by the ceann comhairle. It is the first instance we see of Cowen not only as a strong orator and local politician, but someone his party trusts to speak on a national issue while also proving himself adept in parliamentary procedure.

All politics is local, however, and eventually an issue comes up that affects constituents, friends or family, and TDs can find themselves making a difficult argument. Considering the Brian Cowen we know today, a speech he made in 1986 in opposition to an increase in duty on spirits being sold in pubs makes interesting reading. These were indeed very different times and it is difficult to imagine Brian Cowen today making a similar defence of publicans. However, in context it was a debate where Fianna Fáil as a party greatly opposed the measure and many exaggerated claims were made by other contributors even to the point of suggesting that pubs were good for family life! Cowen's contribution in this context was more measured: 'I should like to express my opposition to this punitive measure which will hurt the licensed trade throughout the country. As a member whose family has a tradition in the licensing trade I am aware of the severe imposition this will be on most rural vintners who at present have to cope with a severe drop in their trade. I wonder if the taoiseach is aware that many country pubs will have to consider closing down for most of the day because of this increase. Many publicans do not do a lot of business during the week and depend on the weekend trade to make a living. Most rural pubs are run by families who are not in a position to employ bar staff.

'Rural publicans must pay heavy local charges because of the severe government cutbacks. Rates and water charges are very high. The taoiseach should take into consideration the fact that many publicans find it difficult to ask customers to leave their premises at 11.10 p.m. because they are only having their second pint. He may find that amusing, but he should bear in mind that vintners who find persons on their premises after hours have their licences endorsed. Does the taoiseach realise that many vintners are having their licences endorsed for after-hours trading which they engage in to try to make a living? He should take into consideration that many responsible people who enjoy a few pints at night cannot do so because of the price of drink. In rural areas the pub is often a meeting place, not just for drinking but for social activities and arranging meetings of the GAA and so on. It is more than a licensed premises; it is a place where people meet to do business for voluntary organisations and so on.

'If this is passed publicans will be at the mercy of a totally unjust law and will be unable to get a renewal of their licence if there are three endorsements on it. This is discrimination against the trade and I do not see any justification for it. It is common knowledge that the price of drink is too high and I do not see how the minister can reduce VAT from 23 per cent to 10 per cent for hoteliers, people who take a greater flow of trade, while publicans, who only supply alcoholic beverages to their customers, will have this further duty imposed on them. The old reliables are being hit once too often. It is no longer a case of people not being able to afford an extra pint in the evenings: the person trying to make a living from the business is in a very difficult situation. I ask the minister to reconsider the matter and I join my colleagues in opposing this measure.'

It is interesting that Cowen did not make the same points or indeed come to the defence of establishments when stricter closing times and drink-driving laws or smoking bans were introduced some years later. However, it is clear to see the pressure that a TD like Brian Cowen often comes under and the fact that sometimes the arguments simply must be made out of a sense of duty even if the argument itself is not all that strong.

The Fine Gael/Labour coalition government was in its final days during 1986. Pressure was building and with an economy that was seeing national debt spiralling, record highs in unemployment and emigration, Fianna Fáil was sensing blood and cranking up the pressure. The following debate took place on 21 February 1986 as part of a motion of no confidence tabled by Fianna Fáil. It is the first example of true debate within the chamber in which we find Brian Cowen engaged. Alan Dukes was a senior minister and within a year would reach the summit of his political prowess when he was elected leader of Fine Gael. He was a seasoned and experienced politician and it is somewhat surprising to see a young Brian Cowen pitted against him. The Fianna Fáil party trusted Cowen, still a backbencher, to lock horns on this issue. Indeed Dukes remarks that it is probably a sign that Cowen is an 'up and coming' politician. The contributions by both men encapsulate the views of both sides of the House at the time with regard to the government's performance and as a historical record are intriguing given that just a decade later the Celtic Tiger was born. It was, however, a major test for Cowen's abilities and provided him with some invaluable experience with regard to such debates.

Alan Dukes was a well-regarded debater and it is difficult to imagine that Fianna Fáil expected Cowen to out-argue the vastly more experienced Dukes at this stage. However, the arguments made by both men reverberate through history, as decisions discussed here were taken, and policies implemented and abandoned, over the coming years, which led to a much-changed economic landscape. Cowen said: 'I am happy that I have come into this House in recent times, times which are more relevant to this country in terms of its financial and economic future. I come from a generation which represents 50 per cent of the population, twenty-five years of age or under. I have no intention of taking up the challenge of government speakers. Since the beginning of this debate there has been a blatant attempt to turn this into a personalised and totally irrelevant debate, in terms of attacking personalities.

'Our motion seeks to remove from the office of taoiseach, Deputy Garret FitzGerald. My sincerely held political opinion is that Deputy FitzGerald should consider vacating his office in the national interest. We do this House, and more importantly the Irish people, a great disservice by the manner in which this debate is being conducted. The tenor of this debate was set by the opening speaker, the tánaiste, and by placing certain government speakers immediately after him to convey to the people an attitude and a series of opinions which I find despicable.

'While I would always hope for cordial and courteous relationships with all members of this House, I cannot but hold those more experienced members in anything but political contempt because of the manner in which they conducted themselves. There is an abrasive side to me and yesterday I deliberately removed myself from the House and made some remarks privately, as I felt that the low personal attacks made yesterday did not give me the right to reply to them in the House with the vindictiveness and invective which it was my misfortune to hear from experienced and otherwise respected members of this House.

'In this debate we are considering the removal of the taoiseach on the basis of the performance of his government since coming to office in 1982. I am glad the minister for justice [Alan Dukes] is here and wish him well in his new post. The remarks of the minister, as minister for finance in 1983, put into perspective our financial situation. Unfortunately debates in this House degenerate into attempts to apportion blame. However, political parties on both sides have had experience in government over the past decade and so should be prepared to point out the mistakes, consider the relevant problems and address the major crisis facing us. The people are more interested in what we intend to do in the future than in the usual puerile debates which take place here. As minister for finance in 1983 as reported in Volume 339 of the official report Deputy Dukes said: "The origins of this budget lie almost ten years in the past."

'Then the minister went on to talk about the oil price rise of 1973 and of 1979–80 and the fact that he felt that successive governments had failed to reduce our standards in view of the transfer of real resources to the oil producers as a result of those oil price hikes. The minister went on to say that: "the position we are in today is not the result of recent developments, or of the sudden change in our circumstances."

'The minister saw his role over the following two or three years as being one of unremitting effort to restore the proper balance between expenditure and revenue and to lay foundations for growth and prosperity in the future.

'We on this side of the House were aware of the seriousness of the crisis and we did not require the minister to moralise. We do not require to be continually told that we should not oppose the policies of this government in view of the great work they are doing. Any self-respecting politician can see the seriousness of the situation when considering the 1986 budget in terms of the percentage of the allocation of resources to various areas. About 21 per cent is to service the national debt and only about 9 per cent is devoted towards services and infrastructure.

'This government set out their objectives in their *Joint Programme for Government* for the elimination of the current budget deficit and a reduction in unemployment. In government they came to realise they could not achieve their objectives. We had a public debate between the minister, Deputy Dukes, and the minister, Deputy Spring, on the current budget deficit in their first budget and a decision was made to review the situation. In *Building on Reality* they reviewed the elimination of the current budget deficit to 5 per cent of GNP by 1987. Like any plan, this plan was based on economic assumptions. One of the central planks of *Building on Reality* was the naïve miscalculation that they could limit public service pay to 1 per cent or 2 per cent per year on average. One must question the political judgment and credibility of a government who put forward a proposal like that. That simply was not a realistic assumption.

'The day before the 1985 budget the minister, Deputy Boland, came to an agreement with the public service which could cost £108 million, so the whole plan was thrown off beam. The minister said at that time that since £20 million had been allocated for public service pay that year, they would proceed to reduce expenditure cuts by another £30 million, and then there was the famous revenue buoyancy of £58 million, all of which conveniently added up to £108 million so that the budget balanced beautifully.

'We must be straight with people or continue with political point scoring. As a result of the 1986 budget we will not attain a current budget deficit of 5 per cent of GNP during the lifetime of this government. Initially the government were going to eliminate the deficit but that proposal was a revised decision. We are attacked by the government for questioning their credibility when it is clear that they cannot and will not achieve that target. The minister, Deputy Dukes, in the 1984 budget said that the economy was now poised on a delicate balance and that until we brought about a considerable improvement in the public finances we would make little progress towards a structured economy and better employment opportunities.

'It is quite clear from the figure of a continuing debt of £2 billion every year, that we are simply not achieving the considerable improvement in the public finances which, in the words of the minister for finance, Deputy Dukes, would have given us a stronger economy and better employment opportunities. The evidence is everywhere to be seen. In every sector we see it. For that reason also we think we are quite credible in requesting that the taoiseach should consider his position in the light of the fact that their economic policies – and there was more than one economic policy in the term of office of this government – and fiscal policies have failed on the basis of their own figures and their own assertions in the *Joint Programme for Government* and after that in *Building on Reality, 1985–1987,* their revised economic plan.

'We have been accused consistently of not providing alternative policies. That is not true. There is an alternative to these economic policies being pursued by the government and if there is not, then the logical consequence of what the government are saying is that, because we have a difficult financial situation, it is not credible to attempt an economic recovery in present circumstances ...

'I would be the first to say that no government *per se* can create employment, but they can and must use the budget and their economic policies as an instrument to provide and create the sort of positive environment to which people can respond. No one is responding at the moment, and that is the basic problem. This government have lost the confidence of decent, ordinary Irish working people who do not want to suffer the indignity of having to queue on the public street for unemployment benefit or assistance and who would regard it as much easier to go out and work a hard forty-hour week for only £10 or £15 more. They want their dignity and a sense of purpose in their lives and they cannot have that sense of purpose if the government themselves are ungovernable. We saw last week the taoiseach, the leader of the country, unable to shift personnel into the departments in which he thought they would be best suited to try to pull the strings and do something better for this country.

'There must be an alternative to the present economic policies being pursued by the government. More importantly, there must be a political alternative to this government. I can assure the House that this party will be the alternative. I travelled my constituency in the past two or three months through our cumainn and our organisation and I was heartened by the response I got from ordinary people whose voices are not heard often enough. They have not the eloquence, the capability or the education to express themselves adequately, but what they want is a government who care. This government do not care. That is the perception out there in the real world ...

'I belong to an open, democratic party and I can speak my mind whenever and wherever I please within my party and my voice will be listened to just as the voice of every member of my party high and low will be listened to. I do not believe in passing remarks about Fine Gael or Labour because I know nothing about the organisation of Fine Gael, Labour, the Workers' Party or the Progressive Democrats.

'I do not see how Deputy Cooney or somebody else can come in here and dictate to me about how my party are run. We are prepared to provide an alternative. We have legitimate aspirations and legitimate reasons why we should seek government and the trust of the people. We will continue to do so no matter what sort of invective emanates from those benches. If one goes through Deputy Garret FitzGerald's record when in opposition one will see that he provided an alternative view to the one he is now putting forward as taoiseach. On the adjournment debate on 29 June 1978 he spoke of the connection between investment and growth. He deplored the fact that there was no increase in the proportion of natural resources devoted to productive capital expenditure. On the adjournment debate in December 1980 he said that he believed it probable that we could not merely sustain the present level of public investment in infrastructure and productive activity, but could even increase it as a proportion of GNP if we not merely eliminated the current deficit but developed a small current surplus to put towards the investment need.

'Here is a man in charge of a government who last year had the greatest current budget deficit in real terms as a percentage of GNP, and he said just before he came into office that he felt he could not only reduce the current budget deficit, but produce a current budget surplus which he could transfer for capital purposes. What has happened in government? In real terms over the past three years the public capital programme has been cut by one-third …

'We need action, for example, in relation to the timber industry. There will be an 8 per cent shortfall in world supply by the year 2000. The European Community are only 50 per cent self-sufficient in their timber needs and import approximately £100 million worth of timber annually. We have 300 hectares of state forest and, despite the stated annual planting target of 10,000 hectares, we seem able only to plant approximately 6,500 hectares annually. We intend, on return to government, to put that state forestry industry under the auspices of a commercially viable semi-state enterprise which will develop a labour intensive industry. It is quite obvious that there is there a great potential.

'We have a government who, in opposition, were full of bright ideas. They were portrayed as the government of all the talents. Even their supporters within the media now say they have more talent on their backbenches than on their front bench and perhaps we should have a few more backbenchers on the front bench. The point is that we have no action. I know the minister is sincere in his attempts, but we have not the action to provide employment to create wealth and encourage incentive. Whatever tinkering they may do with their budgets, it is not enough. If a radical reappraisal is required, so be it. Let us not be hung up on the ideological problems which continue to persist within the inter-party government. We simply do not have unity of purpose in this government. We have heard from the government benches about vetoes on the change of ministries. It is quite clear where the vetoes now are in this government in relation to the re-allocation of ministers' jobs.

'It is important to say that we have an agricultural industry which, unfortunately, has not been getting the sort of priority it should be getting in this economy. With the CAP (Common Agricultural Policy) under attack in Europe it is sad, when one looks at the budget figures, to find that only one half of 1 per cent of total GNP from natural resources is ploughed into industry. We depend almost totally for our investment in agriculture on European funds. Most of those funds are simply to ensure guaranteed prices. The time has come for a major effort to create greater wealth in our agricultural industry. I do not know why this has not happened and I will not berate this government for that, but quite clearly, in view of the difficult investment climate, we will not get the job creation industries we got in the past. Other countries are vying for those industries as well. We must go back to developing native industry, primary industries which we must take on board and for which we must provide the structures that will generate wealth and employment ...

'We should get down to the business of dealing with the merits or demerits of the policies of the parties in this House. Let us finish, once and for all, with the old politics. People out there simply do not want them. No matter how well they present themselves – and we hear so much about the style of this government – that style must be replaced by substance. If it is not more impressionable or attractive, let them not worry about that. In the national interests we require action now. In view of all the circumstances, I request that the government call a general election because the time has come for a radical change. If it will not come under this government, then let us have another one ...'

Mr Alan Dukes: 'I had not intended to make any specific comments on remarks made by deputies in this House. However, out of courtesy to Deputy Cowen, there are one or two things which I would say following the remarks which he has just made. I am quite sure that he is a very sincere deputy. A little of his discomfort in the rather histrionic ramble we have just heard arises from the fact that he does not really believe in the amendment to the motion which his party have put down. He said at one stage "even if the government were to remain in office" and at another stage that under certain scenarios things would be rather easier for the government over the next eighteen to nineteen months.'

Mr Cowen: 'In reality.'

Mr Dukes: 'Of course, it does not lie in Deputy Cowen's hands, but it is perfectly obvious that he does not believe the amendment which the Fianna Fáil Party have down to the motion is going to succeed. He has been given the job of engaging in a half hour of histrionics in this House because he is probably being marked down as one of the rising young men of the Fianna Fáil Party … He is being given an outing. I wish him the best of luck in doing so.'

Mr Cowen: 'Let us not patronise.'

Mr Dukes: 'If I may presume to do so, I think Deputy Cowen would be far better off if he did not work himself into quite the passion he reached at one or two points in his address, but took a slightly more relaxed view of what he was saying and thought a little more through it. He did me the honour, for I am deeply grateful, of quoting from my analysis of the situation when introducing the budget in 1983, where I pointed out that we were, and still are, suffering from the hang-over, the continuing effects of what happened in oil markets in 1973 and through the period up to 1979. Deputy Cowen should have enough "cop-on" to read and analyse that for what it is worth and get the message from it and not to take the easy course of characterising it afterwards as moralising. I cannot see how it helps the debate to take an analysis, whether it be economic or political, or the analysis of any problem, and dismiss it as moralising simply because the message does not change every second day to suit the mood of the opposition or what they perceive the mood of the country to be.

'Ireland, with the most open economy in Europe, is particularly open to influence by what is happening in the world around us. When we have an event in the world, as we did in 1973 and again in 1979, that inherently brings about a major shift in purchasing power between the people who produce oil and the people who have to buy all of their oil, it is something we cannot leave out of the reckoning. It is not moralising to point out, as I have consistently done since December 1982, that we did not properly come to terms with that issue over the period. It is part of the analysis that we must make of our problem.

'Deputy Cowen also referred to certain assumptions on which he thought the national plan *Building on Reality* was based. He mentioned one, there are a whole series of others. The basic economic assumptions in fact turned out to have been on the conservative side because in relation to three of the key areas of the influence of international factors on the Irish economy the climate improved rather faster than we had expected it to improve when we put that plan together. But of course it has never suited the opposition to analyse it from that point of view because they are very very short on analyses. The opposition seem mostly to take their views, as indeed Deputy Cowen is tempted to do, from what is happening in the media. We get presented here time after time, as we did from Deputy Cowen today, with a collage of the popular wisdom of the media, selecting the commentators in order to get a particular effect, but without any input of an intellectual, political or analytical nature from the people who populate those benches over there.

'Contrary to what Deputy Cowen and some of his colleagues may think of me, I am deeply conscious of the fact that the benches over there are populated by people, not by numbers, ciphers, spokesmen or spokeswomen, but by people, all of them having an internal life of their own, a capacity to think and imagine and most of them are making absolutely no effort to do that. They are just following these attractive collages that are put in front of them by the media and stringing them together to suit whatever debate happens to be going on in the House. That is not a worthy occupation for elected representatives. It is the one thing that has most disappointed me about the people on that side of the House since I came into this House in June 1981.

'Deputy Cowen claims that there is an alternative to the government's economic policy. What is it? A new radical reappraisal. That is fantastic. That is a phrase that has a real ring of thinking about it.'

Mr Cowen: 'An increase in capital expenditure.'

Mr Dukes: 'What do you get after that? What is the new radical reappraisal? There is no answer. There has not been an answer from that side of the House in the period from December 1982 to date. There was no answer to it in the period from December 1979 to June 1981. "New radical reappraisal" is a nice attractive phrase that is trotted out but there is no foundation for it. When people come forward with new radical reappraisals they confirm what I said three years ago is still the situation, the reaction to it is that you have stopped thinking or you are not using your imagination. One could say that we need a new radical reappraisal of the condition of the world, maybe they were right to say it is flat, that would be a new radical reappraisal. If we started off on the basis that the world was flat instead of round the new radical reappraisal would do absolutely nothing for us. The opposition are guilty of the use of that kind of catchphrase without ever thinking out what should follow the claim that we need this reappraisal.

'Deputy Cowen fell into the trap that so many of his colleagues have fallen into time after time. He had a nice, plausible, glib line giving out about my colleague, the minister for health, who comes into the House regularly and explains in detail what is being done in the health services, how much is being spent, what the costs are and what is being achieved. Deputy Cowen wants to know why we are spending so much on the health services this year. Is Deputy Cowen saying that he actually wants to hear the minister for health explaining how he is reducing expenditure on the health services, explaining how he would like to see us restrict expenditure there even more? I am sure he could make a good case for this. If that is what he is saying to the House he should say it and have the guts to put his feet where his mouth is, which he does much of the time anyway – I am talking now in voting terms. He should vote for the kind of policies he is talking about and not try to play the two ends off against the middle as he did here.

'Deputy Cowen also agrees with the necessity of looking more stringently at capital projects. I agree with that entirely and I am glad to find that I have the odd disciple on the benches opposite. I did not have many of them during the three years when I had the privilege to be the minister for finance in this House and arguing these issues with the opposition, quite the contrary, I found that whenever I came into this House arguing the case for a more economically based assessment of capital expenditure projects before we committed public or borrowed money to them we should know better what is going to be achieved by those projects. Deputies opposite took exactly the opposite line from Deputy Cowen. They represented that kind of approach as variously monetarist, unfeeling, crude, cold and all these lovely adjectives that they picked up from assiduous reading of the newspapers and they applied them without once thinking what the basic objective is. But when it suits them in a debate like this they can try to gain credit for themselves through the disappearance of plausibility and concern and say, "Oh yes we must get better value for public expenditure", but they have not got the guts to follow it up when it actually comes to making decisions.

'On the question of various areas of specific expenditure, for example the county roads which are giving a lot of difficulty in all areas of the country, as in my own constituency, Deputy Cowen can find out if he does not already know, which I am sure he does, that the situation is and has been for quite a long time that the maintenance of county roads is a matter for the local authorities … he says incentives may reduce net tax but that is better than having no tax at all. Of course, it sounds like a self-evident proposition … what it omits is the substitution effect. There is absolutely no point in saying that you are going to get more revenue if you take less tax from this and have more activity unless you take account of the effects of what you are proposing in other areas of the economy in other areas of taxation. Deputies opposite seem to think that if you juggle enough things around by some miraculous procedure you will increase the total amount of resources available, when in fact we know that that on the whole is not the case. The only reason that the deputies opposite fall into that trap is that they consistently refuse to sit down and try to put together in any kind of logical, coherent order the sum of what they are saying about all these areas of taxation, of economic policy, of public investment policy and so on.'

The debate was certainly a point-scoring exercise for both sides, and as always in politics, depending on your viewpoint, either side would claim victory. It is a remarkable debate, however, and shows how far Brian Cowen had come in a few short years. It is even more remarkable that Alan Dukes devoted so much time to repudiating Cowen's speech: Cowen was not even a frontbench spokesperson at this stage of his career. Unlike some of his colleagues, however, Dukes was not dismissive of Cowen – he pays a number of back-handed compliments similar in nature to those paid by Cowen himself, but seems to pay particular attention to taking Cowen on head to head. Perhaps the emerging threat of Cowen's ability and 'passion' made Dukes feel like it was an opportune time to try to take him to task. There is no doubt however that Cowen had now become a major Dáil asset to Fianna Fáil just two years after his by-election victory.

The remainder of 1986 saw Brian Cowen make two more serious contributions in terms of policy debate in the area of divorce and social welfare. It is notable however that during the divorce debate the Fine Gael TD Professor John Kelly went to great lengths to point out that while he disagreed with Cowen, he complimented his contribution, saying: 'Deputy Cowen is one of the youngest members of his party and I say sincerely that everybody in the House knew and respected his father. Although he is in a different party from me and I regret that he is not in mine, and although his victory in the by-elections about two years ago was a defeat for us, I was glad to see him getting a chance. I do not believe that anybody on this side was so begrudging as to speak otherwise about him. I hope that he will have a successful and brilliant career here. The sobriety and objectivity with which he presented his material this evening makes me think that he will.'

This suggests that by the end of 1986 Brian Cowen had risen from obscurity to a highly rated young politician. He had earned the respect of those on all sides of the House, even if they did not always agree with him. The following year saw Fianna Fáil return to government, but if Cowen had emerged as an asset in Dáil debates and established himself among the many more senior TDs, he still was not appearing on the radar of Charles Haughey, the Fianna Fáil leader. One might expect that a fresh young face that had performed so well might be rewarded with a junior ministry or even chairmanship of a committee, but that did not transpire. As a backbench government TD there was little need for Cowen's oratorical skills in the chamber and he almost disappears off the radar, tabling only one question in 1987 on grant and mortgage subsidies and one question in 1988 with regard to social employment schemes. While it is not uncommon for backbench government TDs to do most of their work off the record it would seem a waste of talent at a national level that a young politician used so readily by his party in opposition to carry the fight would then find himself in relative obscurity when the party returned to government.

APPOINTMENT AS MINISTER

Politics is as much a game of timing, luck and patronage as skill and ability. Brian Cowen was a Fianna Fáil backbencher in 1991, but in the November of that year the then minister for finance, Albert Reynolds, decided to back a motion of no confidence in Taoiseach Charles Haughey. It is hard to imagine just what an earth-shattering event this was in Irish politics at the time, but although Reynolds lost initially and lost his seat in the cabinet, by February 1992 the chain of events had led to Charles Haughey's resignation.

Albert Reynolds was elected taoiseach and commenced his term by completely overhauling the front benches. Reynolds was aware that many of those at cabinet had soldiered too long with Haughey to adapt to his leadership and wanted to bring in new people who would work to his agenda. Charlie McCreevy, Noel Dempsey, Joe Walsh, Michael Smith and David Andrews were among those promoted to shape the future of Fianna Fáil and indeed the country. But perhaps one of the biggest surprises was the sudden promotion of Brian Cowen to a full cabinet portfolio as minister for labour. It was a clear sign of Reynolds' faith in the young Offaly TD. Cowen went on to become one of Reynolds' most loyal supporters and most valuable aides.

There are few cabinet postings that will not land a politician in the firing line very quickly. By April of 1992 the banking sector in Ireland was experiencing one of the most bitter industrial disputes of recent years. Brian Cowen was thrust into the midst of this and on 7 April he outlined the background of the dispute to the House and the policy of government in relation to it: 'This dispute has a particularly long history and has been the subject of investigation by two bank tribunals before eventually being the subject of a Labour Court recommendation. Prior to this the Labour Relations Commission were involved and have been involved more recently. The Labour Court in their recommendation did not concede the IBOA claim for a straight salary increase, but recommended an alternative approach under the terms of the Programme for Economic and Social Progress which involves a 6 per cent increase from 1 May, 3 per cent basic and 3 per cent local bargaining, a lump sum of £750 and an extra day's annual leave in return for extra opening hours … As I said on a number of occasions, a resolution of this dispute must rest in the end with the banks and the IBOA and third party intervention can only be as effective as the parties to the dispute will allow. I regret to say that at present I do not see any real desire by the parties to enter meaningful dialogue but I would again call on both sides to sit down immediately and open discussions in a spirit of goodwill and co-operation.'

For a minister it was crucial not to be seen to take sides and to try to offer a route to resolution that both sides could trust. However, as Ruairi Quinn pointed out, the reports of intimidation of staff and the amount of debate taking place publicly made this difficult: 'Is the minister aware that the banks are currently engaged in a campaign of intimidation and are among other things, taking cars back from managers who refuse to sign declarations that they will not participate in the strike; that officials who were in fact granted examination leave have been transferred in such a way that they no longer qualify for it and that what is at issue, from his point of view as minister for labour, is the defence of the fundamental right of people to organise themselves in a trade union? Is the minister aware the banks are engaged in constructive dismissal, which is in breach of the Unfair Dismissals Act? In view of the gross intimidation that is now occurring in one bank, of which I have documentary evidence, will he open a confidential telephone line in his department to enable harassed bank officials to report instances of intimidation that are occurring on a daily basis?'

Mr Cowen: 'I have been concerned about the reports which have been communicated to my department since the strike began ... I agree that to organise and take free decisions is a fundamental right of every employee in any industry or service industry ... I believe it is very difficult to resolve matters in the atmosphere that has been building up over the past twenty-four hours.'

Mr Quinn: 'Will the minister investigate complaints?'

Mr Cowen: 'As far as I am concerned, any complaints that come to the notice of my department can be dealt with. However, let me point out that if we are interested in resolving this dispute it is important that I do not get involved in recriminations or counter-recriminations. I am trying to ensure that an atmosphere of goodwill and trust prevails in order to resolve this dispute. The chairman of the Labour Court referred in the Labour Court recommendations to the very poor industrial relations atmosphere which has been a dominant feature of the banking system for some time and stated that when this dispute is resolved – hopefully shortly – that issue should be taken up in detail by the Labour Relations Commission. In the interest of seeking to resolve this dispute, which is our primary objective at present, I am anxious not to heighten tensions but to try to create an atmosphere in which the dispute can be resolved.'

While the banking sector in Ireland was an integral part of the state it was also an area in which the minister or the government had very little influence. Cowen clearly recognised the right of workers to organise and take free decisions, but his aim was to become a facilitator for a resolution rather than an active participant in the dispute or an advocate for the rights of either side. While such an approach would not be unusual, it is a key feature of Brian Cowen's style to be a facilitator rather than adopt a more hands-on or dictatorial approach; he expects to be kept well informed and provided with sufficient advice to make timely decisions, but he never seeks to become embroiled in micro-management. It is the first evidence of a trait that can be seen on a number of occasions throughout his ministries.

Ireland had suffered greatly in the 1980s from industrial strife. The bank dispute was the last major industrial dispute for some years thanks to the success of the partnership approach, through national wage agreements. As minister for labour, Cowen was a keen supporter of the whole idea of partnership and on 10 July 1992 he outlined his beliefs in the system: 'A good industrial relations environment is essential not only in maintaining competitiveness but in building investor confidence. Investor confidence is very susceptible to the perception of instability and uncertainty arising from industrial disputes ... It would be foolish in the extreme to think that in the area of employer-employee relations disputes and strikes can be totally eliminated.'

Cowen was a firm believer that the figures relating to Ireland's growth at the time were in the main due to the wage agreements: 'The competitive cost and good industrial relations environment in Ireland in recent years has a very beneficial impact on overseas companies already established in the country. As a result these companies play a crucial role in giving positive recommendations to potential new overseas investors.'

The latest national wage agreement in 1992 was the Programme for Economic and Social Progress and it contained many measures that dictated the agenda of work facing the new minister for labour.

In the same debate he outlined the measures that he would be taking: 'The Programme for Economic and Social Progress commits the minister for labour to bring forward certain legislation during the currency of the programme. Arising from these commitments, legislation dealing with part-time workers, and the payment of wages, was enacted last year by a previous minister for labour. I will follow these achievements by placing on the statute book the remaining legislation committed in the programme. These are the amendments to the unfair dismissals and employment equality legislation … the other labour legislation due for amendment under the programme is the employment equality legislation. Work on proposals in this area is ongoing and involves the preparation of a single piece of legislation that will replace both of the existing statutes and the succession of statutory instruments made over the past sixteen years. These developments will ensure that the basic principles of equality law are accessible and comprehensible to the public.

'The Programme for Economic and Social Progress also commits me, as minister for labour, to review the existing legislative arrangements as they relate to holidays, employment agencies and agency workers, conditions of employment and protection of employment. Work on the review of legislation in each of these areas has commenced.

'In addition to legislative commitments in the Programme for Economic and Social Progress, there is an undertaking to provide on a statutory basis for leave from employment for adoptive mothers …'

There is little doubt that Cowen was eager to put the agenda of work on the record and to set clear targets. He was an ambitious minister and had a certain reforming zeal, but this was kept firmly in check by working within the confines of clear policy documents. He also used the opportunity to illustrate a clear commitment to the European ideal and a belief that Ireland had much to be thankful to Europe for. Another minister might simply have outlined his targets and aims for the area generally: 'As the minister with responsibility for the European

Social Fund, I have a particular interest in ensuring that it continues to centrally contribute to vocational training and education provision post-1993. We have benefited very significantly from Social Fund transfers to date … Ireland will have received in excess of £1 billion from the Social Fund. When matched by the exchequer contribution this will fund training and employment programmes for an average of 150,000 people each year. Training is being provided by a range of agencies to enhance the employment opportunities of participants. That training seeks to anticipate and address the manpower needs of the different economic sectors – the industry and services sectors, the tourism sector and the agricultural sector.'

It is difficult to assess a record for Brian Cowen in relation to his term as minister for labour, other than to say that he clearly believed that there was much work to be done with regard to reform. Probably the biggest message he sent was that partnership and co-operation was central to Ireland's success going forward. He was not alone in this and it was part of a wider rethinking of industrial relations where trade unions and employers began to work together on a scale that had not been witnessed in the past. Cowen was not afraid to set an agenda, but was also cautious in his approach, sticking closely to the accepted wisdom of the day.

Of course Cowen was only minister for labour for nine months. Allegations by Des O'Malley and counter-allegations by Albert Reynolds (at the Beef Tribunal) brought down the Fianna Fáil/ Progressive Democrat coalition government. The mood at the time was particularly emotive on all sides. As the relationship between the government parties disintegrated, the highly charged atmosphere transferred itself to the floor of the Dáil where Des O'Malley laid out his case against Albert Reynolds. Brian Cowen took up the position of chief defender and, in an emotional contribution, he outlined his personal beliefs in defence of Fianna Fáil, his unwavering support for

Reynolds and, quite clearly, the level of enmity and distaste he held for O'Malley: 'When this election is over I hope we will get rid of moral indignation in politics, the attempt to put oneself above the rest. I will not concede my integrity to Deputy O'Malley or anybody else. He does not speak on my behalf in relation to integrity. I have been reared in a political tradition which is as true as it ever was. I am the third generation Fianna Fáil man in my family and the esteem in which I and my political tradition are held is something I am prepared to put before the electorate at any time. If it suits Deputy O'Malley's political agenda, let it be in three weeks' time. I suggest to Deputy O'Malley that it is time to rid the country of this superfluous attempt to indicate moral indignation at every twist and turn. He indicates a persecution complex in respect of the difficult circumstances in which he has lived for the past three years and he claims that finally he had to give way. I have been proud to be a member of government for the past eight months. Under this taoiseach we will fight this election and go to the people. We expect a result which will reflect the common sense approach that he espouses and we will take no more moral indignation from Deputy O'Malley or anybody else.'

It was fighting talk ahead of a bruising and punishing election for both Fianna Fáil and Fine Gael. During the debate the late Niall Blaney probably summed up the view that makes most sense with hindsight: 'We have had many crises in the past two or three years which have been more serious than this one. When one considers the events of last June and last week, it is clear that two people, using very different terms of language, said exactly the same thing about each other, each calling the other a liar. That is the way I see it. Neither of the two is as great as the crisis that follows from it and I suggest they should call it quits. No doubt each believes the other a liar. So what?'

No one was in the mood to take the advice of Deputy Blaney, however. General elections are almost always a gamble: they depend largely on the prevailing mood of the time, they can be swung on a single issue or comment, and the final result can often be surprising. 1992 was certainly no different. While Fianna Fáil and Fine Gael lost heavily, the real winners were the Labour Party. While many presumed that Labour would join in a rainbow coalition with FG and the PDs, the Labour Party, and in particular its leader Dick Spring, surprised everyone by agreeing a coalition government with Fianna Fáil. It was a new departure in Irish politics and, although the relationship between the parties broke down only two years later, it was a successful and reforming partnership while it lasted.

Fianna Fáil sacrificed valuable cabinet posts to attract Labour. By this stage Cowen had quickly established himself as a firm favourite of the party faithful, a fearless man who was proud of the Fianna Fáil party and never felt any need to apologise for it. Once politicians manage to establish themselves in this light with their own supporters it becomes very difficult to shift them. Reynolds knew that he could depend completely on Cowen, and the party membership felt he was a man they could trust implicitly. His appointment as minister for transport, energy and communications was seen as a promotion and just reward for his political work. However, while Cowen had now proven himself in the political cut and thrust, he still had to establish himself as a minister and to demonstrate abilities in the discharge of the duties of government.

As the new minister for transport one of the key difficulties facing Cowen was the situation at Aer Lingus. The state airline had enjoyed a dominant market position for many decades, but changes in the world air travel environment and increased competition both at home, in the shape of Ryanair, and abroad, had left Aer Lingus staring into an abyss. The company was facing financial ruin and the government needed to find a rescue plan that could save what had once been the jewel in the crown of the semi-state sector.

On 12 March 1993, Cowen outlined his views on the company and spoke about the appointment of Bernie Cahill as chairman and the agreement reached with him to take on the task of saving the company: 'At the outset, I want to say that it is in Ireland's strategic interest to have Aer Lingus as a substantial airline to serve trade, tourism and overall national needs. The relationship between the government and Aer Lingus has historically been a close one. The airline has been supported by successive governments since its foundation. It has brought mutual benefits to the employees of Aer Lingus, to the government and to the people of Ireland. Aer Lingus was founded by Seán Lemass and it has carried the name of Ireland with distinction to every corner of the world.

'The government has supported Aer Lingus in its expansion and development over the years. This company has been a critical part of our commercial semi-state sector which has been fostered and encouraged to develop by successive governments ... successive governments have nurtured Aer Lingus as the national carrier in its formative years and, subsequently, endorsed the decision to expand into businesses which were not part of the core activity. This expansion was carried out with the blessing of the governments of the day in a spirit of partnership aimed at the successful development of the company. This strategy proved to be enormously successful with benefits for all those involved in the partnership: the government, the employees of the airline and the taxpayer ... What must be understood by all those involved, however, is that the context in which that co-operation will continue has fundamentally and irrevocably changed. This is something to which we all will have to adapt.'

Drastic action was now needed due to the changed circumstances in which the airline was operating. Cowen went on to lay out what he saw as the changed role of government in terms of involvement in the air travel sector and showed a keen understanding of the developments that would place Aer Lingus under increased pressures to compete in the following years: 'Since 1 January any EC national can set up an airline in Ireland or elsewhere in the EC on meeting certain financial and safety criteria; any EC airline can fly on any route within the EC into any Irish or EC airport without any restriction on frequency, provided slots are available; community carriers can now set their own fares without government control, and the right to operate internal services, known as *cabotage*, in another member state is being phased in over the four years to 1997.

'The role of governments is, therefore, concentrated on ensuring that the market operates in a fair and open manner. For this purpose, safeguards have been put in place to eliminate unfair competition in the market such as abuses of dominant positions, excessively high fares or predatory pricing. Governments no longer have the authority to regulate air transport in favour of their own carriers.'

In the course of the speech Cowen returned to the mantra that the problems can only be overcome in a spirit of mutual co-operation: 'In a sense, the problems facing Aer Lingus represent a microcosm of the problems at a national level to which I have just referred. They can be resolved in the same spirit of mutual co-operation … the core business, air transport, excluding once-off items, will lose over £40 million this year, resulting in losses for the fourth consecutive year. The air transport operation is incurring losses even before interest charges. In addition, the group debt is currently in excess of £500 million with an annual interest bill in the region of £50 million.

'In the past, Aer Lingus has been able to absorb losses on its air transport operations with profits from its ancillary activities. This is no longer the case. Businesses such as the hotels are pro-cyclical with the airline business and their results have also been hard hit by the recession. Group losses in the current year will be of an unprecedented level.

'In addition to the ongoing losses, Aer Lingus is burdened with a major overhang of debt resulting mainly from rapid fleet replacement over recent years ...'

Cowen again favoured the role of facilitator rather than anything more hands-on. It was his view that commercial decisions are best left to those who have experience in the matter and without undue influence from those at a political level with limited knowledge of the business. This was a core plank in his recovery plan for Aer Lingus, as he outlined when he went on to discuss the appointment of Bernie Cahill. The executive chairman had been given absolute discretion in terms of increasing yields, disposing of assets not essential to the core business and in achieving savings on the company's cost base.

Although the problems now facing the airline were clear, the opposition was adamant that it was government inaction in the years preceding the current difficulties that had caused the problem. Michael Noonan, the Fine Gael spokesman, was quick to implicate Cowen in this: 'No matter how the minister tries to obscure the truth it is clear Aer Lingus is on the fringe of disaster. The minister, though newly appointed, must share collective responsibility for this as he was a member of the last government which procrastinated in such a disgraceful manner while Aer Lingus moved closer to catastrophe.'

The opposition was not altogether pleased with the appointment of Bernie Cahill either or the powers afforded to him. Again Michael Noonan made the point: 'A most extraordinary aspect of the minister's statement on Tuesday night was that he had given absolute discretion to Mr Cahill to increase yields to dispose of assets not essential to the core business and to achieve savings on the cost base of the company, we presume, through redundancies. Will the minister confirm that when Mr Cahill was first approached he refused the poison chalice presented to him, that he only agreed to take on the task when he was guaranteed he would have *carte blanche* to sort out Aer Lingus as he saw fit and that he finally agreed to take on the task only when he had assurances that the minister would back his actions and not procrastinate as his two predecessors had done? Is it not an amazing turn of events that a man who both the taoiseach and tánaiste wanted out when Mr Haughey was taoiseach is now in such a strong position that he can dictate terms to the government?

'The appointment also begs the question as to why Mr Cahill was so inactive as chairman of Aer Lingus in the last eighteen months ... Was he in conflict with the board, the chief executive or the department of transport, energy and communications? What has happened now to spur him to action after eighteen months of inactivity? Is there really a rescue plan for Aer Lingus or are we looking at the biggest fire sale ever conducted in this country on the instructions of certain financial institutions?'

But if the government had failed to listen to Bernie Cahill in the past the mood had certainly changed now and Cowen was determined that he was the man who could save the airline. The minister also believed that a balanced and sensible approach to competition was what was needed and perhaps showed a misunderstanding of the pricing and fares model that would come to dominate the industry when he said: 'There has been overheating in the market as a result of the excesses of competition between Aer Lingus and Ryanair. The Aer Lingus strategy to replace a relatively old fleet with an all-new fleet in a short space of years has proved to be a major factor in its current financial problems.

'Offering the consumer fares which the airlines cannot afford and opening new markets without a well developed strategy have also proven to be costly exercises for Ryanair and Aer Lingus. These problems have left the industry structurally weakened for the future despite the best efforts of government to promote a sensible and balanced approach to change.'

The problems at Aer Lingus would not be solved in a single swipe. The airline underwent dramatic change in the following years. While Ryanair went on to become Europe's largest airline, Aer Lingus struggled to find its feet and re-invent itself against a backdrop of industrial relations problems. However, it is beyond doubt that the airline had a very doubtful future in 1993. The appointment of Bernie Cahill proved to be shrewd and successful; he held the post until his untimely death in 2001. Without such intervention there is little doubt that Aer Lingus might not have survived at all. The episode shows that while Cowen could indeed be blamed under the rules of 'cabinet collective responsibility' for not having supported earlier action, once he was handed the task he moved swiftly and comprehensively. His approach was considered and realistic, and by avoiding getting drawn too deeply into the situation and giving Aer Lingus, and Bernie Cahill in particular, the freedom to get on with the job, the airline was saved.

Other issues soon took centre stage. Cohesion funds were made available by the EU to the four so-called cohesion countries, Ireland, Spain, Greece and Portugal. The idea of cohesion funds was to transfer wealth to these countries to enable them to come up to a social and economic standard that would allow them to partake in Economic and Monetary Union. Ireland had been the main driver in establishing the principles of cohesion and received more than any other country in per capita funding. During the campaign for the Maastricht referendum, the Irish government had argued that involvement in Europe would be worth IR£6 billion in funding. The referendum was easily won on this basis. In late 1992 Albert Reynolds announced that they had secured IR£8 billion. This was seen as a resounding success. However, the European Commission were later to row back on the mathematical basis upon which this figure was calculated. This led to a heated dispute between the government and the Commission, and offered the opposition an opportunity to attack the government for overselling a deal they had not finalised. The next partnership agreement, the Programme for Competitiveness and Work, was based on the money that would flow from Europe. It led to heated argument and Brian Cowen was in the thick of it: 'I listened with interest to Deputy Cox refer to the four windmills. I presume he would describe with certainty, when he is not in command of all the facts, that we would get no more than £5 billion as a broken-down sluice gate at this stage. A totally synthetic storm has been raised over the National Development Plan. The bottom line is that we will be receiving at least £7.2 billion in EU aid between 1993 and 1999 …'

Miss Harney: 'Is it 1993 or 1994?'

Mr Cowen: '… easily the largest amount ever negotiated for Ireland. It is also freely acknowledged that we are getting the most per capita of the four cohesion countries. Only this week that was reported by the French newspaper *Le Monde* …'

For many this summed up the debate: from an opposition point of view the government had announced £8 billion but was not delivering that. The opposition also pointed out that the government's inclusion of 1993 funds was inappropriate as these related to earlier negotiations. On the other hand the government and its supporters were clear that no matter what way it was perceived, a big injection of cash into the Irish economy between those years had the potential to transform the state. It also contended that irrespective of what formula was used to establish the final figure, the negotiations would give Ireland its biggest ever haul of cash from Europe and it would remain a significant achievement.

Cowen was adamant that the criticism amounted to no more than jealousy and that he once again displayed his partisan approach to such criticism: 'When did Fine Gael in government ever negotiate from Brussels a fraction of the sums we negotiated in 1989 and again today? They mostly got pious aspirations and promises of good will, but little hard money. It is no harm for those who have built up the politics of goodwill to dip in now and again.

'Over the last fifteen months the opposition deputies have been consistently engaged in trying to sabotage and denigrate one of the greatest negotiating achievements this country has seen in terms of EU funding secured for Ireland. When the European Parliament elections come around in June we are going to ask the people if they want to elect representatives who are going to spend the next five years systematically selling the country short, trying to undermine Ireland's case in Brussels, trying to ensure that we get less money, all for the sake of petty political advantage at home.

'I find Deputy Rabbitte's new found advocacy of wimpish style negotiation particularly hard to take.'

When Cowen finally turned his attention to the subject matter itself, namely the new programme, he described it and the challenges facing the economy in far more visionary terms. It is ironic that he made this speech as Ireland was about to embark on a period of unprecedented success, yet he could easily have supplied the lines to Brian Lenihan for his budget speech fifteen years later: The Programme for Competitiveness and Work is about performance and acceptance of change. It is about recognising that to be able to compete effectively in the world we live in today requires constant top-quality performance and a willingness to embrace constant change.

'This demanding and challenging environment affects everybody. There are no categories of industry, business or administration that can afford to feel complacent or insulated from this environment. Traditionally only private enterprises competing on the open market were considered to be vulnerable to competitive pressures, but that is no longer the case. Today the semi-state sector, the public sector and the civil service find themselves coming under increasing competitive pressure and they too must be prepared to change and redirect their efforts … it is no good hoping that things will get easier tomorrow. It is no good expecting that conditions will soon get back to normal. Waiting for the global economy to pick up or for the recession in Europe to bottom out is not a credible or productive stance. We must act now. We have to plan on the basis that the way things are in business today is the way things will be tomorrow, the day after and the day after that. The Programme for Competitiveness and Work recognises this reality and sets out in a practical and pragmatic way the basis for action to create sustainable jobs and increased wealth here … the only choice is to respond and adapt to the environment as it exists now. We must recognise that the environment will shape our business behaviour far more than we can shape the business environment. If we seek to do otherwise we will not survive as a trading nation in an open and increasingly competitive worldwide economy.'

Cowen displayed a significant understanding of how to use rhetoric and also of the need for economic change on the part not just of the government, but of the individual and those in business. He went on to singularly praise the work of the semi-state sector in adapting to this new environment and becoming a catalyst for change in the country; particular mention is even given to Aer Lingus in this regard: 'The most obvious recent example of market force change has been the turnaround in Aer Lingus. I have already paid tribute to the staff and employees of Aer Lingus for the flexible and courageous response to the traumatic demands made on them. Here again the necessary decisions will have to be continuously augmented by the ability to react to the marketplace and competition.'

In career terms Brian Cowen was on the rise. His reputation was enhanced by his handling of opposition questions, his bullish defence of the government and most importantly by his handling of his ministerial portfolio. But a crisis is never far away in politics.

The mining company Arcon was to open a mine in Galmoy, County Kilkenny. A report made by independent Scottish consultants on the suitability of the site had a line amended and Cowen soon found himself at the centre of a political storm with the accusation of deliberately interfering to assist Arcon to get planning permission. At the time it was being described as Cowengate: 'Officials of my department ... contacted RPS Cairns about the matter and in particular raised the interpretation which might, in isolation, be put on the sentence. My department, however, made it absolutely clear to RPS Cairns that they were not being asked to alter their report nor to do anything which would be at variance in any way with their professional ethics. Given the construction which might, in isolation, be put on a sentence, RPS Cairns were asked if they wished to reconsider their report. RPS Cairns themselves decided voluntarily to delete the sentence [risk of dam failure due to the presence of karst features and the effects of de-watering beneath the impoundment] and to submit an amended report which my department then forwarded to Kilkenny County Council. They did so on the basis of a clear acknowledgement that the deletion of the sentence in question did not materially alter the report.'

Cowen was determined to clear his name and was eager to take the opposition spokespersons to task over their allegations: 'At no stage was I personally involved in any of this process. However, the particular slant which was put on the issue raised by Deputy Hogan might be interpreted as a slur on the professional reputation of the officials in my department and those in Kilkenny County Council. This would be totally unacceptable to me and, I am sure, to every other Member of this House. I am, therefore, in the light of my clarification asking the deputy to withdraw his remarks.'

Phil Hogan was in no mood to accept Brian Cowen's version of events, however, and was not willing to withdraw his remarks. For the first time the opposition had Cowen on the ropes and they contended that either this was a clear case of political favouritism or definitive evidence of poor judgment from the minister. According to Mr Hogan: 'The minister for transport, energy and communications is in the House to apologise for the second day in a row about matters pertaining to his department …'

Mr Cowen: 'That is outrageous …'

Mr Hogan: '… that subsequently meant planning permission could be granted … Is the minister aware that this sentence was altered in his department? Is he aware that if it was not altered in the Cairns report, planning permission could not be granted by Kilkenny County Council? Was he aware that the document by RPS Cairns was the final report on the EIS submitted by Arcon and that it passed through the Geological Survey of Ireland and his department without comment until he was alerted by Kilkenny County Council that there was a problem in relation to the tailings pond? I put it to the minister that he was fully aware of this serious matter when it was brought to his attention by Kilkenny County Council and that he took a hands-on approach in ensuring this material matter was changed which subsequently meant planning permission could be granted.'

Mr Cowen: 'An attempt is obviously being made for the second day in a row to denigrate …'

Mr McCormack: 'Tell the truth.'

Mr Cowen: 'I have no problem telling the truth. For the second day in a row Deputy Hogan has suggested without substantiation, and under the privilege of the House, that I instigated, was involved in and took a hands-on approach in changing a consultants' report which he claims would have resulted in planning permission being refused had this not happened. I will repeat this one more time for Deputy Hogan. If he believes that to be true I ask him to repeat it outside the House, otherwise I will deem it to be an abuse of privilege.'

Mr Hogan: 'The minister has already admitted he was wrong ...'

Mr Cowen: 'Deputy Hogan asked who in my department altered the consultants' report. I am stating unequivocally that no one in my department altered the RPS Cairns report. I refer the House to the statement I made that RPS Cairns voluntarily withdrew that part of the report following consultation and discussion. RPS Cairns will verify that if the deputy bothers to ask them ...

'They confirmed it verbally to my department today. Those are the facts. The question put to me was if I, as minister, had a hands-on approach in changing or deleting a sentence in a report. I am saying clearly that neither I nor my department participated in that. That will be verified by the authors of the report. I suggest to the deputy that if he is not prepared to withdraw the remarks he made under the privilege of the House he should repeat them outside the House ...

'I was not involved in the detailed technical assessments in regard to this matter as I have no function or expertise in this area. I reiterate that there was no interference by me, the minister of state, Deputy Treacy, or anybody in my department in the proper discretionary functions available to the county manager or the planning officials in Kilkenny County Council who deal with the planning authority. We are statutory consultees in this matter, as are others, and we are seeking to assist the planning authority through the provision of technical and other data so that the largest EIS ever to come before a local authority on a mining project is dealt with adequately, with full information available. That is the clear position.

'To suggest that a planning authority would deny itself proper discretion under the law or do so under direction gives a very low opinion of the people in Kilkenny County Council and the professional staff in my department dealing with this matter ...'

Cowen's defence of his position was robust and the matter came to nothing in the end, but the allegation was not withdrawn and continued to hang over him for some time. Other events of much greater magnitude were soon to take centre stage, however. It was now November 1994 and the appointment of Harry Whelehan as president of the high court had caused the collapse of the government. Fianna Fáil had lost two by-elections which changed the Dáil arithmetic, allowing Labour, Fine Gael and the Democratic Left sufficient numbers to form a coalition. This was far more appealing to Labour than the original rainbow with the Progressive Democrats. The collapse of the government resulted in the resignation of Albert Reynolds as taoiseach and leader of Fianna Fáil. Cowen took this blow personally and continued to stand by Reynolds as his mentor and a man he trusted wholeheartedly. A change in leadership is not often good news for existing cabinet ministers and Cowen would have been unsure of his standing with the new leader Bertie Ahern. On 16 November 1994 a motion of no confidence was tabled in the Dáil. Cowen sat through the debate, clearly annoyed and angry, heckling speakers at every opportunity.

While the contributions to the heated exchanges do not tell us much about the policies of Brian Cowen they do illustrate the depth of his loyalty and passion. Without doubt this was a man who was very different to many of those who surrounded him. Charles Haughey was the personification of calm collectedness in the Dáil chamber, while Albert Reynolds was content in his belief that history would be favourable to him if he took decisions for the right reasons and only became particularly animated when his personal integrity was impugned. Bertie Ahern was not a strong orator and was not at ease getting into such dogfights. None of the three were the type of politician to make an impassioned plea on behalf of Fianna Fáil or to believe so deeply that their party was inherently a force for good. Cowen on the other hand did. He was frequently annoyed at what he saw as a demonisation of a party he clearly held a deep affection for beyond that of simply being a representative of it. He held personal friendships and trust in high regard.

There is a sense that Cowen was not always able to take criticism on board, and appreciating the views of others did not come naturally to him. To a certain extent it is indicative of a politician who is decisive, but not always considerate of any view that challenged the pre-eminence of his party's position. Cowen certainly does not display any rose-tinted glasses with regard to his own or the Fianna Fáil record and readily admits failings, but the struggle was always pitched against a tide of criticism which he felt was entirely unfair. This could be argued as stunting his ability to address those shortcomings within the party itself. Cowen was loyal and he did not agree with public shows of disloyalty. For someone so closely associated with Albert Reynolds, the return of Ray Burke to the Fianna Fáil front bench under Bertie Ahern must surely have been a bitter pill to swallow, as Burke had been a thorn in the side of Reynolds and his supporters since Burke's sacking in 1992. Cowen did, however, swallow it, displaying admiral loyalty to the new leader Bertie Ahern and to his party. But this episode alone indicates just why such a policy is not always the best option: perhaps if Cowen had opposed the appointment of Burke he could have saved his party a lot more grief in the long run.

Brian Cowen had a short term of just under three years as a government minister. He was, however, now clearly established as a heavy hitter on the political scene. While questions may have been raised, the Dáil record gives the impression of a man who was on top of his briefs, a central figure in government and someone who could point to a reasonable record of success without any major disasters.

OUTSTANDING IN HIS FIELD? – COWEN'S AGRICULTURE RECORD

The collapse of the government in 1994 came as a shock to all of the Fianna Fáil organisation. In a matter of a few short weeks they had gone from highly successful government to opposition. Bertie Ahern took over the party and had the luxury of being in opposition and the opportunity to make more front-bench appointments than if he had been in government. One of the moves that surprised people the most was the appointment of Brian Cowen as agriculture spokesperson. There have been many theories on this, ranging from an initial distrust by Ahern of Cowen's ambitions, to the fact that Ahern needed to shore up the agriculture vote and required a strong voice. Based upon the fact that Cowen had held industrial/economic portfolios before this, and that his family background was in the pub trade, it seemed unusual to appoint him to agriculture with not much to recommend him for the post other than the fact that he represented a largely rural constituency in Laois/Offaly.

Some people felt that Cowen slipped from the radar slightly during his term in opposition and that he was only a shadow of his former self during this period. However, it is also the case that perhaps his subject matter simply did not demand the column inches any more, because the Dáil record certainly gives lie to the assertion that Cowen was not as active as before.

While it might not be an area that would have been Cowen's first choice, he demonstrated an ability to understand the problems facing the agriculture sector and to digest large sections of complex information. His appointment also gives us the chance to observe some very interesting debates with one of the oratorical stars of the Fine Gael party of the time and the minister for agriculture, food and forestry, Ivan Yates. Yates was a very different style of politician to Cowen and their approach to government and negotiations was often at odds. They were two partisan politicians in the debate, both with very set agendas and both able speakers. Yates certainly had the measure of Cowen in terms of his own popularity and charisma, but he was not about to be brow-beaten by the heavy hitting former minister. The stage was set for much political point-scoring by both sides. It was October 1995, however, before we find a debate of real substance, when both men locked horns on the question of milk quotas. On 11 October, Cowen and his colleagues tabled a number of questions for Yates: Cowen asked when legislation to provide for the ring-fencing of milk quotas in disadvantaged areas would be introduced; Bobby Molloy asked about the reason for the delay in enforcing ring-fencing of milk quotas in the disadvantaged areas; Brendan Smith asked when he would introduce the necessary regulations to ring-fence the milk quota in the disadvantaged areas. Yates replied: 'I am pleased to inform the House the legislation which provides for the application of the principle of ring-fencing in the operation of the milk quota system was signed by me on 4 October.

'The statutory instrument concerned updates and consolidates all the provisions relating to the operation of the milk quota system in Ireland.'

Mr Cowen: 'The minister promised to do this last February and I presume he is aware of the many farmers who relied on the availability of temporary lease quotas from co-ops for the past number of years. They were not told until mid-July what their position would be this year. What will the minister do for the main dairy farmers, with small and medium size enterprises, who are now being offered 3,000 to 5,000 gallons lease quotas instead of 10,000 to 20,000 gallons lease quotas? What were they supposed to do? They should have been notified of the situation last March, not halfway through the main production season in mid-July. What will the minister do for these farmers? Will he pay their super-levy?'

Mr Yates: 'I will not pay anybody's super-levy.'

Mr Cowen: 'There is no fear of the minister doing that. He looked after the big boys; the commercial boys were looked after …'

Mr Yates: 'Regarding the question raised by the deputy about small farmers, I took the exceptional step today of introducing measures which will have a 10 per cent clawback on private leases for cheque-book farmers. This will involve a 10 per cent deduction for people who had temporary leases and who will have them in the future.

'I am not satisfied with the situation whereby all the milk in the restructuring scheme is being siphoned off when milk is making as much as 60p a gallon. As the deputy is aware, that is cheque-book driven. I have taken this exceptional step and the legislation will be put in place soon. It is a new measure which has been checked by the office of the attorney general and the EU Commission. It meets fully the ultimate legal powers I can take in this regard.'

Mr Cowen: 'How many gallons are involved in any such clawback? How many gallons are people demanding, given that they had a certain number up to now and that they were sure they would get it again, based on the minister's statements last February? Why has he not been in a position to deliver for those farmers, who were not told about their position in mid-July? Was it another promise made in the early flush of ministerial office? Can the minister explain the position to farmers who are worried out of their wits about how they will work out their quota and the over-supply of milk? Will the minister meet the demands and will he be in a position to look after those people before they sell every cow they own?'

Mr Yates: 'The purpose of the 10 per cent clawback is to cut down on the number of temporary leases ...'

Mr Cowen: 'It is a drop in the ocean. The minister is indulging in semantics.'

Mr Yates: 'We are exceeding our quota. As the deputy is aware, this is because there is now a record price for milk. Milk farmers were never doing better with 109p a gallon.'

Mr Cowen: 'It has nothing to do with the minister ...'

Mr Yates: 'The current market for milk is so buoyant that the dairy farmers are delighted with the minister.'

Cowen was laying out a stall for what would be his main position in the time to come. He did not dispute the figures of the minister in any substantive sense, but he was conscious of the political weakness as he saw it of the minister's position, in that farmers had not been told that the over-supply could occur. He was also establishing himself as a defender of the small farmer and an opponent of the larger corporations and companies operating in the sector. This may simply be a reverting to type for Fianna Fáil, who were taking advantage to lay claim to small farmers as a voting block that was traditionally supportive of the party. Yates was quite clear in his argument, however, and made the point that the buoyant milk market was what had caused the problem. It is difficult not to feel that while Cowen was making a forceful argument couched in rhetoric, it was not something that he entirely disagreed with the minister on. So much of agriculture policy is decided at European level and operates within such tight guidelines that most argument relates to its implementation and perception rather than any real argument to suggest different or alternative core policies.

By November there were considerable problems in the sheep sector. Cowen tabled a motion in relation to this on 7 November, taking the opportunity to criticise the minister's approach to European negotiations, his level of activity in relation to initiatives to boost the profile of the sector, and to display his distaste for what he sees as PR-driven politics: 'We have a serious crisis in the Irish sheep industry which requires urgent remedy. It is a crisis that will require sustained negotiating on behalf of the minister at council level to ensure that the emergency issues are dealt with and that the cash prices which have bedevilled sheep producers throughout the country are addressed. He should be more pro-active in an area where there have been serious difficulties under his stewardship, an area in which one would have expected he would have shown some flair, given that many of his constituents are seriously affected by what has happened, and is happening, in the Irish sheep sector ... Since 1991 we have seen the reform of the CAP so far as sheep are concerned. At that time we also had the introduction of the quota regime and – with the full support of everyone concerned – a ewe premium calculated across the European Union rather than on an island-only basis, whereby each member state would do its own calculations. That was introduced in the belief that Irish prices would rise to meet French prices; in other words, there would be convergence in relation to the price, and the ewe premium would be the support mechanism which would be uniformly applied at every level throughout the community.

'Since 1991 our experience has shown that the theory does not work so far as Irish sheep producers are concerned. In 1992 there was a collapse in lamb prices. In December of that year the then minister, Deputy Joe Walsh, obtained a top-up premium of over £6 per ewe to meet that situation. Therefore, the minister has a precedent if he wishes to look at it as to how it is possible to get recognition for the special status and the vulnerability of the Irish sheep sector in those circumstances. That precedent was set by his predecessor, Deputy Joe Walsh, in December 1992. In 1993 and 1994 prices were static. In 1995 there has been a collapse in early lamb prices due to currency differences, cheap hogget meat and the lower prices in France.'

Cowen obviously felt on firmer ground here and was convinced that the minister was failing in his approach. He goes on to take a slightly more personal swipe: 'Certainly no marketing strategy on behalf of the minister or An Bord Bia or anybody else in the department is responsible for the favourable fluctuations, because nothing was done by the department or the minister during the year. The only initiatives from this minister were two aids to private storage schemes which took out a minimum number of hoggets from the marketplace but they did nothing for price ... The minister cannot continue to be a policy taker – as he has proven himself to be – rather than a policy maker. He cannot say he has inherited this problem and there is nothing he can do. He inherited the benign situation in the milk industry, to which he never adverts when he and his PR people are talking to people around the country; he inherited excellent situations in the cattle and pig industries and he will probably claim credit for the fact that world prices in grain have lifted above EU prices. The minister will probably tell us he ensured that the sun shone for three months of the year.'

Interestingly Cowen then goes on to espouse an economic measure for the sector: 'Given the high national reserves, we have advocated a reduction in interest rates to help improve our competitive position *vis-à-vis* the sterling area. This would be of crucial significance to sheep farmers next year. If we do not deal with this issue sheep farmers will continue to be at a 7 per cent disadvantage next year, and this will be in addition to everything else that has gone wrong in that sector. The government can achieve this reduction in interest rates if it has the political will to keep its public expenditure programmes under control. If Fianna Fáil was in government it would avail of the opportunity to reduce interest rates. Such a move would be welcomed not only by sheep producers and processors but by all those involved in the indigenous food sector.'

He goes on to finish with what is now a trademark flourish: 'We put down this motion to ensure a proper discussion on this issue. As can be seen from what I said, using the word "crisis" to describe the problems in the sheep sector is not an exaggeration. The minister can take emergency measures to alleviate this crisis yet the measures taken so far this year have achieved nothing. The minister should indicate to the vested interests that he is serious about taking hard decisions regardless of whether he can achieve consensus on them. He should do something about these problems and ensure that farmers do not have to protest on the streets of Dublin during the winter months because of his inactivity and incompetence.'

Of course Ivan Yates as minister was not about to concede the argument. He met the issues with regard to his record head on: 'I do not need to be convinced of the importance of protecting the future of our sheep sector. It is operating in an increasingly difficult and competitive market with pressure being exerted not only by exporters in other production countries but also from other meats. The difficulties for the sector are not as a result of a decline in political supports – there was a cut in export refunds in other areas – but are due to market difficulty. No minister can be held responsible for the market price of sheep.'

Cowen and Yates almost seemed to enjoy the verbal banter between them as the debate progressed. In these early exchanges the partisan approach by both Cowen and Yates makes it difficult to ascertain the real views of either man. Cowen also had the luxury of opposition on his side. His main success was in ensuring that matters were debated at length and an ability to force his opponent to engage at a very substantial level. Yates was an able opponent and for all Cowen's skill in the sphere of debating, Yates managed to survive and score points. Landing a punch on Yates was a very difficult thing to do.

However, in recent decades Fianna Fáil has had the advantage of more government experience. This often translates itself into the argument that Fianna Fáil personnel are more experienced at EU level in particular. This kind of perception, certainly within Fianna Fáil, allowed Cowen to identify the reforms being tabled under the Common Agricultural Policy as a potential Achilles heel of Yates. On 5 December 1995, Fianna Fáil tabled a motion calling on the government to provide a cogent and focused response to the reform proposals under CAP. Cowen took up the debate: 'In contrast to the cogent, focused response from government this motion reasonably seeks, we have what is now a complete policy chasm between the government partners. The furious row between the tánaiste and minister for agriculture, food and forestry on reform of the Common Agricultural Policy is the latest manifestation of government disarray on the range of issues defining our relations with the European Union. Despite having been repeatedly promised since last spring, the publication of the government White Paper has been long-fingered again. It is evident there is no agreement in government on issues fundamental to the totality of our relations with the European Union.

'The squabble reported in today's papers between the tánaiste and the minister for agriculture, food and forestry leaves our entire negotiating position in a state of chaos, the tánaiste reported as having said that European Union enlargement was not only a political necessity but would present new markets and chances for Ireland. In flat contradiction, the minister is reported as saying that backward eastern states would never be compatible with membership. It is against that background of in-fighting and incompetence on the part of members of the government that the vital issue of the Common Agricultural Policy is being debated publicly for the first time ...'

Cowen clearly believed that planning and preparation was the key to a successful outcome in negotiations: 'The lack of coherence in the broader areas of foreign policy, if not tackled, will have a serious impact on our ability to successfully articulate a cogent response to reform of the Common Agricultural Policy. The internal structures of the European Union are also being subjected to reform, agricultural spending at present ring-fenced until 1999 resulting from intergovernmental agreement. However, in an evolving European Union, in which the parliament will have increased powers, that type of commitment may be impossible to achieve and its potential consequences for Irish agriculture extremely serious.

'Fianna Fáil demand that the government articulates its definitive position on these crucial structural problems. We must avoid a scenario in which, because of a lack of planning on the part of the minister, the government of the day in 1999, will be placed in the position of running around endeavouring to rearrange the deck chairs on the *Titanic* ... '

Cowen then followed up his defence of small farmers and his opposition to the idea of a small number of large farmers regardless of the efficiencies that this might bring: 'Another disturbing trend is that the prohibitive price of quota is keeping new blood out of the industry. Prior to the introduction of quota, for every two people leaving milk production, one new entrant was taking up the enterprise. The trend has been not only to bigger and fewer units but away from the disadvantaged areas. The acute lack of policy that characterises this minister's performance is evidenced by the 10 per cent clawback on quota introduced by him. It will have no effect on the continuing haemorrhage of quota from disadvantaged areas. This is a classic case of a policy that is in direct variance with what is required. The minister's apathy should not obscure the fact that there are many policy instruments available at national level. What is required is preparedness on the part of the minister to stand up to vested interests.

'Not only is the national quota slipping into fewer and fewer hands, but a real chance to get more quota and to do something for people on the margins of the industry is being allowed to pass ...'

Cowen was particularly aware of the dangers of the more competitive environment for these farmers: 'It is time we made hard choices, took a pro-active approach and went into the country to talk to farmers' representative organisations and to farm families, and took some tough decisions to ensure we do not end up with a land clearance policy which it seems will be the outcome of the CAP reform. We do not know where we will stand after 1999. Whatever about plan B? Plan A is a blank sheet at the moment and this is not acceptable.

'There are opportunities. The on-farm investment schemes should be a powerful instrument for policy to help secure viability on smaller holdings. We have failed to give priority to those areas where there has been a serious lack of investment in the last few years. Those farmers cannot and will not be able to compete in the second phase of CAP reform if we are not in a position to allow investment in those farms to make them more competitive.'

Ivan Yates was obviously in no mood to take a lecture on EU negotiation. The thrust of Yates' argument was aptly summarised in the closing paragraph of his contribution. He may have felt under some pressure on this issue, but he was intent on fighting it. He was, however, in more defensive mood than normal, although we pick up the debate with Yates using the old political trick of saying something by saying he won't say it: 'I will not take a cheap shot by inquiring with regard to what was done in relation to the national milk quota between 1984 and 1994. However, am I to suddenly parachute into Brussels and obtain an extra milk quota for Ireland? The milk quota regime is embedded. I would be interested to hear from Deputy Cowen with regard to what is Fianna Fáil's direction in relation to milk?'

Sometimes in politics, however, someone else gives you help you never expected. If Ivan Yates had kept Brian Cowen at bay and defended his actions successfully, he was effectively sabotaged in his efforts. Cowen was always on the lookout to expose any hint of weakness. Fine Gael's partners in government at the time, Democratic Left, scored an amazing own goal in terms of agricultural voters. Any efforts at building an image of a government doing its best for agriculture on Yates' part was put firmly on the back foot by Democratic Left's Kathleen Lynch's comments on 21 February 1996 during a debate on the beef industry: 'Judging by the motion before us, obviously Fianna Fáil has decided to abandon the struggle and return to its roots, but what about the farmers? Notwithstanding the difficulties faced by some producers – which I fully acknowledge – large farmers have never had it so good. As an urban deputy, representing PAYE workers and those without work, I am constantly bemused by the extent to which the farming sector can benefit from a variety of grants, perks, tax breaks and the like.

'A short two weeks ago, in reply to a parliamentary question, the House was informed that in 1995 the average income tax take from a PAYE worker was £4,087 while that from a farmer was £1,031, clearly demonstrating that PAYE workers pay through the nose in terms of taxes and higher food prices to support an agricultural system long out of control.'

Mr Cowen: 'What about the average farm income?'

No matter what terms it was couched in, it was an argument that would never be well received by anyone involved in agriculture. It was something that would play right into Cowen's hands in terms of rallying the farming vote to the Fianna Fáil banner. He was quick to raise it on the order of business some days later. Cowen is adamant that the only way to reassure markets is by direct intervention at a political level by visiting them. While Cowen may have often favoured the role of detached facilitator, in this case he clearly believed in a different approach: 'The minister should go on a political mission to those markets to inform them there is nothing wrong with the Irish beef processing industry and stand over Irish beef as a pure and premium product. I cannot understand why the taoiseach has not sent the minister to do so as I am sure he would be willing to do it if he was asked. There seems to be an appalling complacency in some quarters of government although I exclude the minister from that because he seems to know what is going on. However, other members of cabinet have no idea of the potential seriousness of the situation.'

Cowen also focused on what he saw as a lack of co-ordination on the part of the government and seemed at pains to point out that this was not a political football and that the opposition would support any measures that may alleviate the problem. However, he also warned that they would not accept complacency from the government in the face of such a crisis: 'The minister can be assured that we on this side of the House will support any meaningful, effective measures the government is prepared to take to safeguard our beef industry, its jobs and the market share for our products at home and abroad. We will be constructive in pressurising the government to honour its responsibilities in this respect and bring forward precautionary proposals as a matter of urgency … This is the House's first opportunity since the recess to debate the crisis affecting the country's biggest industry. Since 20 March last, BSE has been the most serious problem facing the Irish economy. It has been serious for all economic sectors, but it has been a catastrophe for farming …'

As he continued, Cowen turned his attention once again to Yates' performance on the European stage, highlighting what he perceived as a chink in the armour of the minister: 'Commissioner Fischler's proposals were published at the end of July. Apart from an unfulfilled promise to bring forward his own proposals, to date there has been no intelligible response to the proposals by the minister, Deputy Yates, or the government. The only quoted response so far has been that the proposals are "not radical enough". The minister should use this opportunity to state the government's exact position in relation to the serious measures which emphasise the issue of controlling supply but which do not do enough regarding increasing consumption …'

Cowen put in an assured performance in applying pressure on the minister by bringing the argument back to his belief that the government had failed to reopen markets. He was active in opposition and was eager to take steps that were seen to be pro-active and to be seen to be solving problems even from opposition. The government felt that this was no more than opportunism, but it showed a dynamism in the approach to the issue that portrayed immense energy on Cowen's part and allowed him to speak with some authority even if he was not in a position to really deliver for farmers: 'Transforming Ireland from a land with 160,000 family farms to a mere 60,000 holdings may be the minister's agenda but it is not mine and it is not this party's. In his time in office his inaction has amounted to a campaign of attrition against small and marginal farms. Investment schemes put in place to make a viable difference to small enterprises have been allowed to wither or collapse. Resources have been withheld from Teagasc to enable it to fulfil its mandate to smaller enterprise …'

Using all his skill as a debater Cowen continued to widen his arguments to increase the pressure on the minister on a number of fronts, introducing details of industrial relations arguments that were being experienced by the department of agriculture: 'Since the minister has been in charge of the department it has suffered more industrial chaos than under any of his predecessors. His bungling, his incompetence and his view of what constitutes modern industrial relations is unbelievable. His description of his staff as "opportunists in the extreme" is an outrageous claim, even allowing for his personal familiarity with opportunism. He should not abuse hard-pressed staff in his department who are trying to keep the show on the road. Unlike the minister, I have spoken to staff members and met them in my home. They are reasonable and would like to resolve this matter with the minister, if they could speak to him, but not alone has he not done so, he has not spoken to the trade union IMPACT which represents 40 per cent of the department's staff.'

Mr Yates: 'I had them to lunch.'

Mr Cowen: 'Those people are trying to keep the intervention grading and carcass classification work going. The minister should meet and talk with them, because there is a solution. The staff told me that at no time did the minister or anyone with his authority suggest to them that they suspend their action on the basis of re-entering genuine talks. Yesterday the minister's spin doctors sought to suggest that informal talks were happening between the trade union and departmental officials but Mr Paddy Keating of IMPACT had to deny that today. This is further evidence of how out of touch the minister is from the real position.'

Yates was under significant pressure at this point. While he put in a very strong performance, he was still undermined by a general feeling that the government was not in favour of farmers. His latest contribution may have been what he saw as a tell-it-as-it-is approach, but it served to cement Cowen's position as the resolute defender of small farmers. While Yates made a strong case in his own defence, Cowen was busy building a reputation for himself. It wasn't all about showing the minister in a bad light – Yates was more than capable of meeting those arguments – but while Yates was defending himself Cowen was free to continue his own visits and discussions with the sector, carefully establishing himself as a real alternative and creating the image that he could indeed do better.

The pressure of the crisis was unrelenting, however, and after Kathleen Lynch's comments it offered Cowen the opportunity to attack a government that was not seen as appreciating the difficulties in the sector. Ivan Yates had also announced a protocol that was agreed with the Russians on Irish beef. In radio interviews Yates seemed to suggest he had handled the deal personally in Dublin Airport and had to make a decision on the spot with as he put it a 'gun to his head'. It later transpired that Yates was not at the meeting and he was referring to phone contact he had had with his officials.

On 19 December 1996, Cowen offered a stark warning that the government had been too inclined toward spending and that insufficient financial arrangements were in place to deal with future hardships. It has perhaps a ring of the problems faced in 2008: 'I wish to share time with Deputy Joe Walsh. We see the relish with which ministers like to spend everyone else's money. The economic growth achieved gives rise to a temptation to spend money to a greater extent. The government is particularly prone to giving in to that temptation. When the economic cycle changes we will not have made prudent financial arrangements to enable us face hardships in the future. The government's political imperative is to give out as much good news as it can before it faces the electorate. We can expect a similar trend next year.'

Cowen then moves on from the general to the specific in the form of agriculture; beef had now overtaken the needs of the sheep sector in Cowen's mind as he finished with an argument criticising Yates for concentrating too much time on the crisis: 'Beef prices are under serious threat but the minister claims he can do nothing for beef farmers until January because of his concentration on the sheep issue. If what we see today is the result of his concentration on the sheep issue, beef farmers need not look forward to a prosperous New Year. In the coming months many people will witness the results of the rhetoric that has been emanating from the minister's department in the past twelve months.'

From a policy point of view Cowen's position as agriculture spokesperson gave him enormous freedom. He did not have the worry of taking the wrong step and facing the repercussions. For the most part Cowen relied heavily on figures and statistics during debates, suggesting perhaps that he felt comfort in arguing on numbers in the first instance and also perhaps that agriculture was not a subject he felt naturally at home debating about.

It is difficult to say if things would have been much different if Cowen was minister, as he never held the post in government. More than anything, Cowen's record in the Dáil points to a versatile politician, a man who believed in the rights of small farmers and a man of action and decisiveness – as his trip to Iran illustrated. We can never say for sure, however, if those actions would have led to any real results or if Cowen would have had a different policy if in government. As a TD from a rural constituency it is evident that he was in contact with the agricultural sector continually and sought to represent what he believed was the majority of farmers. He had an able opponent in Ivan Yates, however, and he never quite outwitted him on the issue, although he did land some punches. Yet, considering that a minister is always under greater pressure and normally defensive, Yates would not be disappointed with his own record. Cowen was a different style of politician and there is a sense that he did not like Yates' polished and media-savvy style. The 'blue-eyed boy', as he referred to him, was certainly a popular figure within Fine Gael and among many of the public too. In the debates we get a sense that Cowen feels too much time is spent on the creation of Yates' image and not enough dealing with issues. But there was a telling lesson in that itself. In a very media-conscious age, where there is only a slight window to reach your audience, politicians must be geared to working through the media. While the public might often criticise this in their politicians, it is the case that strong arguments, assembled with much fact and figures, and hours spent researching and working will count for naught if they are not combined with a simple media-savvy style. There is no doubt that

Cowen was a strong performer in his role as agriculture spokesperson and that the record shows little fault on his part, but he could perhaps have taken a lesson or two from the more laid-back Yates on how to present the message. Interestingly, within a few years, Ivan Yates had left politics to look after his business interests while Brian Cowen went on to become taoiseach, illustrating perhaps, most of all, that Cowen had a passion and belief in what he did that outweighed that of Yates, and more importantly the ambition to match it.

ANGOLA (AKA THE HEALTH SERVICE)

1997 was to be an election year. Fianna Fáil had spent just over two years in opposition and as a party that had never been in opposition for longer than one term they expected that they would soon be returning to government. The Rainbow Coalition was not unpopular in itself but it had faced some very tough difficulties in living up to the expectations that had been set. Fianna Fáil under Bertie Ahern seemed a new and revitalised organisation. Health was seen as a major issue for the public and Ahern decided in early 1997 to move Brian Cowen to the health portfolio. It was seen as a more central role in government for Cowen and afforded him the opportunity to attack the Rainbow Coalition on what was probably their weakest point.

Some viewed it as an effort by Ahern to launch an exocet at the government in an attempt to sink them before the election. Cowen was seen as the man who could carry this argument with most force. However, after a successful election when Fianna Fáil did indeed return to office Ahern surprised many observers by seemingly going against the accepted logic and appointing John O'Donoghue and Brian Cowen to justice and health respectively. It is generally thought that an opposition spokesperson who performs well and has been outspoken should not be appointed to that same post in government, as they will inevitably have given too many hostages to fortune and will be open to criticism. Some thought it was Ahern's way of dealing with potential leadership rivals.

It does, however, give us a unique opportunity to assess Cowen's policies and positions both from opposition and government point of view. There is little doubt this was arguably his toughest ministerial posting as problems were mounting in a health service weighed down by bureaucracy and vested interests. Any advances in healthcare would come at a cost and would also be slow and painful for staff and patients, and in many people's eyes could be the political death of a minister. Cowen is reputed to have dubbed the department 'Angola' because of the amount of unexploded landmines that lurked in the health services.

The issues that were covered in the period were wide-ranging and serious, from medical cards and nurses' strikes to CJD [Creutzfeldt-Jakob disease] and tribunals.

No assessment of Cowen's performance both in opposition and government would be complete without reference to the Hepatitis C scandal involving the Blood Transfusion Services Board. This must surely rank as one of the worst scandals in the history of the state, when infected blood products were given to people in need of blood transfusions, and their subsequent treatment by the state left a lot to be desired. In particular, even after the initial story had broken and a tribunal been established it was the emergence of the details of the case of Brigid McCole that was to shock the nation. Cowen was in opposition when the scandal hit the minister for health, Michael Noonan. It would deeply affect Noonan's career, including him apportionin'g some of the blame for the disastrous Fine Gael election in 2002 to the fact that a TV show portrayed the events in an unflattering light in the run-up to the election.

On 4 March 1997, we find Brian Cowen as opposition spokesperson on health putting forth the first questions relating to the events that impacted upon the state most directly: 'There is a need for the minister for health, Deputy Noonan, to give full information to the House on the latest revelation in the Hepatitis C controversy. There is a need for him to clarify, as a matter of extreme urgency, the circumstances surrounding the infection of persons in 1970-71 with the Hepatitis C virus. It has been reported in the media that a woman infected with Hepatitis C as a result of a blood transfusion at that time subsequently died and that her family received compensation from the Hepatitis C compensation tribunal. This revelation is significant, as up until now the Hepatitis C infection scandal has been associated with events since 1976.'

At this point, as a tribunal had been established, Noonan was unwilling to give a statement: 'As the deputy will be aware, the terms of reference of the tribunal of inquiry on the Hepatitis C infection of blood and blood products specify at paragraph 1 the following matter of public importance: "The circumstances in which Anti-D, manufactured by the Blood Transfusion Service Board (BTSB), was infected with what is now known as Hepatitis C and the implications thereof, including the consequences for the blood supply and other blood products."

'I expect to receive the final report of the tribunal of inquiry shortly. In the meantime it would be inappropriate for me to make any comment which may be seen to pre-empt the findings or recommendations of the tribunal which was established on foot of a motion passed by both Houses of the Oireachtas.'

By 20 March the tribunal report was before the Dáil and the details of Brigid McCole's case were public knowledge. Michael Noonan moved the motion to accept the findings of the tribunal and in his contribution stated: 'The report gives us a coherent account of what has occurred and why, but it is considerably more than merely a history. It is an unemotional indictment of past procedures at the BTSB, and is unequivocal in its apportionment of blame to certain named members of staff.'

In his speech Noonan explained that the tribunal report had changed everything that he had been told and therefore he had agreed a change in stance with victims' group 'Positive Action': 'As deputies will be aware, I met with representatives of Positive Action last evening in response to a letter it sent to me on 14 March last outlining its views arising from publication of the tribunal report. Positive Action has requested a full reappraisal of the compensation tribunal. The reappraisal upon which the government is embarking is required principally because the state of knowledge has been altered by the publication of this report.'

However, Noonan was quick to defend his position and state his case. He made the point that he had acted in accordance with the best advice and that the tribunal had not found him culpable: 'The tribunal concludes that the quantitative information "did not constitute new, dominant or fundamental medical evidence" and "did not form a foundation for any particular conclusion which would not have been reached without them in regard to the general wrongdoing in the use of the plasma for patient X". It further concludes that my decision not to set up a tribunal of inquiry at that time "was an adequate and appropriate reaction to the facts as they then were". In addition, the tribunal indicated that "the attitude taken by myself and minister O'Shea in reply to the Dáil questions in relation to this issue would appear to have been correct".'

Noonan was correct in this point and also made the case that once the tribunal had been established he had to await its outcome and report before proceeding. New information came to light during the tribunal and he argued that he could not pre-empt its findings. However, Noonan was in a tight corner and while public opinion was looking for a vent for the shock that was felt he also came up against an unforgiving Brian Cowen. In what is arguably one of Cowen's finest and most well-structured arguments, he takes the entire government to task only weeks before an election would be called. It was certainly Brian Cowen's strongest performance from the opposition benches despite consistent heckling: 'The government, in putting this amended motion to the House, has made a significant concession. It has conceded something which, as a matter of principle and policy, it refused to concede since this debacle happened under the stewardship of the former minister for health, Deputy Howlin. The minister, Deputy Noonan, stated he has agreed to the setting up of a statutory tribunal. That is a major victory for the victims who have to suffer as a result of the criminal negligence of a state agency. However, let it not be seen as a generous response proactively provided by this government. It is, in fact, a somersault of a huge magnitude, given the minister's stated position and the policy of this Administration when he was questioned on this issue at the tribunal some weeks ago …

'On page 160 of the transcript of the tribunal report the minister, Deputy Noonan, was asked by counsel: "In relation to your dealings with Positive Action, could I ask you about the period in November 1995 when you were in negotiation with them? Would you agree with me that at that point in time they were seeking a statutory basis for any compensation provision?"

'The minister replied that was correct; it was one of their requests. In response to further questioning, he confirmed it had not been conceded and that it was his position, as a matter of policy, not to concede it. When asked if he would agree that in his dealings with Positive Action he conveyed to them at all times that he was prepared to give them everything besides a statutory scheme of compensation, the minister replied he did not think that was correct. Asked if he had indicated to Positive Action that all issues in relation to compensation were negotiable, save the issue of a statute, the minister replied that in the formal negotiations that took place between himself, the department and Positive Action it was said that there were issues of principle which were not negotiable.

'The minister has now conceded the principle he claimed was not negotiable as a matter of policy by his administration and during his tenure as minister. It has been dragged out of him by the courageous women who fought the valiant fight and won their battle this morning ...

'The terms of reference of the tribunal circumscribed the ability of Mr Justice Finlay to make any comment on issues relating to political accountability in this House or the primary responsibility of ministers for health to answer this House for the way they carried out their responsibilities during their tenure of office throughout this crisis. He was circumscribed in his comments in terms of determining the adequacy or otherwise of those responses by reference to the strict terms of reference insisted upon by the minister.'

Cowen proceeded to dismantle the argument that the tribunal had found no fault with the minister: 'The basis on which the tribunal was established was such as not to address the political accountability issue. This was deliberately done by the minister when he delimited the terms of reference of the tribunal to exclude Question 5 in the McCole family's letter of 8 October 1996, which got to the heart of the matter. It stated: "In their letter 20 September 1996, the Blood Transfusion Service Board did two things, they admitted liability and apologised, but only in the context of a threat that were she (Mrs McCole) to proceed with a case for aggravated/exemplary damages and not to succeed, they would pursue her for costs." What was the justification for this threat?

'This question was excluded from consideration by the tribunal. What justification was given by the strategists who were devising the defence by the state in the Brigid McCole case? What was the justification for threatening to pursue that dying woman for costs when she insisted on having her day in court?

'That question was not put to the tribunal and was not included in its terms of reference. All on the other side of the House, the so-called political progressives who wished to ensure that the women's rights were vindicated, voted down an amendment moved by my party and supported by others that this question be included in the terms of reference. It was excluded because it would have meant that Mr Justice Finlay would have had to investigate deep in the labyrinth of the department, the minister's office and the office of the chief state solicitor to ascertain who gave the political directions for that strategy to be devised and implemented …'

Cowen widened the argument to include former health minister Brendan Howlin: 'Regarding what the report has shown, what we know about the approach and behaviour of the minister, Deputy Noonan, in the McCole legal action, his insults to the victims which led them to walk out of the gallery of this House and his deliberate exclusion of Question No. 5 in the McCole family's letter, it should be a matter of personal honour now for him to go. The limiting of the tribunal's remit to technical issues also explains why the minister, Deputy Howlin, escapes the criticism he justly deserves. Unless the terms of reference were narrowed, why would Mr Justice Finlay have ignored the fact that the former minister for health, Deputy Howlin, misled his cabinet colleagues in an *aide mémoire* to the government of 9 March 1994? In a memo circulated to the government, the minister, Deputy Howlin, failed to mention he had been informed two weeks previously that there was also a problem about Anti-D infection in 1991. I was at the meeting and to my certain recollection no oral evidence relating to that matter was given at it. That was not mentioned in the memo which states "a problem does exist for 1977 but indicates a low prevalence of antibody positive for Hepatitis C among women who received Anti-D in years other than 1977".'

Cowen may not have been viewed as a sensitive man in his own right, but he displays a moral vigour on the issue that more than compensates for this: 'Before the minister, Deputy Noonan, begins any celebrations he should recall the pain and misery suffered by the victims. More than 1,000 mothers caught Hepatitis C from contaminated blood products. Those mothers contracted a serious and potentially life-threatening virus for which there is no effective cure. Half of those women have the full virus, while more than one dozen children of the mothers and some partners have also been infected. More than 500 others have been infected with Hepatitis C through blood transfusions. People who thought they were getting a new lease of life with a transfusion of blood were infected with a serious virus. Those people include women at childbirth, transfusions administered to children, car accident victims, those who received transfusions during serious operations and those with rare blood diseases. Haemophiliacs and kidney dialysis patients have also been victims of this virus … The most abhorrent fact to emerge from the judicial inquiry was that the BTSB was so aware of the problem in 1977 that somebody decided to keep a list of the destinations of the infected batch 238. This list was to facilitate the recall because they knew there was a serious problem but nobody shouted "stop". Dr Jack O'Riordan, Dr Terry Walsh … did not shout "stop". In 1991, nobody not shouted "stop" when the Middlesex letter arrived. Dr Emer Lawlor told the tribunal: "It just totally slipped my mind." Approximately thirty people would not have the virus if that fax from Middlesex had been acted on.'

Later in this speech, which was unrelenting in intensity and pressure, Cowen referred to the fact that the blood bank was still experiencing unacceptable errors: 'Last year it emerged that the blood bank knew a Kilkenny nurse was infected with HIV from a contaminated blood transfusion in 1985, but failed to inform her. She found out while she was in a foreign country on holiday. The blood bank, in an attempt to trace the batches of HIV infected blood products that infected the nurse, wrote to hospitals but deliberately omitted to say that the problem related to HIV. A separate tribunal of inquiry into this affair is to begin soon …

'The minister for health, Deputy Noonan, and his predecessor, Deputy Howlin, made much of the actions they took with regard to the BTSB. The tribunal supported the current minister for health in his work in reforming the blood bank, using words such as "adequate" and "appropriate" to describe his actions. In the context of this latest episode, apart from the other ones in the last year, this conclusion of the tribunal is not correct. I say this because the upshot of all the episodes is that the public does not, unfortunately, have confidence in the BTSB. While there are still many donors – thankfully, citizens want to supply blood to ensure there is a blood supply for the health services – the real measure of confidence is that of the public and of recipients of blood and blood products.'

When the scandal had first come to light, Brian Cowen had been a cabinet minister in the Fianna Fáil/Labour government. Brendan Howlin was then the health minister and it is in this regard that Cowen issued some of his strongest words: 'In Minister Howlin's case the tribunal notes serious failures on his part. They were put in muted language but were nevertheless serious. His failures include the fact that he left the state response in the hands of those who caused it – a pretty basic error; he did not inform the Dáil, the government, the GPs or the public that the 1991 infection had also occurred. I disagree seriously with the tribunal on this point. It is extraordinary there is no criticism of the minister's failure to disclose such a central fact. How could it have been adequate, as Justice Finlay has said, to withhold this information? The president of the Irish Medical Organisation has said that if the department of health and the minister had received information that raised a significant question about the safety of any products, he would consider it wrong not to have informed the medical profession. There is a persistent belief that only the 1977 infection occurred because this information was withheld at the start. This may explain the reason there are still missing victims as people are not aware that in 1994 the current batch of Anti-D was also infected. The former minister, Deputy Howlin, withheld this information even when questioned by victims about it in June 1994. In the transcript he said: "I may have given partial information." This is from a minister who had a reputation for being open, transparent, competent and willing. When asked about it he did not answer. Who will be accountable for that? As a cabinet colleague at the time I am disgusted the minister was making top of the head decisions about a killer disease …

'The minister failed to make considered judgments on the advice he was getting, especially in relation to independent counselling for the victims. The explanations he has given on that issue do not amount to much …

'It has been said in this saga that the former minister, Deputy Howlin, has shown the moral fibre of a second-hand car salesman, although that is probably doing an injustice to second-hand car salesmen …

'Is anyone seriously suggesting to me that a minister's responsibility is met when he is not prepared to confront those who have been involved – on his own admission on 25 February – in covering up a scandal unprecedented in the history of the state? He admitted that he did not have any direct contact with the BTSB from the time the problem entered the public domain in February 1994 until he left the department in December 1994. That is some statement. He admits that the letter of 25 February – one week after the initial problem had been brought to this attention, written by the then chief executive of the BTSB to the secretary of his department, Mr Hurley – was brought to his direct attention. That letter of 25 February confirmed the further admission that the BTSB had broken all its own protocols by taking blood from patient X who had jaundice. On receiving that letter Mr Hurley described its contents to the tribunal as "the single most significant event in his career as a civil servant". Knowing all of that, the then minister for health, Deputy Howlin, did not see it as his responsibility then, or throughout the remainder of his period in office, to satisfy himself that the contaminated product had been withdrawn from the market.'

Cowen was systematic in his approach to Howlin's evidence at the tribunal and his actions: 'The minister, Deputy Howlin, also brought forward an *ex gratia* expenses scheme for victims. He was told in September 1994 that the expenses scheme was not meeting the needs of victims. He indicated they should consult their community welfare officers. He was surprised when these officers told the victims they could do nothing for them. The minister explained that "… it was a suggestion that was made if you like, on the top of the head at the time … " No general alert was given to the community welfare officers who worked under him in the department of health when the officers' reaction to the victims was brought to his attention. However, he assures us that anyone who came to his clinic or wrote to him was followed through by the department. Who says the politics of *clientelism* are dead and gone, or are with Michael O'Leary in his political grave? … With regard to finding out what happened, the minister, Deputy Howlin, agreed with counsel that it was vitally important that what went wrong would not go wrong again. He admits he was aware from the very beginning of the crisis that the chief medical consultant had got a letter in December 1991 which should have alerted him to this problem and that Dr Walsh did nothing about it. By 25 February we had scandal on our hands and in addition to the 1991 letter, it transpired that blood had been taken from a woman who had jaundice. He turned his attention to finding out what had happened on the Monday 21 February. He decided to set up an expert group to find out as a matter of urgency what happened. He consulted just three people – the secretary and assistant secretary of the department and his adviser, Mr Collins. He was told in June 1994 – such was the urgency involved in finding out what had happened – that the BTSB was not co-operating. He could not compel witnesses or demand that documents be given to the expert group which had been asked by him to find out what had happened as a matter of urgency …

'The minister for health's failings are more considerable. It is because of him there had to be a judicial inquiry. Although he was the first minister to have all the information, he refused to give it to the Dáil. The tribunal had to get it out of him and the state agencies under his aegis. He knew the BTSB had no defence for a legal action but he aided and abetted it in the cover-up in the McCole case. He established an *ad hoc* compensation tribunal despite the opposition of victims and the promise of the coalition government to pay fair compensation. He unilaterally announced the scheme of compensation while still in negotiation with the victims. When he announced it he did not mention health care, which was a primary consideration of the victims. The minister continues to believe this is all about money and lawyers. This is a flawed belief which explains to a large degree his mishandling of the affairs. The compensation scheme continues to fail the fairness test on many counts but, despite numerous calls in this House and from the victims, the minister refused to make any substantive changes until this morning.'

There was a serious question over what the BTSB knew in 1976. The so-called 1976 file was the source of much contention: the government maintained that no new medical evidence was contained in the file, but the question was whether it showed that the BTSB was aware of the problem. In the event it was the McCole case which seems to lend weight to the opposition argument as Cowen pointed out: 'The critical question relating to the 1976 file was put to the minister by Mr Rogers. He considered the critical question to be whether the expert group knew whether the BTSB knew in 1976 and the minister agreed with him. During a further half-an-hour of cross examination the minister studiously avoided answering it. He seeks refuge in the fact that no new medical information came as a result of the discovery of the 1976 file. However, that was not the opposition's contention. Our contention is that the importance of the 1976 file was that it showed the state of mind of the BTSB as far back as 1976. Once it was produced in the discovery documents in the McCole case the state's case collapsed. It showed unequivocally that the state had no defence, although it pursued a legal strategy which brought the woman involved to her death bed and threatened her with costs if she dared seek her rights in court. The 1976 file is not significant for the circular argument in which the minister engaged at the tribunal, seeking to talk about the fact that there was no new medical evidence. Although it was arguable, it was not contended that that was the fundamental point whether or not the infective Hepatitis breached their protocols in terms of not allowing that donor to continue donating.

'The critical issue is that the McCole case was won when the discovery documents, including the 1976 file, were produced. The reason there are aggravated damages is that the defence of the claim by the state is such that justice demands that aggravated damages be paid in all those cases ...

'The minister's contention was that there was nothing new in the 1976 file. If there was nothing new in the 1976 file in April why was a tribunal set up in November? What happened in the interim was the McCole case and the tragedy which unfolded in front of our eyes. Everyone was appalled by the bully-boy tactics adopted by the legal team under the direction of the minister who was a defendant in the case. It is incorrect to suggest that this matter was at arm's length from the minister. People do not go into court and defend the position of the state without taking instructions from the state ...

'As the minister said, this is an outrageous wrongdoing by the state and its agencies. It requires full accountability. The administrative accountability has been dealt with under the terms of reference of the Finlay tribunal and it will be further dealt with by reference to the DPP and the garda commissioner. However, the question of political accountability still remains to be dealt with. I have outlined in some detail the major questions regarding the way in which this matter was handled by the people concerned. Rather than calling for the resignations of ministers which will not be forthcoming, the tribunal of public opinion should decide this matter. We should ask the public if this is the way it expects its state to deal with its most vulnerable citizens.'

The damage to the Rainbow government from this entire episode was significant in the long term. From the point of view of the opposition it was a case of the right man, in the right portfolio, at the right time. Some had questioned Cowen's ability to land blows from the opposition and there was a view that he was only truly effective with the gravity of a ministry behind him; this episode proved the opposite. Fianna Fáil clearly had its most potent attacking machine back in play.

During May there was much further argument surrounding the McCole case. In particular Cowen and Fianna Fáil believed that the minister and government should waive the privilege clause it was invoking and lay all letters and correspondence regarding the McCole case before the House. Fianna Fáil tabled a motion in private members' time calling on the government to waive their claim of privilege in this instance. Cowen laid out the case for the motion: 'This is the thirtieth time in the past two years that there has been a major debate in the

House about the Hepatitis C affair. At the end of each debate the victims hoped that it was the last time they would have to trudge in to Dáil Éireann and that their simple demands for justice and truth would be granted. They were certainly of this view when the tribunal of inquiry was mooted and believed that, at last, everything would come out into the public domain. However, on the morning the terms of reference of the tribunal were laid before the Dáil, 17 October last, it quickly became clear that the cover-up would continue. Buried in paragraph 9 were the words "in so far as these questions relate to the terms of reference above". This was a reference to the questions put by the family of the late Brigid McCole.

'To the uninitiated, this appeared like a simple, straightforward focusing of the tribunal. However, the words were much more sinister and, as events have unfolded, prove that the government planned the tribunal in such a way as not to fully expose the deep-rooted cover-up perpetrated against the citizens of the state. It is abundantly clear that the establishment of the tribunal in a limited way was part of the cover-up, not the end of it. It is necessary to outline some of the background to illustrate the point. Following their mother's death, the McCole family wrote to the minister for health on 8 October last. They put five questions to him which they believed deserved to be answered. Question No. 5 asked the justification for the BTSB threatening their mother while she lay on her deathbed with an action for costs if she pursued a case for aggravated or exemplary damages. By inserting the words "in so far as these questions relate to the terms of reference above" the minister for health and the government effectively excised question No. 5. The "terms of reference above" related to the BTSB and the infection of Anti-D with Hepatitis C but did not allow for any investigation into the political handling of the affair or the legal strategy involved …

'There would have been no tribunal of inquiry or promise of a statutory compensation scheme but for the courage of Brigid McCole.

For this reason there is an obligation to secure the truth in the McCole case.'

Perhaps the difficulty for all politicians was highlighted by Michael Noonan's position. The public often expect simple and forthright answers, but ministers must act in areas in which they themselves are not necessarily expert. It is clear that Michael Noonan relied heavily on legal advice when formulating his position and legal advice rarely takes account of the human issues or the need for a minister to engage with the public. Noonan's response illustrates this point: 'I have been subject to criticism which has centred on the state's defence of the High Court case taken on behalf of the late Mrs McCole. The state did not admit liability in Mrs McCole's case. My strong legal advice, both orally and in writing from independent senior counsel, was that the state, as distinct from the BTSB, is not liable and that an admission of liability should not be made. The state's agents are obliged to follow the law in using public funds; this is a country governed by laws. If I had acceded to the demand that I admit liability on behalf of the state in that case and similar cases, I would be accepting liability contrary to legal advice on behalf of all ministers for health over the years and in relation to pending court cases back to 1970 in respect of the Hepatitis C infection of the Anti-D product. If I were to admit liability I would be acting against all legal advice in a way which would be contrary to overall public policy for which I, as minister for health, have functional responsibility ...

'In the motion tabled by Fianna Fáil it is suggested the state adopted an offensive legal strategy in the McCole case. It has in the past been alleged by the opposition that the state delayed and obstructed the plaintiff from beginning to end. I deny this because it is simply not true ...'

While this position clearly had merit in a court of law and most likely represented sound legal advice, the minister's problem was that he was now in the court of public opinion, and defences of discovery and evaluation held little water. The public were demanding simple explanations and did not want a legal argument from an elected minister. Noonan did go on, however, to give a strong defence of the reasons why privilege would not be waived: 'The House is aware that the government, while recognising a person's right to take court proceedings, has put in place a non-adversarial compensation tribunal for certain persons who had contracted Hepatitis C since December 1995. While the state is still a defendant in those other similar proceedings, it would not be appropriate for it to disclose legal advice on this litigation where comparable litigation is pending before the courts.'

This scandal and the debate of the fallout continued to the end of Michael Noonan's tenure and any issues arising in the future would be for Brian Cowen to handle. Having been so outspoken, Cowen could expect that he would face serious questioning on the issue and on 9 October Alan Shatter, as Fine Gael's new health spokesperson, queried the delay in bringing the commencement order for the statutory tribunal before the Oireachtas. In his reply Brian Cowen made the point that he had insisted that all elements of the tribunal be finalised to avoid confusion even if this was not entirely necessary: 'The preparatory work on the regulations and the settlement arrangements under Section 8 of the Hepatitis C Compensation Tribunal Act, 1997, which is being carried out by my department, the attorney general's office and the compensation tribunal is almost complete. These regulations will cover, *inter alia*, the establishment of the statutory tribunal, the establishment of the reparation fund and matters relating to costs and expenses. Although it is not necessary to have settlement arrangements under Section 8 in place in order to establish the statutory compensatory tribunal, it is my intention that on the establishment day, all benefits accruing to claimants will be immediately available.'

Cowen also extended the tribunal to persons outside the state: 'The deputy will be aware that on 16 September last I amended clause one of the non-statutory compensation scheme. The effect of the amendment was to allow access to the non-statutory compensation tribunal to persons who, in particular circumstances, appeared to have contracted Hepatitis C from the administration of blood or blood products outside the state. At this point I am aware of only one such case. However, in the interests of fairness I consider that sufficient time should be made available to allow any other person who might be covered by the amended clause to make a claim.'

One would expect that any minister who has been so vociferous on an issue would ensure that all bases are covered in government. However, the opposition were all too aware that systems can fail, and as the threat of the human form of BSE [bovine spongiform encephalopathy], namely CJD, was a significant concern. Alan Shatter raised the matter on 20 November. In his reply Cowen appears to have done his research: 'CJD is an exceptionally rare disorder of the brain which causes rapidly progressive dementia and eventually death. Research has shown that CJD is caused by a unique prion protein which exists in a non-infectious form in all humans. The mechanism whereby this non-infectious prion protein becomes infectious and causes CJD has been under intense study for many years. Four types of CJD have been identified to date, including sporadic or classical CJD, the cause of which is uncertain, and new variant CJD. New variant CJD has only been identified in the past three years and is associated with a variety of symptoms and signs different from those found in sporadic CJD. There have been no cases of the new variant CJD identified in the country to date ...'

Problems were never far away, however, and the emergence of another contaminated blood product was raised on 16 December. In his statement Cowen said: 'Amerscan Pulmonate II is a product used in the diagnosis of abnormal lung perfusion in patients. Certain batches of this product have been recalled by the Irish distributors. The Irish Medicines Board was informed on 18 November by the UK Medicines Control Agency regarding the relevant batches of Amerscan Pulmonate II Agent. The board took immediate steps on 19 November in co-operation with the distributors of the product, to quarantine the unused products and ensure their full recall. All nine hospitals involved have confirmed to my department that none of the product was used after that date …

'The delay which occurred in the Irish Medicines Board notifying the department is a matter of concern to me. I have already made it clear to the board that in future I require to be informed immediately of any similar incident and the nature and extent of the board's response to it.

'The number of vials of the relevant product which was used is 268. Following the decision to advise patients, taken on 12 December, my department has now been in contact with each hospital involved and has established that hospitals may treat more than one patient with each vial, depending on the circumstances of each patient. Accordingly, the information from the hospitals today suggests that the total number of patients who will have to be contacted and counselled is up to 467. I have issued a statement this afternoon clarifying the position with regard to the numbers involved.'

This is an area where the new minister was determined that there would be no slip-ups. Thus his concern about the delay in the IMB informing him was made evident, as was his wish to be informed immediately. There is little doubt that Cowen saw this as an area with the potential to do serious damage. From his response, however, it would appear that all those involved in such systems had learned a clear lesson: 'I am informed by eight of the nine hospitals concerned that they have already identified all the patients who were diagnosed using the product in question. The remaining hospital has almost completed this task. A clinical information pack is being prepared and will be sent to each of the hospitals. This pack will consist of briefing material on the scientific data in relation to Amerscan's composition and operation, and on the clinical issues in relation to new variant CJD and the possibility of transmission through this product. Each hospital is being asked to arrange with the appropriate consultants, generally the treating consultants responsible for the care of patients known to have been treated with the relevant batches, to meet each patient individually and to brief them fully on their circumstances using, as appropriate, the background information contained in the clinical information pack. I take this opportunity to request the full co-operation of medical consultants and other hospital staff in carrying through this sensitive task.'

Later in the debate, during an interaction with Róisín Shortall of the Labour Party, we get a unique insight into Brian Cowen's *modus operandii* and expectations as a minister: 'Deputy Shortall supported a government which introduced the strategic management initiative and the devolution of functions to agencies. However, the culture in this country is such that if a problem arises in IMB the public will hold me responsible politically. I have made this clear to Mr Kelly and any other agency that wishes to listen. That is the system. I do not have a problem with it.'

Mr J. Bruton: 'The minister is good at that.'

Mr Cowen: 'This is a serious point. We all set out to strategically improve the state agencies, entailing the devolution of functions and day-to-day management. However, if a problem arises it comes to me, not Mr Kelly. With regard to these matters it is crystal clear that I am to be informed immediately.'

Ms Shortall: 'That is not a procedure.'

Mr Cowen: 'My idea of a procedure is not to establish a joint interministerial task force to tell somebody how to do something. It is a direct order that is well understood and comprehended.'

We are given the impression from this that Cowen is the type of politician who believes in issuing orders and has absolute faith that he will be respected and obeyed. This shows a high degree of confidence both in himself and in those who work for him, but it is a policy that is not without its risks.

There seemed little scope for error within the reformed institutions and Cowen could be thankful that he took over the service when he did. However, he did seem to pay particular attention to this area and was obviously aware that the opposition was only waiting for the first error.

Many people felt that posting Brian Cowen to health was a big risk. There would have been many who would have felt that after such virulent attacks on the failures of the BTSB and Minister Noonan, Cowen would be a sitting duck as health minister. But whether it was purely for political expediency or whether he did indeed feel moral outrage at the events, is for any individual to assess. What is clear is that on becoming health minister he was determined that he would not be found wanting in this particular area. It is safe to say that although he had the distinct advantage of working with institutions that were already reforming, he hastened the process and laid his position clearly on the line. If failures happened he wanted to be informed and he wanted to take immediate action and be seen to handle them with authority. Considering the potential there was for getting something wrong or errors in an area where he had given so many hostages to fortune while in opposition, the Dáil record points to a man who was in control of this part of his portfolio.

Not all areas of the health service would be as responsive, however. In the late 1990s, well before the Treatment Purchase Fund was introduced, the issue of waiting lists was one of the most intractable problems facing any minister for health. Shortly before the 1997 general election, Cowen had raised the issue and clearly wanted the latest waiting-list figures published before the country went to the polls: 'I am grateful for the opportunity to outline my difficulty in obtaining details of waiting lists up to the end of March. The inadequate replies to my parliamentary questions on this matter gave me no option but to raise the matter on the adjournment.

'Five weeks ago I tabled a parliamentary question to the minister for health in which I asked for the hospital waiting lists to the end of March. The minister said that they would be circulated to me shortly. When I did not receive the details by 20 April I tabled another parliamentary question in which I asked the minister why the hospital waiting lists to the end of March were not available in view of the advances in technology. On 22 April the minister replied to my question by giving endless excuses and effectively blaming the consultants for the delay. He added that a significant proportion of the information on the waiting-list figures was compiled and validated manually. He again promised to provide the lists as soon as they became available.

'I have still not received the lists two weeks later. I believe the lists are being withheld because the figures are bad. When the figures are good the lists seem to be published much quicker. Hospital waiting lists are obviously out of control. In December 1994 when the Rainbow Coalition took office there were 23,700 people on the waiting lists. This figure had been reduced from more than 40,000 through intensive action and an investment of £30 million by the previous government. This progress has not been maintained by the coalition government. Only £20 million has been spent in the past two years, and this has not even been sufficient to maintain the number on the waiting lists at 23,700. At one stage the number had increased by almost one-third or 32 per cent to 31,519. Even though the figure was reduced to 26,000 in December this was still an increase of 2,300 on the 1994 figure. The figures to the end of March are likely to have increased again due to the cancellation of procedures during the nurses' dispute and the ongoing chaos in hospitals.'

However, as minister for health himself in May 1998, during a debate on a Fine Gael motion in regard to the health service, Cowen was forced to defend the latest waiting-list figures: 'Some deputies made a number of claims last night about waiting lists on which I would like to comment. Deputy Shatter noted that waiting lists rose by 6,000 from 26,000 at the end of 1996 to 32,000 at the end of 1997. He blamed the government for the increase, but conveniently forgot to mention that the great bulk of the increase occurred in the first six months of 1997, when his party and other parties were still in office. His claim that waiting-list figures "started to shrink during the lifetime of the previous government" sounds unconvincing when waiting lists rose by 4,500 during the final six months of his party's participation in government.

'The reason for this increase of 4,500 is quite clear – the last government cut waiting-list funding by £4 million in 1997 from its 1996 figure. When I became minister I increased this funding to £12 million for 1998 and this represents a 50 per cent increase in the waiting-list allocation over that provided for last year by the previous minister for health, Deputy Noonan. I also made the funding available to agencies much earlier in the year than my predecessor did.'

This would become a feature of Cowen's term as minister for health, he would frequently compare his record against that of his predecessors. In his mind the only way to evaluate the success of a minister was to place their record against that of those who served before them. As regards waiting lists, he believed that he inherited a problem that had been exacerbated by a cut in funding for the waiting-list programme. The acid test of this theory would, however, be whether the additional funding would have any impact on the waiting lists themselves. Labour spokesperson Liz McManus had a tetchy relationship with Cowen in the Dáil; in the same debate she accused him of having failed on his promise to tackle waiting lists: 'Fianna Fáil was quick enough to sense the public desire for action and it promised to tackle the waiting lists when in government. However, now that it is in government it has taken a U-turn on this promise. The minister for health and children lacked the necessary leadership and determination to make radical changes in order to achieve significant improvements in this area. His defence is robust but the record is plain. The objective is clear to members who are committed to radical change. It is outlined in the health strategy of 1994 which states that access to health care should be determined by actual need for services rather than the ability to pay or geographic location.'

A month later Cowen seemed to be able to show some slight improvement with regard to cardiac services waiting lists, but he was experiencing similar problems to his predecessor in getting up-to-date information: 'At the end of December 1997, the most recent period for which information is available, there were 1,150 patients awaiting cardiac bypass surgery. Information is not routinely collected by the agencies in the format requested by the deputies. However, I am consulting with the hospitals involved about the possibility of getting data in the format requested and will communicate with the deputies on the matter in due course.

'In 1997, my department allocated a sum of £1.7 million under the waiting-list initiative with the specific aim of reducing the national cardiac surgery waiting list for adults and children. A combination of approaches was used by hospitals to achieve this objective. As well as purchasing additional cardiac surgery procedures, patients were also reassessed with a view to using alternative therapies such as interventional cardiology or medical treatment, as clinically appropriate. I am pleased to say this initiative was very successful in reducing the adult waiting list by 203 between September and December 1997.

'This year a sum of £3 million is being made available specifically for cardiac surgery patients.'

But the difficulties would continue; instead of being reduced waiting-lists in general were on the increase, leaving Cowen in a very exposed position. Alan Shatter of Fine Gael tabled the following motion on 13 October 1998: 'I move that Dáil Éireann deplores the scandalous increase in the hospital waiting lists, which on 30 June 1998 stood at 34,331, an increase of over 13 per cent since this government took office, and the failure of the minister for health and children to implement the broad range of reforms necessary to end the waiting lists crisis.'

Fine Gael blamed the problem on two issues: firstly that hospitals scaled back services and did not work at full capacity due to seasonal changes at particular times with regard to staffing, etc.; and secondly they believed the minister was failing to introduce reforms to this area.

Cowen was of course prepared to defend his position vigorously. He based his arguments around the fact that he had allocated significantly more money to deal with the issue and he believed that underfunding had been the problem in the past and this had to be addressed in the first instance. Perhaps Cowen himself was surprised by the problem, but it seemed to emerge that the result of the extra funding had not been as one might expect – a direct impact on the numbers waiting – but instead it had affected the length of time the patients were waiting: 'While the actual numbers on public waiting lists have been on the increase recently, little, if any, attention has been paid to the length of time that patients must wait. The length of time spent by public patients on waiting lists in a number of important specialties has actually been reduced in recent months and in other specialties it has remained static.

'For example, waiting times for adults requiring treatment in cardiac surgery, general surgery and urology fell between March and June of this year. Similarly there were improvements in waiting times for children in cardiac surgery and ear, nose and throat procedures. It is vital from the very beginning of my contribution to stress that looking solely at numbers will distract us from the real issue of how long patients are waiting for treatment. That is the issue for every individual referred to by each deputy as regards their own regions – how long must they wait?

'In addressing the question of waiting lists and waiting times, we must remember that they are an international issue. No country has wiped them out, nor can any country claim that it is easy to reduce them very quickly. A number of practical difficulties arise, irrespective of how much funding is available to deal with waiting lists.'

Cowen was quick to revert to his standard comparison of his performance against previous governments: 'I allocated £12 million for waiting-list work this year, which represents an increase of 50 per cent over the funding made available by the previous government in 1997. The additional funding will result in an extra 15,000 procedures being carried out during the current year. Again, I caution against the simplistic approach of counting numbers only, with no regard to waiting times, but it is quite clear that adequate funding is required to support a sufficient level of dedicated hospital work to reduce both waiting lists and waiting times.'

A concerned Cowen goes on to explain the difficulties in assessing the performance of the health service based solely on the waiting-list numbers as they appear: 'I would like to place the numbers on waiting lists and the performance of the waiting-list initiative in context. First, the number of people on waiting lists on 30 June 1998 was 34,331. Within this figure there is a wide spectrum of ill-health among the patients waiting for different procedures. In this context the length of time waiting is not the sole determinant of access to treatment. The severity of the person's condition is also important and, irrespective of which criterion is used to determine access to treatment, it is clear that a large number of patients are waiting too long for surgery.

'While the current numbers on waiting lists are clearly not satisfactory, this figure must be set against the total number of patients who have been treated over the past year. In 1997, for example, there were over 535,000 in-patient discharges from acute hospitals and a further 250,000 day cases. The waiting-list figure of 34,331 represents 6.4 per cent of all in-patients and 13.7 per cent of day cases seen in acute hospitals last year. When the total activity of 535,000 in-patient discharges and 250,000 day cases are combined, the numbers on public waiting lists represents 4.4 per cent of all such activity.'

Considering the climate of crisis that had surrounded the health service for the last decade, the sheer enormity of the figures and the number of people treated are a credit to a much-maligned system aside from the political arguments.

Cowen made his case, but it is evident that he still felt himself that waiting lists were something that he must begin to achieve results on. It was a weak link in his ministry and he made it clear that he was open to discussing various options. We are also given a first insight into a long-term vision of the health service where the current system of multi-purpose acute hospitals was no longer viable: 'I am willing to discuss strategies on how best to address the waiting-list issue with all interested parties throughout the health system and central to this is an acceptance that the rate of change in medical and surgical has moved on substantially. The model of the acute hospital system as a single multi-purpose facility for treatment, recuperation and rehabilitation is simply no longer valid. Patients need a continuum of care involving all components of the system. We must work on the basis that co-operation between all sections of the health system is critical and that waiting lists are not just an acute hospital issue. The interdependencies between sectors is vital and must be recognised by all concerned. The long-term strategy proposed by the review group will have an impact on all levels of our health and personal social services and it is essential that the relevant developments are planned and implemented effectively.'

Under questioning a month later Cowen still had a problem on his hands and little good news to tell: 'The number of adults on hospital waiting lists for more than twelve months on 30 June 1998 was 12,314 and the number of children waiting for more than six months was 2,413. The remaining persons on public in-patient waiting lists were waiting for less than twelve months and six months, respectively. I am committed to taking all appropriate steps to addressing both waiting lists and waiting times. Since taking office I have taken a number of initiatives in the operation of the waiting-list initiative.

'In addition to these steps, I established a Review Group on the Waiting-List Initiative, which was the first major formal analysis of the area since the initiative was launched in 1993. I received the report and we had a debate in the House on this matter. I have since been preparing proposals for its implementation.

'I will shortly bring these proposals to government, after which I will announce full details of how I intend to proceed ...

'There will always be an argument for increased resources for the health services, no matter what government is in office. Unless we are prepared to submit to the budgetary disciplines the same as other departments, these health agencies cannot plan for the improvements which the deputy, I and others in the House seek. As regards dealing with some of the outstanding problems, if people on the other side propose to throw budgetary discipline out the window and continue to provide funds regardless of how we plan our services, clearly that will not solve the problem either.'

Cowen's remarks are another of his hallmarks as minister for health. For those who supported him they saw a man who was taking necessary action on behalf of the taxpayer; he was trying to combat inefficiency and unwilling to allow spending spiral without some form of evaluation. He believed that this was achieved through budgetary discipline and contended that with finite resources one cannot allow any department to simply spend as it wishes. For his opponents this was an accountancy-based approach that only took account of the bottom line and failed to address the human angles and suffering often experienced in a very sensitive area.

During a confidence vote in the minister in February 1999, which we will examine in more detail later, Cowen seemed to indicate that he felt he finally had the machinery to tackle waiting lists: 'The issue of waiting lists has received much attention. No country has solved the problem and all the most comprehensive studies, both here and abroad, emphasise that there are no simple, quick fix solutions. Despite these hard facts, I have been subject to some extremely simplistic and poorly thought out criticisms from the other side of the House on this matter. I wish we could have reasoned debate on this issue, rather than the extraordinarily ill-informed approach taken by the opposition. Despite its complaints, it loses sight entirely of the fact that I have provided two and a half times more funding this year than it did before it left office in 1997.

'The review group has pointed out what needs to be done in the short, medium and long term. The government is providing the funds to ensure that happens. The measures I have taken were not in place in 1998. Nevertheless, the information available to me on the position at the end of last year indicates that the overall numbers have stabilised and that numbers in many specialities and, importantly, waiting times are being stabilised. We will now attack that problem on the basis of the review group's recommendations and the funding which the minister for finance has made available to me.'

While it is only fair that this would take some time to have an impact the world of politics is unforgiving and there was more bad news one month later on 2 March: 'The number of persons on in-patient waiting lists on 31 December 1998 was 36,883. I am forwarding a detailed breakdown of this figure by hospital and by speciality to the deputies.

'While these figures show an increase over the September position, I again remind the House that there is no simple, immediate or quick fix solution that can be applied to the problem of lengthy waiting lists. The Review Group on the Waiting-List Initiative, which I established to advise me on these issues, emphasised in its report that an integrated series of short-term, medium-term and long-term initiatives must be taken to address this issue. Towards this end, I have taken a number of important steps for the financial year. These include allocating £20 million this year for the treatment of patients on waiting lists …'

It had taken Cowen a considerable period, most of his term in the health portfolio in fact, but he still believed that he could now begin to address the issue: 'I am determined to take the necessary medium- and long-term steps to tackle the underlying causes of unacceptably long waiting lists and waiting times. This will take considerable effort on the part of many agencies, but I believe we will now begin to show progress in what is a complex problem.'

In October 1999 the health services were hit by the biggest industrial relations dispute in the history of the state, as nurses went on strike. This episode will be evaluated on its own, but it did have an obvious impact on waiting-list figures. On 11 November Alan Shatter placed a question with regard to the effect of the strike on waiting lists. However, Cowen was unfazed by the query, as while the dispute may have impacted negatively, in the normal course of events the trend was showing a reduction in the numbers on waiting lists and one of the thorns in Cowen's side for his period in the health brief finally appeared to be showing some positive results. Cowen would maintain that while it took some time to get to grips with the issue he did seem to finally be having an effect: 'The provisional total numbers on in-patient waiting lists on 30 September 1999, shortly before the nurses dispute commenced, are now to hand. They stood at 33,381, a decrease of 343 over the figure for 30 June. This brings to 3,302 the reduction in numbers since the beginning of the year. My department sought initial total figures on the number of persons awaiting in-patient treatment on 31 October 1999, some days after the ending of the industrial action. These figures are provisional estimates only and will be subject to validation. They indicate that there was a total of 37,200 on in-patient waiting lists on 31 October, an increase of 3,619 over the September figure. Information provided by the health boards and hospitals during the course of the industrial action indicated that approximately 3,300 procedures were cancelled during the dispute.

'Since the conclusion of the nurses' dispute my department has been working with the health agencies to ensure that services to patients return to normal as quickly as possible. This includes measures to address any backlogs emerging as a result of the industrial action …

'Having inherited an escalating waiting-lists problem, we not only stabilised it but were starting to reduce it for the first time in five years.'

This would be his last report on the issue, as in January he moved to the department of foreign affairs. Detractors will point out that Cowen did arrive in health from an opposition position, where he had promised to deal with waiting lists; and that in a time of significant exchequer buoyancy it took over two years before he had some good news to report. He certainly had resources at his disposal to tackle waiting lists. On the other hand Ireland has faced many problems during its Celtic Tiger years and many ministers have failed to deliver any impact even with resources, so Cowen could argue that in dealing with an area that was historically underfunded, and in a department with procedures so rigid that any turnaround required more space than an aircraft carrier, he could point to the positive effects of his policies. Once he managed to get the machinery in place he could begin to tackle the issue. It would have been interesting to see how he would have handled the problem going forward and if he could have had further impact. His transfer to a new department robs us of that opportunity, but it is obvious that his party colleagues at least believed that he was having a positive impact. The jury may be out in terms of the time delay and the resources, but at a basic level the Dáil record does point to some success, eventually, for Cowen with regard to waiting lists, albeit not as much as he might have hoped.

But while all issues taken in isolation can paint a positive picture, Cowen's term as health minister was far from a walk in the park. Taken as a whole, the health service came in for much criticism due to its failings. Cowen was always under pressure to lay out a long-term plan for the sector. However much time was spent fire-fighting issues rather than debating what kind of health service Ireland should have in the future. There was also a historical problem of under-resourcing in this area and, while Cowen desperately tried to ensure budgetary discipline, he was keenly aware of the fact that the health service needed funding to address this historical deficit. He was minister at an early stage in the Celtic Tiger when Ireland was beginning to acquire the resources to allocate to such areas. Cowen's heavy investment in health continued into the future and while value for money would always be an issue it is clear that a large portion of Ireland's wealth went towards addressing problems in the health service that had accumulated over the previous twenty years.

However the performance of the health sector in general was what he would be judged upon. On 20 November 1997 we see Cowen getting tough with the health services. While he was in a position to allocate significantly more resources to the sector, he obviously felt a need for reform. We find him imposing the rule of sticking to budgets and insisting that under-performance could not in his view be rewarded whatever the circumstances. He was very aware that even in such prosperous times he had a limited budget, and he expected all units of the health service to play their part in meeting this target. That meant, however, that seasonal problems such as crises in A&E during winter might not have resources available at the end of the year. If anyone had expected that the government could not ignore the issue and therefore would be forced into allocating extra resources they had misjudged the minister: 'The Eastern Health Board has a co-ordinating role in relation to the provision of accident and emergency services by six major hospitals in the Dublin area. Arising from the work of the Accident and Emergency Steering Group, the board has requested funding for a series of proposals aimed at relieving pressure on the accident and emergency services during the coming winter. These proposals refer mainly to anticipated spending in 1998 and my department will consider the board's request as part of its overall consideration of estimated budgetary requirements for the coming year.'

Mr Shatter: 'Will the minister accept that the steering group has advised him that, to ensure that the accident and emergency services will be in a condition to meet the expected demands to be made on them this winter, this extra financial injection is required, that it is important in the context of forward planning that the health board is advised at a very early stage as to whether this funding will be made available, and that it is not adequate that a decision should be made and funding made available only some time after the new year? It is essential that this issue is immediately addressed by the minister, decisions communicated and the necessary action taken so that the accident and emergency services know they will be in a position to cope.'

Mr Cowen: 'I agree that of course it would be far better had the Eastern Health Board been able to provide funds which would not have required it to wait for the 1998 allocation since it has been involved in positive measures in 1995–6 and 1996–7. However, far from having the allocation in reserve, the deputies will be aware that the ability of health boards to keep within budget has been problematical, but it will have to be done from now, given the accountability legislation.'

Cowen started the process of shifting the emphasis onto how hospitals are managed. As he was the first minister to really apply a high level of funding to the service he was probably the first who was in a position to pose this question. We also see during the debate that Cowen was preparing to introduce higher fees for attending A&E so as to ensure people did not use it as a substitute for attending their GPs, who at the time would have been more expensive. It would be a step for which he would be criticised, but his mind was clearly made up: 'The definition of adequate funding is often dependent upon the level and quality of management one is prepared to tolerate. Nothing is adequate if it depends on other criteria not being met.

'There is an important problem to be resolved in the accident and emergency services in Dublin hospitals which will require a great deal of co-ordination and a mechanism for taking away from the equation those who are clearly inappropriate attenders. At present it is cheaper to attend an accident and emergency service than to go to a GP for the most basic requirements. That has been ducked for a long time and it needs to be addressed if we are serious about trying to ensure that those who require accident and emergency services can avail of them. It is quite clear, from speaking to people on the front line in those wards, that there are people attending who are depriving them of the ability to deal with those who should be there.'

Mr McDowell: 'Is the minister considering an increase in the outpatient charge to those using accident and emergency services?'

Mr Cowen: 'I certainly am.'

On 20 November Cowen laid out his agenda for increasing the amount of consultants' positions available in hospitals: 'The number of consultants in the health services in Ireland has increased steadily in recent years. Between 1984 and 1996, the total increased by 19 per cent and it can be expected that the numbers will continue to increase in light of new service developments, expansion of existing services, the introduction of new medical technologies, increased activity levels in individual specialities, the service requirements towards ensuring regional self sufficiency in medical and surgical specialities, and requirements regarding postgraduate medical training.

'Towards ensuring that there is an appropriate framework in place to facilitate a medical manpower plan, the issue is being addressed and discussions are currently taking place with a range of appropriate organisations in the areas of training, education and regulation of the medical profession designed to match consultant numbers to service and training requirements.'

It is plainly evident that nothing happened fast in the department of health, but Cowen was busy addressing a range of issues and his approach seems to be with emphasis on the longer term rather than immediate or short-term measures.

However, that December we find an interesting debate. Cowen, who had been a spokesperson on agriculture in the past, was faced with a dilemma as minister for health. Evidence showed that there was a very small risk that CJD could be contracted from consumption of meat on the bone. On the one hand the risk was so small and the potential to harm consumer confidence in beef so large that there was a strong argument for saying nothing until further research was available. However, on the other hand, evidence saying there was a risk was now presented to the minister for health, who had a responsibility for public health, and it was something the public would be keen to know about.

It is clear that Cowen regarded his current portfolio to be of primary importance and he was not going to risk being told he had hidden the material if there was a case of CJD: 'On Wednesday last, 3 December, the United Kingdom ministry for agriculture, fisheries and food – MAFF – received new advice from the Spongiform Encephalopathy Advisory Committee – SEAC – based on the findings of continuing research into BSE.

'An experiment designed to re-check which parts of cattle may contain BSE infectivity has detected infectivity in nervous tissue called the dorsal root ganglia which lie within the bones of the spinal column and which would be left with the bone when meat is cut off the spine. The dorsal root ganglia are not currently covered by the specified bovine restriction – SRM – which ensures that all tissue in which infectivity is detected is removed from the human food chain.

'Further new findings, still being evaluated, indicate that infectivity may also be found in bone marrow in cattle which are at a very late stage of the disease and are already showing clinical symptoms. Although, in its advice SEAC emphasised that the risk to the consumer is very small, the United Kingdom minister for agriculture, fisheries and food decided to opt for the deboning of all beef, whether from home suppliers or imported, before sale to the consumer. He also decided that the bones should not be sold, given to consumers or used in the preparation of food.

'As minister for health and children, my primary concern and first priority in relation to food is to ensure that all food on sale to the consumer is of the highest standard of safety and is fit in all respects for human consumption …

'Having examined the information available in relation to the latest United Kingdom research, the CJD group made a number of recommendations to me … and a recommendation that immediate arrangements be put in place to ensure that no meat with the backbone (vertebrae) be sold to the consumer; that the most practical way of ensuring this is to require it to be carried out at the retail level, for example, by butchers; that bones removed in this way should be disposed of as not fit for human consumption; that the issue be raised at community level as a matter of urgency; and that there is a need for further information, notably in relation to the findings on bone marrow, to allow more detailed consideration of this issue ...

'I emphasise that my primary duty as minister for health and children is the protection of public health and my main concern in dealing with this issue is to ensure that consumers are kept informed of any risk, however small, to food safety.'

Ms McManus: 'Would the minister not agree that the fact that he made his statement to consumers and butchers in a very inadequate manner was not helpful and that since then there have been alternative opinions expressed by highly reputable experts? For example, would he not agree that Mr McNulty or Miss Darina Allen have made statements which, if not casting doubt on the minister's position, would certainly present a different view to the consumer and that this should lead him to consider that he needs to do more ... perhaps the minister would indicate whether he was in a position on Friday evening last to go to the supermarket and discover that a normal part of the Irish diet was suddenly taken away and that our consumers were not given adequate information for the reason that was being done.'

Mr Cowen: 'I shop locally in small grocery shops all over my constituency.'

Ms McManus: 'How often?'

Mr Cowen: 'Often. I might be permitted to make a couple of comments in relation to this issue. I issued a press statement on Friday last, which comprised clear and simple precautionary advice. Deputy McManus has suggested that that statement was inadequate in some way. In my statement I pointed to the fact that the position here was totally different from that in the United Kingdom. I spoke about the much greater control mechanisms that obtain here, the banning of meat and bonemeal and the fact that we have a very low incidence of CJD compared with the United Kingdom. Any suggestion that I was in any way equating our position with that in the United Kingdom is wrong.

'The second line of criticism was that I slavishly followed the UK position. It seemed to come as news to some of the people making this criticism that we have our own CJD expert group which advises me on these matters. Those two criticisms, therefore, simply do not stand up to scrutiny. The question of adequacy or inadequacy is a subjective test. My press statement is more than adequate. It sets out the position precisely in simple terms. My primary responsibility is to public health matters and, as minister for health and children, it is my duty to inform. We have come through an extremely traumatic experience in relation to a public health failure involving the blood system precisely because there was failure to inform.'

Cowen had one eye on the problems his predecessors had faced with the BTSB and he was intent on ensuring that he would not be found wanting in his duty to inform the public, irrespective of the consequences. We would see a similar approach when Cowen was taoiseach in 2008 and a possible contamination of pork products was considered. It is clear that he believes that there is no acceptable level of risk that can be left to chance when it comes to food safety, irrespective of the consequences. Fine Gael, however, were not convinced by his actions and felt that he had jumped the gun – damaging the beef industry in the process; but Cowen had little doubt about his position and when pushed further he again alluded to problems in the BTSB: 'I would advise as a precaution the practical step of taking out the bone, which would eliminate the risk, however small. That is practical advice that should be given, which need not and does not cause a major inconvenience and would deal with the matter on the basis of the knowledge we have at present. That is the reason I gave that advice. It would have been easy for me to do nothing about it.'

Mr Sheehan: 'It would have been the wisest thing for the minister to do.'

Mr Cowen: 'That is a matter of opinion, deputy.'

Mr O'Dea: 'That is the Fine Gael position.'

Mr Cowen: 'That type of approach has created public health disasters that we do not wish to revisit. The advice given was practical and precautionary. The monitoring that will take place will be carried out by the industry and the department in the normal manner. I have not sought to be prescriptive at this stage in terms of, for example, amending food hygiene regulations.'

It was an interesting performance from a man who had become so close to the beef markets issue while agriculture spokesperson. Two things were evident. From a policy point of view, Cowen believed in taking steps and action as soon as a matter of public health became a concern. He had learned a lesson from the BTSB. Secondly, Cowen was not going to put his own political reputation at risk for any argument or sector. Such debates must have been a welcome distraction in the overall scheme of the health service. Cowen's planning and implementation of various programmes may have been beneficial in the longer term, but there is little doubt that the lack of tangible success in dealing with everyday issues and generating confidence in the hospital services in the short term was causing Cowen much difficulty.

On 29 January 1998 he was questioned on plans to increase hospital staffing: 'The public hospital system currently employs 3,852 doctors and 27,265 nurses. The number of doctors in the system has been increased by 17 per cent since 1990 and the number of nurses has increased by 10 per cent in the same period. This increase in staffing has been accompanied by an increase in the quality of service provided as well as an increase in the range of services available to patients ...

'Letters of determination setting out funding levels for 1998 were issued to health agencies in December of last year. My department is now examining the service plans submitted by the agencies, as required by the letters of determination. The service plans will be the subject of intensive discussions between officers of my department and the health agencies. Overall numbers employed, including medical and nursing staffing levels, will be discussed with the agencies in this context.

'Future medical and nursing staffing requirements will be the subject of study as part of a general review of medical staffing structures and as part of the work of the Commission on Nursing.'

The Commission on Nursing would cause its own problems for Cowen, but his reply is indicative of the enormous amount of planning and consultation that goes hand-in-hand with every decision in the health service. This is because of the large numbers involved in terms of money, staff and patients.

Cowen showed an ability to work with the opposition in certain circumstances, accepting a Fine Gael bill dealing with the report of child abuse, albeit with some amendments as recommended by the department. Such episodes were rare however and Cowen was usually involved in pitched battles with his opposite numbers in Fine Gael and Labour. One of the issues that many governments had dealt with was that of Tallaght Hospital. For years the agreement and construction of such a hospital was a matter for debate and indeed a problem. Considering how many hospitals were constructed in the private sector over the following years with little fuss, the development of Tallaght Hospital did not show publicly-funded and -run projects in a positive light. However, Brian Cowen would be minister for health when the hospital would finally open its doors. He discussed plans for the opening in April 1998: 'The new hospital at Tallaght is the largest project in the history of our health services. It has been built to a standard on a par with the finest acute teaching hospitals in western Europe. A process of continuous consultation with the user groups, who will be providing the services at the new hospital, has informed the planning and commissioning of the hospital.

'At the start of the commissioning phase of the hospital earlier this year a range of adjustments and some additional works were identified by users. This is not unusual in a project of this size. These works were confirmed by senior management as necessary for a variety of reasons, including adjustments necessitated by improved health and safety standards. The funding required for the completion of these essential additional works, which have been agreed as necessary to facilitate the opening of the hospital on 21 June, is being made available and the hospital is agreed on the arrangements to do this.'

It is clear that the government hoped that the opening of Tallaght would be a positive news story and a help in alleviating problems as the new state-of-the-art hospital came into operation. It was badly needed as the continuing problems with accommodation in hospitals were never far from the agenda, as illustrated by Róisín Shortall's question to Cowen on 30 April 1998. Ms Shortall asked Cowen what immediate steps, if any, he was taking to tackle the hospital bed crisis. Cowen replied: 'According to the latest provisional information available, the total in-patient bed stock in 1997 was 11,861 beds. This is based on the average number of in-patient beds available for use over the full year, taking into account beds temporarily opened or closed. I am satisfied that this is adequate to meet national acute hospital needs.

'In this context, I emphasise that in looking at acute hospital service delivery it is appropriate to consider overall levels of service rather than focus solely on bed numbers. This is reflective of major changes in medical practice which have resulted in shorter average in-patient lengths of stay, a marked shift from in-patient to day case surgery, and increased treatment at outpatient level …

'In the current year, I have made a total additional investment of £44 million in acute hospital services to provide for ongoing developments, including improvements in accident and emergency services, to commission new units completed under the capital programme and to tackle waiting lists and waiting times for access to in-patient services.'

As Shortall presses Cowen on the issue stating that it appears he is taking no action, she highlights the fact that reports suggest people are being turned away from hospital as there are no beds. Cowen does not believe, however, that more beds are the answer: 'The deputy seems to suggest that increasing bed numbers alone will solve the waiting-list problem. That is not the case, because if one examines how the health service has developed over the past ten years one can see that there has been an increase in productivity in our hospitals. When that was subjected to an OECD [Organisation for Economic Co-operation and Development] test it came out in a favourable light.

'It is fair to say the hospital system is under pressure at any given time. We cannot plan for the peaks in every circumstance. We must plan across the board and try to provide a basic level of service. I agree waiting times for certain procedures are too long. We must get the information system in place to find out how we can resolve that problem rather than approaching it in a haphazard way which will not result in waiting lists being reduced.'

On 27 May 1998 we find Brian Cowen defending the role and performance of the health service with an argument that is not often heard: 'It is almost inevitable that when there is debate about the health services the concentration is on deficiencies in the service. However, we should not dismiss our current level of achievement. A high number of people benefit every year from the availability of quality health and personal social services. Shortages and deficiencies exist in most health services, many of which absorb much greater amounts of money than our own.

'The OECD recently gave a positive assessment of our health services relative to those in other countries. Its conclusion was: "The Irish health system ... has resulted in a good provision of health care at a relatively low cost to the taxpayer." Therefore, there is much to be proud of in the core service provided. I do not wish to deny that problems exist in specific areas. However, the government will not walk away from addressing those issues. It has set out clearly in *An Action Programme for the Millennium* its resolve to address, in a targeted fashion, the improvement of key aspects of our health and personal social services. Very significant increases in both capital and non-capital funding were provided in 1998. These increases have allowed me to make significant progress in implementing the government programme.'

During the speech we get a summary of some of what Cowen regards as his key achievements up to that point: 'In the acute hospital sector I made funding available for high-cost drug treatments many of which, although very expensive, are of a life-saving nature. The sum of £3 million was made available for such drugs and a further sum of £2 million went towards the treatment of young haemophiliacs.

'Progress was also made in the childcare area, in particular, the problem of homeless children and children with emotional and behavioural difficulties. A total of £4.5 million was provided on an ongoing basis to cover the additional costs incurred by health boards in caring for these children and to introduce targeted measures intended to alleviate this problem. Funding of £6.9 million was provided to health boards to allow them to meet the increasing demand for subventions toward the cost of care of older people in private nursing homes. A package of once-off funding was also provided to meet pressing needs in relation to the disabled and the elderly at the end of 1997. The sum of £4.8 million was provided for the purchase of equipment, aids and appliances by voluntary organisations working with people with physical and sensory disabilities and with older people. A further sum of £4.5 million was made available in relation to services for people with physical and sensory disability. That funding went towards the elimination of historical funding deficits in voluntary organisations which had built up over the previous years.

'On taking office I was very concerned at the serious under-investment in our capital programme which has occurred in the past. An extra £23 million in capital funding was provided in 1997. Among the issues this allowed to be addressed was the replacement of urgently required hospital equipment, the purchase of which had been postponed in previous years under the previous administration, and tackling the serious backlog in fire prevention and maintenance works which had also built up.

'The year 1998 has been the first full year in which the government was able to address the necessary improvement in our health services. The net non-capital provision for health in 1998 shows a 10 per cent increase over and above the 1997 outturn. Further progress has also been made on the capital programme wherein we have achieved a 12 per cent increase over the 1997 outturn. I do not have sufficient time to set out all the progress that this has allowed during 1998. However, I wish to refer to some of the areas raised in the opposition motion to assure the House the government is already committed to addressing these issues.'

As a minister from outside Dublin, Cowen could not be blamed for bringing the case for balanced regional services to the debate: 'On taking up office I was very concerned that there would be imbalances between services in different parts of the country, particularly in relation to hospital services. The government is very conscious of the need to achieve regional self sufficiency in the specialities where it is possible to do so with high quality facilities. This is in keeping with the principles of the national health strategy. The government's actions bear out its commitments in this regard. For example, I have proceeded with the implementation of the national cancer strategy which has as one of its main aims the provision of consultant oncology and haematology services in appropriate areas throughout the country. I have also announced that a cardiovascular strategy will be prepared and work on it is already well under way. As a practical indication of the reduction in regional imbalances, I announced plans for the provision of cardiac surgery and radiotherapy in Galway. Similarly, the major capital projects at various stages of development in Galway, Castlebar, Mullingar, Tullamore and Roscommon are testament to the government's commitment to developing services in a targeted way throughout the country.'

Cowen always maintained that he did all within his power to prioritise service for the handicapped, and he outlined this in his speech: 'A number of deputies have accused the government of failing the mental handicap sector. I immediately refute these accusations. The moneys available to this sector in 1998, a sum of £16 million, are equivalent to the investment made in 1997 by the previous government. However, the 1997 figure was the largest given by that government during its term. I have matched this figure in my first year.

'In addition, for the first time, I have agreed a major capital programme of £30 million for mental handicap services to be invested over the next four years. This is the first time there has been a multi-annual capital programme specifically for mental handicap services. The £5.25 million capital funding provided this year is the beginning of the programme of investment and will allow for the continued implementation of the assessment of needs report. By utilising all the resources available to me the mental handicap services can be assured that the facilities and support services required will be available.'

This is a particular piece of his record that he has guarded jealously. There is little doubt that he brought significant investment to the sector. On 10 November, when Fine Gael proposed a motion criticising progress in respect of services for the mentally handicapped, we find Cowen in combatative mood once again while outlining his approach to the issues: 'The philosophy which underpins the development of services to persons with a mental handicap is that people with a mental handicap should be given the opportunity to live as full and independent a life as possible, and to live with their families and as part of their local communities for as long as possible ...

'Since my appointment as minister for health and children, despite the many competing demands which are made on the resources available to my department, and in particular in relation to waiting lists for services in the acute hospital sector, I have consistently identified as one of my priorities the provision of the additional residential, respite and day services outlined in the *Services to Persons with a Mental Handicap – An Assessment of Need 1997–2001*. I have, in the past twelve months or so allocated an additional £25 million to the services ... My department will spend approximately £271 million in 1998 on services to persons with a mental handicap and while acknowledging what still needs to be done, it must also be seen in the context of the existing level of expenditure ... The provision of additional respite services is vital if families are to be supported in caring for their relatives at home. As well as the provision of additional residential places for respite, this also involves the enhancement and expansion of the various "share a break" or "breakaway" schemes and the home support services. This approach will build in both a flexibility in responding to individual needs and an element of choice for carers.'

But it was the capital programme in which Cowen took most pride: 'In late 1997 I put in place a major capital programme of £30 million for mental handicap services to run over four years in tandem with the assessment of need report. This is the first time we had a multi-annual designated capital programme for mental handicap services. During the next four years this capital programme will provide for: new residential and day care facilities and the up-grading of existing facilities; the provision of alternative accommodation for persons with a mental handicap who are accommodated in St Ita's, Portrane, St Raphael's, Youghal, and other psychiatric hospitals, and the up-grading of existing facilities which will continue to be used in the medium to long-term future; and the provision of facilities for persons with a mental handicap who require specialist services in a secure environment.

'Yesterday I announced the first of a number of measures which are being taken to fulfil the commitment I made, as part of the national capital programme, to provide alternative and refurbished accommodation for persons with a mental handicap in psychiatric hospitals and other inappropriate places.'

Despite the arguments of the opposition the Dáil record portrays a man who would not compromise on his record in this area and it would seem that he felt it was one of his strongest achievements, even though as he admits himself, there was more work to be done.

Outside of hospitals Cowen could point to other achievements in his term, such as the establishment of the Food Safety Authority. This was an important body – given the level of doubt and fear that existed among consumers following salmonella and BSE scares. Proposing the bill to establish the authority Cowen said: 'It is clear that consumers are concerned about food safety and it behoves any government to listen to and respond appropriately to these concerns. I assure the House that this government will not be found wanting in this regard. The protection of public health is an absolute priority for me, as it is for all of my colleagues in government. Any threat to the safety of the food we eat, whether it be real or potential, will be responded to robustly and with transparency. It is therefore imperative that we have a structure in place that can adequately identify and assess the risk in a competent, professional manner and then communicate clearly and effectively with both consumers and providers.'

By 8 October 1998 it had become clear that there were major problems in the budget for Tallaght Hospital and money was now coming up short. Mr Shatter asked Cowen, as minister for health and children, the steps, if any, taken by him to address the financial crisis affecting Tallaght Hospital: 'The deputy will be aware the board of management of Tallaght Hospital has had discussions with officers of my department with regard to the budgetary difficulties facing it. This issue is, in the first instance, a matter for the hospital. The deputy will be aware of the determination process which is now in place in making allocations to all health agencies, whereby service plans must be submitted to my department within approved levels of funding. The hospital is now saying it has cost more to open the new hospital at Tallaght than was envisaged when it submitted its service plan earlier this year and it has advised my department of some immediate steps which it is taking to address the problem.

'The hospital's outturn for the month of July 1998, which was its first full month in operation at its new site in Tallaght, showed a significant overrun against budget and the board of management, having been asked to review the figures, confirmed the hospital's budgetary difficulties on 24 September last. As minister, I am extremely concerned at the degree of the projected deficit for 1998 which has been presented and the reasons given for the overrun.

'I was pleased when the board of management set 21 June last as the opening day for the new hospital and every possible support was given by my department and many of the health agencies in Dublin to support the hospital in achieving this date. I am particularly appreciative of the enormous effort made by the staff of the hospital at all levels to ensure the smooth and safe transfer of patients to the new hospital and the commencement of services at Tallaght.

'However, it is vital that the hospital now establishes itself on a proper footing at Tallaght. It is for that reason I have initiated an independent review of the data recently submitted by the board of management. This review, which will be carried out in the context of the recent merger of the base hospitals and the move to Tallaght, will also examine the arrangements within the organisation for service planning and associated staffing and financial budgets. The review will also look at the process, systems and practices for reporting and control. It is expected the review will be completed within three weeks.'

What should have been a good news story was turning into another problem. There was a consistent problem across the health sector in predicting budgets; Cowen did not believe such overruns were acceptable. Tallaght would be forced to come to terms with budgetary procedure and there was certainly to be no special treatment. Cowen's insistence on an independent review of the data illustrated a lack of trust in the board and just how seriously he took the problem of the cost overrun. He was to remain strict on instilling the principle of adherence to budgets and, on 19 November, during statements on the health service, Cowen probably gave his most comprehensive view of how he saw that sector: 'Planning, management and control are essential in implementing the longer-term strategy. The government will use the 1996 legislation to control non-capital expenditure within the limits agreed by government and approved by the Dáil. It will ensure that available resources are distributed as objectively as possible, consistent with real needs, and it will not allow the agenda to be dominated by those who are best placed to make the loudest noises about their needs. It is not an unplanned or rudderless service. It is far better integrated than many health systems and is acknowledged by the OECD as an efficient, well organised service.'

Cowen also made the case that capital expenditure in the past had been inadequate: 'In regard to capital, I have negotiated a three-year programme. This is the first time any minister for health has been in a position to work with such assurance in relation to capital developments. This will be of immense benefit to the system as my department and the agencies can plan on a much more orderly basis. The actual amounts for each year of that programme are: £147 million in 1998, £155 million in 1999 and £165 million in 2000. Over that three-year period the total amount of extra investment over the original 1997 figure of £108 million will be a total of £143 million. Indeed, the figure for the year 2000 represents an increase of 53 per cent over the 1997 original figure introduced to the Oireachtas by former minister Deputy Noonan. All of this reflects the government's recognition that the health capital programme has not been adequately resourced in the past.'

He proceeded to describe the benefits of extra funding and the achievements being made by hospitals: 'The acute hospital sector consumes about 50 per cent of total expenditure. This sector is getting its fair share of resources having regard to the need to meet other priorities, many of which have been relatively neglected until recent years. The hospital system continues to expand with more patients being treated every year. This year alone has seen an increase of 9 per cent in day work with a 1 per cent growth in in-patient activity and with an overall average increase of over 3 per cent.

'While the acute hospital sector continues to receive the largest single share of the funding devoted to the health service, the benefits of this funding are clear. In recent years, the acute hospital system has treated a steadily increasing number of patients. A recent study by the OECD has shown that the Irish hospital system has become more productive and efficient. The average length of a hospital stay has declined. Better management of hospitals has resulted in increased occupancy levels. Hospitals have taken advantage of developments in medical practice to increase the level of day-care in Irish hospitals almost four-fold since 1986. The impact of these improvements can be seen in the fact that the number of patients treated in acute hospitals has risen by 3 per cent a year since 1987. In the twelve months to the end of August 1998, 539,900 patients had been discharged from our acute hospitals, almost 17,000 more than in the same period last year.'

The patient numbers indicate the sheer scale of the health service. But Cowen also believed that those who could afford to pay more must do so, and he showed his intentions to ensure that those seeking private rooms in public hospitals met their fair share of the costs: 'I announced yesterday an increase in charges for private rooms in public hospitals. Let me make it absolutely clear again that I have no apologies to make for this increase. The increase still leaves a gap between the charges and the cost of providing services to private patients in public hospitals. As minister for health and children, am I expected to allow these charges to be frozen and thereby continue with subsidies for private practice or should those charges not reflect the realistic cost of providing services? There are already considerable subsidies in place for the private sector, including tax breaks, and I will not allow a situation to continue whereby the taxpayer must pick up an ever increasing proportion of hospital costs while the private sector does not meet its fair share.'

He then comprehensively outlined his thoughts on governance, management and budgeting: 'I now turn to the key tasks of governance and management and set out the level of performance I want to see achieved throughout our services. Everyone accepts that health management is a complex and difficult task. It has perhaps been the focus of most public debate in the acute hospital sector. One area which has received insufficient attention to date is that of governance. No manager, however skilled and well supported by clinicians, can deliver appropriate and effective services without clear directions from his or her board. There is an absolute need for every health agency to be explicit about the values and principles which underpin the service it delivers and by which it will measure itself and those it employs.

'The accountability legislation brought a sharper focus than ever before to the issue of governance as it now affects health board members and management. This year my department has embarked on a general programme of governance development with a number of the major voluntary hospitals. This is long haul work, but I am certain it will be a vital part of our future success and our continuing ability to deliver quality services within defined budgets …

'The managers of health service agencies must also live within their budgets. I accept that the management of acute hospital services poses significant and difficult challenges. The activities to be managed are largescale and complex. The acute demands that may be made on the system are unpredictable. However, none of these demands are new. We have been here before and we have managed these problems.

'There is a degree of predictability in what faces each acute hospital every year. The surge in demand for acute services in January and February of each year is a well-observed phenomenon. The drop-off in demand for elective services in the summer is also well known. The fact that facilities have to be taken out of commission for maintenance or refurbishing is known. At the beginning of each year it should be possible to devise a plan which matches known available resources to these demands. However, a plan drawn up in December or January cannot simply be put on a wall or a shelf and left there to gather dust …

'We must put the patient at the centre of the system, even if that means changing the type of contracts people have, the hours they are required to cover, the ways in which they interact with other service providers and the processes through which work is done. Those responsible for governance must assure themselves that the service is good and safe and is seen as such by the patient. Management must provide the environment and the infrastructure through which people are likely to give of their best, as well as complying with their statutory obligations and those delivering the service must show flexibility and responsiveness in a dynamic and necessarily rapidly changing service.'

However Cowen's approach to management reform and in particular to budgeting did not meet with universal acclaim, far from it. Alan Shatter clearly disagreed with the minister's interpretations: 'The minister and his officials in briefings in recent days referred, as the minister did this morning, to the 1996 legislation passed by the previous government, which prevents health boards exceeding their budgets allocated at the beginning of the year and prevents them from raising overdrafts. This legislation was rightly put in place to enable central government to determine financial allocations for the health services and to prevent health boards arbitrarily running up overdrafts which they could not discharge out of their own resources ...

'The 1996 legislation does not act as a barrier to a minister for health providing additional financial allocations to hospitals forced to close beds in the month of December for budgetary reasons. It does not prevent the minister in the middle of the year from reviewing the state of the hospital waiting lists and considering, in the context of unexpected financial inflows to his department, whether additional funding should be made available to facilitate the undertaking of additional procedures at a time when waiting lists are growing. An efficient and competent minister would have conducted such a review and would, given health levy buoyancy, have allocated additional funds to tackle the waiting-list crisis earlier this year.'

Cowen was clear on the objectives of his policy however: 'I have no problem explaining that we will not go back to the situation that obtained up to recently when we had to plan and develop health services on the basis of allocations made long after the start of the financial year and deputations trooping into ministers mid-year to bid for more moneys because expenditure was above what was targeted for. In the interest of greater transparency and accountability, the policy of successive governments since 1993, when historic deficits, totalling £120 million, were eliminated, has been to bring forward prompt payment legislation to ensure small suppliers to the health services do not have to wait ten or twelve months for payment because budgets in the health sector are way out of line. That legislation had the support of everybody in the House and everyone accepted it had to be done. We introduced the Health (Amendment) Bill, 1996, the purpose of which is to make sure we deal first with situations where people get allocations and letters of determination prior to the start of the financial year, to give an opportunity to the health agencies to draw up a service plan, not three or four, during the year, based on the allocation made.

'The purpose of these legislative frameworks is to bring some semblance of planning into the health service … It has been my contention since I became minister for health and children that the capital base, valued at more than £4.5 billion, the infrastructure which we use to try to deliver a health service, requires major capital investment. We cannot have a situation where equipment is replaced only if it breaks down, paid for with money taken out of revenues. We have to put forward a designated capital budget for that purpose. I have decided on a £10 million re-equipment budget every year to bring more capital investment into the health service so that we can improve morale in the service which has not seen a capital investment programme worth the name for years. Those are the facts. If we want to improve morale in an organisation perhaps we should put more money into the physical environment in which people work. The only way to do that is to enhance the capital programme.'

Cowen's approach was controversial and led to further accusations of an accountancy-led approach to hospital management. He did not believe that this is the case: 'I will address the point that the hospital service is being run by accountants. I will introduce an initiative shortly to try to bring clinicians into management. With the type of high-technology hospital service available as we approach the twenty-first century and the regional and tertiary centres being developed around the country, a greater partnership is needed in the management process. The old hierarchical system and stereotypical view of how hospitals are run – the general surgeon and the administrator and a case of never the twain shall meet – is an unfair assessment of how matters stand. However, that is not to suggest we do not have a sufficiently integrated service in terms of management. In some hospitals, such as St James' and Cork University Hospital, I have seen multidisciplinary teams of executive management and clinical directorates working together. That is in line with best practice and is needed throughout the hospital system as it would benefit both managers and clinicians. The idea would be that clinicians would be in charge of budgets as well as patients. That brings its own disciplines and challenges and both sides have their reservations. However, everyone involved in the pilot schemes agrees it is a better system of management and that they would not revert to the old system. That is in train and should be accelerated in the interest of good patient care, if nothing else.'

But the need for budgetary rules was never far away: 'We provide a very good service compared to many. It has many problems but we will continue to work to solve them. However, the experience of the late 1980s and up to 1993, when the historical deficits were cleared, showed that such deficits in such difficult years seriously arrested the development of the health service. This was because of the overhanging debt on health boards and the consequent debt repayments which had to be contended with. This was at a time when health boards were already working on tight budgets and when there was less economic growth and strength.'

The health service was still undergoing a process of change and for many the real problems still lay in the cuts and underfunding of the past. However there was merit in the argument that debt also placed a heavy burden on the health sector.

There is a view in certain quarters of Leinster House that you are never truly a minister unless you have faced a substantive motion of 'no confidence'. It is a right of passage that heralds you as a serious enough player that the opposition deem you worthy of such time. If that is the case, then Brian Cowen got his on 16 February 1999, compliments of Liz McManus: 'I propose a vote of "no confidence" in the minister for health and children, Deputy Cowen. I do not do so lightly but because we, in the Labour Party, are seeking the approval of the House for a fresh start in the area of health. It is clear this minister has failed abysmally to live up to the rigours of his office and that those who depend on health care and those who provide it have increasingly lost faith in him.

'Our motion is grounded not on some abstract political expediency, but on the reality that too many sick and vulnerable people have suffered needlessly – some have even died needlessly – and will continue to do so into the future unless the taoiseach seizes the initiative and establishes a new basis for our health care system under different leadership.

'Everyone understands that ministers are constrained by the general economic climate within which they operate and the competing and conflicting demands for resources. Nowhere is this more true than in the area of health care. Each minister must be able to make choices in order to resolve immediate problems while, at the same time, creating a vision for the future. Ministerial leadership has been described as the place where the dream starts and the buck stops. The minister, Deputy Cowen, has proved himself gravely lacking on both counts. His focus is more on accountancy than on accountability, more on financial management than on medical care. His role is part of the problem rather than part of the solution at a time, when, for the first time ever in the history of the state, the country's prosperity offers us a real opportunity to address the inequities and failings of our health care system.'

McManus pulled no punches in her attack of Cowen and her speech was a compendium of the problems in the health service: 'The question the sick and vulnerable can legitimately ask is "what has happened in our acute hospital services since this government took office?" I will let the record speak for itself. Far from tackling the hospital waiting lists, this government has presided over a steeply escalating rise in the number of patients waiting for hospital procedures. In some cases, patients have literally died for want of a hospital bed. Those who can, have gone into debt to raise a loan to access treatment. The remainder are still waiting in ever increasing numbers.'

The arguments were emotive and hinting at what was perceived to be Cowen's main weakness – a lack of sensitivity in such a vital portfolio as health. McManus continued: 'I can say with some certainty that when the minister for health stands up to speak, he will reel off his set piece for yet another time about what the Rainbow government did or did not do. I acknowledge he has put more money into the system so the real question is why is he not more successful when he has all this money to spend? Why is he not doing the business? ...

'When things got busy in 1998, it was clear that neither the minister nor the department had prepared for the pressures that built up in accident and emergency units and which led to extreme overcrowding. Patients were left on stretchers and slept on trolleys, some of them for literally days on end. In one case an elderly man died just five days after he had been left on a trolley for fifty-six hours.

'Plans were not made by the department in time to enable hospitals to cope in terms of keeping beds open and providing step-down beds in nursing homes which, according to hospital consultants, had spare capacity of approximately 500 beds at that time.'

But McManus maintained that the catalyst for the tabling of the motion was the financial problems in Tallaght Hospital and the minister's handling of the affair. She cited the Deloitte & Touche report into the matter: 'On page 26 of the Deloitte & Touche report the consultants state: "In our view the decision to base the 1998 Determination on the cost structure of the three base hospitals plus certain additional monies was inappropriate." The report goes on to state: "The Determination process does not lend itself well to a situation of major change; such as the opening of a new hospital." Earlier it is described as a "relatively blunt instrument". Today I received further confirmation of this and this point needs to be stated. The Deloitte & Touche report shows that from the department's notes it knew in March 1998 the amount set was not enough. The notes record that it thought it had put enough funds aside. While it does not look like that now, the amount is set and it is a case of "tough luck, Tallaght".

'Tallaght Hospital is a state-of-the-art, modern, technologically superb hospital. It is a Rolls Royce of a hospital, yet it is being forced to manage on a Morris Minor budget … The minister is reported in today's newspapers as saying he will not make up that shortfall. Even at this eleventh hour he persists in his obduracy, yet he has the statutory authority to make it up without any difficulty.'

It became apparent that it was Cowen's adherence to budgetary policy that was McManus' main bone of contention: 'The impression one gets is that the minister for health and children would shed no tears if he was moved elsewhere. He is a man of undoubted ability and intelligence with an unprecedented amount of money at his disposal, which raises an obvious question, namely, why is he unsuccessful in meeting the requirements of his brief when all the circumstances are such that his position should be absolutely secure? No minister in recent times has received so much criticism, in a whole area of concerns, as the minister, Deputy Cowen. Yet the circumstances in which he is operating, economically and in other ways, have never been so good.'

Of course the government was in a strong position and Cowen had the full support of his colleagues. He had no problem in ensuring that a counter-motion of confidence was passed in his performance as minister. He faced the arguments in typical style: 'I face a dilemma. Do I react and deal with the petty political agenda being followed by those who want to use the issues within the health service as a political football or do I ignore the nonsense and concentrate on what concerns the public? I have taken the view that it is best to ignore the politics and get on with the job. I intend, therefore, to ignore the political jousting that is of no interest to the majority whom we aim to serve.

'Those working in the health service have become cynical of the extent to which the services are increasingly used as a political football. They know that issues now being exploited were also issues during the opposition's time in government. There was a persistent failure by the previous government to address them over a number of years. The major difference between the government's approach to the health service and that of its immediate predecessor is that it is committing resources, instead of uttering platitudes. I lay down the challenge that no matter how the opposition pours over the respective figures it cannot fail to be embarrassed when a comparison is made between the government's investment in the health service and what happened under its stewardship.'

Ms Shortall: 'What about waiting lists?'

Mr Cowen: 'The additional resources provided by the government are double the increase provided by the parties opposite.

'I do not deny there are problems in the health service that have to be addressed. The government is determined to address them in a structured and planned fashion in partnership with all those interested in improving the health service. There are those who seek to portray a systematic and reasoned approach to reform of the health service as indicative of inertia and lethargy, to use a favourite phrase of Deputy Shatter. On the contrary, I make no apology for diagnosing problems, identifying solutions and implementing reforms in a structured way so that the progress achieved endures. Our strategy for the health service is based on three key elements: a substantial increase in the resources provided; proper planning of the use of these resources; and a partnership approach to the resolution of problems with interests of the patients the overriding consideration.'

Cowen then came as close as he probably can to displaying a personal conviction and sensitivity he is supposed to be lacking: 'I care deeply about preventing illness and providing good services for those who need them. I have a special responsibility to those for whom there are few advocates and who do not have major interest groups to plead their cause. I take the concept of equity seriously. The major initiative I have taken for public patients – an all-out assault on waiting lists – is the one which was subjected to a significant reduction in expenditure by the previous government. I have done much and I hope to do much more for the mentally handicapped, the physically disabled and older people. Public patients should enjoy the best standards of physical accommodation and be treated by fully trained doctors. On these issues, I ask deputies opposite to reflect on what they failed to do when they had the opportunity and were fully aware of the need.

'The health service is a soft target from within and without. It is subject to easy black propaganda and much hyperbole. It will never be perfect, but it can always be improved, provided the improvement is designed with the needs of patients at the core of the initiative. That is my mission.'

Cowen dismissed what he saw as an overhyping of the problems and proceeded to deal with the central issue of Tallaght Hospital: 'All politics is local and we tend to focus on what is nearest to us. In doing so, we forget to make objective comparisons. The organisation, cohesion, impact and value for money of the health service are properly regarded by those who have examined it objectively, as providing good quality at relatively low cost to the taxpayer. Critics tend to highlight what it may lack. They rarely acknowledge the considerable strengths which come from a centrally funded, well-planned service, staffed by a well-trained and highly committed workforce. For example, significantly more people were treated in our hospitals in 1998 than in previous years. It is right that the gaps in the service should be addressed. That is what I am doing far more quickly than those who are criticising me. We should not talk ourselves and health service staff into artificial depression about imagined crises.

'Deputy McManus stated that Tallaght Hospital is the catalyst that sparked her move. Given the extent to which the opposition has deliberately misrepresented the difficulties at Tallaght Hospital, let me briefly give the salient facts before informing deputies of the latest welcome developments.

'The board of the hospital failed to produce a service plan within the determination for 1998. It initially indicated a shortfall of £900,000. It then claimed to be short £5.9 million and after less than three months in operation it informed the department that it would require an additional £21 million in 1998, of which £16.4 million was attributed to non-capital. It was in these unprecedented and alarming circumstances that I commissioned the Deloitte & Touche report. The hospital, the board and senior management created the conditions which made this review essential. Any other presentation of the root cause of the current difficulties is not a reflection of what happened.

'The report which was received in early December was critical of issues relating to governance and top general management at the hospital and pointed to serious deficiencies in these areas. It did not deal with clinical issues at the hospital. The determination process used by the department in relation to the hospital for 1998 has been the focus of critical comment. I invite reflection on the following points. The report states, on pages 25 to 27, that the determination was a relatively blunt instrument in relation to the development and commissioning costs. This represents about 10 per cent of the total determination.

'The alternative method regarded as preferred by the consultants – in effect a zero-based budgeting approach – was not feasible. The hospital had not geared itself to make such a submission to the department. It was its responsibility to do so, if it wished to provide an alternative model. It did not recruit a director of finance until September 1997.'

He later picked up on the expenditure estimates for the hospital in 1999: 'The hospital was notified of its non-capital determination for 1999 on 23 December 1998 in the sum of £64.69 million. A further £3.916 million was approved in respect of the spending in the federated Dublin voluntary hospitals. Almost all this latter amount refers to staffing at the Tallaght Hospital. The total amount available to the hospital for 1999 is, therefore, £69 million … I am pleased to inform deputies that at a meeting held earlier today, the board agreed to a service plan for 1999 which, on the basis of the information now available to me, will comply with the requirements set out in the letter of determination. The plan provides for the full delivery of the approved level of services during 1999. There will be no enforced redundancies and the shedding of excess staff will be linked primarily to the completion of their short-term contracts. There will be no bed closures, other than those which occur seasonally.'

Cowen would appear to have ensured that his objectives were adhered to by hospital management. But he was not willing to let Liz McManus get away with comments she had made on the radio: 'In her radio interview this morning, Deputy McManus sought to make much of our relative position in the EU league table of health spending. I remind the deputy that the expenditure figures are based on the situation which prevailed in 1995 when the last government was in office.'

Later he suggested that the health policies of the USA would not meet with his approval: 'We need hardly look beyond the state of health agencies in the USA to see that high *per capita* spending does not automatically equate to a high-quality, equitable and comprehensive system.'

Support for the minister was of course forthcoming from his cabinet colleagues including this contribution from Jim McDaid, the minister for tourism, sport and recreation, outlining the costs involved in health service provision: 'In 1997, a time when it cost £3 to £5 per prescription, £11 million was spent on 2,502 artificial hip operations, representing an average of more than £4,000 per joint replacement.

'Let us take the example of a patient with increasing chest pain and invalidism, a feature of progressive coronary heart disease. There was a time when such patients were told – I did it myself – to put a tablet under the tongue, being reassured that they would be all right once they remained at home and never moved out. This disability is no longer acceptable. A patient can be whisked into hospital, his chest opened, the diseased heart vessel bypassed rendering the patient mobile again and pain free. It costs more than £10,000 to £12,000 per operation and over 1,006 such operations were carried out here last year …

'We, the politicians, stand indicted before the public for failing to spell out the escalating costs of high-technology medicine and for failing to educate the public on this subject. We are the people who should be indicted, not the minister for health and children. As I said to Deputy McManus, this is just a personalised attack on the minister and will not do one iota for the health service.'

In the debate we find the first mention of the 'Angola' reference on the floor of the House and also an example of Cowen's tough skin when it comes to insults. This time it was at the hands of Green Party TD, John Gormley. Gormley was an outspoken critic of Fianna Fáil, but would, of course, some years later lead the Green Party in coalition with Cowen.

Mr Gormley: 'I thank Deputy Higgins for sharing his time with me. There are many stories circulating about the minister for health and children. Some of them may well be apocryphal; some may be true. There is a story that the minister referred to the department as "Angola".'

Mr Cowen: 'The deputy should get a sense of humour.'

Mr Gormley: 'There is a story that in respect of the minister's most recent appearance on *Morning Ireland* he did not want to go out to the studio, but would prefer to take a phone call in bed.'

An leas-cheann comhairle: 'Deputy Gormley should not cast reflections on a Member of this House.'

Mr Cowen: 'Do not worry about it. I thought the deputy had a bit more intelligence.'

Obviously with the full support of his government colleagues Cowen was not threatened by the motion.

While there were many issues facing the health minister at the time, one area that did not cause him much trouble was that of medical cards. Indeed, not so long ago it would be hard to justify an inclusion of debates surrounding medical cards at all. That all changed with Budget 2009. In 2001 the then finance minister, Charlie McCreevy, extended an automatic entitlement to a medical card to all persons over seventy regardless of income. Brian Cowen had left the health portfolio the previous year and as such could only claim to have been part of the cabinet who approved the measure rather than having direct responsibility for it. We do not find any statements from him during 2001 regarding the change on the Dáil record. In 2008 as taoiseach he was closely involved in Brian Lenihan's preparations for the budget. Now as the country experienced one of its worst downturns, people were shocked when it was proposed to end the automatic entitlement to a medical card. Such was the outrage that the government was forced to revisit the decision and while they still ended automatic entitlements, the income limits were increased dramatically.

But perhaps an analysis of Cowen's record on this issue while minister for health, would have indicated that the move would not be such a shock. Cowen made clear, as far back as 26 January 1998, that he personally was not in favour of automatic entitlements. When Ms Clune asked the minister for health and children if he would provide a medical card to all persons over the age of seventy-five years, Cowen replied: 'Entitlement to health services in Ireland is primarily based on means. Under the Health Act, 1970, determination of eligibility for medical cards is the responsibility of the chief executive officer of the appropriate health board. Medical cards are issued to persons who, in the opinion of the chief executive officer, are unable to provide general practitioner, medical and surgical services for themselves and their dependants without undue hardship.

'Income guidelines are drawn up by the chief executive officers to assist in the determination of a person's eligibility and are revised annually in line with the consumer price index. It should be noted that these guidelines are higher for persons aged sixty-six to seventy-nine and higher again for those aged eighty and over. However, these guidelines are not statutorily binding and even though a person's income exceeds the guidelines, that person may still be awarded a medical card if the chief executive officer considers that the person's medical needs or other circumstances would justify this. Medical cards may also be awarded to individual family members on this basis.

'In view of this special provision it is felt that it is not justifiable, on health policy grounds, to extend an automatic entitlement to a medical card to any specific group without any reference to their means, particularly as a general rule, in view of the many areas of pressing need in the health services and the limited resources available to meet them. It is open to all persons to apply to the chief executive office of the appropriate health board for health services if they are unable to provide these services for themselves or their dependants without hardship.'

On 16 June the matter was raised again with a similar result. Jim O'Keeffe asked the minister for health and children what plans, if any, he had to introduce medical cards for all those over the age of seventy-five, and, if so, when this would be introduced.

Mr O'Keeffe: 'Do I take it the minister is unsympathetic to the proposal to extend medical card eligibility to those over the age of seventy-five? Will he accept that there are now only 30,000 or so in that category and that eligibility could be extended for approximately £7 million? Will he accept it is a reasonable proposition to extend free medical treatment to people over the age of seventy-five?'

Mr Cowen: 'I am not unsympathetic to the argument that it should be considered. It was mentioned, uniquely, in our programme and was not in the programme of any previous government. I cannot be accused of being unsympathetic to a proposal that is now getting consideration for the first time. The general rule is that, because of the pressing needs on the health services, we do not decide on eligibility for medical cards beyond income eligibility. There are income limits but a residual discretion is available to the chief executive officers in cases where people are above those limits. In relation to the principle, I am far from being unsympathetic, but I am anxious to get the views of the chief executive officers on this matter before decisions are taken.'

However by 2 March 1999, Cowen appears to have considered the matter and decided on a three-year course of action aimed at raising thresholds but leaving a means test in place: 'Subsequent to the announcement in the 1999 budget, which was in line with the commitment given in the Programme for Government to review medical card eligibility for the elderly, the chief executive officers of the health boards have decided to implement, from 1 March, changes in the income limits for people over seventy consistent with the budget statement.

'At present, 80 per cent of persons aged seventy and over, that is, about 231,000 individuals, have medical cards and it is estimated that figure will rise by 30,000, to 90 per cent, at the end of the three-year doubling of the existing income limits referred to in the budget.'

Cowen is clear that he does not believe in abolishing income limits as Alan Shatter pushes the matter further: 'I also welcome this scheme, but I ask the minister to clarify the reason the age of seventy was chosen and whether it is the minister's intention to reduce that incrementally? In other words, might we see elderly persons over sixty-five or sixty-six being brought into this scheme next year? What are the minister's proposals in this context? Does he envisage ultimately abolishing the means test in the context of the medical card?'

Mr Cowen: 'No. The commitment in the budget statement is to double the income eligibility limits for all people over seventy within the next three years. There will be a 33.3 per cent increase each year to eventually achieve a doubling of the eligibility limit. There is no proposal to abolish income eligibility limits. That would involve changing the health act. I do not believe that is necessary in any event. We simply want to ensure that old-age pensioners, particularly those who have small state pensions or other small pensions along with that, who up to now have been rendered ineligible for a medical card, will now be eligible in the vast majority of such cases.'

On 22 April 1999 he made it even clearer that it was his belief that the current government did not intend extending an automatic entitlement to any group: 'In common with previous governments, this administration does not feel it is justifiable on health policy grounds to extend an automatic entitlement to a medical card to any specific group without any reference to their means or, in the case of children, to their parents' means as a general rule. It is open to all persons to apply to the chief executive officer of the appropriate health board for health services if they are unable to provide these services for themselves or their dependants without hardship.

'Those who do not hold medical cards are entitled to a broad range of health services, including an entitlement to public hospital and public consultant treatment, subject only to modest statutory charges and out-patient services free of charge. There are a number of schemes which provide assistance towards the cost of medication.'

He went on to further explain his reasons for not extending automatic entitlements: 'The deputy also referred to the elderly. I was glad to be in a position to ensure that the eligibility limits will be doubled over this and the next two budgets. This move was justified and it was a good proposal. However, it did not negate the basic principles of the scheme. The decision was to double the eligibility limits rather than move towards automatic entitlement because questions of inequity could arise. Elderly people with means should not be automatically entitled to a medical card when there are many people who are under sixty-five and slightly over the limits who are not automatically entitled to a card.

'One can make cases for specific groups and one would have sympathy with many of the arguments. However, more has been done in this area by this administration than any other government. This matter is ongoing and the arguments will be raised when I am in opposition and there is a different minister.'

The points Cowen makes on this issue are interesting. A clear policy belief and stance is evident. Considering the government then took the decision to give an automatic entitlement in 2001, it is hard to imagine Cowen supporting it. One can only wonder whether, if his views were so entrenched, the measure would ever have seen the light of day had he remained as health minister. It has often been criticised as a move by Finance Minister Charlie McCreevy in order to court the grey vote. The new health minister, Michael Martin, obviously did not share his predecessor's objections. In any event Cowen had moved on from the health portfolio and while he was part of the cabinet who approved the measure, it would be difficult to imagine him opposing it from his new position as foreign affairs minister if the ministers for finance and health and the taoiseach had agreed it. Nonetheless it is clear that in 2008 Cowen allowed his own views on the matter to resurface. It does perhaps hint at an overall disapproval of universal entitlements regardless of income.

For all the debate we have seen with regard to health, however, one issue in particular was to define Brian Cowen as minister for health. It was to be his toughest task and represented a career-threatening crisis. He was the first minister to face a strike by nurses and it was to be the biggest industrial relations dispute in the history of the state. To assess Cowen's record, we must go right back to his time in opposition in 1997 when Michael Noonan, the then minister of health, faced the threat of strike action by nurses: 'I welcome the decision by the Labour Court to issue a recommendation tomorrow night in the nurses' dispute and I hope a satisfactory resolution can be reached. The Labour Court is working under immense pressure and I wish it well …

'Even though the dispute has been looming for six months, it is only now that the department of health and the management of the health services are developing a contingency plan. A major mistake was made by the minister for health in leaving the development of cover procedures until the last minute. Trying to put these in place just days before potentially the most serious strike in the history of the state is very bad management. Efforts were made by the nursing unions some time ago to develop contingency plans for the health service but these did not receive a response from the department of health. Likewise, even though there is a provision for a code of practice in the Industrial Relations Act, 1990, for disputes in essential services, the department of health also did not act on this …

'Fianna Fáil wants to see justice done to the caring profession. Nurses play a vital role in the health services. They are integral to its functioning and their work is of immense value. In the past, when Fianna Fáil has been in government, there have been disputes where more rigid national agreements and more difficult fiscal conditions applied in the economy. Amongst these were disputes involving the ESB, radiographers, dental assistants, fire brigade staff and hospital doctors. In each instance the disputes were resolved with political will and imagination despite the limitations of the Programme for National Recovery and the Programme for Economic and Social Progress ...

'If a national nursing strike goes ahead, the entire health service will grind to a halt, probably within hours of the strike starting. The chaos that will result is unthinkable. The minister for health and the health service managers at the Labour Court must be conscious of this.

'It is very unfair to leave the Labour Court in the unenviable position of trying to resolve this dispute at the fifty-ninth minute of the eleventh hour. The minister was wrong to remain at arm's length from the dispute for so long. After two rejections of the pay offer, he should have got directly involved and tried one last effort. He should have responded to the request from the unions to hold a direct meeting with them and he certainly should have taken up the offer from the general secretary of SIPTU [Services, Industrial, Professional and Technical Union] for a commission on nurses' pay and conditions. This could and probably will form part of the ultimate solution.'

Brian Cowen certainly gave some hostages to fortune on the issue. On 18 February Michael Noonan outlined the scale of the Labour Court recommendations: 'In view of the threatened strike action by nurses with effect from 10 February 1997, the Labour Court decided to use its powers, under section 26(5) of the Industrial Relations Act, 1990, to carry out an investigation into the reasons for the proposed action. The recommendation of the Labour Court issued on 7 February 1997 and provided for improvements in the package of proposals which had emerged from independent adjudication in September 1996 as follows: in respect of staff nurses, a new ten-point salary scale to a maximum of £20,350 in addition to one long service increment of £650 for nurses who are on the maximum of the scale for three years – this is effectively a maximum scale of £21,000; the deletion of proposed lower entry points on the staff nurse scale; improvements in three areas in respect of early retirement – that up to 200 nurses per annum be allowed to retire at age fifty-five, subject to thirty-five years service; the age for application for the previously proposed pre-retirement initiative be reduced from fifty-seven to fifty-five; the pensions commission give priority to the nurses' pensions claims; and that temporary nurses be allowed to progress to the seventh point of the incremental scale – incremental progression for temporary nurses and other health service grades has hitherto been capped at the fifth point of the scale.

'The court also recommended that 2,000 temporary nurses be offered permanent positions. This is an increase of 300 from the previously proposed number of 1,700. It further recommended that a commission on nursing "become a reality within one month from acceptance of the court's recommendation".

'The present position is that the unions decided to defer strike action, pending a ballot of their members, on the revised proposals incorporating the additional gains recommended by the Labour Court. In the case of SIPTU this decision was taken on 8 February 1997. In the case of the Irish Nurses Organisation, Psychiatric Nurses Association and IMPACT the decision was taken on 9 February 1997. No recommendation on the revised proposals is being made by the unions.

'The government has accepted, in full, the terms of the Labour Court recommendation, including the establishment of the commission on nursing for which chairmanship and terms of reference have been agreed. It is my earnest hope that there will be a favourable outcome to the ballots currently taking place, enabling us to proceed with implementation of the pay increases due and to allow the next phase of the process of addressing grievances in the profession to commence through the work of the commission. The contingency planning arrangements drawn up for the threatened strike on 10 February remain in place. My department continues to be in direct contact with all of the affected agencies in relation to contingency plans and regional centres have been established to provide an ongoing flow of information on a daily basis to the department. These arrangements will remain in place until such time as agreement to the terms of the Labour Court recommendation is confirmed by the unions representing nurses.'

Fast forward to 8 October 1998, when the Commission on Nursing, which was central to the original nurses' dispute, reported. Brian Cowen was now minister for health: 'When the report of the Commission on Nursing was presented to me, I indicated that the government accepted the broad thrust of the report and that I wished to talk to the nursing unions about a partnership approach to its implementation. As an indication of that commitment to the report I also announced an action plan aimed at implementation of its clear recommendations. The government's position on the pay issues arising from the report is that these can be dealt with in a way that is consistent with the directions set down in the taoiseach's address to the social partners last July.'

It did not bode well. The government were determined to hang tough on the idea of partnership. There was a fear that any pay claim dealt with in isolation would lead to a series of pay claims across the public sector. Cowen's claim that in earlier times Fianna Fáil had avoided disputes through political will and imagination now appeared little more than rhetoric from the opposition benches as he found himself facing a very intransigent union. This would undermine partnership as there was little point in having a wage agreement if separate increases were negotiated outside of it in any event. The matter was referred to the Labour Court for an independent opinion. The nurses rejected the findings of the Labour Court and Cowen believed that all the machinery of state was now exhausted. The options open to his predecessor had now been used up and he had to decide whether to face the strike which would be damaging in the extreme or come to an external agreement that could undermine social partnership. It was in this dispute that Cowen showed his mettle. For many it was a defining moment as to whether you disliked him or respected him for his actions. It was debated by the Dáil on 30 September just ahead of the strike and Cowen made his position clear: 'The Labour Court finding of 31 August 1999, rejected by nurses, includes among other elements: (a) increases of 10 per cent for ward sister and other higher grades; (b) significant improvements in annual leave, namely, an extra three days for staff nurses and an extra four days for promotional grades; and (c) a lump sum of £1,250 for all nurses contingent upon acceptance of the recommendation. When the latest Labour Court finding is implemented, the maximum salary of ward sisters will have increased by more than 37 per cent inclusive of general and special increases since before the 1997 settlement. The maximum pay of staff nurses has increased over the same period by almost 26 per cent. Many staff nurses and a significant number of ward sisters also stand to benefit from substantial increases in location and specialist qualification allowances recommended by the court in February 1999.

'The Labour Court's finding represented the culmination of a lengthy negotiating process on nurses' pay and conditions that has taken four years to complete. The court itself acknowledged that over the past two years nurses have justifiably improved their position not just financially, but in terms of gaining recognition for the enhanced role of the profession.

'I am glad to have this opportunity to reiterate that the government is committed to paying the full terms of the Labour Court finding and as far as the government is concerned that offer remains on the table. However, there is no possibility of improving upon the terms of the Labour Court finding. The government also remains fully committed to implementing the recommendations of the Commission on

Nursing which are designed to tackle the underlying problems within the profession and develop nursing and midwifery as a key profession within the health services.

'Once again, I ask all nurses to reflect and consider the full implications before voting for strike action. Not only would such action be in direct breach of the industrial peace clause of Partnership 2000, it would endanger the entire national partnership approach which has served the country so well and above all it would inflict considerable hardship on patients and their families.

'Last week the taoiseach outlined a credible alternative to confrontation and a way forward that will provide a better outcome for all. That alternative is renewal of our commitment at national level to social partnership and a series of practical steps to a new partnership agreement. That national position must be combined with an approach to public-service pay which is imaginative in ensuring that the income of public servants more closely reflects their performance and is not based on so-called traditional relativities. This is the context within which the aims and aspirations of public servants, including nurses, can best be met. However, if nurses vote for industrial action there is no avenue open to me to avert such action. All avenues have in fact been exhausted. In 1997 the Labour Court intervened to avert industrial action, but on this occasion nurses have rejected the Labour Court finding …

'The justification of a claim one way or another can only be resolved in the context of independent arbitration. The Labour Court, under the Industrial Relations Act, 1990, has that authority. The government is honouring it and committed to it. It is also committed to implementing the report of the Commission on Nursing and to implementing all of its obligations under the established industrial relations procedures. What more is the government to do if it wants to maintain – as I presume other Members wish to maintain – the social partnership which has been the cornerstone of some of our economic success? That is the position.'

The opposition piled on the pressure on 12 October with a private member's motion. Alan Shatter led the attack: 'The effects of this damaging dispute are already being felt. Patients are being sent home from hospitals, hospital beds are being left vacant, scheduled operations are being cancelled, people with life-threatening illnesses, such as cardiovascular disease and cancer, are being told that essential in-patient hospital procedures are either being postponed or cannot be scheduled. It should never have come to this, but it has because of the gross incompetence of the minister for health and children and his failure to play a proactive role in the running of our health service.

'The nursing dispute should be put in context, it cannot be understood in isolation. As at 30 June last, 34,000 patients were waiting for in-patient hospital treatment during the term of office of the minister and at a time of unprecedented economic prosperity. The public in-patient hospital waiting lists grew from 29,000 to 36,500. In June 34,000 patients were affected, 5,000 more than at the date of the last general election.'

Enda Kenny added his voice: 'The government, of which I was proud to be a member, when confronted by the possibility of a nurses' strike paid out £85 million on the recommendation of the Labour Court and following the involvement of others, but more importantly established the Commission on Nursing to analyse and consider the structural deficiencies in the nursing profession and to make recommendations on how these could be rectified. The government has said that it will pay the full amount recommended by the Labour Court, but the key to settlement of this dispute lies in dealing with the structural deficiencies in the nursing profession, including the recognition of expertise and incremental payments in respect of courses followed at one's own cost.'

However, Cowen had set his face against any compromise and insisted the dispute could only be handled within the context of social partnership: 'I welcome this opportunity to set out in clear and unambiguous terms the position of the government on nurses' pay and, in particular, to reiterate our determination to protect social partnership.

'Social partnership has delivered major benefits. For this country, it has been a winning formula, and there is no reason to believe that it cannot continue to do so. It has provided the framework within which economic and social goals can be agreed and achieved. The benefits we now enjoy through high levels of employment, low inflation and reduced taxation did not happen by accident …

'The overall numbers employed in our health services are now at an all-time high, including the number of nurses employed. Social partnership and its fruits have given us the confidence to embark on long-term strategies to tackle the main causes of sickness and death: cancer and cardiovascular disease. There is scarcely an area of the services that is not enjoying a period of development …

'Outside social partnership, it is difficult to envisage how we could find a formula through which we can, in a controlled way, break out of an iron circle of pay relativities in the public sector and agree a basis on which reward is more closely linked to contribution and performance …

'The history of nurses' pay talks is a long one, punctuated by a series of offers followed by rejection. In order to provide a context for the situation now confronting us, it is necessary to go back to 1994. Discussions with the Nursing Alliance under the PCW [Programme for Competitiveness and Work] restructuring clause commenced in late 1994, when management offered nurses a down payment of 1 per cent, effective from 1 April of that year, the same as had been offered to other public sector groups. This was accepted by the nursing unions who then broke off talks to consider progress. Talks resumed in February 1996, during which management tabled a conditional offer of £20 million. This offer was rejected following a ballot by nurses. In March 1996, following intervention by the Irish Congress of Trade Unions, talks took place at the Labour Relations Commission, which resulted in agreement on a set of proposals costing £33.5 million. This enhanced offer was rejected by the Nursing Alliance following a ballot.

'Direct discussions between management and the nursing unions were resumed in June 1996. The nurses' pay issue was subsequently referred to an independent arbitration board established by the government and the Congress of Trade Unions to hear outstanding pay disputes. This adjudication board recommended a package worth some £50 million to nurses. This package was accepted by SIPTU and the PNA [Psychiatric Nurses Association], but rejected by the INO [Irish Nurses Organisation] and IMPACT. Strike notice was then served to expire on 10 February 1997. The Labour Court then intervened and on 7 February 1997 issued a recommendation containing a package costing £85 million. This was accepted by nurses on the basis that a Commission on Nursing would be established to examine and report on the role of nurses in the health services.

'The Labour Court finding of February 1997 provided for special pay increases of up to 17 per cent for the grades of staff nurse and ward sister, with similar level increases for other grades. These increases were substantially in excess of the 5.5 per cent cap on restructuring deals under the PCW agreed by the then Rainbow Coalition government and the Irish Congress of Trade Unions. The Labour Court justified the award of such large pay increases to nurses on the basis that their pay scales, to quote directly from the court's recommendation: "have fallen significantly behind other groups". This statement clearly demonstrates that the Labour Court regarded nurses as a special case deserving a special pay award.

'I would like to highlight one particular aspect of the court's finding relating to long-service increments at that time. The adjudication board had recommended a salary scale for staff nurses with two long-service increments. The Labour Court subsumed those two increments into a new ten-point salary scale for staff nurses and added a new long-service increment to the new scale. I am left wondering to what extent staff nurses were made aware that long-service increments had been conceded to them at that stage.

'The Commission on Nursing was established in March 1997. Its membership included representatives of the four nursing unions. Seven of the fourteen ordinary members of the Commission were drawn from the nursing profession. The Commission's final report, entitled *A Blueprint for the Future*, was formally presented to me in September 1998. At the launch of the report, I announced, on behalf of the government, that it had accepted the broad thrust of the report and that it was committed to implementing its recommendations. That remains our position …

'The fundamental fact that needs to be emphasised here is that the Commission on Nursing did not recommend that staff nurses should be given additional long-service increments …

'The Labour Court issued its final determination on the nurses' pay issue on 31 August last. The court's package included an average increase of about 10 per cent for ward sisters and higher grades; a lump sum payment of £1,250 for every nurse employed in the public health services, conditional on acceptance of the Labour Court recommendation; additional annual leave for all nurses linked to service, up to three days for staff nurses and up to four days for ward sisters and higher grades; a personal allowance payable on a red circle basis to serving nurses in certain grades to compensate for the apparent loss of existing differentials under the proposed pay structures; and an interim award of 4 per cent to nurse tutors pending the report of the Nursing Education Forum.'

Cowen was insistent that he acted fairly and expediently: 'At the

February 1997 Labour Court hearings, the Nursing Alliance sought to link the pay of staff nurses with that of the Grade Vs in the health services, which is a supervisory-administrative function. Moving the goal posts like this is a totally unacceptable way of conducting industrial relations business. They want to negotiate, in effect, another new claim, having rejected the arbitration finding in respect of the claim they argued for four years on a totally different basis.

'I have been portrayed as having being opposed to negotiations. The issue of nurses' pay has been four years in the negotiating process. I have spent more time on industrial relations issues relating to nursing since I became minister than on any other industrial relations matter.

'The government's approach to the nurses' pay issue and the threat of an all-out strike is correct and responsible.'

He would not let the opposition have it all their own way either: 'Deputy Shatter, however, is now calling on me to do something which his own party colleague would not and could not contemplate when he was in office. Deputy Quinn has gone even further; he has completely reversed his position from the time he was minister for finance and subsequently. In November 1996, he warned the country's nurses that they were making a gross error of judgment if they thought the government could offer them more than the £50 million pay package that they had just rejected.

'Deputy Quinn's own views on the management of public service pay were published in a report of an interview with him which appeared in the 5 February 1998 edition of *Industrial Relations News*. He is quoted as saying that as minister for finance "he looked at the economy both as the ringmaster and the paymaster" and that it took him "about 15 months to realise that there was no one managing the public sector side of the equation". I want to inform Deputy Quinn that we did not take 15 months to figure that one out. My position as minister for health and children …'

Mr Connaughton: 'It is hard to know what we were at.'

Mr H. Byrne: 'The deputies opposite have not got a leg to stand on.'

Mr Belton: 'The deputy knows where he will be standing shortly.'

Mr Cowen: '… is to manage my side of the public service and, as a member of the government, to be fully involved in managing the entire public service.'

Later, Cowen continued the point: 'The record shows that when Deputy Quinn was minister for finance, he was not anxious to move beyond the £50 million package that was on offer to nurses in late 1996 and early 1997.

'In a radio interview on 12 November 1996, Deputy Quinn said, "As far as the government as management are concerned, we have exhausted all of the room for manoeuvre that existed for us as one of the signatories to the PCW and I would not like any impression to be given that one extra push or shove might result in additional monies being put on the table. That would be an error of judgment if people were to think that such an additional movement or push would bring about extra money."

'When the £85 million package was finally agreed in February 1997, Deputy Quinn levied public services to pay for the nurses' pay increase.

'I ask the House to compare his stance then with his recent statements which called on the government to give nurses what they are looking for and worry about relativities later.'

Cowen later outlined the current levels of pay that were on the table as a result of the Labour Court findings: 'The Labour Court finding of 31 August 1999, together with an earlier finding on specialist allowances and significant improvements which have already been conceded on overtime payments and incremental credit, will cost approximately £110 million in 1999 and £70 million a year thereafter.'

Mr McCormack: 'The minister is only filibustering.'

Mr Cowen: 'This is on top of the £85 million award of February 1997. The combined value of all these improvements on an ongoing basis is more than £150 million and equates to an average increase of approximately 23 per cent.

'This is in stark contrast with the restructuring increases to other groups of workers which were limited to 5.5 per cent under PCW. The restraint shown by the rest of the trades union movement in accepting this difference in recognition of the exceptional position of nurses is not likely to extend to any increase above and beyond the recent Labour Court finding. Everybody needs to understand that under the present arrangements it is not possible to disregard existing relativities. Nurses' pay cannot be dealt with in isolation from other public service groups.'

By 19 October the strike was under way. The opposition were quick to lay the blame at Cowen's feet. Mrs B. Moynihan-Cronin said: 'The date 19 October 1999 will be remembered as one of the worst days in the lifetime of the government. It is, as one senior representative of the nursing unions stated, "a black day for our industrial relations". In this era of unprecedented wealth the government has allowed the nurses dispute to fester for months and let the unthinkable happen. It has forced our 28,000 nurses out on strike through its ineptitude. They have a proud record of serving the people in our hospitals. The government, to its shame, is the first administration in the history of the state to allow a national nurses strike to take place, and it is the biggest strike in the history of industrial relations.'

Caoimhghín Ó Caoláin of Sinn Féin offered his support to the nurses: 'I extend my solidarity and that of my colleagues in Sinn Féin to the nurses and hope that their action is successful in achieving justice, their basic claim.'

Joe Higgins of the Socialist Party agreed: 'The Irish Congress of Trade Unions should, by all means, facilitate discussions, but the Irish Congress of Trade Unions should be out in front, leading public support for the nurses, giving voice to it to such an extent that the government will listen and pay up.'

In his contribution, however, Brian Cowen announced the first signs of a settlement. It would be agreed within the terms of the partnership agreement and could be seen as a significant victory for Cowen. He did not want to portray it as such: 'This is a very complex and difficult dispute. In saying this, I am not only giving my own view of this dispute, but I am also giving the view of the trade union personnel who are also dealing with it from their side. If it were not a complex issue, we would have found a resolution to the difficulties long before now.

'The first point I want to make abundantly clear is that there has been no change in the position of the government. Our position has been consistent throughout. It has never been a case of calling on the Nursing Alliance to simply take or leave the Labour Court findings. The government want the Labour Court findings accepted and to move on to the other issues in the context of the Commission on Nursing report and social partnership.

'On 23 September, the taoiseach outlined a credible alternative to confrontation and a way forward that will in my view provide a better outcome for us all, including for nurses. That alternative is a renewal of our commitment at national level to social partnership and a series of practical steps to a new partnership agreement. That national position must be combined with an approach to public service pay which is imaginative in ensuring that the income of public servants should more closely reflect their performance and not be based on so-called traditional relativities. This is the context in which the aims and aspirations of public servants, including nurses, can best be met. It would also be the best context within which to set the progressive implementation of the report of the Commission on Nursing.

'It was not until last Saturday that I heard, for the first time, an explicit acknowledgement from the Nursing Alliance that it recognised that the government obviously has difficulties in dealing with this matter in the way that the alliance had been asking it to do up to then. In the course of being interviewed last Sunday on the RTÉ *This Week* programme, I made the following statement: "I am saying very clearly, and it has always been the government's position, that if the Nursing Alliance unions recommit themselves to social partnership, acknowledge that we cannot pursue issues in isolation from the wider public sector pay implications, acknowledge that we cannot tear up existing agreements, if that is the position of the Nursing Alliance, then clearly there is a whole range of possibilities open to them to pursue their agenda."

'I have been at pains all along to let everybody know that the problem in dealing with this issue is that existing social partnership agreements must be honoured, and that the primacy of the Labour Court as a means of settling disputes must be upheld. At three o'clock last Sunday, the Nursing Alliance issued the following statement: "The Nursing Alliance wishes to reiterate that it is cognisant of the government's difficulties in further addressing the outstanding pay issues for nursing grades against the backdrop of existing social agreements.

'"The alliance also realises that any discussions will have to consider those difficulties while also providing a forum and process which will address, in a meaningful way, the outstanding pay-related issues from the Commission on Nursing.

'"In the above context we state once again we are available for talks."

'Later that evening I issued a statement noting this recognition by the Nursing Alliance, and indicating that if the alliance was genuine in its desire to identify a process by which these issues might be addressed within the parameters of pay partnership, then I would be available to meet the alliance the following day, which was yesterday.

'I met the representatives of the Nursing Alliance at 3 o'clock yesterday afternoon in the department of health and children in Hawkins House. The most important achievement coming from yesterday's meeting was the mutual recognition of the problems that exist on both sides. It was a good working meeting and I certainly found it helpful and constructive and it provided for a useful exchange of ideas. Both parties agreed to go back to the social partners and talk to their own sides in the partnership and seek help in trying to find a process that will allow for the resolution of this dispute on such a broad basis ...

'Because of the number of people, or groups, lining up behind the current nurses' claim, it is important to ensure that arguments which may seem specific to nursing now are not later used by any of these groups to advance their particular case within the next number of weeks or months. I do not see this route as a lengthy process but it should be comprehensive so that both sides do not simply keep arguing over old scores.

'I am most anxious to ensure that any new process or any new concepts which might be involved in progressing the situation do not interfere, or be seen to interfere, with the primacy of the Labour Court. I have always maintained and I still maintain, that the Labour Court should be the court of final appeal. While I am anxious to devise a new way of resolving the current problems, I do not see this process operating as if the Labour Court did not exist.'

He then takes a more conciliatory tone: 'I would also like to put on record that the co-operation between the management and union sides, where they have agreed and provided emergency cover, is very much appreciated. Those plans were put in place to try to keep the inconvenience to the public to the absolute minimum.'

He is also clear on his own record and puts this before the House: 'Since I became minister for health and children, a particular priority for me has been the greater involvement of nurses and other health care professionals in the management of our health services. Last November, I launched the Clinicians in Management Initiative and provided £2.5 million to get it up and running. This initiative is all about the better running of hospitals and other health care institutions through the participation of clinicians in the decision-making process. This involves devolution of responsibility, a process of empowerment for front-line staff and an openness to change. For nurses, it means getting rid of the traditional hierarchies and giving them more power in decision making in their own wards and units.

'Clinicians in Management is an initiative that involves nurses of all grades. My department and I stand ready to work with nurses in moving this initiative forward and providing nurses with empowerment across a range of hospital and community setting.'

Supporters of Brian Cowen's position saw him as a staunch defender of social partnership, the taxpayer, particularly the taxpayer in the private sector, and of the economic achievements that come from wage restraint. However, his opponents saw him as a grim breaker of union resolve, a man who had set his face against one of the 'caring professions' and refused to bow. Tackling groups such as nurses is a difficult business, but Cowen clearly showed he had resolve and the courage of his convictions. It was a resolve that many felt deserted him, however, in the early stages of his leadership in 2008. But none the less here his record on health stands for judgment.

INTERNATIONAL RELATIONS

Brian Cowen's appointment to the foreign affairs portfolio could safely be assumed to be a promotion. His stature had never been higher within Fianna Fáil and he was already being discussed as a potential leader. However, many people outside of the party wondered if Cowen had the diplomacy and skill that is necessary for the role of taoiseach. It was all well and good to be a tough, no nonsense minister, but could he display an ability to compromise and unite, the way leaders normally do? His appointment as minister for foreign affairs would put this to the test.

On 27 January when he was nominated for the post, his peers had plenty to say about him. Ruairi Quinn urged him to lead the debate on the new emerging Europe: 'How the constitutional balance of the emerging European Union will take shape in a manner that recognises the identity of nation states yet sensitively pools their sovereignty while respecting the necessity for some form of democratic accountability will be a major task. Sadly, the taoiseach, to my knowledge, has not engaged in it.

'Deputy Cowen, the new minister for foreign affairs, has an opportunity, because he undoubtedly has the ability to engage in that debate. Indeed, he will be expected to lead that debate and not, as some of his Fianna Fáil predecessors did, quietly sit back and allow the debate to proceed until such time as Irish interests were threatened and only then make an intervention.'

Mary O'Rourke had no doubts about his success: 'What can one say about my midlands friend, Deputy Cowen, the new minister for foreign affairs? He will be a great success. He will bring to the department his intelligence, wit, pugnacity – which is needed in any department – and sense of purpose.'

Ivan Yates challenged him to bring a new purpose to Northern Ireland: 'I have not ceased to be amazed at the outgoing minister of health and children's ability to hide his intellect behind his pugnacity. Nevertheless, I wish him well and hope that the endless hospitality and finger food in Iveagh House will not bore him to death. He is out of Angola now, so to speak, and faces an onerous job in regard to the next phase of reconciliation in Northern Ireland. I hope Deputy Cowen will be part of a process which will broaden the sense of Irishness, one which will make Mr David Trimble as Irish as someone whose grandfather fought in the GPO in 1916.'

A man he was traditionally close to within the party, Noel Dempsey, referred to his health record: 'I congratulate Deputy Cowen on his appointment as minister for foreign affairs. I could say many nice things about him, but I know he would only blush and be embarrassed as he is here with me at present. He has shown a capacity for leadership in his previous ministries. He has an obvious determination and tenacity in the jobs he has been called upon to do. It is recognised by all Members of this House that the job of minister for health and children is not an easy one, and he served in that role with distinction. His intellect and strength of character will be necessary in his role as minister for foreign affairs representing this country abroad. I have no doubt he will be able to fulfil that role. His commitment to the mentally handicapped and the programme he put in place – including the provision of funding – will be a lasting legacy of which he can be proud. It will be remembered by everybody in the years ahead. He had to fight many vested interests to prioritise this issue, but he succeeded in doing that. His achievement has been well recognised by all sides of the House, the service providers and advocacy groups. I have no doubt that in his new role at the department of foreign affairs he will leave further legacies.'

Pat Rabbitte was a mix of compliments, humour and criticism: 'Ever since Deputy Andrews announced his decision, wherever more than two or three people met around the country and asked who has the natural skills, diplomacy and track record to take over at Iveagh House, they automatically said Deputy Cowen. Asking Deputy Cowen to take over the diplomatic service is like asking Mike Tyson to stand in for Michael Flatley in *Riverdance* or *Lord of the Dance*. He knows, of course, I do not mean that. Deputy Cowen is a man of considerable ability. He has not been a good minister for health and children, but he has the intellectual ability and commitment to politics to be a good minister for foreign affairs and I wish him well.'

Mary Harney and Monica Barnes obviously agreed that substance should be more important than style. Mary Harney said: 'Deputy Cowen is being promoted to the department of foreign affairs. He is one of the most able people to have served in ministerial office. I am amused when I read that there is supposed to be a certain formula if one wishes to become minister for foreign affairs. The world of diplomacy does not operate on the basis that everybody smiles at everybody else, that one just tells people what they want to hear or one goes about one's business in a particular way. We should be mature enough in this House to know what is required to be a minister in any department. Deputy Cowen is tough, decisive, has his own views and is not afraid to outline them. That is much more important in ministerial office than some of the qualities that are perceived by others as being necessary. We will soon get to a stage where if one is not a certain size or does not look a certain way, one will not be able to serve in the House.'

Mrs Barnes: 'Hear, hear.'

So Brian Cowen commenced his term as minister for foreign affairs with no shortage of praise and just a little criticism ringing in his ears. In opposition, Cowen never lost interest in the Northern Ireland question. His leanings towards the nationalist position were always evident. But as minister for foreign affairs a more conciliatory approach was necessary. Northern Ireland had dominated the role of foreign affairs ministers for decades. The peace process went through many different stages and encountered numerous problems along the way. By the time Brian Cowen had assumed the foreign affairs portfolio the Good Friday Agreement was in place, but the task of implementing it was proving just as difficult. If Cowen had nationalist tendencies, he would be forced to dig deep to avoid them clouding his judgment.

On 15 June 2000, Cowen set out his first statement to the Dáil that encompassed his views on the way to move the peace process forward: 'On 5 May the Irish and British governments issued a statement expressing our belief that the remaining steps necessary to secure full implementation of the agreement can be achieved by June 2001. A letter setting out the governments' proposals and commitments in the areas of rights and equality, security, policing and justice and prisoners was also circulated to the parties. This was an important step towards creating a context of confidence in which others could make their intentions known. It paved the way for the statement issued by the IRA on 6 May and for the decision to re-enter the executive taken by the Ulster Unionist Council on 27 May. The restoration order signed by the secretary of state returning power to the Assembly and Executive entered into force on 30 May. All the institutions under the agreement are now back working to their full capacity, taking forward the important work to be done in each of their respective areas of competence.

'As a result of these developments we are now closer than ever before to achieving full implementation of the agreement and have a secure and agreed basis on which it is to be achieved. There are difficult issues which remain to be addressed.'

Without doubt considerable progress had been made during the month of May to ensure that the process was back on track after some very difficult problems. Cowen later points out that policing was going to be the next major issue for all parties: 'In discussions with the British government, including in my meeting with the secretary of state on 31 May, and in consultations with the parties, I have stressed that if it is to achieve the representative, accountable and effective police service envisaged in the agreement it is vitally important that the legislation give full effect to the Patten recommendations …

'The Patten proposals suggest a new model for policing in Northern Ireland distinct from the system in operation in any other part of the United Kingdom, where the chief constable is the focus of authority in local constabularies. Under the new model, authority would be vested in a policing board representative of both communities. It would also have independent members and have accountability mechanisms built in to ensure it would herald a new beginning in policing in Northern Ireland in a way that would allow those members of the RUC who have behaved professionally in the past to pursue their careers and representatives of the broad nationalist community in particular to encourage its members to pursue policing as a profession in this new context.

'I have indicated on a number of occasions the concerns we have expressed since the policing bill was published. There were indications in the second stage speech of the secretary of state, of movement in certain areas. There are issues under discussion. I have been in direct contact with the SDLP and Sinn Féin in relation to their concerns. The government wishes to see faithful implementation of the Patten proposals to ensure there will be a police force which will be representative and provide a basis for full participation and its full acceptance by everyone in Northern Ireland.'

Cowen was unambiguous in his position that the Patten report had to be implemented in full if policing was to become acceptable to all communities in Northern Ireland. He applied heavy pressure on his British counterpart in this regard.

If the government had hoped to implement the Good Friday Agreement in full by 2001 they were to be disappointed. Progress on many issues was painfully slow. However, the important fact remained that at least progress was being made. It was once thought that the IRA would never consider decommissioning – 'not a bullet' was the refrain. But on 22 March 2001, Cowen was able to report that perhaps the first steps in that process had been taken: 'As deputies will be aware, following several months of intensive discussions, the two governments – led by the taoiseach and Prime Minister Blair – and the pro-agreement parties in Northern Ireland met in Hillsborough on 8 March. While our talks did not enable us to reach a complete and comprehensive resolution of the issues we face, we had a very useful and productive exchange of views. Throughout a long day, it was obvious that, although several continue to face difficulties within their respective constituencies, all of the pro-Agreement parties remain firmly committed to securing the full implementation of the Agreement and are acting in good faith in their efforts to secure that outcome.

'At the end of our discussions, the two governments issued a statement setting out a framework for continuing work, which would help increase momentum behind the implementation of the Agreement, and we urged all concerned to respond positively.

'Our statement welcomed the IRA's announcement that it intended to enter into further discussions with the International Commission on Decommissioning and expressed our view that discussions should start promptly and should lead to agreement on the ways in which arms will be put completely and verifiably beyond use. We also said that we looked forward to receiving early and positive reports from the Commission.

'The IRA's announcement that it has since met with the Commission is, therefore, to be welcomed. However, as I have said before, it is important not only that these discussions take place but that they lead to meaningful progress. A positive report from the Commission would make an important contribution to building confidence and to enabling us to make progress across the range of issues.

'There can be little doubt that continuing progress on the scaling back of British military installations, particularly in some high-profile and sensitive locations, will also help us to unlock difficulties elsewhere. In our joint statement, the British government restated its commitment of May 2000 to continue progressively to take all the necessary steps to secure as early a return as possible to normal security arrangements, consistent with the level of threat, on which it will consult the Irish government.'

When it comes to dealing with Northern Ireland, successive taoisigh have normally taken the credit for the bulk of the work, and in general this is only right. However, the work of the various foreign ministers should not be forgotten in this regard and Brian Cowen was certainly playing a central role in the process. Policing was still causing problems, however: 'On the policing question, a lot of the discussions on the outstanding issues are linked in that nothing is agreed until everything is agreed. A very intensive attempt was made since the new year to try to get a comprehensive agreement on all these issues. It is true that there are still outstanding matters as far as Sinn Féin is concerned that would require some legislative change. It is true to say that it is unrealistic that would happen before the forthcoming British election expected to be held in May.'

Brian Cowen was careful not to assume anything when it came to Northern Ireland and he approached negotiations and discussions on it openly without falling into the trap of pre-judging the outcomes: 'There are certain commitments and understandings on various issues, including flags, emblems and other matters which are, as the deputy would be aware, of crucial importance in terms of whether people recognise there is a new beginning in relation to policing. There are outstanding issues in relation to cases which are well known, on which the SDLP has a particular view and which have yet to be addressed adequately as far as it is concerned. There is a number of issues.

'As regards the Sinn Féin issues, the question of the accountability mechanisms, how they interact, the powers of the chief constable and the powers of the police board, there are still some discussions in the areas for improvement. Similarly, as the deputy will know, the issue of district police partnerships is important from its point of view. Basically, we are continuing discussion to try to see if we can sign off in a way which will bring about acceptance by everybody that the policing issue has been dealt with.'

On 19 June Cowen reported on another intensive round of discussions following elections in the UK and the need to drive the process forward. Cowen was mindful of the need to create momentum in the process: 'As the House will be aware, the governments and parties are currently engaged in an intensive round of discussions to find an agreed basis on which outstanding elements of the Agreement are to be implemented.

'Last Wednesday I met Secretary of State John Reid in Dublin and on Thursday the taoiseach met Prime Minister Blair at the European Council in Gothenburg. Yesterday the taoiseach, the prime minister, the secretary of state, the minister of state, Deputy O'Donnell, and I met the main pro-agreement parties in London and we will follow up on these discussions in the days ahead.

'The election results highlight the urgent need for us to make progress now. Regardless of the imposition of deadlines or ultimatums, the arrangements under the Agreement cannot thrive unless we can put our difficulties behind us.

'The issues we need to address are well known – policing, demilit-arisation, the operation of the institutions and decommissioning. We were able to make some progress before we broke for the elections and we are now seeking to take that work forward.'

Negotiations on Northern Ireland were often difficult because of the background against which they were set. Both the British and Irish governments struggled to keep all the parties at the table despite huge misgivings on both sides. The dogged persistence of both governments was what often kept the process alive. In October 2001 Brian Cowen updated the Dáil on the latest developments and it appeared that while progress was being made with regard to policing, it was the institutions and decommissioning that now seemed to have taken a backward step: 'Following our intensive discussions with the parties at Weston Park in July, the two governments put a package of proposals to the parties at the beginning of August which we believe can deliver the full and early implementation of outstanding aspects of the Agreement. We have since been working to secure further progress.

'On policing, we have reached a situation where appointments, in-cluding representatives of both communities, have now been made to the new policing board and a chair and vice-chair have been appointed. I am disappointed that all parties did not feel able to make nominations at this point. As I have said before, and as I firmly believe, all that is now available can, if implemented, comprehensively deliver the spirit and the substance of Patten. I commend the parties that have made nominations and I hope that when they see how matters evolve, others will also decide to come on board.

'On the institutions and on decommissioning, however, the situ-ation remains less clear. Deputies will be aware that having failed to have a motion to exclude Sinn Féin passed by the Assembly and having withdrawn its ministers from the executive, the Ulster Unionist

Party [UUP] has said its members will now resign from the executive. This would be a most serious development. It is crucial that all parties ensure the institutions are allowed to operate fully, on a stable and inclusive basis.

'On decommissioning, and while the agreement reached between the IRA and the Independent Commission on Decommissioning in August on a method for putting arms beyond use was a hugely important development, the decision to take it off the table was disappointing. The government, however, took considerable encouragement from the subsequent IRA statement in which it undertook to intensify its engagement with the Commission. The reality remains that, as the governments said at Weston Park, putting arms beyond use is an indispensable part of implementing the Good Friday Agreement, and this matter must be resolved in a manner acceptable to and verified by the Independent Commission ...

'It is vital that confidence and momentum be restored and that all parties, collectively and individually, do all in their power to overcome the present impasse and to demonstrate to all sides that politics can be made to work, including in the critical demilitarisation area. The government will remain in close contact with the parties and the British government to see what more can be done to advance the situation.'

If Albert Reynolds and Bertie Ahern were believers in the process and seldom doubted that they would get results in the end, Cowen was more of a pragmatic negotiator. In response to questioning from Austin Currie, we do not find any blind faith on Cowen's part that this will all work out, or a rhetoric about his belief in the future. Cowen approached the problem from a point of view where he would do everything he could to bring about agreement, but he was never blind to the realities and equally was never sceptical of the chances for success: 'It is open for people to be sceptical and to remain convinced as regards this step in terms of actual decommissioning and the need for it to occur. People can have their doubts if they wish based on their experiences or their understanding of the situation. It is true that in the implementation of this indispensable part of the Agreement, we are talking about historic shifts being made by people who in the past have perhaps indicated that there was no prospect, certainly prior to negotiating the Good Friday Agreement. However, efforts are being made to ensure the Agreement is implemented in all its aspects, including on this issue.

'We have seen at times – too often perhaps – an attempt to relegate this Agreement to a single item agenda, which it is not. By the same token, it is not possible to suggest that the Agreement does not include this item. Given the deputy's own experience, it would, therefore, be better for us to wait and see if those who have influence in these matters can bring the necessary trust and confidence that is absent back into the process and that there would be reciprocation on the other side regarding its commitment to work to the full the institutions as envisaged and as agreed in the Good Friday Agreement. The reduction of the security threat that would represent would accelerate further normalisation measures, particularly in the areas of demilitarisation.'

If persistence was the key to resolution in Northern Ireland then it certainly looked to have finally paid off by 24 October 2001. We find Brian Cowen outlining the position in the Dáil. He was commenting on what was the single most important piece of good news in the peace process since the Good Friday Agreement itself. The IRA had just completed its first act of decommissioning: 'I have the honour to make this opening statement on what has been another very good day for the peace process. That the House has scheduled this debate at such short notice reflects the exceptional interest and support all parties have demonstrated in the progress of that process ... Without that constant support over many years of successive governments, it would not have been possible to achieve the progress that has been made. On behalf of the taoiseach and my other colleagues in government, I express our deep appreciation for that consensus support which sustained us on the bad days and encouraged us on the good. The events of yesterday were enormously significant and 23 October 2001 will rank among the seminal moments of the peace process over the past decade. ... Yesterday the IICD [Independent International Commission on Decommissioning] confirmed it had witnessed an event it regarded as significant during which the IRA had put a quantity of arms completely beyond use, including arms, ammunition and explosives. As the government statement indicated, this represents unprecedented progress in the resolution of the arms issue. To fully appreciate the shift involved, we need to bear in mind that the IRA did not consider itself to be party to the Good Friday Agreement. In the immediate aftermath of those negotiations it issued a statement to the effect that there would not be decommissioning. That statement received pithy expression in the murals which appeared in the republican areas stating "not a bullet, not an ounce". Therefore, we should not underestimate the enormity of the move made by the IRA yesterday ...'

Cowen himself had an understanding of just what this meant to the nationalist community. He laid out his view on what happened to make this a possibility: 'The required context was finally brought to fruition with the publication on 1 August, following the talks at Weston Park, of the two governments' proposals on addressing the outstanding issues from the Good Friday Agreement: putting arms beyond use; normalising security arrangements on the ground in Northern Ireland; establishing a policing service that attracts and sustains cross-community support; and ensuring the stability and inclusive operation of the agreement's political institutions. Yesterday's developments provided the catalyst that allowed us to fully deliver on all of those outstanding dimensions of the agreement.

'As I have indicated, the events of yesterday would not have been possible without militant republicanism acquiring the vision and generosity to stretch itself for the public good, without the creation of a political context that enabled that shift, and without the various political leaders on these islands who took risks repeatedly. Neither would it have been possible without the professionalism, integrity and endurance of General John de Chastelain and his colleagues on the IICD.'

Cowen was eager to get on with the job; now that decommissioning was finally happening we get a sense that he believed we had truly reached 'endgame': 'The 23 October was the day on which we collectively drew a line under the difficulties in implementing the Good Friday Agreement and resolved to get on with finishing the job. There is now no substantive reason we should not continue delivering all the commitments contained in the Agreement ...

'For too long we have lived back to back on this small island, cut off from one another. It is time for us to start working side by side on the basis of respect for the diversity of our traditions and for the constitutional architecture set down in the Good Friday Agreement in the common interest of all our people. That is a challenge for everyone on this island which we must now take on and meet.'

But such high hopes were to be dashed just twelve months later when a series of sectarian murders and attacks caused tensions to rise and eventually resulted in the British government suspending the institutions once again. It was a frustrating development and, despite all the talk of redoubling efforts, concerns had entered everyone's mind as fatigue set in. But Cowen held the line and showed the grim determination and patience that was the hallmark of both governments: 'I am disappointed to have to address the House under these circumstances. Yesterday's announcement and the developments which gave rise to it have highlighted the fact that we are, once again, entering a period of difficulties in the ongoing implementation of the Good Friday Agreement. However, these difficulties are not insurmountable and the Agreement has not been suspended. It is still the only agenda, and I have every hope the Northern Ireland institutions will be restored in the near future.

'As the taoiseach and Prime Minister Blair said yesterday, the two governments believe it will be possible for the institutions to be restored "in a way that will last without further disruption once trust within the parties has been established". The breakdown in trust between those involved will not be a simple issue to resolve. There are many layers of trust which need to be woven together on all sides and at all levels, from community relations at the interfaces to power sharing at the highest level …

'Suspension is a serious development and not an outcome that any supporter of the agreement would have wished for. However, in the absence of sufficient trust between the parties let us focus our energies on the extremely challenging business in hand. It is not in anyone's interest to allow a political vacuum to develop. Having brought the process to such an advanced state of progress, we cannot now renege on our responsibilities and let matters descend inexorably into stalemate …'

He goes on to lay down the strategy for the future: 'One of the ways in which the two governments will continue to co-operate bilaterally is provided for under the Agreement under strand 3 of which the British-Irish intergovernmental conference was created. It allowed for the creation of the Conference and its standing secretariat. The Conference provides a platform for co-operation between both governments on all matters of mutual interest. However, it particularly recognises the Irish government's special interest in Northern Ireland and the extent to which issues of mutual concern arise in that regard. The Conference is tasked with meeting on non-devolved Northern Ireland matters, including *inter alia*, the areas of rights, justice and policing. Meetings of the Conference are to be co-chaired by the secretary of state for Northern Ireland and the minister for foreign affairs, and it is our intention to meet in this format in the very near future.

'However, I emphasise that, contrary to some unhelpful speculation, the British-Irish intergovernmental conference is not, by any means, a method for the creation of joint authority by stealth or a way in which power-sharing might be taken off the agenda in favour of an intergovernmental track. The conference provides a basis for the ongoing co-operation that will facilitate the two governments in the management of the process until the restoration of the institutions. While co-operating through the conference, our ultimate aim is directed towards the full operation of the institutions, including the restoration of the Assembly and the Executive.'

Any accusation that Cowen was not capable of being diplomatic and patient while also being tough and single-minded was fast disappearing: 'As we work to bring a speedy end to the period of suspension, we need to make continuing progress on other aspects of the agreement where full implementation has yet to be achieved. In this category, for example, I cite the bill of rights for Northern Ireland, which has yet to be brought to fruition. In addition, in the area of security normalisation, there may be scope for further progress on the removal of intrusive installations without any negative impact on the capacity of the security forces to counter the operations of those who are determined to undermine the Agreement.'

Working with the British secretary of state for Northern Ireland, Cowen was at the core of efforts to get all parties back to the table for dialogue in an attempt to find a solution. On 13 November he outlined his efforts to the House: 'As deputies will be aware, the government regrets the suspension of the devolved institutions in Northern Ireland on 14 October last and the decision of the IRA to suspend contact with the Independent International Commission on Decommissioning on 30 October. I reiterate, however, that the Agreement itself has not been suspended. It remains the template for progress and both governments remain wholeheartedly committed to its full implementation. They also share a determination, as expressed in the joint statement of the taoiseach and Prime Minister Blair, to protect the many achievements of the agreement and restore the devolved institutions in Northern Ireland as soon as possible …

'In recent weeks, I have undertaken a round of intensive bilateral meetings with the pro-agreement parties in Northern Ireland and the British government. Together with the minister for justice, equality and law reform, I participated in the meeting of the British-Irish intergovernmental conference held at Hillsborough on 22 October. In addition, I met the new secretary of state, Mr Paul Murphy, in Dublin on 6 November.

'This afternoon the secretary of state and I issued invitations to the parties to participate in round-table talks in Belfast on 21 November. These talks will represent an important opportunity for all the parties to constructively and comprehensively address the range of outstanding issues on which progress is required, thereby renewing confidence in the political process.'

After what seemed like an endless stream of talks, particularly involving the secretary of state and minister for foreign affairs as opposed to the taoiseach and prime minister, in March 2003 progress finally seemed to be happening: 'The talks over recent months have taken place in various formats, including bilateral, trilateral and collective formations. These discussions also made it clear that the current difficulties in the process could not be reduced to a single-item agenda and could best be addressed in a comprehensive framework that advanced and resolved all outstanding issues of the Agreement.

'As deputies will be aware, the past few weeks have been particularly intensive and have culminated in the talks earlier this week and this morning in Hillsborough. A substantial amount of progress was made over the course of two long days and I pay tribute to all of the parties who constructively engaged in those discussions. We managed to bridge or substantially close the gaps in a number of key areas, including policing, criminal justice and the human rights and equality areas. While all of the parties did not sign up to every aspect, there is nevertheless a shared understanding among them of the broad parameters of the steps necessary to achieve the required acts of completion on all sides. In Hillsborough, the consistent approach by the two governments was to provide clarity and certainty and to set down the obligations and commitments necessary to restore full confidence and trust ...

'On account of the need to accord some more time and space to the parties to facilitate their consultations, the Assembly elections will be delayed by a few weeks and will now take place on 29 May. I believe that this modest postponement is both appropriate and reasonable. Our aim is that when the people go to the polls on that date, they will see before them an agreement that is in full working order, a demonstrable end to the instability of the past few years and a clear prospect of sustainable political institutions that will deliver a better and more prosperous future for all.'

On 15 April, in a statement to the Dáil, Cowen gave some flavour of the slow steady progress that was being made and the kind of pressures involved as all sides stood agonisingly close to a deal but still just short of the line: 'In dialogue with the pro-Agreement parties, the two governments have undertaken a huge amount of work auditing the progress that has been made over the past five years and bench-marking it against the objectives and undertakings of the Agreement. This work was undertaken in various formats: bilateral, trilateral and round-table meetings – implementation group meetings as they were known where all the parties who have an interest in this matter in terms of the full implementation of this agreement – were held over several months to develop a broad consensus of the kind of steps that were required to constitute an overall acts of completion package.

'From these discussions, two things were clear. First, that the question of the transition to exclusively democratic means was a key issue of confidence that had to be resolved if the institutions were to be sustainable. Second, that it could only be addressed in the enabling context of the full implementation of all aspects of the Agreement ...

'Arising out of the progress made, the governments have now developed a comprehensive package of proposals which, we believe, could provide a solid basis for the necessary acts of completion. However, for this package to have the desired political impact, it must be clear that the consequential acts of completion will have the required confidence-building impact. That is why the taoiseach and the prime minister laid such stress last Thursday on obtaining the required clarity and certainty.

'Assuming that sufficient responses are forthcoming, it must be equally clear that the Ulster Unionist leadership will positively embrace the package as a reasonable and sustainable basis for participation in inclusive government. The stop-start phase of the operation of the agreement must be seen to be over. As the taoiseach and the prime minister said on Saturday, fulfilling the promise and potential of the Good Friday Agreement is a collective responsibility.

'Last Thursday was the fifth anniversary of the Agreement. I know this House shared the disappointment of many that it did not prove possible for the taoiseach and the prime minister to return to Northern Ireland on that day to publish their proposals. However, there would have been little purpose in doing so if publication did not achieve the quality of response that would have the potential to break the current impasse. The two governments, therefore, judged it necessary to defer publication until there was sufficient clarification about the nature of those responses.

'Some encouraging progress has been made since then. The government has been keeping in close touch with the parties. All the pro-Agreement parties are to be commended for the responsible way they have dealt with the situation in recent days.

'As the House will be aware, the two governments sought clarification on a number of issues arising from the text of an IRA statement which we received on Sunday night … If we can make the judgment that sufficient clarification of positions has been obtained, we will publish our full proposals.'

But by 7 May frustrations were clear, as a deal, however close, just could not be reached. Assembly elections were cancelled. Many accusations were levelled and there was much recrimination. Independent TD Finian McGrath suggested that Cowen had not done enough for nationalists; however, Cowen was clear that he stood as a 'constitutional nationalist' and showed no fear of any kind of criticism on the issue: 'The underlying aim of all the work undertaken by the two governments and the parties in Northern Ireland since last October has been to address the deficit in confidence which had arisen about the commitment on all sides to the full and inclusive operation of all aspects of the Agreement. We undertook this work in the full awareness that it would be difficult and might not be resolved quickly. Our intensive engagement continued through the months that followed and, after much painstaking effort and slow grind, a full and complete audit of all areas of the Good Friday Agreement which remained to be fully implemented was developed.

'This blueprint, which was published last week as the Joint Declaration by the British and Irish governments, was part of an overall package which we described as acts of completion. This requires a renewed and clear commitment to a definitive end to all paramilitary activity. It also requires an unequivocal commitment to the full and inclusive operation of all of the institutions of the Agreement.

'The last weeks have seen detailed discussions and contacts among the governments and the parties, and we eventually arrived at a situation which came close to securing a resolution of the problems that have bedevilled progress on repeated occasions. That was not part of a pretence or charade. It was part of an attempt to resolve the matter to everyone's satisfaction, but, to the regret and disappointment of all sides, despite great progress and advances which went far beyond what might have been imagined possible by the naysayers and cynics, it was not possible to achieve a final agreement at this point …

'The clarifications provided throughout the process by the Sinn Féin leadership have been helpful and positive. I welcome as a positive development the indication in yesterday's IRA statement that the answers provided by the Sinn Féin leadership accurately represented their position.

'There remains an ambiguity about whether the full range of activities described in paragraph 13 of the Joint Declaration has been dealt with. Unless this aspect of the issue is addressed to the satisfaction of everyone, the prospect of inclusive partnership government being restored is unlikely to be translated into reality.

'It was in this context that the decision was taken by the British government not to proceed with the Assembly elections which had been scheduled for 29 May. As the taoiseach made clear in his statements, the government disagreed with the British government on the postponement of these elections. That opinion was made clear to the British government throughout our contacts, including at two meetings by me with Secretary of State Paul Murphy in Belfast on that Monday, 28 April. I was not involved in a pretence or charade when I represented the government's views on that matter either. They were sincere, straightforward, consistent views of the government that were put to the British government on that occasion.'

Mr F. McGrath: 'Ask the Northern minority what they think.'

Mr Cowen: 'The deputy was not there. I am telling the House what happened. I will not have my good faith or my honesty questioned by anybody in or outside this House. The government does not deserve that and will not take it.'

Mr F. McGrath: 'The minister should remember his job and represent the citizens.'

Mr Cowen: 'I tell the deputy that I have not been involved in any charade or pretence since I took this job, nor have my predecessors nor the people with whom I work in government, nor the taoiseach. The taoiseach is working on behalf of the people, with others, trying to move might and main to achieve a solution to this problem. When I make the effort and recognise the contribution of others I expect the contribution of the government to be given the same generosity of spirit. I am prepared to give that recognition to anybody who sincerely tries to resolve this problem.'

Efforts were unrelenting, however, and nothing was spared in trying to find a solution. The following October intense talks once again came agonisingly close, but still failed. A tired but optimistic Cowen suggested the experience could be banked: 'I wish to put the events of yesterday in some perspective. In this way, we can bank the significant progress we have made and identify the remaining obstacles to the full and complete implementation of the Good Friday Agreement.

'The Agreement has proven to be a resilient accord. It should be noted that, with the sole exception of one party, no one has called it into question as the defining social contract governing relations within Northern Ireland, between north and south and between Ireland and Britain. There is not even disagreement about the obligations it imposes on everyone.

'The obstacle we encountered yesterday is not the first of its kind and may not be the last, but it is important to recognise what gives the Agreement its resilience. Its strength derives not from the modesty of the demands it makes on parties to it but from the ambitious challenges it presents to them. Its ambitions may have contributed to the difficulties of its implementation. The challenges in creating a new and peaceful Ireland are not shirked but faced head on. However, I believe that is why the Agreement will stay the course, the foundations it lays will be enduring and that it will be seen as one of the defining achievements in Anglo-Irish relations.

'At its core, the Agreement demands that everyone plays by the same rules, that the only acceptable methods of pursuing one's political objectives are through peace and democracy, that every tradition be respected and that all be treated equally. It seeks no less than the ending of the use of physical force to achieve political objectives and the forging of a new and historic relationship between the traditions on this island.

'I welcome, therefore, the statement made yesterday by the leader of Sinn Féin, Gerry Adams. His statement, endorsed by the IRA, made a number of key points. He recognised that political parties must be held accountable. He stated that he was committed to ending physical force republicanism and that: "We are opposed to any use or threat of force for any political purpose." He underlined that the republican strategy, including that of the IRA, was creating a purely peaceful alternative to achieving republican objectives. In a most significant contribution, he stated that the Agreement, democratically endorsed by the people of both states on this island, provides the context for the full and final closure of the conflict. The leader of the UUP, David Trimble, was, therefore, right to recognise and welcome these comments.

'However, both governments have been acutely aware that, if we are to establish the necessary confidence, especially on the part of the unionist community, words must be accompanied by actions. A key part of the approach of both governments was, therefore, to secure another major act of decommissioning on the part of the IRA so that the unionist community would understand in word and deed the significance of what was unfolding yesterday. Under the aegis of the IICD, a major act of decommissioning was sanctioned by the IRA and was carried out yesterday. That this was a significant event was clear from the statement issued by the IICD. The quantity of arms was greater than the quantity put beyond use by the second act of decommissioning. This second act was, as reported by the IICD, varied and substantial. In terms of the third act of decommissioning yesterday, General de Chastelain and Mr Sens reported to both governments that the arms decommissioned included light, medium and heavy ordnance and associated munitions. In other words, it spanned the range of operational equipment in the possession of the IRA. They went further and stated that what was decommissioned included automatic weapons, ammunition, explosives and explosive material.'

In time of course the elections were held and the institutions restored. But the Northern Ireland peace process was a long and tortuous process. At some of its toughest moments Brian Cowen was there; he did of course have to play a supporting role to Bertie Ahern who was taoiseach, and he did not seek plaudits for his efforts. But it was an example of his own determination, perseverance and diplomatic skills and he does indeed deserve some credit for the part he played. In that at least, Ireland owes him, like all the other participants, a debt of gratitude.

But Brian Cowen's horizons would spread far beyond Northern Ireland. After one of the most remarkable feats of Irish diplomacy, Ireland was selected to sit for a term on the UN Security Council. The year was 2001. Now there were many years that Ireland could have served previously and perhaps not all that much would have happened. But maybe it was fate, or perhaps Brian Cowen may wonder why the gods conspire against him at every opportunity, but it certainly made for interesting times. The date of 9/11/2001 would change the world forever. From the world trade centre to Afghanistan, Iraq and Shannon, Ireland was to be right in the thick of things. Eamon de Valera, the founder of Fianna Fáil, had always felt there was a danger in such activities and maintained that small nations should not get involved in the affairs of larger ones. But in the globalised world it was no longer an option, Ireland whether it liked it or not would always be seen to be on some side.

But before the term on the Security Council there were ongoing concerns about Iraq. In 2000 there was little chance of another invasion; however, heavy sanctions had been imposed on Iraq for not complying with UN resolutions. While in later times much talk would centre around the fact that after an invasion no weapons of mass destruction were found, it remains an even worse crime that the Iraqi regime of Saddam Hussein refused to allow inspectors into Iraq or to comply with resolutions, thereby inflicting enormous hardship on his own people, when in fact he had nothing to hide and was simply playing a callous PR game that caused the deaths of thousands of Iraqi citizens. The sanctions were known to be having such a devastating effect that on 15 June 2000, the issue was addressed by Cowen, the new minister for foreign affairs: 'The suffering of the people of Iraq, especially children, and the problems in implementing the United Nations humanitarian programmes in Iraq are of deep concern to the government.

'The taoiseach and I raised our concerns about the effects of the sanctions on the people of Iraq with the US secretary of state, Mrs Madeleine Albright, in Washington in March, and urged the United States, as a permanent member of the UN Security Council, to seek to reduce the delays on needed medicines and spare parts for infrastructure. Mrs Albright expressed sympathy with these concerns and at the same time pointed out the lack of co-operation by the Iraqi authorities with the positive humanitarian provisions in Resolution 1284, which was adopted by the Security Council on 17 December last, but flatly rejected by Iraq. Our concerns have also been presented in discussions at official level with British counterparts.

'We consistently advocate further reductions in the number of refusals and delays by the sanctions committee in clearing supplies contracted under the Oil for Food programme, and continue to raise within the United Nations and the EU the urgent need to improve the conditions of the general population in Iraq ...

'We support the UN Security Council, therefore, in demanding full compliance by the government of Iraq with the terms of its resolutions, which require the verification of the elimination of Iraqi weapons of mass destruction.'

The Irish diplomatic corps has a proud record in defending human rights and raising humanitarian issues. But even at this early stage Ireland's approach to such matters was evident. They would stick firmly to the stance of the UN and whomever was believed to be legally correct. Brian Cowen saw no merit in altering this approach. For a small country taking a radical stance could have serious repercussions; it was also true that Ireland was not privy to the information or sources of the larger members and therefore the only sensible approach was to stick rigidly within the structures while always promoting peaceful resolution and humanitarian issues. Iraq was not willing to let the UN investigate its weapons capability, however, and the major powers were reluctant to ease the sanctions.

That was the kind of environment into which Ireland would step as it approached its membership of the Security Council. On 18 October 2000 Brian Cowen outlined the significance of Ireland's selection and the value we could bring: 'All members of the House will agree that Ireland's election to non-permanent membership of the United Nations Security Council for the 2001–2002 term is a major achievement and a recognition of the esteem in which Ireland is held internationally. The international community has bestowed a tremendous honour on Ireland and we deeply appreciate it. I thank all of the states who voted for us and gave us every support and encouragement during the campaign. I also appreciate everyone in Ireland who supported our campaign.

'Membership of the council will place Ireland at the centre of decision-making by the body with primary responsibility for the maintenance of international peace and security ... We are also conscious of the trust placed in us by the membership of the United Nations as demonstrated by our election on the first round against stiff opposition. We will seek to remain responsive to the concerns of the wider membership during our time on the council.

'Peacekeeping is at the heart of Ireland's contribution to the United Nations. For more than forty years we have participated continuously in United Nations peacekeeping operations, and Irish personnel have served under UN command in the Middle East, Africa, the Americas, Asia and Europe. This experience will enable us to speak with authority when peacekeeping issues come before the council. The principles of reconciliation, mutual respect and partnership which have informed our approach to the peace process in Northern Ireland will guide our consideration of issues before the council. African issues are a significant part of the current Security Council agenda. Ireland, through her long-standing support for political and economic development in Africa, will bring an informed view to the council.'

On the same day, Michael D. Higgins tabled another question on the sanctions against Iraq, clearly believing that perhaps Security Council membership meant that Ireland could have an impact on the issue. Cowen maintains his position on the issue: 'The suffering of the people of Iraq, especially children, and the problems in implementing the United Nations humanitarian programmes in Iraq, continue to be of deep concern to the government. We have consistently raised within the United Nations and the EU the urgent need to improve the conditions of the general population in Iraq. The Security Council clearly needs to take full account of the grave humanitarian situation of the Iraqi people in its further consideration of the sanctions issue.

Our policy has been to advocate further reductions in the number of refusals and delays by the sanctions committee in clearing supplies contracted under the Oil for Food programme.'

Some months later, on 22 March 2001, the situation in Iraq had become so grave that an adjournment debate was tabled. From this we get the most comprehensive analysis of Brian Cowen's views on Iraq pre-9/11 and also a summary of the feelings and fear that existed at the time: 'The situation in Iraq, especially the enormous hardships faced by its people, is of major concern to the government. I welcome the exchange of views on Iraq which took place in the Seanad on 8 March and I am pleased to be able to take up the issue again in this House. A number of deputies tabled questions on Iraq for reply today which were not taken due to the decision to hold this debate. I intend to address the substance of those questions in this statement.

'There are two separate but closely related issues which lie at the heart of the debate on Iraq. There is the urgent issue of the humanitarian crisis there and the terrible suffering of its people, as witnessed at first hand by members of the Oireachtas Joint Committee on Foreign Affairs during their visit last December. There is also the question of the approach the international community has taken over the past decade to address the proven threat to international peace and security posed by the Iraqi regime following its aggression against its neighbours, especially Kuwait. This approach is set out in the decisions of the UN Security Council which detail the commitments required of Iraq and also established the sanctions regime as a response to Iraq's failure to meet those commitments.

'As a member of the UN Security Council, Ireland's approach to the situation in Iraq is informed by both these issues. We want to see an end as soon as possible to the suffering of the Iraqi people and we wish to see the government of Iraq co-operating fully with the United

Nations ... However, until such inspections take place, the jury must remain out on the question of whether Iraq maintains or seeks the capacity to build and use weapons of mass destruction ...

'The issue of the legality in international law of the no-fly zones and the recent military action in Iraq by the United States and Britain in support of these zones needs to take due account of this reality. There is, unfortunately, no agreed view in the Security Council on the issue. The United States and Britain argue that the establishment of the no-fly zone arrangement is legally justified on the basis of the provisions of a series of UN Security Council Resolutions 678, 686, 687 and 688. Other members of the Security Council contest this interpretation. On the basis of the legal advice available to my department and given that none of the Security Council resolutions concerned unambiguously authorises the no-fly zone arrangement, it appears that no definitive legal interpretation is possible ...

'The economic and development needs of the Iraqi people do not have to be put on hold pending full compliance by Iraq with the Security Council resolutions. We want to see a system in place which would allow these needs to be fully met within the constraints required to ensure Iraq does not further develop weapons of mass destruction or threaten its neighbours. We recognise, however, that, as long as sanctions remain in place, there is no alternative to the Oil for Food programme in providing for the humanitarian needs of the Iraqi people ...

'From the outcome of my meetings there is an emerging view, including on the part of the new US administration, in favour of examining possible new approaches to the continuation and implementation of sanctions. I am hopeful that this will include the approach favoured by Ireland. I anxiously await the outcome of the policy reviews in Washington and elsewhere. I have instructed Ireland's Security Council delegation to play an active and constructive role in bringing this issue forward in New York and to work in the Security Council and the sanctions committee to ensure progress is made in taking the necessary additional measures to eliminate the humanitarian cost of the sanctions.'

Of course any reforms in the sanctions would have been a major boost for supporters of the humanitarian cause and in particular for Ireland, as it could certainly claim to have helped contribute to this through its voice on the Security Council. Cowen and his officials believed in a definite tactic. This effectively meant that he did not believe in calling for items unless there was a reasonable chance of success: Cowen and, it is safe to say, the department of foreign affairs believed that it was more effective to work behind the scenes until a consensus could gradually be built. Ireland has become a very strong player in this regard through its experience of the EU, where Ireland generally is able to assemble broad support for a position by the fact that it rarely finds itself off-side with particular countries. It is a pragmatic approach which Brian Cowen could readily identify with, but many opponents disagreed from the strict position of principle and demanded more outspoken action.

In an overall sense, though, there was much ongoing work on the Security Council. A lot of this work the department of foreign affairs would have anticipated. On 15 June 2001, Cowen seemed particularly proud of the smooth operating of his department and the effect Ireland's new position was having: 'I am informed on a weekly basis of the work being done. By its nature, it is painstaking, diplomatic work and takes place in the background. It is a matter of making sure our representatives are making our views known, and that they are doing so in accordance with the many foreign policy approaches that have been followed by successive governments.

'I refute suggestions that Ireland is wasting its time on the UN Security Council. We are making an important contribution. We are acquiring levels of expertise that we would not have acquired were we not full-time members of the council. We are working assiduously with our colleagues and are seen to be constructive in every respect. They respect the fact that we make our case objectively. It has not ever been suggested that we are playing to anyone else's agenda. We are playing to the agenda that we were elected to adhere to – peacekeeping and promoting humanitarianism, as in Afghanistan. Where African problems are concerned, we have a strong standing among fellow members of the general assembly. They feel we keep them informed and assist in what are very difficult circumstances, not just political circumstances, but those relative to poverty, AIDS and other serious developmental problems. Our contributions were consistent and detailed.'

But if Ireland's year at the Security Council was going smoothly, matters would soon change. The 11 September terrorist attacks shocked the world and changed people's attitudes to world security forever. On 18 September Brian Cowen gave his reaction to the attacks: 'It is safe to say that no event in recent history has had such an instant and widespread impact on people worldwide as the dreadful tragedy which struck the United States on Tuesday last. A series of calculated and deadly assaults on the proudest symbols of the most powerful nation on earth was broadcast on live television across the globe. Thousands of innocent civilians going about their daily business were slain in a merciless assault driven by vicious hatred ... These attacks will go down in history as the most appalling act of international terrorism ever committed ...

'Immediately the news of the attacks broke last Tuesday, my department established a special emergency centre to assist Irish people seeking information about friends or relatives who might have been involved. A telephone helpline service was set up and a team of over fifty volunteers worked around the clock answering calls and building up a database of over 2,500 Irish people who were possibly affected.

'In the United States our embassy in Washington and our consulates in New York and Boston also established a special emergency service to assist Irish citizens caught up in the terrible events. They, too, have been working around the clock for the last week dealing with queries from relatives in Ireland and the United States.

'Working closely together, the emergency centre in Dublin and our missions in the United States have helped to narrow down the list of potential Irish victims of the attacks. The overwhelming majority of the 2,500 persons reported to the emergency centre in the first days after the attacks have proved to be safe and well. There have been some heartening stories of people who were thought lost turning up alive. Tragically, there has been a small number of cases where the news has not been good and where it looks as if our worst fears will be realised.

'I pay my own tribute to the many officials of my department at home and abroad, the staff from other departments, the health board representatives and the locally employed staff at our missions in the United States who participated in the emergency services during this crisis. Their commitment and dedication have demonstrated the very highest standard of the Irish public service. The public can be proud that it has people of such ability and generosity working in its service.'

Once again Cowen leaves no one in any doubt as to his respect for the staff in the department. There was little doubt in anyone's mind that this attack would not go unpunished. Across the world governments braced themselves for what many saw as the legitimate right of the US to respond. America did not seek unilateral action at this point, however, and instead was generally concerned that world opinion should be on-side. Therefore the UN Security Council would prove pivotal. Ireland as a member would have some say, but it was also clear that Ireland would have to abide by the rules of the council and support any UN resolution wholeheartedly: 'We will support action in conformity with the UN Charter or in pursuit of Security Council resolutions against those who planned, supported and carried out these acts. The US government has made clear that it is embarking on a long and difficult campaign which will be pursued on a wide front, using diplomatic, military, economic and police assets. The United States has recognised the need to build the support of a broad international coalition to act in a targeted manner and offer clear justification for any action, should it prove necessary.

'We will work with the international community at the United Nations and with our partners in the European Union in a concerted effort to stamp out international terrorism wherever it is found ...'

There certainly was an onerous responsibility on Ireland, a small country thrust into the heart of a major international conflict. Brian Cowen showed no fear of the challenge and no doubts about his own principles, whether others disagreed or not. Cowen most definitely was shocked by the events and his heart most certainly sided with western democracy and America on the issue, but he also strove to encourage an avoidance of armed conflict, and a concern for humanitarian issues within a framework where he also believed that action was necessary. On 3 October he spoke further on the attacks when he reported on his visit to New York: 'Last Thursday evening I stood on ground zero in lower Manhattan, New York. Up until three weeks ago, this had been the site of one of the great landmark buildings of the world; a centre of global enterprise with an international work force, a commercial United Nations. What I saw, through the hazy smoke of the fires which still burned below ground, was an enormous mound of twisted steel and broken rubble under which were buried the bodies of more than 5,000 human beings.

'It was for me a traumatic, emotional and deeply saddening experience.

Nothing could have prepared me for the sheer immensity of the destruction to property, but even far more shocking was that on this spot, on that terrible Tuesday morning, thousands of innocent people going about their daily business had been slaughtered in the name of an evil hatred.

'More than three weeks on from the attacks, the scale of the devastation is still only being guessed at. Estimates of the number of people killed in the World Trade Center are still imprecise. The figures are being revised downwards but, sadly, not by much …

'We are already beginning to feel the tangible economic impact of what took place on 11 September. Business confidence has been shaken, international travel has fallen off and in Ireland, the tourism industry has experienced the direct impact of the atrocity. Given the commitment of the United States and its friends not to give in to terrorism or to give comfort to those who would seek to terrorise them, I hope they will show the necessary resilience in bringing things back to normality as quickly as possible.

'However, there is a less obvious but more fundamental implication for what has happened. The international community has experienced a direct assault on the universal freedoms and values on which our increasingly global society is based. The terrorists who struck on 11 September exploited many of these freedoms – freedom to travel, freedom to seek employment, freedom of financial movements – to build up their networks for their attack on the free world.'

It would be unfair to portray Cowen as an eager supporter of war. While many people believed that US foreign policy was to blame for the attacks, it was an argument that was fundamentally unsound for any politician in Cowen's position. Thousands of innocent people had been killed – it was not an attack on politicians or the military, but an attack on civilians and a society. Like a large proportion of people it seems that Cowen believed that terrorism had no place in the modern world, and that America was entitled to defend itself, but he also believed that while weeding out terrorists was important, addressing conflicts that breed terrorism and humanitarian issues were central going forward: 'Yesterday, when I addressed the general assembly of the United Nations, I argued that the fight against international terrorism needs to take place on three levels. First, as member states of the United Nations, we must do all we can, in accordance with Resolution 1368, to bring to justice the perpetrators, organisers and sponsors of the attacks of 11 September and to prevent further such atrocities. Second, we must combine in a longer-term initiative to defeat the monster of international terrorism by choking its funds, cutting its supply of munitions and technical support and denying it the bases from which it plans and prepares its actions. Third, we must redouble our efforts to put an end to the many conflicts and injustices, which, while they can never, ever justify the horrors of 11 September, are exploited by the terrorists to garner support for their warped philosophies ...

'My meeting with the Secretary of State Colin Powell on 26 September primarily focused on actions to counter terrorism in the aftermath of the attacks on the US, particularly through our joint efforts in the Security Council. We also reviewed the situation in the Middle East and in Iraq. I took the opportunity to update the secretary of state on the Northern Ireland peace process and to express appreciation for the strong and continuing support of the United States. We both agreed there is an urgent responsibility on all sides to live up to their obligations and to ensure the full implementation of the Good Friday Agreement ...

'Secretary of state, Mr Powell, told me the US government was enormously gratified by the support of bodies such as the Security Council, UN general assembly, the EU, the organisation of Islamic states and a wide range of countries. Support for the campaign against terrorism would be varied but the US welcomed support according to each country's ability to offer it. The secretary of state was very clear in his perspective that the international campaign against terrorism would be multi-faceted. He was equally clear that any military response should not be seen as a clash between Islam and the west. The vast majority of Muslims world wide were just as horrified as anyone else at these atrocities.

'The secretary of state, Mr Powell, cited President Bush's determination to engage in a long-term campaign against terrorist networks located in many countries. He regretted the Taliban regime's failure to respond to the demand of the Security Council to hand over Osama bin Laden. He assured me that if military force is used, it will be careful and calibrated. I emphasised to the secretary the imperative, as Ireland saw it, that any military response be measured, proportional and avoid as far as possible the risk of inflicting civilian casualties …

'The UN Security Council has been demanding the closure of terrorist camps in areas controlled by the Taliban for the past three years. The Security Council has also been demanding that Osama bin Laden be handed over for trial. The council has been rebuffed in both these demands, despite the imposition of stringent sanctions by the international community against the Taliban regime. Those who committed these acts of terror and those who supported them can no longer be allowed to defy the will of the international community.

'The government is extremely concerned about the plight of the Afghan people. There are already millions of Afghans living as refugees in neighbouring countries or as displaced persons in their own country. They are the victims of drought, civil war and, in some cases, the Taliban regime which controls 90 per cent of the national territory. The current crisis is causing further population movements out of the major cities and towards the frontier.

'Over several years Ireland has consistently sought to highlight the humanitarian situation of the Afghan people at the UN. In part due to our efforts, the Security Council has decided to keep the situation under constant review. Let there be no doubt as to those primarily responsible for the hardship imposed on the Afghan people. The UN secretary general has firmly laid this responsibility on the Taliban regime.

'A £2.8 million grant aid package for Afghanistan was announced on Monday by the minister of state, Deputy O'Donnell. This package, the largest ever for a single emergency, will continue to support the work of Irish NGOs and the main international agencies in responding to the crisis in Afghanistan. Along with the £1.2 million already provided since January, this brings the total assistance provided by Ireland Aid for Afghanistan in 2001 to £4 million.'

On 16 October Cowen had the opportunity to outline the role Ireland was playing in the fight against terrorism: 'The multifaceted campaign against international terrorism is being pursued across a wide front. Ireland is particularly involved through the United Nations and the European Union. We are also active at a national level. The UN Security Council reacted swiftly to the events of 11 September by unanimously adopting Resolution 1368 which condemned the attacks and called on all states to work together to bring the perpetrators to justice and prevent and suppress international terrorism.

'Following on from Resolution 1368, the Security Council unanimously adopted Resolution 1373 on 28 September. The resolution imposes obligations on member states under Chapter VII of the UN Charter and particularly emphasises measures which must be taken to combat the financing of terrorism. Member states are obliged to report on actions taken to those ends within 90 days. As president of the Security Council, Ireland moved quickly to ensure the establishment of the committee provided for in Resolution 1373 to monitor the implementation of the resolution. Both UN resolutions reaffirm the inherent right to individual and collective self-defence under Article 51 of the UN Charter ...

'On 21 September EU heads of state or government reaffirmed their commitment to take concerted action against terrorism and make it a priority objective of the European Union. They agreed to pursue a wide range of judicial co-operation measures. These include Commission proposals for council framework decisions on combating terrorism and the introduction of a European arrest warrant ... The government has moved quickly to set up internal arrangements to co-ordinate the follow through on our national responsibilities under the UN and EU initiatives, including seeking to provide additional time in the House to deal with the necessary legislative measures.

'On the security front, the United States and its allies began military action on 7 October against the military assets of the Taliban regime in Afghanistan and the terrorist bases of Osama bin Laden's Al Qaeda network in that country. I regret that such action proved necessary. However, the Taliban has refused for two years to comply with demands of the UN Security Council that it hand over Mr bin Laden and his associates and close terrorist camps operating in areas under its control. It continued its defiance even after the terrorist attacks of 11 September, which Mr bin Laden has since openly applauded.'

Ireland was in an unenviable position, but it was clearly trying to establish some form of lead on the issue. While it could not influence the war, a serious attempt was being made to address humanitarian issues. He expanded further on Ireland's position within an EU context later: 'The general affairs council, which met in Luxembourg on 8 October 2001, declared its full solidarity with the United States and wholehearted support for the action being taken in self-defence and in conformity with the UN Charter and UN Resolution 1368. The council stressed that the carefully targeted action launched on 7 October was not an attack on Islam nor the people of Afghanistan, whom the European Union is determined to support and sustain ...

'I very much hope the United States will not find it necessary to undertake military action beyond the targeted action under way in the areas of Afghanistan controlled by the Taliban regime. The government is firmly of the view that military action should be undertaken only as a last resort after all other means of persuasion have been exhausted. Regrettably, military action against the Taliban was the consequence of its sustained refusal to respond to the demands of the international community, even in the face of UN sanctions, to hand over Osama bin Laden and close the terrorist camps operating from within the territory under its control ... I am not aware of any evidence which demonstrates that other states were knowingly involved in harbouring those who planned or executed the 11 September atrocities. It has not been mentioned in my contacts with the US or its military allies, that other possible targets for military action are under active consideration.'

The fear was obviously abroad that the US intended expanding the war against other countries. This put Ireland in a very problematical situation. While it is difficult to believe that the US did not have other possible targets under consideration one has to accept that the sources of information available to Ireland were limited. The extensive experience of dealing with countries in peace times was of limited value when caught up in a conflict involving a super-power. As a neutral country Ireland held little military influence and was not privy to information from that point of view. The 9/11 attacks were felt deeply in Ireland due to its connections with the US. There were many Irish-American casualties in the attack on the twin towers and in light of the support America had given to Ireland with regard to resolving the Northern Ireland conflict, the cut was even deeper. The combined military powers of an international coalition led by the US and Britain, did not take long to achieve initial military success in Afghanistan. But military success is only half the battle: securing and creating a sustainable system would be a much greater challenge. Brian Cowen was very much aware of this as he made clear on 15 November: 'At the request of the House, I would like to make a statement on Afghanistan. We meet today as events in Afghanistan are unfolding by the hour. The international community is presented with an enormous challenge. With military success comes great political and humanitarian responsibility. There have been too many atrocities in Afghanistan over the past twenty years, too much bloodshed and too little respect for human life and dignity. The international community needs to act decisively to ensure a new beginning for the people of Afghanistan which will ensure political stability, economic prosperity and the vindication of the fundamental rights and freedoms of the long-suffering people of Afghanistan ...

'Against the background of the rapidly evolving situation, the Security Council last night adopted a new resolution on Afghanistan. This affirms the central role of the UN and expresses support for the process initiated by Ambassador Brahimi, the UN special representative to Afghanistan. It also supports the efforts to form a transitional administration leading to the formation of a broad-based, multi-ethnic and fully representative government. It stresses the need for emergency humanitarian assistance and for long-term reconstruction and rehabilitation. All parties are called on to refrain from acts of reprisal, and to adhere to international law and human rights obligations.

'On Tuesday, I represented Ireland at the ministerial meeting on Afghanistan. I emphasised our hope that the military campaign against the Al Qaeda terrorist network and the Taliban regime that shelters it will achieve its objectives in as short a timeframe as possible and that every effort will continue to be made to spare civilian casualties ...

'On the political transition, the solution must come from the Afghans themselves. Discussions between the various Afghan groups will be brought together quickly under the UN to decide upon the means to establish a transitional administration … I emphasised that a visible and effective humanitarian strategy was necessary, as was prompt donor disbursements. I paid particular tribute to the bravery of the UN and NGOs and condemned the Taliban's harassment of humanitarian officers. Human rights abuses, especially of women and girls, have to be reversed and the new administration held to international standards. I committed us to continue to provide all possible support, nationally at the UN and with our EU partners …

'I have emphasised that there must be a visible and effective strategy for meeting the humanitarian needs of the Afghan people over the coming period. This will provide a basis upon which the move from providing international emergency relief to supporting national reconstruction can take place. This will be an ongoing process, not a once-off project. As the initial step in this process, we cannot afford to waver in our delivery of humanitarian assistance. It will be an important building-block in creating the conditions for a new national dispensation for the people of Afghanistan …

'An estimated 52,000 tonnes of food aid are needed each month to meet the requirements of the vulnerable people of Afghanistan. We commend the untiring efforts of the UN agencies, the International Red Crescent and Irish and international NGOs to overcome the obstacles they face to the delivery of this aid in the field. We must give them the strong support they need, at all levels, in this major humanitarian endeavour at the outset of this century. Above all, we must consolidate each step taken so that what we do now will have a lasting, positive effect and be of lasting benefit to the Afghan people.'

While the war might have been an issue on which few people would heed Ireland's input, the after-effects and humanitarian efforts were another matter – one in which the Irish view was respected. Simon Coveney of Fine Gael complimented Cowen for his handling of events: 'I congratulate the minister who has done a very good job for Ireland during our chairmanship of the Security Council, who continues to do a good job and is extremely informed on what is happening. As a result we are focusing on the areas where we have credibility. We are constantly highlighting humanitarian issues in the UN and we are being listened to. It is perhaps fair to say the humanitarian effort would have been far less significant had it not been for the role Ireland played on the Security Council during October. The consultation process which took place in the Security Council would not have been as comprehensive if Ireland had not shown leadership in how it chaired the Security Council. I congratulate Richard Ryan in particular, and the minister. We must also play a role in finding political answers to what is a very complex situation in Afghanistan which is constantly developing and changing.'

When it came to navigating a course through the rough seas that it found itself in during the immediate aftermath of 9/11, Ireland could indeed be proud. It had stood up with considerable effect for the humanitarian cause and backed it up with considerable funds for a small country. Once again Brian Cowen had proved himself capable of high-level diplomacy and statesmanship in international relations. But the situation was evolving fast, leaving little time for many countries to prepare. The US would soon divide the world opinion it had so carefully brought onside. In October 2002 pressure was mounting over Iraq. The US was losing patience with Saddam Hussein's refusal to allow weapons inspectors to investigate; they were convinced he was hiding something and the argument was that affording him time may only be allowing him expand that capability. Britain supported that position. Other countries such as France and Germany were not so sure and were in favour of giving more time. One thing was clear, however, the UN was getting to 'endgame' one way or another on this issue. Brian Cowen outlined developments to the Dáil: 'The gathering crisis over Iraq has been several years in the making. Its root cause is the aggressiveness of the current regime. This aggressiveness has manifested itself in repression at home and attacks against its neighbours abroad.

'Iraq has fought two major wars against other countries in the region. It invaded Iran in September 1980 and it invaded and occupied Kuwait almost exactly ten years later in August 1990. The number of casualties inflicted in these two wars was enormous, amounting to a million dead and wounded. The Iranians fought Iraq to a stand-still after eight years of heavy fighting, one of the longest and bloodiest wars of the second half of the twentieth century. Kuwait was powerless to resist the invaders who were ejected only after the international community put together a massive coalition force which fought a brief but intense war against Iraq.

'Iraqi aggression against its neighbours on both these occasions, as on others, was in complete violation of international law and the Charter of the United Nations. It was destructive of every effort since the Second World War, and earlier, to build up an agreed code of behaviour among states under international law. Under this code it is forbidden to use force and to seize territory. Furthermore, the proliferation of weapons of mass destruction is forbidden, as is the massacre of civilians and the abuse of human rights. Iraq has broken virtually every rule of international law and of universally accepted standards of behaviour.'

Ireland was clearly taking its line from the UN. It was a position close to American thinking, but not at variance with world opinion at the time: 'In May of this year, the very important Resolution 1409 was adopted. This resolution completely changes the basis on which the sanctions are operated so as to target the regime and minimise civilian suffering to the greatest extent possible. Ireland has been particularly concerned about the impact of sanctions on innocent civilians. As a member of the Security Council we have been actively involved in all the efforts so far to refine the system of sanctions so as to take into account the humanitarian dimension. We worked hard to obtain a comprehensive and timely solution which would impact as little as possible on the lives of Iraq's civilian population. We were particularly engaged in developing Resolution 1409. We recognise that, as long as sanctions remain in place, however, there is no alternative to the Oil for Food programme in providing for the humanitarian needs of the Iraqi people. The government will continue to strongly support practical measures aimed at ensuring the delivery of assistance to children and other vulnerable sectors of the population in Iraq. First and foremost, Iraq must live up to its responsibilities to fully utilise the funds available and co-operate in ensuring that the necessary assistance reaches those most in need.'

The difficulty was clear. The UN were not happy with Iraq, but there was some resistance to what people saw as a ramping up of pressure by the US. While Cowen was unequivocal in stating that a war should be avoided, he was also stating a case against Iraq. A case which suggests that he saw no reason to trust Saddam Hussein or to believe that he should be left alone: 'The Iraqi regime has an appalling record of violating human rights. This is not only terribly wrong in itself, it is a further threat to the international order. Respect for human rights is a core dimension in preventing conflict. It is part of the very foundation on which peace and security are built. One of the major objectives being pursued within the international community is to reinforce respect for human rights as part of the rule of law and as a norm of civilised behaviour. Iraq's record is an affront to conscience.'

As his speech progresses we can see that Cowen certainly hoped this would be resolved and he also sounded grateful that it was the UN that would take a decision, as this would make a policy decision on the situation much easier: 'This is most certainly not a time for hasty or ill-considered decisions. Events must not be allowed to escape our direction.

We see it as imperative that the Security Council should remain in control of developments. For this reason, we welcomed the fact that President Bush brought the issue to the United Nations and that we are now working within the framework of the Security Council.

'We have also welcomed the efforts of UN Secretary General Kofi Annan to convince Iraq to accept weapons inspections. As the secretary general told the general assembly, this would be the indispensable first step towards assuring the world that all Iraq's weapons of mass destruction have been eliminated, and they must be eliminated and seen to be eliminated beyond doubt or question.

'We also welcomed Iraq's agreement to the return of inspectors, without conditions. This is a highly important development, but it has to be put to the test. Unfortunately, past experience with Iraq shows that nothing can be taken for granted. Instead, words must be backed with deeds. The time for Iraq to act is now. It must co-operate fully with the inspectors, end its evasions and allow full, free and unfettered access to all sites, as well as to personnel and documentation. There can be no exception for presidential sites. Nothing less than immediate and complete access can carry the necessary credibility …

'We continue to believe that diplomatic means offer the best hope of resolving the crisis. In this respect, we welcome President Bush's assurance on Monday that he is willing to make another effort to find a solution through diplomacy. We will strongly encourage that. In our view, every possible effort should be made to avoid the use of military force. We would be seriously concerned that the use of force could destabilise an already volatile region, particularly in view of the conflict between Israel and Palestine. We consider, therefore, that multilateral co-operation in the application of sanctions remains the best approach in tackling the problem of Iraq …

'Ireland wants very much to see a peaceful solution to this crisis. We are working together with the other members of the Security Council to accomplish this objective. This goal is the overwhelming wish of the international community. The purpose of the UN resolutions is to bring about disarmament, nothing more. Ireland is working within the framework of these resolutions. We do not see that there is a UN mandate for any further end, such as regime change. We believe that UN action against Iraq should be halted as soon as Iraq comes into compliance with the resolutions of the Security Council and implements the council's decisions in full.'

This could suggest a belief on Cowen's part that Iraq would eventually comply once enough pressure was applied. Regime change was not on the agenda. If the weapons issue could be sorted then the crisis should be averted. That was Ireland's position. This does raise a question, however. If Ireland did not believe in regime change, then was all the discussion surrounding Saddam's crimes against his own people just idle chat? It seems to suggest that if the weapons inspectors had been successful in their task, Ireland would have been happy for Saddam to do as he pleased within Iraq's borders. Clearly what was exercising Irish minds at the time was finding a solution to the current impasse.

By 13 November the situation was becoming increasingly worrying. In the Dáil Cowen outlined the purpose of Resolution 1441: 'On Friday, 8 November, the United Nations Security Council unanimously adopted Resolution 1441 on the situation in Iraq. The government supported this resolution which we believe offers the most likely means of achieving the three goals we set ourselves, namely, to obtain Iraq's voluntary compliance with its disarmament obligations, to avoid a military conflict and to preserve the primary responsibility of the Security Council for the maintenance of international peace and security. The resolution represents the outcome of nearly two months of painstaking negotiations in the council in which Ireland played an active part.

'The resolution provides for a clear sequential process whereby the inspectors will report back to the council on Iraq's compliance with its obligations under Security Council resolutions. It has decided that Iraq is already in material breach of its obligations, but notwithstanding this, has afforded Iraq a final opportunity to comply with its disarmament obligations. Accordingly, further acts of non-compliance by Iraq will be reported immediately to the Security Council by the arms inspectors. Such reports will then be assessed by the Security Council which will consider the position to decide on any further steps to be taken to bring about full compliance. This was a principal objective of Ireland and other like-minded countries. The agreed text of this resolution contrasts sharply with the original draft which provided that any failure by Iraq to comply would automatically authorise member states to use force.'

The process was now clear for Ireland. The weapons inspectors would report and any further action would then be considered by the council. This gave a degree of control, but the fact that it differed from the draft shows the pressures being applied by other countries. Ireland was clearly happy with the outcome, however.

But as questioning proceeded problems arose with the resolution: 'It will still require a report from the inspectors to be brought to the Security Council in making an assessment of a material breach suggested by anyone on the council or any member state. The idea that – as I saw in some commentaries – in the immediate aftermath of the resolution any one state or a number of states could decide on a material breach having occurred thereby providing a trigger mechanism for military force, is not a correct reading of the resolution … Regarding the question of pre-emptive strikes and their legal validity, the deputy will be aware there is not an international legal consensus on this. Some states suggest that a mandate for military action exists based on existing resolutions, which have already been passed. If there were any move towards military force, everyone would be best advised to come back to the Security Council for consideration and for the approval of the Security Council in order that it would have the widest possible support and legitimacy in international law. Clearly a resolution such as this, which has brought about an outcome of a fifteen to nil vote, involves compromises by everybody in order to reach agreement. Our interpretation of the resolution is that we should come back to the Security Council for such authorisation.'

Effectively a dispute now existed on whether strikes could take place in advance of Security Council authorisation. The hope that everyone would come back to the Security Council is clear, but for Ireland the lack of an international legal consensus posed a problem; there would be no black-and-white issue on this if it occured.

As Ireland's eventful term on the Security Council neared its end Cowen took the opportunity to outline some of the achievements: 'We have sought to ensure that the human rights of individuals and the humanitarian needs of populations remain central to discussions at the council and have stressed at all times the need to address the root causes of conflict and to respect the principles of international law.

'This approach has … enabled Ireland to make a very positive and substantive contribution to the work of the council and has brought a fresh perspective and an objective approach to its work which has been welcomed and respected by other member states, in and beyond the council, and by the NGO community.

'Two substantial resolutions on Iraq have been adopted by the council in 2002 with active Irish engagement. Resolution 1441, adopted on 8 November, gives Iraq a final opportunity to comply with its disarmament obligations through compliance with a reinforced inspections regime. In so doing, it offers the best possible means of avoiding a recourse to military action and preserving the primary responsibility of the Security Council for the maintenance of international peace and security. Resolution 1409, adopted on 14 May, made changes to the system of economic sanctions against Iraq designed to reduce their impact on the civilian population. This was a major goal for Ireland on the council.

'During Ireland's time on the council, twelve resolutions have been passed on the situation in the Middle East, most recently Resolution 1435, which condemned terrorist attacks and expressed support for the work of the quartet. The council is working towards a two-state solution and is actively supporting the work of the quartet on a road map leading to a Palestinian state within three years.

'Ireland has played its part fully in the serious work in the international fight against terrorism that has been undertaken following the terrorist attacks of 11 September 2001. We have been active in discussions on the reconstruction of Afghanistan where we were successful in seeking to focus the council's attention on the humanitarian situation of the Afghan people.

'African issues have been a consistent priority for the Security Council during Ireland's period of membership. Significant progress has been made towards resolving the conflicts in the DRC, Angola, Sierra Leone and Ethiopia-Eritrea, and the challenge now is to consolidate that progress and avoid a slide back into war. Important issues which need to be tackled include the dire humanitarian situation in many conflict countries, grave abuses of human rights, the use of child soldiers, and ongoing insecurity, often as a result of the uncontrolled flow of small arms and light weapons across borders.

'The illegal trade in conflict commodities, such as diamonds, is an issue which has been tackled by the Security Council in Sierra Leone, Angola and the DRC, and must be kept under constant review to ensure that conflicts do not become self-financing and self-perpetuating. As chair of the Angola sanctions committee, Ireland made a significant contribution to bringing to an end the military action by UNITA which has caused so much suffering to the people of Angola.

'Ireland took a particularly firm position on the situation in

Western Sahara, where we have refused to support proposals which could have called into question the right of the Saharwi people to self-determination.

'Membership of the council has also afforded us the opportunity to work to improve UN sanctions regimes. While there is no doubt that specifically targeted sanctions play an important role where flagrant breaches of international law occur or there is a threat to international peace, there is a strong balancing objective to ensure that the civilian population of the country against whose government the sanctions are imposed does not suffer.

'In the remaining weeks of our term, we will continue to promote Ireland's values and objectives in the pursuit of international peace and security and human rights for all.'

While Ireland has had a generally positive influence, the potential for conflict in Iraq was still overshadowing all questions in relation to Ireland's involvement on the Security Council and under questioning from Gay Mitchell, Cowen discussed his knowledge of Iraq's capability for weapons of mass destruction: 'In relation to the evidence we have regarding Iraq's access to weapons of mass destruction, a number of assessments, including evidence gathered by previous work carried out by arms inspectors in Iraq, are available. The assessments we have seen, such as that in the British independent report of the Institute of Strategic Studies, paint a disturbing picture. Although they do not present conclusive proof that the threat is immediate and pressing, they reinforce concerns we already have. It will not be until the arms inspectors return to Iraq that a reliably accurate and independent assessment can be carried out.'

Continuing diplomatic efforts meant that by December there was a glimmer of hope that war might be avoided. Iraq sent a declaration to the Security Council which was to be examined. As some elements of the report by the weapons inspectors contained material about building weapons of mass destruction it was decided only to pass these elements to those countries that already had such a capability. Otherwise, there was a fear, presumably, that Brian Cowen could have turned Ireland into a world power overnight: 'The complete text of the Iraqi declaration contains sensitive information, including material on how to set about building weapons of mass destruction, and it was decided by the full Security Council that the text would only be seen by the weapons inspections teams and the permanent five, who possess the necessary expertise. This was intended to guard against leaks. Ireland is a very strong proponent of non-proliferation and we accept that the circulation of such information must be kept to a minimum. The material to be withheld by the inspectors will relate only to how such a capability could be built, it will not deal with whether Iraq has done so.

'Ireland and the other members of the Security Council expect to see a revised version, with any sensitive material removed, in the next twenty-four to forty-eight hours. We expect to be given a clear picture by the inspectors of the extent and nature of any material which has had to be withheld. Equally we expect that all the members of the Security Council will be given complete access to any information required for them to fulfil their responsibility to determine whether Iraq has complied fully with its obligations under Resolution 1441. We have seen no evidence that undue political pressure will be put on the inspection teams. In any event, we have complete confidence in their integrity and professionalism.'

The difficulty of course for Ireland was that it was being asked to judge the capability of Iraq in a field in which Ireland had no expertise. Assessing the information from an Irish perspective was an impossible task, as the country did not have the requisite technical knowledge: 'We will be primarily relying on UNMOVIC [United Nations Monitoring, Verification and Inspection Commission] and the IAEA [International Atomic Energy Agency] who will report to the Security Council. They are the people charged with an assessment of the situation. We will defer to them on this matter for an independent assessment …

'I will emphasise two points: the IAEA and UNMOVIC have been given the full report and they will report to us. We will refer to them when it comes to assessing the independence of the evaluation. The extent and nature of the information will be made available to us by those who have the capacity and expertise to examine it and provide an independent report.'

This was a return to normal practice for Cowen. On many occasions throughout his career he believed that politicians could intervene, facilitate, and make decisions, but all of this had to be informed by people with relevant expertise in an area. Cowen never believed a politician should get in over their head in day-to-day business; it was their job to decide based on evidence presented. For instance, he could appoint Bernie Cahill to Aer Lingus and agree its future framework, but he would give him free reign to introduce reforms he felt necessary without undue interference. Cowen wanted to be informed of any problems in regard to blood products or food safety so he could take a decision, but there is little evidence of him questioning their advice. Therefore this situation with the Security Council would make perfect sense to Cowen, who would have to have taken advice from someone else in any event. This is a wise course of action and has brought Brian Cowen much success in his career. However, as we will see in later chapters, a similar approach in banking would let him down as the advisers got it wrong.

But for the time being Ireland was ready to play its part in assessing the situation in Iraq based upon the advice available. By January 2003 the situation was becoming critical and Cowen was coming in for some criticism for not doing enough to stop what many saw as an inevitable march to war on the part of the US. We join the debate on the issue as

John Gormley attacks Cowen, who shows his thick skin when it comes to attacks: 'Despite all this evidence, the minister for foreign affairs, on a radio programme, dismissed the idea that this could be about oil. I listened very carefully to what he had to say and he very quickly jumped to the defence of the USA. The minister has become very good at jumping. The only question now is, how high? That is determined by George W. Bush. There is something rather pathetic about this self-styled rottweiler, now a performing poodle.'

An ceann comhairle: 'The deputy should withdraw that remark about the minister.'

Mr Cowen: 'It is based on the deputy's usual gratuitous insults.'

An ceann comhairle: 'I ask the deputy to withdraw that remark. He must not refer to a minister in that way.'

Mr Gormley: 'It is normal parliamentary language.'

An ceann comhairle: 'It is not normal parliamentary language to refer to a Member of the House in that way.'

Mr Gormley: 'It is perfectly acceptable. I referred to him as a performing poodle. Tony Blair has been referred –'

An ceann comhairle: 'I ask the deputy to withdraw that remark.'

Mr Gormley: 'That is absurd.'

An ceann comhairle: 'The deputy may feel it is absurd, but I will not allow personal remarks of that nature to be hurled at any Member of this House at any time.'

Mr Gormley: 'The minister understands perfectly well that it is not a personal remark, it is a political remark. Tony Blair has been referred to as a poodle and I am saying that the minister is behaving in a similar fashion.'

An ceann comhairle: 'The deputy should be more tempered in his language.'

Mr Cowen: 'There are much more objectionable things he could say.'

There was an increasing unease about the war in Iraq. The use of facilities in Shannon airport by the US military was becoming a contentious issue: 'I will speak shortly about the current situation with regard to Iraq. Before doing so, however, I wish to deal with comment and speculation on current arrangements to allow for access to Shannon Airport by transiting US military aircraft and personnel.

'Let me begin with the historical and geographical background. Ireland's geographical position places it on the main flight path between North America and Europe. Shannon was initially developed as a refuelling point for transatlantic flights, when limited aircraft range obliged most aircraft to touch down in Ireland when travelling to and from the US.

'For many decades, military aircraft of various nationalities have been refuelling at Shannon or, as aircraft ranges have extended, overflying Ireland on their way to or from North America. There has also been a practice, again going back decades, for civilian aircraft carrying US and Canadian military personnel and civilian staff to refuel at Shannon on their way to and from various bases around the world. Shannon has continued to be popular because of its efficient and friendly service. This business has brought jobs and income to the wider Shannon area and generated revenue for Aer Rianta …

'Ireland's recent prosperity and the staunching of the haemorrhage of emigration is partly due to US investment. Our newfound peace is in no small measure due to the support received from successive US administrations, Congress and private interests. These facts do not make us a military ally of the US, nor do they require us to uncritically support US foreign policy. They are factors which no responsible Irish government, conscious of the interests of the Irish people, would wish to ignore.'

Cowen had set out his stall early. The use of Shannon was not likely to be revoked. It was a measure that had been used for some time by the

US and any change to this would appear like Ireland was aggressively objecting to the US policy. Cowen saw no need to offend the US. He believed that Ireland's interests lay with America and that the Iraqi people would be best served by an end to sanctions brought about by Iraqi compliance. It was to be a controversial policy that seemed for many to put our own interests above principles. But in any event it was a no-win situation for Cowen. Ireland's geographic location meant that withdrawing overflight permission would seriously hamper flights from the US to Britain and Europe and would be seen as an impediment to the war effort. Indeed some would probably claim it as an act of assistance to Iraq. Equally, Cowen was aware that while France and Germany would object to the US policy they would still afford them the right to landing facilities. Nonetheless, it did call into question Ireland's neutrality in this new global world.

Later in the debate Cowen outlined how the overflight system developed and was working: 'The specific arrangements that apply to the United States regarding overflights were agreed in the exchange of letters in January 1959 between the then minister for external affairs, Mr Frank Aiken, and the US ambassador. Under this agreement, the US is granted blanket permission for overflights of unarmed military aircraft. The terms of the permission specify that the aircraft be unarmed, carry only cargo and passengers and comply with the navigational requirements and flight patterns specified by the government of Ireland under the International Civil Aviation Organisation. The blanket permission includes a stipulation that the permission will be subject to reconsideration in the event of a serious deterioration in the international situation ... Another point needs to be made in relation to the overflight and landing of foreign military aircraft. On 21 September 2001, the taoiseach, with my full agreement, announced that the state would facilitate military aircraft operating in pursuit of UN Security Council Resolution 1368 by waiving the normal conditions that apply to the granting of permission for landings and overflights by such aircraft – that they be unarmed, carry no ammunition or explosives, not be involved in intelligence-gathering and not engaged in military exercises. Deputies will recall that in this resolution, the Security Council classified the terrorist attacks of 11 September 2001 as a threat to international peace and security and called on all states to work together urgently to bring to justice the perpetrators and organisers. In the event, no request seeking to avail of this waiver has been received. The US has continued to follow standard procedures, notwithstanding the availability of this exemption from normal requirements …

'It came to the notice of my department during the course of a review of arrangements, initiated at my direction, that US troops travelling by civilian aircraft were often accompanied by their personal weapons, a matter to which I referred in a recent statement. The US authorities made clear that such weapons are not loaded, are normally stowed in the hold and are not taken off aircraft while on the ground in Ireland and that troops are issued with ammunition only on arrival at the ultimate destination. It was pointed out to the US authorities that the airlines concerned were nevertheless obliged to seek the permission of the minister for transport to carry such weapons and ammunition and the department of transport wrote directly to the carriers concerned reminding them of this requirement. The civilian carriers involved are now routinely submitting advance information on side-arms and any other military cargo to the department of transport to facilitate compliance with the terms of the 1973 order. This accounts for the reported rise in the number of authorisations issued by the minister for transport for the shipment of so-called "munitions of war".'

As the debate progressed, Cowen outlined a number of changes he had made. John Gormley was not impressed, however, as the changes were retrospective and indicated an evolving situation rather than a clear stance from the beginning: 'Another matter on which I have acted to tighten the application of regulations relates to the wearing of military uniforms by foreign troops. Under section 317 of the Defence Act 1954 military personnel are forbidden to enter or land in the state while wearing a uniform except with written ministerial permission. Following discussions between my department and the United States embassy, ministerial permission to wear duty uniform in the "immediate vicinity of an arrival-departure airfield" was sought and granted. Any requests for exceptions to this policy are to be submitted to my department.'

Mr Gormley: 'When did that happen?'

An ceann comhairle: 'The deputy should allow the minister to continue.'

Mr Cowen: 'That happened on or around 13 January last.'

Mr Gormley: 'I knew it.'

Mr Cowen: 'The deputy should allow me to explain the matter.'

Mr Gormley: 'The minister has explained.'

Mr Cowen: 'I hope that this description ...'

Mr Gormley: 'I have heard all that I need to know.'

Mr Cowen: 'The deputy needs to know more.'

Mr Gormley: 'I knew that it was all retrospective.'

Mr Cowen: 'I hope that this description of arrangements ...'

Mr Gormley: 'The minister has been caught with his pants down.'

An ceann comhairle: 'I will take action if Deputy Gormley does not allow the minister to speak without interruption.'

Mr Cowen: 'I have listened to Deputy Gormley making some very objectionable remarks and I want to answer them. I do not have much time. I have just as much conviction and integrity as Deputy Gormley. I hope that my description of arrangements will make clear for the House the precise arrangements which apply in relation to overflights and landings. I hope it will be recognised that the government has done more than all its predecessors put together ...'

Mr O'Dea: 'Hear, hear.'

Mr Cowen: '… to ensure that the practices and arrangements built up over the years are operated in strict compliance with the precise legal requirements …

'We stand on the brink of a third Gulf war, the consequences of which, if it takes place against our wishes, could be very grave. Apart from the horrific human suffering that is likely to accompany the outbreak of war, there is a risk of destabilising an already volatile region. Support for terrorism could grow and economies may suffer.

'The Irish government does not wish to see war take place. We have raised our voice and used our influence in every forum available to us to urge the need for a peaceful solution. We are determined to discharge our international obligations, both in trying to avert conflict and in carrying out the decisions of the Security Council.

'Ireland's approach to this crisis is based on our long-standing commitment to international peace, justice, security and stability upheld by the rule of law, peaceful settlement of disputes and respect for human rights. These are the principles which have informed Irish foreign policy under successive governments ever since the foundation of the state. Ireland is a strong supporter of the system of collective international security set forth in the United Nations Charter. We regard the United Nations as the centre of this system of collective security. We attach particular importance to the role of the Security Council as having primary responsibility for the maintenance of international peace and security. In carrying out its duties under this responsibility, the council is acting on behalf of the entire membership of the United Nations.'

A clear divide had already emerged among politicians and indeed the public. Those who saw Saddam Hussein as a despot who should be dealt with in any event for the benefit of the Iraqi people, and those who believed that although he may be a despot the reasons for any attack on Iraq were wrong and the Iraqi people would suffer. It was a debate that would not go away.

Later on Cowen again returns to the issue of whether the Security Council will sanction military action or whether it will go ahead regardless. The lack of clarity here is clearly a concern to Ireland and Cowen still hoped that the matter will be returned to before any action was taken: 'The resolution does not specify that a further resolution is required to authorise the use of force. This would simply not have been acceptable to either Britain or America, both of whom hold veto power on the council, and was not attainable. These two countries have long held the view that earlier Security Council resolutions already mandate the use of force and that no further authorisation is required. There is no international legal consensus on the validity of the different interpretations. There is no definitive position of the international community on what is still a hypothetical question. Regardless of the legal arguments which have been advanced on both sides, Ireland considers that there is an overriding political need for the Security Council to determine whether its resolutions have been breached and to take a further decision on what measures should be adopted in response.'

Cowen continued to outline the difficulties in the evidence from Iraq and it is clear that he saw a serious problem developing because of the discrepancies reported by the weapons inspectors: 'All of us in this House hope that military conflict can be avoided. It has to be said, however, that there is still some considerable way to go before this danger can be averted. On 7 December the Iraqi government submitted its declaration on weapons of mass destruction to the Security Council. Two days ago, the arms inspectors made a report updating the council on the progress of inspections. The report delivered by the head of the International Atomic Energy Agency, Dr El Baradei, was fairly positive and took the view that Iraq does not have any current nuclear weapons programme. However, he did cite the need for more active Iraqi co-operation with the inspectors.

'The report delivered by Dr Blix, head of UNMOVIC, the main weapons inspection body, was far less positive and raised a number of serious questions. He pointed out that Resolution 1441 required Iraqi co-operation to be immediate, unconditional and active. He then made it clear that such co-operation had not been forth coming. Dr Blix reported in his own words that, "Iraq appears not to have come to a genuine acceptance – not even today – of the disarmament which was demanded of it and which it needs to carry out to win the confidence of the world and to live in peace." He went on to say that "Iraq has decided in principle to provide co-operation on process, notably access", but that "[a] similar decision is indispensable to provide co-operation on substance".

'He then listed a whole series of areas where the Iraqi declaration is incomplete or Iraq has failed to produce evidence to support its claims that it has destroyed weapons or that they are absent. He pointed out that it was for Iraq to produce credible evidence to this effect and not for the inspectors to prove the contrary. Among the discrepancies he listed were 6,500 chemical bombs containing 1,000 tonnes of chemical agent, holdings of VX nerve gas precursors, quantities of anthrax and 650 kilograms of bacterial growth media sufficient to produce 5,000 litres of concentrated anthrax as well as numbers of Scud missiles and further missile development.'

On 11 February 2003 the matter was back on the Dáil agenda. Iraq, while found to be in breach of Resolution 1441, was afforded another chance. Nations like France and Germany were concerned that although the weapons inspectors were being hampered and items seemed to be withheld from them, there was still nothing to show any weapons of mass destruction existed. At the same time the US was growing impatient with the extra time and chances being afforded to Iraq and remained convinced that the only reason for such truculence was that the weapons must exist. Brian Cowen updated the Dáil:

'Resolution 1441 decided that Iraq was already in material breach of its obligations under earlier resolutions. Despite this, it afforded Iraq a final opportunity to come into compliance. Iraq was required to provide an accurate, full and complete declaration of all aspects of its weapons programmes. Any false statement or omission, together with failure to co-operate, would constitute a further material breach and would be reported to the council for assessment.

'The resolution also decided that Iraq should provide the arms inspectors with unconditional access to sites and persons. It directed the heads of the arms inspection teams to report immediately any interference or failure to comply. The council was to convene immediately on receipt of such a report. The resolution then recalled that the council had repeatedly warned Iraq that it would face serious consequences as a result of its continued violations of its obligations. The resolution did not, however, provide automatic authorisation for military action; rather, did it deliberately place the threat of serious consequences in the context of the circumstances surrounding the reconvening of the council ...

'The government has spoken out and used its influence at every opportunity, in every forum and in all its meetings and contacts to urge the need for a peaceful solution. It has insisted that all means short of force must be tried, and that force may be used only as a very last resort. It has repeatedly warned of the dangers which would inevitably result from military conflict. It has called attention to the threat of large-scale loss of life, casualties and human suffering. It has pointed to the risk that conflict could destabilise a region which is already volatile. It has pointed out that extremists and terrorists would seek to exploit growing tensions between the Muslim world and Europe and the United States. It has spoken of the possible disruption of economic growth. It has laid particular emphasis on humanitarian concerns, as it always has in such circumstances. It has sought and obtained confidential briefing from the UN secretariat on the extensive plans it is making to deal with a possible humanitarian crisis. It maintains regular contact with the key UN relief agencies and is ready to take part in a humanitarian conference on Iraq to be held in Geneva on 15–16 February at the initiative of the Swiss government.

'Last week I conveyed these views to President Bush's special envoy on Northern Ireland, Ambassador Richard Haass, when he visited here. It is our strong view that the inspections should continue as long as the inspectors and the Security Council consider that they serve a useful purpose. At the same time, we recognise that the inspections cannot continue for ever. The question of increasing the number of inspectors has been raised but, as Hans Blix has pointed out, the real issue is not the number of inspectors but whether Iraq is willing to co-operate actively with them.'

Later in the debate Cowen gives us an idea of the proposals that were being offered to the Security Council: 'A draft resolution has been tabled in the Security Council by Spain, the United Kingdom and the United States. The clear thrust of this text is that Iraq has been warned that it would face serious consequences if it continues in violation of its disarmament obligations, that Iraq is in further material breach of these obligations and has consequently failed to seize the last opportunity offered by Resolution 1441 to comply with its disarmament obligations. The draft resolution does not speak of continuing arms inspections, nor does it specify what should happen next. Both that and the intention of the Security Council will become clear when the draft is introduced by the sponsors, is placed in context and is followed by a debate.

'At the same time, the council has a memorandum before it, prepared by France, Germany and Russia, which foresees the continuation of inspections for a certain period. The arms inspectors are due to deliver their next report on 7 March, which will have an important input into the debate in the Security Council on the draft resolution likely to take place next week. It is not known when or if a vote on the draft resolution, on an amended text or on some other text will take place. The government will decide its own view in the light of the inspectors' report and the considerations of the Security Council. Should the Security Council adopt a resolution, Ireland would be bound under the Charter of the UN to accept and carry out the decisions of the Security Council.'

The debate over the need for a second resolution raged and Ireland was clearly at a loss due to the lack of any international consensus. As John Gormley pushes him for answers, Cowen shows some of the frustration on this point: 'My position will be that if the Security Council is able to discharge that responsibility, we will support it. That is the requirement under the UN Charter.'

Mr Gormley: 'The minister is hiding. He is refusing to come out with his position and it is frustrating to sit on this side House and listen to him. We are asking direct questions, to which we are not getting answers.

'Will the minister give his legal opinion on the second resolution. An opinion has been given in Britain by Ms Cherie Blair's law firm which said that the UN resolution sponsored by the US and UK does not authorise the use of force against Iraq and that any military action without UN Security Council authorisation would be a clear violation of international law. Does the minister agree with that analysis and does he further agree with the opinion given today by Irish lawyers which states that the government is in breach of international law and that this is an indictment of his position?'

Mr Cowen: 'As a poor small-town lawyer myself, I am afraid I must humbly disagree with whatever Irish lawyers are talking to the deputy about our breach of international law. I would not be as eminent as the people to whom the deputy speaks.

'Regardless of the legal debate – and law is an inexact science – the government's position is that we want to see a second resolution. We regard it as politically important that happens so that we can ensure this regime understands that the resolve of the international community is such that he will have no option but to comply with these resolutions. It would also ensure that the message is sent loudly and clearly and that there is no miscalculation by the regime in relation to our resolve as an international community. As a minister, I make no apology for discharging my responsibilities by taking our position as to what we feel should be happening, as we try to resolve this matter peacefully in the context of the closing window of opportunity.'

On 5 March 2003 Cowen outlined aid given by the Irish government to Iraq for humanitarian purposes: 'Ireland Aid has contributed more than €700,000 in humanitarian funding for the people of Iraq since 2000. Funding has been targeted at relief programmes in nutrition, water and sanitation and rehabilitation of health services. These programmes have been implemented by UNICEF, the International committee of the Red Cross and Red Crescent, and Trócaire's local partner CARITAS.'

By 20 March, war was due to commence. Cowen made his views on this known, as well as on the situation with regard to Ireland providing facilities at Shannon: 'That we stand on the verge of military conflict is both a tragedy and a failure. A tragedy because any conflict, no matter who its protagonists may be, and no matter how worthy or unworthy its aims, brings suffering and death to combatants and civilians alike. A failure, because for twelve years, and as restated by Resolution 1441, the objective of the international community has been the complete disarmament of Iraq by peaceful means.

'Our failure has been a collective one, in that it is through the United Nations that the nations of the world seek to act together to maintain international peace, stability and security. The credibility and prestige of the United Nations has suffered a heavy blow through the inability of the Security Council, so impressively united in the autumn, to agree now on an appropriate way forward.

'The permanent members of the Security Council have a particular weight and authority within the United Nations. It is deeply regrettable, therefore, that they have been unable to work together to agree a path to the disarmament of Iraq without resort to force. It would be neither useful nor appropriate to speculate as to whether, if this or that had been done differently, it would have been possible for them to agree. The absence of a common approach among the permanent members left the Security Council without a clear compass by which to navigate. The international machinery of the United Nations is only effective when there is clear leadership from those member states entrusted with the heaviest responsibilities. The secretary general has played a quite outstanding role in seeking to build and encourage this consensus, but his capacity to do so is ultimately defined by the willingness of the member states to facilitate his efforts.

'It is a matter of the greatest regret to Ireland that the Iraqi crisis has now reached a point where military conflict has begun. This is exactly the outcome which we had worked to avoid during our time on the Security Council and since. The government has consistently opposed the use of force, except as a last resort after all other possible means have been tried and failed.

'There was a characterisation of our policy position over the past few months as being in some way sitting on the fence when in fact what we were trying to do was to encourage those within the Security Council to muster the necessary collective political will to progress this matter on an agreed basis as the only reputable way forward. ... In relation to what we were seeking to achieve, the idea that one backs one crowd or the other within the Security Council was never going to resolve this problem and that is precisely the issue. If one wants an effective multilateral response then one has to build for a consensus approach within the Security Council. We did it on Resolution 1441. It was not possible on this occasion precisely because there were many, not just in this parliament but in other parliaments and other democracies, who were trying to suggest that one country had the monopoly on virtue and wisdom. One does not go in there simply protecting national interests within the Security Council. One has a responsibility to the wider international community.'

The absence of a second resolution did not sit easy with the government: 'Ireland has repeatedly stated its view that if Iraq continued in its non-compliance, a second Security Council resolution should be adopted. We believe that this is what should have been done. The United States and Britain have long held the view that earlier Security Council resolutions already mandate the use of force and that no further authorisation is required. They are now acting on this belief. It is clear that there is no generally accepted view on the validity of the different interpretations and it is unlikely that agreement on this point can be reached.'

This is what put Ireland in most difficulty. Had Brian Cowen been able to attain a definitive legal view that the war was in breach of UN procedure he could have extricated Ireland from any association with it easily enough and had an excuse for withdrawing any landing and overflight facilities. However, Ireland relies heavily on taking its lead from the UN; when no clear lead could be provided and all nations disagreed, Ireland was uneasy finding its own way. Cowen now had to decide and he came down in favour of continuing to facilitate any flights and offer a reserved support for the US: 'I recall that we urged the member states of the Security Council to consider three questions: What precisely did Iraq have to do to meet its demands? How long did it have to do it? How would the Security Council discharge its responsibility if Iraq did not comply? We asked those questions last January. If they had been asked within the collegiate of the Security

Council at the same time I believe we would not be in the position we are in today. When people talk about entering into the logic of war by asking those questions, my response is that this was a final chance resolution, this was about immediate and full co-operation. Instead of allowing, as happened on all sides of the argument in my opinion, the use of the inspectors' report as a means of validation for their own particular positions, they should have been sitting down in a collegiate way answering those questions and reaching a compromise in relation to their respective positions in order that the prestige of the United Nations could have been upheld ...

'I am profoundly saddened that we have arrived at this point. Everything I said and did over recent months had a single purpose, to promote a multilateral solution and bolster the resolve of the Security Council to face up to its responsibilities. Having arrived at this point, hard choices must be made. That is the responsibility of government, a heavy responsibility we must discharge with the utmost seriousness. ... We hope that the humanitarian consequences of the conflict will be limited. Those participating in the military operation have a duty under international humanitarian law to ensure that they are minimised.'

The debate would run for some time both inside and outside Leinster House. It sparked a heated debated about Ireland's policy of neutrality in many quarters. On 9 April Cowen outlined his views on neutrality, in particular that Ireland is not ideologically neutral: 'I am satisfied that Ireland's long-standing policy of military neutrality, as followed by successive governments, is fully protected. As recently as last October, it was upheld by the amendment to the constitution approved by the electorate in the context of the referendum on the Treaty of Nice. This confirmed the central and defining characteristic of the government's policy in this area, that is, non-participation in military alliances. A commitment was made not to enter into a common defence arrangement in the EU unless the people decide otherwise in a referendum.

'Irish neutrality is a policy choice. It is not defined exclusively on the basis of international legal instruments, such as the Hague Convention of 1907; neither is it described in the constitution, nor should it be. Arguments about whether an action was compatible with a policy of neutrality as referred to in the constitution would give rise to endless legal challenges and take decisions out of the hands of the government and the Oireachtas where the constitution has placed them ...

'Successive governments have also made clear that Ireland is not ideologically neutral. Neutrality policy has also been informed by the view that military neutrality on its own is not sufficient to maintain conditions of peace and security internationally. This is especially so in the context of the fundamental challenges to global peace and security which the world currently faces. Ireland, notably through the United Nations and now also through regional organisations such as the European Union, has sought to play a proactive role in preventing and managing conflicts and keeping peace.'

Aengus Ó Snodaigh: 'I find the minister's reply interesting as it is the first time I have heard a Member of the government state he or she does not accept the Hague Convention's definition of neutrality. If, when it was pursuing the second referendum on the Nice Treaty, the government had explained to the people that it did not accept the definition set out in the Convention, but was, instead, preparing to sell off what remained of neutrality in this state, they would not have supported the Treaty. Time and again, during the Nice Treaty campaigns and beforehand, we were told the state is militarily neutral. I find odd the minister's refusal to accept that there is an internationally accepted definition of neutrality, namely, that contained in the Hague Convention. Why is the government not willing to accept this definition? What definition of neutrality does it accept?'

Mr Cowen: 'I am forced to reiterate my reply as the deputy seeks to misrepresent what I said. I stated that Irish neutrality is a policy choice and is not defined exclusively on the basis of international legal instruments such as the Hague Convention of 1907. In other words, if the deputy, in his efforts to understand our neutrality policy, restricts his understanding to the view that the Hague Convention encapsulates our policy, he is grievously wrong and all the empirical evidence on the exercise and conduct of our neutrality policy since its initiation and as pursued until now by successive governments is against him. That is the basic failure of comprehension on the part of the deputy as he seeks to redefine neutrality policy by defining it exclusively within the framework of a convention laid down in 1907. He may have heard of a number of international instruments, including the United Nations Charter, which have been passed since then.'

Irrespective of the rights or wrongs of the position, by 29 May attention was turning to what happens after the war. Michael D. Higgins asked Cowen about the government's position on control of the Iraqi oil resources and in particular the government's views on a Security Council resolution which would give control of such resources to the occupying powers, and the arrangements he favoured to follow the Oil for Food programme which was due for renewal in early June 2003. Cowen replied: 'The government believes the natural resources of Iraq should be returned to the stewardship of the people of Iraq as soon as possible, and that the Iraqi people have the right to determine their own political future. Security Council Resolution 1483, to which the deputy refers, takes this as its starting point. This resolution also recognises that until the Iraqi people are in a position to exercise these rights, the occupying powers have specific authorities, responsibilities and obligations under international law.

'The resolution does not give control of Iraq's oil revenues to the occupying powers. On the contrary, it provides that all export sales shall be made consistent with international market best practices and that this will be independently audited. It also provides that all proceeds from such sales shall be deposited into the development fund for Iraq until such time as an internationally recognised representative government is established by the people of Iraq. The development fund for Iraq will be subject to the scrutiny of an international advisory and monitoring board. Its members will include representatives of the UN secretary general and the international financial institutions, including the director general of the Arab Fund for Social and Economic Development.'

We can see that Cowen felt much more at home dealing with this issue than that of the war. But as the debate continued we can see that already the lack of any weapons of mass destruction was causing problems. Cowen tried to outline his position in relation to this: 'As regards the other wider issue to which the deputy refers, in regard to weapons of mass destruction, in its Resolution 1441 last November, the United Nations Security Council recognised the threat posed to international peace and security by Iraq's weapons of mass destruction. This view was based on the fact that since 1998 Iraq had refused to permit the return of the weapons inspectors with the consequence that they had been unable to fulfil their mandate. Subsequent to this resolution and when faced with the threat of force, Iraq accepted the return of the inspectors. However, the degree of co-operation ...'

Acting chairman: 'I must ask the minister to conclude.'

Mr Cowen: 'It is an important point. However, the degree of co-operation which Iraq extended to the inspectors was described by them as less than full. The reports of the inspectors made it clear that many questions remained unanswered about Iraq's holdings of weapons of mass destruction. Whether weapons of mass destruction are discovered in Iraq will not alter the fact that the mandate of the arms inspectors remained unfulfilled at the time of the US-led invasion.'

Like many others Cowen had been swept along on an assumption that if Iraq had nothing to hide it would have complied. It was a major criticism of many world leaders that no weapons had been found when people had been led to believe it was almost a forgone conclusion. The embarrassment felt by many countries, even if they still supported the war, meant that change would have to come to the UN to prevent countries taking action without full consent of the Security Council. Cowen reiterates the fact that, whether or not the weapons existed, the problem of Iraq's non-cooperation still existed. We get a sense that Cowen felt compelled to act in advance without knowing what the future would bring, which is the nature of politics and he finishes with an immortal line on statesmanship to Michael D. Higgins: 'The second point I want to make in reply to Deputy Higgins is that the issue of non-compliance by the Iraqi regime with successive UN resolutions meant they were not meeting their disarmament obligations, regardless of whether the weapons of mass destruction were in existence then or before.'

Mr M. Higgins: 'That is a new tune.'

Mr Cowen: 'It is not a new tune. I heard no one in this House suggest that the UN was wrong to suggest they were not getting sufficient co-operation.'

(Interruptions.)

An leas-cheann comhairle: 'We must proceed to the next question.'

Mr Cowen: 'No one contested that issue. The benefit of hindsight does not turn you into a statesman.'

Perhaps it was a suggestion that if he had his time again, Cowen would have done some things differently. In any event Ireland would be much more capable at dealing with the events outside of war, and in November Brian Cowen underlined Ireland's commitment to the humanitarian agenda in Iraq: 'At the Madrid conference Ireland pledged up to €3 million to the future humanitarian and recovery needs of Iraq. It is intended that this pledge will be mainly channelled through the UN window of the international reconstruction fund facility for Iraq, and through valued partners such as UN agencies, international organisations and NGOs. Discussions will take place over the coming months with these partner organisations to examine sectors and priorities on a needs basis. This pledge was in addition to €5 million in humanitarian assistance delivered to date in 2003.'

The war in Iraq was a defining moment in world history. America lost much of the support it had established before the Afghanistan conflict. It would hurt both George Bush and Tony Blair along with many other leaders by association. It also damaged the view of the UN. Ireland was indeed in a very difficult situation. For many people Ireland should not have co-operated with the US; for many others Ireland's stance was entirely correct. That debate will rage *ad infinitum*. Brian Cowen did emerge from the issue intact, which was remarkable. He showed particular ability in the aftermath of 9/11 and the lead-up to Afghanistan. If Cowen and indeed Ireland seemed to lose its way as the world moralised over the rights and wrongs of the war it was perhaps somewhat understandable. Hindsight does not indeed make one a statesman and while there are certainly criticisms that can be levelled at Cowen as a result of the Iraq war, it is difficult to imagine that any other ministers, regardless of their view in opposition, would have taken any different action when presented with the situation.

It was of course not the only challenge that Cowen would face in foreign affairs; if Northern Ireland and the Security Council were not enough then there was also the changing nature of Ireland's position within the EU. For many previous foreign ministers, Europe had been the means to negotiating big deals that would help deliver funds to transform the economy. But that was all set to change. Whatever people might feel about quality of life or value for money, the simple fact was that Ireland had indeed become a wealthy country. As the EU expanded to take in Eastern European states, Ireland would find itself in transition. Instead of being the receiver of help from other

EU countries, Ireland would become one of the givers. Of course there is no such thing as a free dinner and the reason all countries choose to give in the first place is because the more they invest in developing poorer economies the more potential customers there are for the businesses of wealthier nations. But could the Irish government communicate this much more complex set of advantages to the Irish people? In looking at this period through Brian Cowen's eyes we can get a flavour for the depth of negotiations, how difficult they really were and why such issues are complex. Critically while looking at the Nice Treaty negotiations we see many elements that affect the Lisbon Treaty and it is an opportune time to study this.

On 15 June 2000 the future of Europe was very much up for debate and Gay Mitchell asked Brian Cowen for his views on the desirable ultimate destination of European integration. Cowen said: 'From its inception as the European Economic Community in 1957, with six founding members, the European Union has shown a remarkable capacity to adapt to changing circumstances. Having increased throughout successive enlargements to fifteen member states and seen a significant extension in Union competencies following the Maastricht and Amsterdam Treaties, the Union over the past decade has faced the task of responding to unprecedented change in central and Eastern Europe. The Union has responded to these challenges with an imaginative strategy for enlargement, and a vigorous programme of internal reform.

'The imperative now is to complete the transformation already under way, through the series of accession negotiations now in train with twelve countries and the process of adapting the Union's institutions to meet the demands of enlargement, through the work of the intergovernmental conference … The organic character of the European Union ensures that it will continue, as it has done in the past, to adapt to changing circumstances. As a union of states and of peoples, it is required to respond to the wishes of the governments and the citizens which make up the Union, to preserve both its credibility and its democratic legitimacy. While it is not possible, therefore, or, perhaps, even desirable, to pre-empt decisions which may be taken in the future on the further development of the Union, the essential point is that it should continue to build on the solid foundations already in place.'

So there was little doubt in the mind of Brian Cowen that Europe could and would enlarge and take new members on board, but his bottom line was that the balance must be maintained and here we can see that he was aware of the threat that could be posed to Ireland in terms of influence.

Cowen was also in no doubt about what the major issues facing the EU would be: the number of commissioners and the extended use of qualified majority voting (QMV): 'Questions of the extent to which qualified majority voting is to be advanced in terms of the decision-making process at the council, the expansion of the Commission and the entitlement of each of the member states to a commissioner, which is a majority view at this stage of the negotiations as expressed by member states, and the re-weighting of votes, are issues which require the full concentration of the member states in order for us to deal successfully with this intergovernmental conference in a relatively short time of twelve months, as envisaged.'

Later that day further questions were asked about the work of the intergovernmental conference. Cowen laid out what Ireland's opening position was in the negotiations, but the size of the task was already evident in his speech: 'The intergovernmental conference began in February of this year with a meeting of foreign ministers and is due to conclude at the Nice European Council in December. The conference has held five meetings to date at ministerial level, while the preparatory group of personal representatives, on which Ireland is represented by Noel Dorr, has met on a further nine occasions.

'The agenda for the intergovernmental conference chiefly comprises those items left unresolved from the negotiation of the Amsterdam Treaty, namely the size and composition of the Commission, the re-weighting of votes in council, the possible extension of qualified majority voting and changes to the institutions necessitated by enlargement. The aim of the intergovernmental conference is to ensure that the EU and its institutions can continue to work effectively following enlargement.

'Ireland's objective for the conference is to prepare the EU for enlargement, while maintaining the carefully constructed balances and relationships between the institutions and the member states which underpin the EU. We, therefore, attach particular priority to maintaining the right of each member state to nominate a full member of the Commission. This is an important element in enhancing the democratic legitimacy of the EU in the eyes of its citizens. I am encouraged by the level of support for this principle among our partners. However, as with all other issues, the question will not be resolved finally until negotiations are concluded ...

'We are taking a constructive attitude to the possible extension of QMV, while insisting that in certain areas, such as taxation, the retention of unanimity is appropriate. Given the range of national positions, it is fair to say there are relatively few articles for which there is universal support for a move from unanimity. However, it remains likely that the final outcome will see a further increase in the already large number of articles governed by qualified majority voting.'

Cowen also made clear that while some people may be caught in an overall vision of the Union or what certain proposals may seem to mean in principle, he was far more concerned with the practice and what the working position would mean to Ireland's interests: 'I am more of a pragmatist than a visionary and I am reassured by Mr Vedrine's suggestion that there is no question of unravelling existing community-wide practices. In other words, what has been achieved on a committee basis will not be compromised by the proposed changes. Therefore, the concerns expressed by member states need to be addressed in that context.'

After a European Council meeting in Feria in Portugal many of the issues were coming into focus. On 27 June, as Cowen answered questions about the outcome of the Council meeting, the concerns of EU politicians are clear: 'One must also take account of the fact that while broadening the Union, the EU's ability to have an effective decision-making process is something to which we are all bound to apply our minds. That is not just a matter for member states but also for applicant countries. We must not end up with a paralysis in the Union's decision-making process which would militate against the continuing progress and prosperity of member states while also militating against the ability of applicant countries to integrate into the new, enlarged Union ... We must recognise that the EU is a union of peoples and states and the shared sovereignty that is part of the decision-making process must continue to be progressed in a way which will maintain a consensus in the Union and allow it to proceed in the way envisaged by the member states at European Council meetings such as in Feria.'

The problems were becoming clear. New countries would bring huge benefits to the Union in terms of its influence, and in terms of trade and the amount of consumers that could be reached. However, while the advantages for business and economics were clear, there was a very big threat to the political functioning of the Union. Getting twenty-seven states to agree unanimously was a lot tougher than twelve. Political leaders, including Cowen, feared that the European Union would become bogged down in an endless stream of negotiations and votes and watered-down decisions that were in nobody's best interests.

At this stage, however, Ireland was still hanging tough with regard to the commissioner, still believing that every state was entitled to one commissioner: 'The number of commissioners and the areas in which qualified majority voting will apply are issues to be considered, as is the reweighting of votes, the new European Parliament of a maximum of 700 MEPs in an enlarged Union and the operation of the court of auditors, the economic and social committee and so on. As we progress into an enlarged Union, these are fundamental issues for the institutions. The overall approach of our government is to ensure that the institutional balance is maintained. We believe very strongly that the Commission is a very important institution in relation to moderating the relationships between large and small states as well as developed and less developed states, but it is also the organ of initiative. The Commission is the guarantor of the treaties and ensures that the EU develops in the way envisaged by the treaties. It is the legal guardian of the legal basis of the treaties.

'Our position is that the retention of one commissioner per member state is fundamental, not on the basis that the commissioner is a representative of the member state, but that the institutional balance within the Union dictates that if one wants affiliation and acceptance of EU decisions in some competitive area, it would be far more difficult to ensure that happens in member states that do not have Commission representation than in those that have. The basis on which the Union has proceeded up to now – the entitlement of every state to a commissionership – has been one which we feel is an absolute requirement for our negotiating position.'

It was clear that negotiations would be long and drawn out, but Ireland remained committed to the idea of enlargement because of the economic benefits it could bring. On 18 October 2000, Cowen reaffirmed this position: 'The government's position on EU enlargement is clear and has not changed since the last time I answered questions on this topic in the House. Ireland is a strong supporter of the current enlargement process for strategic reasons of peace and for economic reasons. We look forward to welcoming the new member states when they have satisfactorily completed their negotiations and have demonstrated their ability to assume the obligations of membership. Enlargement will provide important economic opportunities for new and existing member states alike. Enlargement will also give us the opportunity to address outstanding problems on our continent, including such vital issues as organised crime and a better functioning relationship with Russia and the states of the former Soviet Union. In addition, an enlarged European Union can play a more important and more credible role in world affairs.'

Cowen believed in the EU project, but stressed that for him integration did not equate to centralisation or federalisation: 'Ireland has benefited enormously from EU membership. We have, at the same time, contributed constructively to the Union's development, politically and institutionally. The decade ahead will bring its own momentous happenings, not least of which will be enlargement. These developments will influence the necessary integration process leading to the further construction of the Union. Ireland views this prospect positively. We are in favour of integration. It does not mean centralisation or federalisation, rather the further development and improvement of the manner in which Europeans freely co-operate and work together while respecting diversity.'

In reply to later questions, Cowen recognised that changes were necessary in some areas of the Union and its decision-making process, but also established the firm position held by the Irish government in relation to taxation. As far as Ireland was concerned, this could not and would not be on the agenda: 'It is recognised, including by the institutions themselves, that there is a continuing need to review existing arrangements and, in particular, to ensure within the Union that issues are dealt with at the most appropriate level. In certain areas, in relation to the single market, for example, this requires that decisions be taken at community level. In others, or in relation to the implementation of decisions taken in a community framework, the responsibility will more appropriately rest at national or regional level. As the House will be aware, we have consistently argued that taxation, for example, must remain a matter for decision at national level, bearing in mind its importance in the overall management of the economy.'

Fianna Fáil in particular has always been loathe to give up national authority, as the party enjoys considerable control in Ireland. However in the EU parliament Fine Gael is actually a member of a much larger and influential grouping, the European People's Party [EPP]. Therefore for Fianna Fáil the influence of national government over issues and decision-making within the EU has always been of primary importance.

The Nice Treaty was to be one of the biggest and toughest negotiations to date and Cowen gave a full appraisal of the situation: 'All partners committed themselves to a successful conclusion to the intergovernmental conference at Nice and reviewed progress across the four main agenda items, namely, the extension of qualified majority voting; the size and composition of the Commission; the re-weighting of council votes and conditions governing the use of closer co-operation.

'Overall, across a range of issues, the council was able to note the possibility of useful progress in extending the scope of qualified majority voting. The taoiseach informed his colleagues that Ireland is prepared to endorse QMV for many of the provisions proposed, including transport, industrial policy, structural funds and certain appointments. He also noted our fundamental opposition to QMV for any aspect of taxation, a position shared by a number of other member states. We take that view because we believe any change in the present arrangements would put at risk the economic model, with its strong emphasis on the partnership approach, which we have followed in this country for many years, and which has contributed to the substantial expansion of our economy.

'The Commission was also discussed in depth, with the taoiseach reiterating our well known support for one commissioner per member state. The larger countries continue to argue for a capped Commission.

'The re-weighting of votes is proving to be one of the most difficult areas to resolve. We have taken a pragmatic approach, but are naturally determined that, while demographic factors are taken into account, existing balances are not unduly distorted. Finally, on closer co-operation, our position was that, while prepared to consider easing the flexibility provisions, we wanted to ensure this would be accompanied by appropriate safeguards for the coherence of the Union. This view was widely shared, and there is strong support for facilitating non-participating members in joining at a later date. Ireland also made known its views with regard to flexibility in the second pillar, in particular our wish to avoid undermining the Common Foreign and Security Policy.'

Ireland's stall was clearly set out. We would be willing to discuss qualified majority voting being extended to a number of areas. This meant in effect that rather than unanimity being required the QMV approach could be used, so a country could not veto a proposal. This posed little problem for Ireland in most areas – Ireland had not used its veto and had always negotiated broad-based support for its positions. This experience probably meant that QMV could actually be an advantage to Ireland. However, QMV was not an option for taxation. There would be no EU controls over taxation policy and Ireland was determined to keep it that way. Finally, Ireland still wanted one commissioner per member state, although there was clear opposition to this from many of the larger states who saw it as unworkable. As all nations would sit down to negotiate, Ireland had an ambitious target if it was to achieve all of these aims.

During the debate Cowen also stated that he saw no issues arising for Irish neutrality and negotiations would not affect this: 'In relation to the Common Foreign and Security Policy, our position has always been, and remains, that we do not believe any Western European Union commitment is required. We do not agree that a mutual defence commitment of any kind should form part of a Common Foreign and Security Policy of the European Union [CFSP]. We continue to hold that view. The flexibility issue, how it will apply and what pillars will apply is still a matter for discussion and negotiation.'

Mr Gormley: 'On the whole question of a possible protocol for opting out for neutrals ...'

Mr Cowen: 'As I said, the Irish position is that we do not see the inclusion of a Western European Union into a defence commitment forming part of CFSP.'

The protocol mentioned by John Gormley would come back to haunt Ireland much later; however, it is clear that at this stage Cowen knew the size of the challenge facing Ireland in the negotiations and did not believe in adding more to the table as regards a protocol for neutrality, which was an issue that he did not believe would be affected anyway.

The five largest states held two commissioner posts; and it was argued that they would have to accept a reduction to one like everybody else. However, in real terms the larger states realised that in the absence of a reweighting of the votes, they would actually be losing considerable influence therefore they were using this as a bargaining chip: 'Regarding the idea of one commissioner per member state, that has not been conceded. There are two very distinct views currently as to whether it should be a capped Commission or a Commission comprising one commissioner per member state. There is no concession made by any of the large five countries relating to dropping their second commissioner, for example, until ...'

Mr J. O'Keeffe: 'They will have to.'

Mr Cowen: '... I am informing the deputy of the facts. The position of the large five countries is that they do not concede the second commissioner ...'

Mr J. O'Keeffe: '... informally they are.'

Mr Cowen: '... I will make a third attempt to get through this point. It will make sense to the deputy when he hears it. They do not concede dropping their second commissioner until such time, in compliance with the protocol of Amsterdam, that there is a decision on the reweighting issue. That was the basis on which they agreed the protocol. Until and unless there is agreement on the reweighting matter, the commissionership issue will not be resolved. Therefore, when I talk about being pragmatic, I mean that we cannot insist on obtaining one commissioner per state, with a reduction of the big five down to one each without a reweighting. That is the basis on which the protocol was negotiated.'

From this we can easily see just how difficult the negotiations might prove to be. It also shows that Cowen was alive to the task and was already thinking of how a workable compromise could be reached.

In answer to questions in November, Brian Cowen presented an intriguing picture of how countries interact at European level. While it is often assumed to be small countries combining against large, he pointed out that Ireland is often in the middle and had shared interests with larger states on some issues and smaller ones on others: 'A number of assumptions must be made if one puts the case the deputy has advanced. If one actually analyses the pursuit of Irish interests at European level, the idea that there are ten small states which are united on all issues in opposition to five large states united on all issues does not reflect the reality of the position. In fact, it is difficult to find any issue on which the five large states are agreed. This reality has been lost in the negotiations because those states with two commissioners are pushing very hard for the reweighting of votes, be it the Italians who are seeking a substantial reweighting or other states which are adopting a more realistic approach. I do not believe that reweighting would result in the diminution of the Irish voice at the table, presuming we can arrive at a modest reweighting proposal which would meet with everyone's agreement.

'Our allies in many of these discussions are not limited to other small states and it is not true that all small states and all large states have the same interests. On a number of issues of fundamental importance, such as the Common Agricultural Policy, the position of large states is very much in line with ours.'

While discussing any possible referendum Cowen recognised that the arguments would be very different from past referenda: 'I accept the point that a referendum in the context of this ICG will be very different from previous referendums in that financial arrangements or transfer of competencies are not envisaged. We are talking about how to get a more effective decision making process in the Commission and in the Council in terms of voting procedures, including deciding the areas which will require unanimity and qualified majority voting. It is linked with the logistics of how the EU will move forward in terms of an historic enlargement phase and how it can continue to operate effectively.'

Brian Cowen accompanied Taoiseach Bertie Ahern to the Nice summit. Anyone who thought it might be a formality would be badly mistaken. And in an era when people across Europe are sceptical of their politicians, it is only fair to point out that the Nice summit was nothing short of a war of attrition in negotiating terms, with all countries fighting tooth and nail on proposals. While people may wonder why texts of treaties are not more readable and much shorter, then perhaps it is best to illustrate that to make them so would be impossible when one considers that the Nice summit began on the morning of Thursday 7 December 2000 and delegates finally emerged with an agreement at 4.30 a.m. on Monday 11 December. The longest summit in the history of the EU, it was a bruising and exhausting process.

On 13 December the taoiseach and minister for foreign affairs reported on the outcome to the Dáil. In summary, from an Irish perspective, qualified majority voting would be extended in line with what Ireland had expected. Taxation was safe. The reweighting of the votes was a solid outcome with Ireland having a much bigger share of the vote than its population would require. But the price for success in these areas was with regard to the commissioner. Larger states agreed to give up the second commissioner putting everyone on an equal footing; but it was agreed that when membership reached twenty-seven states the number of commissioners would be capped so not every country would hold a post. The sweetener for Ireland was that it would be on a rotation basis and all countries small or large would at some stage lose their commissioner for a term, levelling the playing field.

Fine Gael felt that Ireland had conceded too easily with regard to the commissioner. John Bruton suggested that he would not have accepted the proposal. Brian Cowen answered questions on the issue: 'I thank those who contributed to the debate. I am glad to take up some of the questions which have been raised. Deputy Bruton made the point that he was prepared to veto the Treaty of Nice on the basis that the right to a commissioner was not being made available for all time. That was his clear position. Deputy Bruton suggests that he knows how to win his friends in Europe on the basis of vetoing the Treaty of Nice on that issue. I would say to him that is probably the most naive comment I have ever heard him make. Even sorrier than that is that Deputy Bruton went on to conduct …'

Mr J. Bruton: 'I said that to the people.'

Mr Cowen: 'I listened intently to what Deputy Bruton had to say.'

Mr J. Bruton: 'I said that to the people at the time – back in the 1990s.'

Mr Cowen: 'The deputy spoke very highly about his presidency of the European Council. He had that privilege and the very best of luck to him on that. He also went on to say that the Commission has the sole right of initiative. That is not correct. Whether he is president of the European Council, leader of the Fine Gael Party or vice-president of the European People's Party and thinks that is the situation in relation to the treaties we were negotiating, I am afraid it shows an enormous lack of knowledge about what are the institutional capacities. I will tell him why because it is not the sole right of initiative, it is fundamentally correct. Therefore the deputy's argument is based on a totally inaccurate assessment and understanding of what is the Commission's capacity or what is the capacity of the council of ministers. An initiative can be taken by member states without reference to the Commission. It requires two thirds of the member states and a qualified majority vote procedure for that initiative to be passed by the council, without any direct input by the Commission.'

Cowen clearly felt that the deal was the best achievable in the circumstances. He based this on the fact that no country emerged from the Nice summit having achieved all its goals: 'We held a hard negotiating line on each of the elements up for debate, as is our job, throughout the whole intergovernmental conference meeting. We then went to the intergovernmental conference on the basis of the options that were to be put by the presidency. No country emerged from the Nice negotiations having maintained in every respect every negotiating position they held on all the issues. Had they done so, we would not have a Treaty of Nice. Those are the facts. It is easy when one does not have the responsibility to step back and say to me that this, that and the other was a failure. We take the negotiating package as a whole and as such it was a successful outcome. It had as successful an outcome for Ireland as any other country can claim for itself.'

Cowen also made clear that Ireland did not have sufficient support to argue the point further: 'If there are people who are prepared to step back and say, "No, we will maintain our own national interest in every respect, regardless of the common European interest that emerges in the consensus", that is fine. They have that luxury. Let there be no doubt that the Commission did not hold to the position articulated by us throughout these negotiations. We have fought tooth and nail a rearguard action from many states and the Commission on this issue.'

It was no easy return for Cowen and Ahern. Any referendum would need Fine Gael support. Whether Fine Gael members would now view it as a good deal was open to question. Depending on your view, either the Irish negotiators, including Ahern and Cowen, failed to press home their point and should have brought the entire agreement down through a veto, or they achieved a considerable deal based on a practical solution, protecting taxation and Ireland's interests while giving up on some over-arching principles in the name of gaining further influence. For some, Nice could have been a lot worse for Ireland, and Cowen could rightly be proud of his part in the deal. For others it was not enough. It is unlikely that that debate will ever be resolved. However the Irish civil servants with over thirty years negotiating experience in Europe seemed pleased with the deal, and the strategy. One could argue those civil servants were the architects of the deal, in any event only those who were at the table can ever say for sure what was really achievable.

On 22 March Cowen informed the House that a referendum would indeed be required and that legislation was being prepared: 'The government has decided, on the basis of the attorney general's advice, that a referendum will be required to allow Ireland to ratify the Treaty of Nice. Work on drafting the necessary legalisation is in hand and it is hoped shortly to publish a bill containing the wording of a constitutional amendment. It is the intention to hold the referendum before the summer. It is understood that in other member states decisions on ratification are likely to be taken by the respective national parliaments.

'As part of the process of providing objective information for the public about the new Treaty, a White Paper will be published next week. This will provide a factual account of the background to the negotiations and the decisions taken in Nice. It is intended that the White Paper, and a concise summary of the White Paper, which is also in preparation, will be widely distributed so as to facilitate access by the public to information on the Treaty ...'

Information provision was already weighing on the government's mind. But the question was how many people were actually interested in following the detail of the negotiations and the meaning of the outcome? How could the government sell such a complex document to a largely apathetic audience.

Cowen went on to state that if a referendum were not required he would not be recommending that one be held: 'I am making my position plain. I do not believe in having a referendum for the sake of having one. We have a referendum because we are required under the constitution to have it. If the legal advice was, as in the case of Denmark and other member states, that it would be possible to ratify the Nice Treaty simply by legislating for it in the Oireachtas, that would be the course of action I would propose to government and ask it to agree on. The fact is that our constitution requires a referendum and the wording and approach will be similar to that taken last time. The discretions involved which are being changed require a constitutional yes vote from the people to safeguard this against legal challenge and we will proceed on that basis.'

On 3 April Cowen brought the enabling legislation for the referendum before the House; in doing so he pointed out that Ireland is the only country where a referendum would be required: 'The Treaty will only come into effect if ratified by all fifteen member states. Current indications are that this will be done by means of parliamentary approval in the other member states: Ireland is likely to be the only country where a referendum is required to complete the process of ratification. It is, perhaps, interesting to note in this regard that Denmark which, like us, has frequently had recourse to referendums is not doing so on this occasion because the Treaty does not involve any transfer of competence from the member states to the Union.'

We can see even from this excerpt that for Cowen, Nice was all about enlargement and allowing other countries to join the Union: 'It goes without saying that Ireland, no less than our partners, has a vital interest in these developments. A peaceful and stable Europe is, clearly, in Ireland's interest. Small countries, in particular, benefit from a settled international order. However, for an open economy like ours it is, in addition, a vital underpinning of our domestic economic well-being.

'We, in Ireland, are in an excellent position to take advantage of the opportunities offered by enlargement. Irish business currently has access to a market of 370 million. With the completion of the current enlargement process this would expand to some 550 million. Irish exporters are already well placed in these markets. Irish exports to the Central and Eastern European applicant countries rose by 337 per cent to £586 million in the five years to 1999. These countries also provide excellent investment opportunities for Irish companies. For example, in Poland Irish investment is already in excess of US$1 billion.'

The economic case that was the driver for countries like Ireland supporting enlargement was compelling, but whether or not these type of advantages would resonate with the public was very much open to question. However, Cowen seemed sure that the Irish people would endorse the argument – based on the fact that they would want to allow other countries an opportunity to join Europe: 'I am confident that the Irish people, for whom the memory of the challenges we faced in making a similar transition some thirty years ago is not so distant, wish these countries well and are ready to extend the hand of friendship, co-operation and solidarity, just as we were helped at the equivalent stage in our development ...

'I am confident that those who fairly consider the issues will conclude that the Treaty is right for Europe and right for Ireland in Europe. It is, clearly, in Ireland's interest that an enlarged Union can continue to function properly and take decisions for which the treaty provides while maintaining in place necessary safeguards in sensitive areas and the fundamental balances that are the hallmark of the Union ... we should not lose sight of the fact that in reality influence in the Council is based on forging alliances with like-minded states, and that issues rarely divide on the basis of size. Ireland, under successive governments, has shown itself adept at protecting its interests.'

Cowen was also unequivocal about Ireland's neutrality: 'In line with the government's policy of military neutrality, the government has made clear that Ireland would participate only in operations authorised by the United Nations, in accordance with the appropriate legislation and subject to Dáil approval. The existing treaty provisions were intended to make the Common Foreign and Security Policy of the EU more coherent, more visible and more effective.'

Cowen then went on to stress the benefits that European Union membership had brought: 'The Treaty of Nice is concerned with preparing for enlargement, but it is, of course, also about the continuing development of the Union, of which we have been a full and committed member for almost three decades. During that period the Irish people have enjoyed substantial economic benefits, reflected in unprecedented levels of employment, growth and prosperity. Our network of roads and services have benefited substantially from Structural Funds assistance, averaging more than 2 per cent of GNP during the 1990s. Similarly, our education and training programmes have benefited greatly under the European Social Fund down through the years. We have gained from and contributed to important advances in areas like the environment, social programmes, equal rights for men and women and consumer protection, all matters of direct concern to every citizen in the country. Nobody seriously believes that these advances would have been achieved to anything like the same extent if we were outside the Union.'

However Fianna Fáil had just had their own difficulties with Europe, as Charlie McCreevy received censure for an over-inflationary budget from the EU. Ireland did not accept the censure as fair and Fianna Fáil in particular had shown a willingness to challenge and question Europe. This did not bode well for encouraging Fianna Fáil members to support Europe at this time. Also, Fine Gael had questioned the deal and perhaps left many of their own members apathetic as a result.

The Nice referendum would of course become part of Irish political folklore. The campaign failed and for the first time Ireland rejected a vote on Europe. For many across the EU this was greeted with shock. This was the country, after all, that had put Europe back on track with the Maastricht referendum after a Danish 'No' vote a decade earlier. A search for answers was already commencing. Looking back with the knowledge and hindsight of Lisbon, the arguments have not changed and both treaties involved broadly similar matters. There was no doubt that, as minister for foreign affairs, Cowen had to shoulder a sizeable chunk of blame and it was a major blow to his tough confident image. For many Cowen had failed to get beyond the technical issues when he spoke and this was a reason for a lack of interest and understanding. On 12 June 2001 he made a statement to the Dáil, finding it difficult to hide his disappointment and frustration: 'Our EU colleagues unanimously expressed concern and disappointment at the outcome of the referendum on the Treaty of Nice and I share their disappointment. I explained that the decision to hold a referendum was based on legal advice provided for the government and informed my colleagues on the general affairs council that the campaign against the Treaty was composed of a variety of disparate elements. Matters raised by them included issues not germane to the Treaty. There were also interpretations given to aspects of it for which there is no Treaty reference. There were, therefore, myriad reasons given as to why the voters may have decided to vote "No".

'I also adverted to the historically low turnout and the unfortunate confusion among sections of the electorate about what the Treaty did and did not contain. Our EU partners accepted my assurances that the vote was in no way a vote against enlargement. They also pledged to give whatever assistance was possible in helping Ireland to find a way forward, taking into account the concerns reflected by the "No" vote.

'At the same time the reality, as reflected in the Council conclusions adopted yesterday, is that none of our EU partners is willing to renegotiate the text of the Treaty. The Treaty took the best part of one year to complete, including four days at heads of government level at Nice last December. All member states and candidate countries remain committed to the Treaty as being the basis for enlargement ...

'Those who have suggested the government can somehow call a halt to this process are fundamentally out of touch with the situation as it stands. Each member state is fully entitled to pursue national ratification in line with its own democratic procedures and principles. To suggest otherwise is contrary to their democratic rights as member states.'

Cowen was clearly setting himself a new task, which was to continue to try to dispel the arguments against Nice; the only purpose of this could be to facilitate another referendum: 'I am convinced that open public debate and consequent understanding of what the European

Union does and how it operates will dispel many of the fears which led people to vote "No" in last week's referendum. I was able to reassure my EU colleagues and all the candidate states in Luxembourg of Ireland's unwavering support for the enlargement process and our continuing commitment to the development of the Union. Unfortunately, the reason it was necessary to give such reassurances was the "No" vote in the referendum, encouraged by some in the House who protest they are in favour of enlargement.'

Cowen was still arguing the merits of the Treaty and had clearly not admitted defeat on the issue: 'Perhaps in Ireland we should reflect on the alternative to a rules-based European Union. It would be a Europe dominated by the large countries where shifting alliances would lead to instability – in other words, the sort of Europe that helped create the conditions historically for conflict and crisis. It should be recalled that even during the present period instability and war are still a feature of parts of Europe outside the embrace of the Union. An enlargement incorporating the present candidates will include one of the former Yugoslav republics. Perhaps more will join in time, each enlargement reinforcing the strength and stability of a Europe voluntarily united on democratic principles.'

Cowen saw no break in the campaign. The process of convincing the electorate began with discussing the defeat. This tenacity and doggedness was of particular value to the 'Yes' campaign. Clearly Cowen had signed up to the mantra 'my head is bloody but unbowed'. The fight would continue: 'The government has stated that nothing in the Treaty undermines our policy of military neutrality. Nothing commits us to a mutual defence pact. Perhaps this reality needs to be further articulated. The issue of democratic oversight of European activities was also a recurring feature in the referendum campaign. We can surely do more at national level. I am thinking in particular of the role of the Oireachtas in scrutinising EU legislation and informing the public of what is being done at European level. I have already told the joint committee on foreign affairs and the joint committee on European Affairs – the chairman is here today – that I would welcome such a development in the interest of democratic debate on EU issues.'

The Nice Treaty hurt Cowen, however. It hurt Fianna Fáil and the level of division in the party later became apparent when Eamon Ó Cuív, a government minister, admitted he himself voted no. We can only imagine what the reaction of Cowen must have been to such news. Perhaps some idea is given to us by a throw-away comment under the order of business on 19 June, as Ruairí Quinn questions recent comments by Charlie McCreevy and Michael McDowell that seemed to support the 'No' argument: 'This is not a game between some members of Fianna Fáil, this is about the future of the European Union and the future of this country and its relationship to other European nations. The deliberate stirring up of a conflict in Gothenburg by the minister for finance has had very negative results for us right across the continent, a conflict that has now been compounded by the attorney general attempting to do as the minister of state, Deputy Ó Cuív, did – private in part and yet having responsibility as attorney general.'

Mr Cowen: 'At least he voted for it.'

It was perhaps a tired and baffled Cowen that at least respected the fact that they supported the Treaty, which was more than Ó Cuív had done.

On June 21 while answering questions on the Gothenburg summit Cowen made clear what was by now a familiar refrain in Ireland, namely that treaties of this magnitude simply cannot be re-negotiated – no other offers would be tabled. It is a line that recent experience would suggest still hasn't been appreciated by the public: 'In relation to some issues which were raised in the debate with regard to the enlargement question, the member states are unanimous in their view that the ratification process must continue on the basis of the text as agreed at Nice and in accordance with the agreed timetable. They made it clear that there could be no question of any reopening of the text agreed at Nice. The Gothenburg European Council confirmed these conclusions while restating a willingness to do everything possible to help Ireland resolve the difficulties which have arisen. Mutual respect cuts both ways. Just as we rightly expect respect for the outcome of our referendum, we must also respect the unanimous view of the other fourteen member states, fully supported by the applicant states. They are unwavering in their conviction that the Treaty of Nice is required for enlargement.'

Cowen was also eager to dispel the argument of a 'begging bowl' in the past. It is probably true that this idea has tarnished the public's impression of Irish negotiators, who, from a variety of political parties and the civil service, negotiated particularly strong deals based on sound economic principles and arguments. Cowen clearly felt that this misunderstanding had led people to believe that Ireland did not get a good deal at Nice: 'A grave disservice is also done to people's understanding of our role in Europe when it is suggested that we are moving from a begging-bowl mentality to some other kind of mentality. No Irish government has had a begging-bowl mentality towards Europe. What was agreed in the Delors Plans 1 and 2 was precisely the economic realisation that, in a single market with its own centrifugal economic force, it was necessary for peripheral regions to be given the economic, social and cohesion funds which would allow them to compete in that single market. That was not a begging-bowl mentality. It does little service to the argument for supporters of the EU – the vast majority of people in this House and in the country – to suggest that we have been engaged on the basis of a handout mentality.'

Fine Gael put an EU bill to the House in late June and when Cowen contributed to the debate we get a greater sense of the Europe he sees and his viewpoint on it: 'The analysis of there being a competing view between those who wish to see a liberal, non-social Europe and those who favour a social Europe which takes on the responsibilities of civilised nations is an attempt to create a gap where none exists. The Treaty of Rome and subsequent treaties incorporate all of these social rights, and all parties have been proponents of pursuing those rights and entitlements.

'We do not do ourselves a service if, in trying to analyse the situation and how we go forward, we try to suggest that there are greater differences between pro-European parties than we would like to be the case. I have seen this kind of analysis articulated in the media for some time. It succumbs to the tyranny of the soundbite in trying to extrapolate an argument from a Berlin versus Brussels analysis which itself does no justice to the speech concerned. It is always a problem that some seek to encapsulate considered policy positions in nice soundbites for editorials. However, such soundbites are not practical in terms of a considered political debate in this House in the aftermath of the referendum or as part of the continuing European debate ...

'I was taken by Deputy McDowell's contribution. Sometimes our analysis over-emphasises points of difference which, when examined, are not as great as some would like to suggest. It is more about people creating a political space in terms of their electoral prospects than it is about the reality. However, it is a legitimate party exercise in which to be involved.'

The Common Foreign and Security Policy came in for particular attention: 'It is worth recalling that Ireland has been participating in consultations and co-operation on foreign policy issues with our partners in Europe since we first joined the EEC in 1973. Starting with European political co-operation, as it was then called, through to the development in the Treaty of Maastricht of what we now call the Common Foreign and Security Policy which came into operation in November 1993, Ireland has had the opportunity to consult, debate, and very often, agree on foreign policy positions or courses of action with our EU partners across a whole range of foreign policy issues.

'On those occasions when the EU member states reach agreement and speak with one voice – for example, in the United Nations on many issues, or in the Organisation for Security and Co-operation in Europe – our combined weight can be very important in building international consensus and in promoting our world view in favour of the peaceful settlement of disputes, democratisation and the protection of human rights and fundamental freedoms. Ireland's experience over nearly thirty years is that our involvement in the formulation of EU foreign and security policy enhances our voice in the world.'

While Ireland may have voted 'No' to Nice, it was clear on 11 December that Ireland was still doing all in its power to facilitate enlargement: 'Ireland is playing an active and positive role in the formulation of the Union's detailed positions in the continuing negoti-ations. Through the so-called "twinning" scheme, a number of Irish officials are, or have been, seconded to work in candidate country administrations, offering practical advice based on our own experience of adaptation to the demands of membership. We offer financial support to their officials to come to Ireland to take part in courses and seminars. We are expanding our network of diplomatic missions in the candidate countries, with the recent opening of embassies in Cyprus, Estonia, Slovakia and Slovenia supplementing those in the Czech Republic, Hungary and Poland. This means that we are much better placed than before to interact with them on an informed and intensive basis.'

Cowen pulled no punches later in the debate as he stated that many of the arguments used to defeat the Treaty had, in his view, nothing whatsoever to do with it: 'In the immediate aftermath of the vote, one thing upon which all commentators agreed was that there were multiple reasons for the "No" vote, and in many cases had little or nothing to do with enlargement or the Treaty of Nice itself. Another critical factor was, of course, the disappointingly poor turnout. These initial impressions were broadly confirmed by the European Commission survey which appeared at the end of October. It revealed alarmingly high levels of public apathy and confusion about the Treaty and about the European Union generally, which underlay both the abstention rate and the "No" vote. While this factor was statistically the most significant, specific fears were expressed about issues such as the alleged loss of national sovereignty, perceived threats to our policy of military neutrality and the power of large member states as against small. It was also apparent from the survey, as from the referendum itself, that most people had found the campaign lacklustre, uninspiring and uninformative. I am by the way amused, but not surprised, that Patricia McKenna, MEP, is so strongly opposed to any attempts to amend the legislation governing the referendum commission so as to improve the quality of debate and to enable the public to be better informed.'

There was certainly no shortage of debate taking place before or after the Treaty of Nice, but Cowen was perhaps understandably disappointed at the coverage it received: 'My one regret is that media coverage of the forum has so far not been equal to the importance of the issues it is addressing and the substance of the contribution it is making. I know, as do all of us in this House, that the dumbing down of the coverage of politics and public affairs is a wider problem, but I find it irritating that very often those who lecture us on the inadequacy of political debate themselves constitute a large part of the problem by failing to report on substantive discussion when it does take place.'

On 30 January 2002 it was clear to everyone that Ireland was heading for a second referendum even if it was not yet official. In the Dáil chamber Brian Cowen was again answering questions on the most recent European Council meeting. The debate is interesting as he chose to focus particular attention on John Gormley of the Green Party who had backed a 'No' vote on Nice. It is interesting because six years later both men would be at cabinet together and Gormley would be backing a 'Yes' vote to Lisbon, a treaty that dealt with and extended the same issues as Nice: 'I welcome the opportunity to report on some of the foreign policy issues dealt with at the European Council at Laeken. In replying, I am always mindful to pick up on some of the issues raised by speakers but the limitation of time constrains all of us. I would never question Deputy Gormley's sincerity about the European project but I fundamentally disagree with him. This evening he has spoken about the inevitability of the worst-case scenarios he predicts, yet he speaks about the ability of other states to bring down the issues he supports while suggesting we are incapable of preventing the vision about which he is concerned. There is a total inconsistency in his argument. He mentioned a scenario where two states could do something with which he disagrees in relation to nuclear safety measures. He had spent the previous eight minutes telling me all the things that will happen on the basis that we will not be able to stop them when, in fact, the intergovernmental conference process confirms that there must be agreement from fifteen governments. Many compromises, which have emerged at Nice and elsewhere, can be regarded as being messy. However, they represent the political consensus of the fifteen governments and that is what determines the pace of development and evolution of Europe, to which Deputy De Rossa referred.

'Deputy Gormley's analysis that the worst-case scenarios he fears will definitely happen is fundamentally incoherent when at the same time he tells us all the things that are not happening because of the intervention of various states. The deputy has a sincere interest in these matters, but he must examine his reasons for continually adopting this approach. He cannot tell the Irish people that all of this will happen when it will not. I cite one point in the Nice Treaty referendum which he would not accept. Every decision on participation by Ireland in European security and defence policy is based on the sovereign decision of government, subject to full parliamentary approval of this House and the requirement of a specific UN mandate. That is a pretty clear statement …

'If Deputy Gormley took neutrality to its ultimate logical conclusion, Ireland would not be a member of the United Nations. Issues can be explained and discussed and, while we may not reach consensus on certain issues, we should be fair to the citizenry and outline the factual position. The great paradox is that the Nice declaration for the first time began to look at the concerns of people like Deputy Gormley by saying we would have a structured discussion on issues such as competencies, the degree of federation or confederation or the *sui generis* nature of the European Union treaties. Pillar I is integrationist in terms of the need for the discipline of a single market and what that has meant for us. On objective economic analysis, the peripheral states have benefited to a far greater extent than those at the centre in every expansion that has occurred …

'If Deputy Gormley wants to be involved in democratic debate, he cannot disregard the consensus of 350 million people. His party has 3 per cent or 4 per cent of the vote, yet he regards me and my party, which now has 42 per cent of the vote, as being part of an elite group. I represent people just as he does and they all have equal rights. If we are to have a debate, the tone, dialogue and discourse should respect the fact that we will have different views.'

On 7 February Cowen warned against the idea that there are no repercussions one way or another for a vote: 'The idea that everything will be hunky-dory one way or the other greatly minimises the damage which will be done to our national interests, a point which I will consistently make. Suggestions to the contrary do not take into account the impact failure to ratify would have, not only on the European Union, but also the members thereof. This is not to say that other member states or citizens do not respect our democratic decision making. It is simply a fact of life. We need to face the fact that we will hold up the ratification of the Treaty of Nice if we are unable to resolve matters satisfactorily by the end of the year.'

On 27 March the Irish strategy was clear as Cowen pointed out that a declaration on neutrality would be sought in advance of a second referendum: 'In summary, and in the context of the government's commitment to EU enlargement and to the ratification of the Nice Treaty by the end of the year, the taoiseach signalled to his European counterparts that the government would seek a declaration from the Seville European Council which will confirm that Ireland's policy of military neutrality is not affected by the treaties.

'Our EU partners responded positively to the taoiseach's statement. The conclusions of the European Council welcomed the approach outlined and reiterated the Council's willingness to contribute in every possible way to supporting the government. Work will proceed on the drafting of a declaration with a view to consideration by the incoming government.'

On 19 June Cowen expanded on the approach Ireland would take towards securing a declaration: 'I am glad to have this opportunity to clarify to the House the government's approach to the declarations we are seeking at Seville – the national declaration by Ireland and the related declaration by the European Council. I emphasise that the texts of the declarations fully reflect the views expressed in the second report of the chairman of the National Forum on Europe. The Forum was established as part of the government's response to the concerns of the people raised in last summer's referendum on the Nice Treaty. Chairman Hayes, in his second report, underlined the importance of assurances that the Nice Treaty did not imply a departure from our traditional policy of neutrality ...'

Mr Boyle: 'On a point of order, that is not true. The minister should not mislead the House.'

Mr Cowen: 'As I was saying before I was rudely interrupted, Chairman Maurice Hayes stated we had no plans to enter a military alliance or participate in the development of a European army and would not do so without the approval of the Irish people …'

Mr Boyle: 'That is not true.'

An ceann comhairle: 'I am reluctant to ask the deputy to leave the House. However, there are very strict procedures which must be observed for this debate.'

Mr Cowen: 'There is no plan to change the basis on which Irish troops participate in peacekeeping and conflict operations. Each and every one of these points is being dealt with by the declarations.

'The national declaration will reaffirm, beyond any reasonable doubt, that the Treaty of Nice poses no threat to our traditional policy of military neutrality. In so doing it will confirm that Ireland is not party to any mutual defence commitment and that we are not party to any plans to develop a European army. It will also reaffirm that we will take our own sovereign decision on whether Irish troops should participate in humanitarian or crisis management tasks mounted by the European Union, based on the triple lock of UN endorsement, government decision and Dáil approval. Moreover, the national declaration will also make it clear that Ireland will not adopt any decision taken by the European Council to move to a common defence or ratify any future treaty which would involve a departure from our traditional policy of military neutrality unless it has first been approved by the people in a referendum.'

Of course the 2002 general election saw Fianna Fáil and the Progressive Democrats returned to government on the back of a massive endorsement by the electorate. The way was clear to proceed and the government now had a mandate upon which to campaign for a second referendum.

On 25 June Cowen was in the Dáil to explain the background to the declaration received at the Seville European Council: 'Common foreign and security positions are precisely that – positions about which a common policy can be agreed. We do not adhere to every area of the foreign policy of France and Germany. Common Foreign and Security Policy is intergovernmental in character. We come to common positions on the basis of agreement. They are about those areas of policy about which we agree, not those about which we disagree. Therefore, to characterise Common Foreign and Security Policy as in some way imposing a uniform foreign policy in respect of all fifteen member states on every issue, is to misunderstand precisely what the position is. … In so far as Ireland is concerned, this area of policy is the one where we can demonstrate, as the declarations do, where we have retained sovereignty because the government decides, on a case by case basis and subject to Oireachtas approval and prior UN endorsement, whether we will participate in any crisis management or humanitarian task which the EU military capability will take on board.

'That is the position and any characterisation to the contrary has no Treaty reference and is not correct, accurate or in conformity with the declarations we have set out … We are putting this point again to the people because of the duty of government to put it to them where we see our essential national interest at stake. This is no way fetters the right of the people to make the sovereign decision on this question. We are simply asking them to consider it once again.'

On 4 September a confident and combative Brian Cowen introduced the enabling legislation for the second referendum, the government was determined not to be defeated again: 'The Treaty of Nice matters. It matters to Ireland, to our partners in the European Union and to the candidate countries. There are many positive reasons we should approve the Treaty and for seeking, through this bill, to ask the people to return to this important issue. The Treaty may be relatively limited in its scope and dry and technical in its details, but it is hugely ambitious in its purpose. If ratified, it will help to transform Europe's economic and political landscape to the advantage of us all. The people will be asked in the forthcoming referendum if they wish to assist in this process or to stand in its way. Ireland has been a success in the Union. Its membership has been a force for progress, jobs and development. Does it make sense to change tack at this important stage of our national development and put that at risk? Do we want Ireland to remain at the heart of the Union as a fully engaged and active member or do we wish to move to the margins? …

'The decision we will make, therefore, is very serious and very real. It will have real consequences for people in Ireland and for people across Europe. Voting "Yes" to Nice is the right thing to do from a broad European perspective. It is also the right thing to do from our own national perspective. We are not being asked to choose between our own interests and those of others. Of course we have a right to make our own choice, but I sincerely believe it would be a major mistake to think that if we vote "No" things will simply go on as before. Every single person in this country is directly affected by our membership of the European Union, whether as a worker, employer, farmer, trade unionist, parent or consumer. Every part of Ireland is affected. Therefore, everyone has a stake in the outcome of the referendum …

'However, we as political leaders bear a particular responsibility. If we are honest, we failed collectively last time to energise and enthuse the public, with a turnout of barely more than one third of the electorate. Analysis after the event revealed that there were many complaints of confusion and lack of knowledge. Whatever outcome we want this time, let us together resolve to do a far better job in explaining what is involved and just why it is so important to vote. Apathy is not just misplaced, it is dangerous. We must strive to ensure that every individual voter sees the referendum as being personally important.'

Cowen was of the opinion that Europe was more important to Ireland at that point than ever before: 'It would be quite incorrect to think that the European Union will become less significant for Ireland in the future. On the contrary, membership of the single market will remain crucial in offering opportunities to Irish companies and in attracting foreign investment. Hundreds and thousands of people at work today depend directly or indirectly on that investment and they will continue to do so in the future. Membership of the European Union has been a key strategic element and this has been reiterated by those involved in industrial promotion. The capacity of any one country to deal on its own with such issues as environmental protection, the fight against cross-border crime and the management of immigration issues will become even more limited and it is vital that collective action be taken by members of the Union.'

To conclude his speech Cowen pointed out that while the issues were complex he did not believe the choice was: 'At the end of the day, the choice is straightforward. This is not the time for us to hesitate or turn away from the path we have followed for thirty years. Europe has been good for Ireland and an enlarged Europe will continue to be good for it. For us to say "No" to this Treaty definitively would damage the European Union, the candidate countries and our own interests. We would lose friends and influence in Brussels and across the continent, which would most emphatically not be in our interests … Ireland needs Europe and Europe needs Ireland, which is why the government believes that the Treaty of Nice should be ratified. A "Yes" vote is a vote for jobs, growth and Ireland's future.'

The second Nice Treaty referendum was comfortably passed and what was seen as a minor hiccup on Brian Cowen's record had now been rectified. Ireland's European partners were assured it was an aberration and the diplomatic work began to repair any damage to Ireland's carefully balanced negotiating positions. On 6 November, when Brian Cowen reported on the next European Council, it was clear that all eyes were on the next round of negotiations and what would turn into an EU constitution and eventually the Lisbon Treaty. Considering Cowen's comments on the matter, it certainly started with high hopes; one can only wonder where it all went wrong: 'We have reached a stage where we clearly need to see – this is what the convention is attempting to do – how we provide a basic text that is understandable and comprehensible to citizens. There is a sense of disconnection, not because the European Union is not doing important work or because it does not have effective common policies. The Union certainly has the latter, but there will always be room for improvement. There is a need to communicate with Europe's citizens about the range of competencies that are exercised by the European Union's institutions, why these are so exercised, what is the appropriate level at which certain decisions should be taken, how is the principle of subsidiarity to be properly addressed, what should be the role of national parliaments and how can we ensure that national parliaments have a role and, therefore, enhance the democratic legitimacy of the deliberations of the Union in all its aspects.

'These are wide-ranging issues which have deep implications. We agreed at Nice to establish the convention, which engaged in a listening phase and is now in the process, through its working groups, of preparing papers. … The second referendum on Nice has occupied most of our time until now. In light of the outcome obtained at the referendum and having seen that the enlargement process will proceed within the timescale envisaged – it is likely to happen by the end of the year – it is clear that we must all give the work of the convention a very high priority.

'To be fair many would argue that significant progress was made on these issues, as we will see, but the public did not seem to agree when the texts were finally presented.'

On 9 April 2003 Cowen gave a clearer picture of how negotiations were progressing. Clearly the route to the eventual Lisbon Treaty was a long one. European treaties are not agreed over the course of a day or a few hours of negotiations, but are the culmination of years of work: 'The government has set out its broad approach to the convention, and the future of Europe generally, on a number of occasions, including in my speech in Brussels last week. We hope that the process which is begun at the convention, and which will he concluded at the intergovernmental conference, will result in a simplified treaty which is more legible and accessible for our citizens. We hope it will prepare the institutions to face the challenges that lie ahead, including enlargement. We have been positive and constructive at the convention and our representative, the minister of state at the department of foreign affairs, Deputy Roche, has been particularly active and engaged in building networks which can help to advance and protect our interests. The taoiseach and I have also had meetings with our counterparts in various member states and, of course, with President Giscard d'Estaing during his recent visit to Dublin.

'The convention has moved into its final drafting phase. Draft texts published to date include the Treaty's general and final provisions. I emphasise that the draft article on ratification will not alter the current arrangements whereby a treaty cannot enter into force unless ratified by all the Union's member states. I do not believe that any other arrangement would have the necessary political or legal legitimacy. I do not support the arrangements proposed in the so-called Penelope Document drafted informally within the Commission for that reason.

'While good progress has been made by the convention, draft texts on important areas have yet to be brought forward. Articles on institutional matters and on CFSP and defence will be published towards the end of this month and debated in May. The European Council has asked President Giscard d'Estaing to present the convention's final recommendations to it at Thessaloniki in June. However, he has asked that there be a special European Council meeting at the end of June and will seek agreement for this in Athens next week. The government is open to some modest extension. However, as I said previously, we strongly believe that, irrespective of when the convention finishes, there should then be a significant period of reflection to allow us to digest its recommendations and to allow for the necessary and important process of public debate.'

The idea of creating networks and discussions with counterparts shows just how Ireland approaches such negotiations. It also shows the depth of thought and analysis that was already going into the negotiations. When one considers that Cowen would later be ridiculed for stating that he hadn't read the Lisbon Treaty from cover to cover, it does perhaps put the need for such reading in perspective.

On 8 May Cowen was answering questions on the Athens European Council. From this we begin to see how negotiations were developing and to see Ireland's position on issues that would become core in the Lisbon Treaty. Clearly Ireland wanted changes on items such as how a Commission president was elected. Ironically the Irish electorate would later reject many of the items Irish negotiators had fought so hard over: 'The informal European Council meeting focused on the work of the European convention. The European Union must be seen by our citizens to work; that is why the work of the convention and the intergovernmental conference that will follow, is so important. It is why the government is taking the work of the convention so seriously.

'Prior to the European Council meeting, a group of seventeen current and future member states met. The meeting was hosted by Prime Minister Verhofstadt of Belgium in the absence of the current president of the Benelux countries, Prime Minister Juncker of Luxembourg. Ireland was represented by the minister of state at the department of foreign affairs, Deputy Roche. The meeting was a follow-on from one which the taoiseach and I attended in Luxembourg on 1 April.

'The seventeen countries agreed a number of fundamental principles which we want to see reflected in the outcome of the convention. These principles draw largely on the Benelux memorandum of last December and on a paper drawn up over recent months by many like-minded states at the convention, in the drafting of which Ireland played a major role.

'The group of seventeen set out its strong support for a European Union that will work in the future at least as effectively and democratically as in the past. The principles that we reconfirmed are the need to ensure the equality of member states and to retain the balance between the institutions, without creating new institutions.

'At the European Council meeting we set out our views as to how these principles could be preserved and strengthened. While there are some differences among us on points of detail, we shared a wish to see the following: a strengthening of the community method and of the Commission; a more open and transparent process of election for the Commission president; the retention of the formula agreed at Nice, especially the requirement for equality as between member states, for the membership of the Commission; and a single external relations representative, with council and Commission membership.'

Proposals and counter-proposals were being submitted from all countries and Ireland was playing a full part in this: 'As the convention enters the final and decisive phase, intensive work is continuing across the range of issues it is addressing. Next week's plenary session will debate the vital issues of the Union's institutional arrangements, foreign policy and defence. The government's representative at the convention has submitted extensive proposals in response to texts published by the presidium in these areas. We will continue to work extremely closely with like-minded countries – and, of course, our allies vary from issue to issue – to ensure that the outcome of the convention is a balanced and appropriate one.'

Cowen later outlined that it was clearly the view and preference of member states to conclude the agreement in Rome and that at that stage there seemed little possibility of negotiations carrying over to the Irish presidency unless agreement could not be found: 'There is a possibility of a summit being called in early October to begin the intergovernmental conference. The question of whether it will be completed during the Italian presidency or continue to our presidency depends on the level of consensus which can be reached on the content and issues to be addressed. The proposal is to complete the intergovernmental conference prior to the accession date of 1 May 2004 as this would feed into the parliamentary elections and the appointment of the Commission and allow everything to come on stream under the new arrangements thereafter. While it is a little early to say what will be the timescale, that is the general plan envisaged.

'The question of what the treaty will be called is a matter for the council to decide. As the deputy will be aware, there is, due to the seminal nature of the treaty, a strong belief among many member states in the Rome to Rome cycle. We take a pragmatic approach. We will take up the obligations of trying to complete the treaty if it passes on to our presidency and simply concentrate on the need to find a genuine consensus that will meet the requirements of the circumstances, rather than worrying about whether the treaty is concluded during our term.'

By 29 May, replying to questions from John Gormley, Cowen was unequivocal with regard to the position on neutrality: 'There is no question of the government agreeing to Ireland's participation in a mutual defence commitment, other than with the approval of the people expressed in a referendum.'

Cowen and Ahern were also clearly worried in the aftermath of Nice that the public should take heed of what was happening and what was being negotiated so that they could engage and understand any possible treaty. On 15 October the crucial intergovernmental conference had begun and Cowen outlined progress in the early stages: 'The Irish people are not naive or starry-eyed about Europe, as they recognise its shortcomings, but they have a basic sense of its enduring promise and of its practical benefits.

'That is the context in which the proposed constitutional treaty should be analysed. It is highly significant but, as is inevitable in a negotiation, it is possible to get too close to the detail. Standing back, the convention draft does not fundamentally alter the nature of the Union as a unique experiment in the voluntary sharing of sovereignty by independent states. It does not fundamentally alter the Union's powers or its relationship with member states, the mix of policies that has worked so effectively for Ireland or the balances between the institutions and among member states. If the people support the Union and our membership of it – and I am sure they do – then they can be broadly happy with the convention outcome.

'The convention itself was an innovative approach to treaty change. A body representative of the peoples, states and institutions of Europe was established rather than having the preparatory work carried out by anonymous officials behind closed doors. All the member and applicant states were represented at both government and parliamentary level and the European Parliament and the Commission were also present. All had their say. Thousands of pages of draft texts and amendments were considered and finally a single text was produced.'

The drawing together of a single text was a monumental task in itself. But Cowen was clearly pleased that, in his view, the position and stance of the EU would be more open and accessible for the ordinary citizen. He felt it brought clarity to the issue, he also felt that the convention had strengthened the role of national parliaments which was always important to Fianna Fáil.

One of the issues that would later cause controversy in the Lisbon Treaty was the position of president of the European Council. Ireland had not initially sought this provision, but after much negotiating, Ireland began to see that it could be of benefit and, after the negotiation of certain changes, Cowen and the government were happy: 'Some smaller countries were among the early advocates of a long-term president of the European Council, for example. We did not seek the creation of this post, but we now think it is defined in a way that protects the interests of the Commission and will ensure that its holder is more chairman than chief. We hope the post will, as its supporters argue, bring more coherence and a longer-term perspective to the work of the European Council. Similarly, a small number of member states believe that a restricted Commission is more likely to be collegiate and effective than one in which every member state is represented. The countervailing and increasingly supported argument – that a Commission drawn from the widest possible range of member states is more likely to be aware of and responsive to concerns on the ground and thus more legitimate – is also very strong.

'The essence of the convention compromise, that all member states should be represented at all times, but with a smaller number of voting commissioners appointed on the basis of strictly equal rotation, is broadly acceptable to us as it builds on what was agreed at Nice. Aspects of the arrangement need to be teased out, however. For example, what would be the precise roles of the voting and non-voting commissioners? On the other hand, many countries are arguing strongly for one voting commissioner per member state. If this can be achieved on terms which protect the genuine equality of all commissioners and all member states, as was agreed at Nice, we would very much welcome it. At the end of this process, we want an effective Commission which embraces genuine equality and serves and reflects the interests of all member states, big and small.

'The question of how a qualified majority is defined is shaping up to be crucial at the intergovernmental conference. We recognise that the proposed new dual majority system would be simpler to understand and more efficient in terms of decision making. We would be quite happy to stick with the more complex Nice formula, but are prepared to accept the convention's proposal. Our influence will always depend more on our capacity to network and on the effectiveness of our arguments than on any arithmetical formula. In practice, votes are rare.'

Cowen's contribution leaves little room for doubt about the depth of thinking that was behind these negotiations or the level of difficulty against which they were set. By 23 October following another European Council meeting in Brussels, Cowen still had high hopes that an agreement could be reached in Rome: 'Ireland supports the ambition of the Italian presidency to complete negotiations by the end of the year. We will of course be prepared to take over and advance any work that may fall to us from January onwards.'

However, the range of issues outstanding suggested that a tough task was ahead and agreement in Rome was an ambitious target: 'The future composition of the Commission was a main topic of discussion. It is clear that there is a range of views on this matter. Ireland and a number of other countries indicated general satisfaction with the European convention outcome, subject to some clarification. Ireland would welcome a move to one commissioner per member state if this can be achieved on the basis of strict equality. Several participants, in particular the accession countries, supported one commissioner per member state. Five of the larger member states and the Benelux countries indicated support for the convention outcome. The retention of guaranteed equality in the appointment of the Commission remains of fundamental importance to Ireland and several other smaller states.

'It is now generally accepted that a post of European Council president will be created. The issue is how the role will be defined and how the individual appointed to the post will make it work in practice. Ireland believes that the current text is broadly balanced. There is also more work to be done on how a presidency will be organised in the future in the various council formations, with significant support for team presidencies.

'The definition of qualified majority voting remains a difficult issue. At the intergovernmental conference the known positions of those seeking to change the convention outcome were reiterated. Ireland's point of view is that we would be happy to keep to the arrangements agreed at Nice, but we can also support the convention outcome. The minimum number of seats allocated in the European Parliament is an issue of particular concern to the smallest members of the intergovernmental conference and Ireland is sympathetic to their concerns.'

Later Cowen focused on the ongoing everyday work that was taking place, giving us an insight into why most Irish political parties believe Europe is so vital to our interests: 'On the economy, the European Council noted that after a period of some uncertainty, there are some positive signals emerging in Europe. An improvement in the international economic environment, low levels of inflation, stabilised oil prices and better conditions in the financial markets have been key factors behind a pick-up in economic activity. However, the situation remains fragile and in this context economic policies should continue to be aimed at job creation and sustainable growth and at enhancing economic and social cohesion. The European Council focused, in particular, on ways of stimulating growth by increasing investment in transport, energy and telecommunications networks and by underlining the need for further structural reform. I welcome its focus on re-launching the European economy. Action to boost growth will create more job opportunities and bring greater prosperity to the people of Europe. I also welcome, in this regard, the European Council's endorsement of the principles of the growth initiative which seeks to increase investment by improving the mechanisms for financing growth-related projects. This initiative aims to exploit the resources of the European Investment Bank more effectively, both to increase the funding available for growth-related projects and to leverage greater private funding of infrastructure.

'The European Council recognises that building modern, efficient transport infrastructures is critical to boosting growth and maximising the potential of the internal market. It recommended, in this regard, that particular attention should be given to proposals on priority projects for trans-European transport networks. In this context the Council suggested that the possibility of a higher rate of community co-financing of such networks might be explored.

'The European Council also considers that the completion of an integrated market for electricity and gas in an enlarged Europe would give a vital impetus to growth through ensuring security of supply and promoting competitiveness. Equally, it views the development of telecommunications networks as being of key importance in promoting growth and, in this regard, considered the availability and promotion of a broadband network to be particularly necessary for the European knowledge-based economy. Viewing innovation, research and development and investment in human capital as crucial to Europe's growth potential, it reaffirmed the importance of action to mobilise investment and put the right regulatory conditions in place.

'The European Council's focus on growth was complemented by its corresponding recognition of the importance of building a more competitive European economy. It reiterated the need to eliminate remaining barriers to the completion of the internal market, particularly in the area of services, which now account for 70 per cent of the growth in the EU economy and in job opportunities ... The

European Council reiterated that action to stimulate growth and boost competitiveness needed to be accompanied by effective social policies and a continuing focus on job creation. It made particular reference, in this regard, to the demographic challenge currently faced by the European Union and the need to secure the long-term sustainability of pension systems. While the formulation of policy on pensions remains the responsibility of member states, the European Council considered that certain benefits could accrue from reinforcing open co-ordination in this area.'

In November, Romano Prodi, President of the Commission, said a rejection of a future treaty could call into question Ireland's membership of the EU. John Gormley was quick to put the question to Cowen. Gormley asked him if a rejection of the EU constitution by Irish voters in a future referendum would endanger Ireland's membership of the EU as stated by Romano Prodi. Cowen replied: 'The proposed arrangements for the ratification of the new EU draft constitutional treaty are quite clear. They involve no change from the existing arrangements. When unanimous agreement has been achieved among governments at the intergovernmental conference, the treaty must be ratified by all member states in accordance with their respective constitutional requirements. Nobody has seriously challenged this requirement at the conference. Ireland will not support an alternative approach … It is obvious that political difficulties will arise if one or more member states experiences difficulty in ratifying the treaty. In such circumstances, all member states will have to come together to see what can be done.'

Cowen would later stick to the line of members coming together 'to see what can be done'. Later under further questioning it would appear that Cowen is tiring of Gormley's position on neutrality – no matter how many replies Cowen gives on the issue: 'An inability to listen to answers is part of Deputy Gormley's problem. The deputy also raised certain defence issues. It is important to point out that we have provided the safeguard clause since Maastricht. We negotiated the clause at Maastricht, as it was clear that there are different defence and security policy traditions in the European Union. The community method involves accommodating those traditions. Deputy Gormley has always failed to acknowledge that successive governments have been involved in successful negotiations. When a defence working group, of which Deputy Gormley is a member, produced a proposal which left me with very little room to manoeuvre, I was capable of negotiating Ireland's position and ensuring that its tradition is respected. The safeguard clause ensures that there is no automaticity involved in such a mutual defence clause, as far as Ireland is concerned. The whole purpose of our negotiating strategy is to achieve that. It is far better to acknowledge that something has been achieved, rather than denying it.'

As fate would have it, the range of difficulties proved too large for a final agreement to be reached in Rome. There was widespread disappointment in Europe as a result of this failure. The incoming Irish presidency would now have a huge task in getting everyone around the table again. But Cowen, in his report to the Dáil on 16 December, appeared upbeat about the prospects, perhaps having seen worse setbacks in Northern Ireland at the time: 'We cannot make any assumptions. We have an incomplete set of negotiations. There was general recognition at the intergovernmental conference's final meeting on Saturday that substantial progress had been made under the Italian presidency. However, people will not sign off on all or part of the treaty until we have a complete negotiated settlement.

'Everyone recognises the work done and the genuine efforts made. It is more the rule than the exception that intergovernmental conferences are not completed in the presidencies in which they begin. We have had an intensive ten weeks of negotiations in the intergovernmental conference, which followed more than sixteen months of consideration by the convention. Unfortunately, it was not possible to complete the negotiations. However, it is important to inform the House that there was no sense of recrimination or failure.'

While Cowen was upbeat, he was still sticking to the same approach that we saw in relation to Northern Ireland, namely just stating the case as it was and dealing with matters in hand with no presumptions about the future and no inbuilt desire to hurry a decision or achieve a specific target, other than to facilitate and promote agreement to the best of his ability.

During Ireland's presidency the negotiations would intensify. On 19 May 2004 the issue of Commission numbers, a hangover from Nice, and the new position of president of the Council were causing concern: 'I do not view the proposed creation under the constitutional treaty of the position of permanent president of the European Council in the context of either the institutional balance between large and small member states or of a movement towards intergovernmentalism. The provisions on the president of the European Council as they developed in the convention debate essentially reproduce the functions of the current rotating president. The role of the European Council president will be to chair the European Council and drive forward its work, to prepare the work of the European Council in co-operation with the president of the Commission and on the basis of the work of the general affairs council, to facilitate consensus and cohesion within the European Council and to present a report to the European Parliament … A broad consensus was reached on the proposals at the convention. Among the original supporters of the idea were Sweden and Denmark, two smaller member states that had recently held the presidency. While the government was not among those advocating this proposal, it recognised from an early point that as the Union continued to enlarge and develop, some change was both necessary and desirable. In the government's opinion the new provisions as finally drafted do not cut across the role of the Commission nor undermine the position of smaller member states and they are acceptable on that basis. No participant in the intergovernmental conference opposes them …

'The [Irish] presidency tabled for discussion this week a paper on the future composition of the Commission. It builds on its report to the March European Council and the taoiseach's subsequent speech to the European Parliament. The presidency's strong view is that any proposals on the Commission must meet the twin needs of efficiency and legitimacy. The discussion paper suggests these twin needs might best be met by maintaining one commissioner per member state until 2014, whereupon a move would be made to a smaller Commission of a pre-determined size, composed on the basis of equal rotation among the member states.'

Cowen saw little threat in the creation of the new position of president of the Council, probably because concessions had been already achieved in relation to this role by Ireland and other states. The Commission proposals were a different matter and Ireland was trying to steer a course that would protect its interests and receive support. According to Cowen they were having success in relation to this. It is important to note, however, that once negotiations were opened the possibility of a worse outcome for Ireland and other countries was always a threat. Clearly it took quite a bit of convincing to ensure that the principles achieved under Nice were still adhered to.

Cowen later outlined the role, function and approach of the Irish presidency to the negotiations: 'The presidency is making available on the world-wide web all its documentation pertaining to those issues where a broad consensus has existed and pertaining to proposals for the orientation-type debates that are taking place. The aim is to inform the presidency and inform everyone of the range of views that exist. This means when the presidency puts forward a proposal, people will have a clear understanding of why the presidency is proceeding in a certain way in an effort to achieve full consensus. In reply to the first part of the deputy's [G. Mitchell] question, those issues will be discussed in plenary session of the IGC [intergovernmental conference] next Monday.

'The last thing Ireland or any small country wishes is the notion of gridlock in decision-making. We need decisions at European level. The integration of the Irish economy into the wider European economy has been the greatest economic development in this country since independence.'

There was still no guarantee that a positive outcome could be reached. On 19 May Cowen outlined the considerable outstanding difficulties: 'The House will be aware that one of the main outstanding issues at the intergovernmental conference relates to the definition of qualified majority voting. We have made clear our view that only solutions based on the principle of double majority are likely to command agreement. Within that framework, and in response to the sensitivities of some member states, we can consider adjustments, including to the member state and population thresholds and to arrangements for transition from the current system. I am aware of media reports setting out possible solutions to this question, and I also am aware that President Giscard d'Estaing has suggested a certain approach. It will ultimately be for us as presidency to table our own proposals. We have not yet done so, and are continuing to consult with partners.

'Two working papers were circulated by the presidency in advance of this week's meeting of the IGC. The first contained those proposed texts which the presidency felt did not require further discussion by ministers at this time. The second contained three areas for discussion by ministers: first, a small number of issues previously discussed by officials, such as the budget, common commercial policy and presidency of the council of ministers, on which we tabled revised proposals; second, the overall QMV/unanimity balance, where the presidency did not put forward new texts but wished to have a collective discussion before moving on to make its own proposals in due course; and, third, on the Commission, where the presidency put forward new texts on some secondary issues and a discussion paper on Commission composition.

'Member states gave a broad welcome to our two papers, and I believe that significant progress was made. While nothing is agreed until everything is agreed, we have, I believe, succeeded in reducing the number of outstanding issues and clarifying the questions which remain to be resolved.'

Once again we can see the level of consideration that was being given by politicians from all countries to the detail of the negotiations. There was no question of Ireland being sidelined; as it held the presidency, it dictated the agenda and was the most central figure. Many plaudits were paid to Ireland's approach and ability to build consensus. Finally, agreement was reached on an EU constitution. It was an outstanding achievement for the Irish presidency and a credit to Irish politicians and to the Irish civil service. For Bertie Ahern it would be a crowning achievement at EU level, but Brian Cowen had played an integral role. On 24 June Cowen outlined the latest position to the Dáil: 'As the House will be aware, the intergovernmental conference reached an agreement on the constitutional treaty. This is both a remarkable achievement for the Irish presidency and a fundamental advance for the European Union. Following intensive work both in plenary session and in bilateral contacts, we were able to put forward final compromise proposals on the outstanding issues which met the specific concerns of all member states and were thus the subject of consensus. Heads of state and government also held an exchange of views on the appointment of the next president of the European Commission. It is envisaged that a decision on this matter will be taken shortly.

'The European Council itself agreed conclusions on a range of important issues, including justice and home affairs, and the fight against terrorism; enlargement; financial perspectives; economic and social issues, employment and environment; the Northern Ireland-related peace funds and external relations issues.'

Ruairi Quinn of the Labour Party was among the first to offer his congratulations: 'I congratulate the minister and his colleagues on the extraordinary achievement in getting the constitution agreed. It is a tribute to successive Irish presidencies and the personnel in Iveagh House and elsewhere. However, it would not have happened without the political input of the minister and his colleagues and they deserve, unashamedly and unreservedly, our congratulations.'

While Ireland basked in the plaudits it was not difficult to see where the opposition in any future referendum would come from. On 30 June Cowen was on the offensive against Sinn Féin: 'I have heard Sinn Féin suggest we should have a Europe of equals with one vote each in the European Council. It calls that equality. So Luxembourg with 400,000 people and Germany with eighty million people should both have one vote and it calls that equality. That would not be equality. It is not just about a union of states but also a union of citizens. The purpose of the new decision-making process is to reflect the need for 55 per cent of the states and 65 per cent of the citizens to agree. That is a weighting system that respects states and citizens …

'I have no problem in discussing with those with a different political perspective from me on the basis of the facts, but not on the basis of some sphinx that is generating hot air that has no relevance to the treaty. I am not dismissive of people in general. However, I am dismissive of people who accuse me of arrogance. What in the treaty indicates that such a big conspiracy took place? It has been suggested here that we have not defended our national interests. Of course we defended out national interests. On every issue on which we had concerns, we won. We won on tax, defence and security, and the institutions, where our concerns have been respected.'

The idea of conspiracy theories and arguments not central to the treaty itself, but based rather on some future direction of Europe, was clearly something Cowen had little time for. Such a line of argument irked him and one already feels that his patience in such arguments was wearing thin. In the final analysis the EU constitution was put to referendum in a number of countries, and the reaction of the general public was mixed: France and Holland voted 'No'. Spain and Belgium voted 'Yes'. For many this issue was seen as far too complex. Politicians argued that the idea of a written constitution would not sit well with countries who did not already have one. Others argued that it was simply too complex and all-encompassing to expect people to take three weeks of a campaign to make up their minds and assess something that had taken experts in the field years to negotiate. The solution was simple enough; the EU constitution was withdrawn but all the measures were simply repackaged as a treaty. This meant that governments could pass the treaty in all countries except one – Ireland. The Lisbon Treaty was heavily defeated in a vote as we will see later. However, after all the years of negotiation by the Irish delegations, after all the questions and debate tabled by the opposition in the Dáil, after all the ups and downs of a tough negotiating process, the Irish public still expressed a lack of knowledge about the treaty. It is ironic that it was a treaty in which the democratically elected Irish government had played a central role in negotiating and finalising. It is unlikely that Ireland will be in such a prominent position for future negotiations and finalising of treaties. It is therefore ironic that while an agreement brokered by the Irish government brought European countries together, a vote on the same agreement by the Irish people threatened to push them apart.

In any event Fianna Fáil had a poor local and European election in 2004. A cabinet reshuffle took place. Cowen was again promoted, this time to minister of finance. Cowen left a solid record in foreign affairs, even if it was controversial. He could be very proud of the role he played in Northern Ireland. He was exemplary in relation to the Security Council and the reaction to 9/11 and Afghanistan, always focusing on the humanitarian needs. However, in the blaze of confusion that was the Iraq conflict, he did suffer some damage to his reputation upon the failure to find weapons of mass destruction and his defence of the use of Shannon airport. People would continue to have grave misgivings on this issue. But Cowen could at least claim he was not alone in his thinking and could rightly argue that it would have been difficult to take another approach, even if it seemed to compromise strict principles. He proved himself a tough and relentless negotiator at European level and could arguably claim to have secured significant protections for Ireland in the new Europe. The loss of the first Nice referendum was a black mark against him, however, as was perhaps an assumption during the negotiations on the constitution/Lisbon Treaty that large amounts of the electorate were actually taking heed of what was going on.

ECONOMICS AND PUBLIC FINANCES

There are certain things all politicians hope for when they start on their careers: to get a nomination, to get elected, to become a minister, and, particularly for Fianna Fáil politicians, to become minister for finance. This is because by now it is seen as a right of passage before the honour of becoming taoiseach can be conferred upon you.

We can be in no doubt that the position of finance minister was a post Cowen wanted and would have been thrilled to get. He had always had a healthy interest in the economy since his earliest days in the chamber.

From the opposition benches on 28 January 1997, Cowen criticised Fine Gael for failing to do anything with regard to the top rate of tax: 'The top rate of tax should be reduced since it applies at a base of £13,200. For many people earning that amount of money, the failure of that party – which claims to be more in favour of private enterprise and the productive sector of the economy than the social services sector – to achieve a reduction in the top rate of income tax is ample testimony to its impotence in conducting negotiations in the lead-up to the budget.'

Later Cowen went on to outline why he believed the electorate would not thank the Rainbow Coalition: 'What people recognise is that they may be better off by £4 to £6 per week. In these buoyant economic times that is not regarded by taxpayers as a particularly munificent gesture.'

Cowen also saw excessive public expenditure as a problem for the Rainbow Coalition: 'Public expenditure increases are too high. Over the past three years it had a real opportunity to get a better mix between increased public expenditure and tax deductions which would make its electoral position better than it is now. Its failure to do anything about it in the 1996 budget and its preparedness to front load everything into this budget will be seen for the cynical political exercise it is. One particular statistic bears that out – £393 million of the £900 million in tax deductions or 44 per cent of the commitments given in Partnership 2000 is front loaded into this year's budget. This is evidence that political imperatives have coloured the government's thinking and economic logic in the presentation of this budget.'

As we will see, however, he would later find that cutting public expenditure is never an easy exercise; but of course by that stage Fine Gael would be making the accusations from opposition. That is the one benefit of opposition, it's easy to criticise. The onus of implementation is much more difficult.

Cowen did go on to articulate some principles that he would apply in time, however. He also displayed some particular allegiances to certain theories, most notably that of the fact that there is 'nothing for nothing': 'When Fianna Fáil returned to office in 1987 there was a need to make swingeing cuts. Our position was so difficult economically that there were serious dislocations in the provision of services which caused great hardship. These were necessary in the interest of trying to return public finances to some state of order. An increase in the provision of public services is seen as an end in itself with no thinking as to how they are provided. Are there other ways in which they can be provided? Are there ways and means by which we can control the level of public expenditure and provide more money in people's pockets and give them the choice as to what services they wish to pay for or to have?

'Fine Gael has failed to get back to a culture where there is nothing for nothing in the running of the economy. We have had the abolition of this and that to service every narrow political constituency, whether it be the 300 people who attend the Democratic Left annual convention or the few Labour Party activists who still have some ideological hang-ups about the provision of local services. They will be paid for some other way and people will have charges imposed on them in other respects because there is nothing for nothing. That has been a great step backwards under this administration.'

While in opposition he also showed a significant commitment to the idea of reducing the national debt: 'The only way we will make a significant impact on tax reform, to get more people back to work and more money in workers' pockets, is to tackle our debt. Half our income tax revenue, some £2.56 billion, goes towards the interest on our accumulated debt. It is an indictment of successive governments that the national debt has gone from £1 billion in 1973 to £30 billion now and the government is projecting it will be £32 billion by the end of 1999. Is it beyond the means of this House to broadly agree to not increase our debt above a certain level and to work within those constraints? We would have a much more intelligent debate about the management and administration of the country if we were prepared to do that.

'Until we reduce the interest bill we will not be able to provide for real sustainable increases in public services and tax reduction. The best way to maintain public services at the level to which we all aspire and require for our constituents is to do something about the interest bill.'

In April 1997 we find him in particularly critical mode of government spending and of the danger to the economy. He gave a few hostages to fortune at this point: 'One would think it would be beyond the ability of this incompetent group to come up with as many ideas for spending taxpayers' money and seeking to bribe the public with their money. Not only are they doing that, but they continue to mortgage the future. The prospect of real tax reform and tax relief for workers in this economy is being put at risk because of the large increase in the budget base, which is not sustainable in the long term. We saw in yesterday's *Financial Times* that even if our economic growth is reduced by 1 per cent between now and 1999 in terms of the projections built into the three multi-annual budget projections brought forward by the minister for finance, we may not meet the Maastricht criteria of staying within the 3 per cent current budget deficit. That is criminal. That is the result of three parties, which one would have thought had very little in common, coming together. Fine Gael is happy to be a partner in this government because it does not have a distinct policy. The taoiseach has said government policy is Fine Gael policy, so they make it up as they go along.'

But he did make two further points which he can claim to have delivered on: 'All this clearly dictates that nothing is being done for the small business sector in this finance bill. Fianna Fáil has set out in its policy document "Rewarding the Risk-takers" the many basic, practical steps which could be taken to improve that dynamic sector of the economy.'

Small business and risk-takers certainly did benefit under later governments. Cowen also laid out a firm belief in cutting taxes. Although it sometimes attracted criticism it was another fact that he could claim to have delivered on: 'This is supposed to be an administration which has some semblance of affinity to workers. The less imperialist elements of Democratic Left, the Labour Party and Fine Gael would claim to have some recognition of what a worker looks like, but the workers have been sold down the river because of the excessive public spending in which this government has engaged. Tax reform has been delayed and denied and we must wait for a change of administration and a Fianna Fáil-led government to ensure workers get their deserved reward for bringing about the economic progress we have seen in recent years.'

However, as I mentioned earlier, it is one thing to attack from opposition, it is quite another to deliver in government. There were certain issues that arose at times which would define Cowen's beliefs with regard to the economy. One of these was social partnership. Cowen was a staunch believer in and protector of social partnership. In a debate on the issue in 1999 he leaves us in no doubt that it is something he believed transformed the country and attacks others for not believing in it at its introduction: 'I am delighted to support the government motion on social partnership. It is interesting, and it would be amusing if it was not so serious, to be lectured on social partnership by Fine Gael which, in that famous coalition government with the Labour Party between 1982-87, left everyone outside the door and told us all that the great guru, Garret, would sort it all out, but left us on the brink of bankruptcy. It galls Fine Gael that the 1987 administration … showed that the political capacity to deal with the magnitude of the problems facing the country could only be taken on board by a party with the political leverage throughout social partnership to build a consensus which was totally absent as we headed into that administration. Were it not for the enlightened leadership of a now-discarded leader of Fianna Fáil, that partnership would have met with limited success, but that is what happens to prophets.'

Mr J. O'Keeffe: 'The deputy should tell us about his leader at the time.'

Mr Cowen: 'The leader of Fianna Fáil at that time was the author of social partnership with the social partners.'

Mr J. O'Keeffe: 'His legacy in the 1980s was a disgrace.'

Mr Cowen: 'We are here to discuss social partnership and it is sometimes important to acknowledge the contribution people make, even if it is not fashionable to do so. I do so unreservedly. In the run up to negotiations for the renewal of social partnership agreements, difficulties often arose because leverage was being sought by all parties to get their priorities included in the deal. When Partnership 2000 was being negotiated, Democratic Left tabled a motion lamenting the imminent collapse of discussions and calling on the Labour Party, of which they are now eminent members, to pull back on the 1 per cent levy imposed and claiming they wanted social welfare cuts changed before there could be any discussions …

'We have achieved unprecedented success in economic and social terms. I also acknowledge the vision and leadership shown by the trade union movement as a corporate entity. It has discarded the old adversarial ways which sought to restrict the influence of labour to wages and conditions. In so doing, it has recognised the social and economic advantage for its membership and their families, and for those political constituencies it seeks to represent – the unemployed and socially excluded – have been achieved under successive social partnership agreements under successive administrations.'

But it was on 29 September 2004 when he was announced as minister for finance that his financial views finally became the most important ones in the country. On his first day Cowen was quick to establish that there would be no changes to corporation tax: 'I want to nail the lie in this debate. People must come up with better ideas. The idea that increasing the tax rates will result in more money from the corporation sector is denied by the facts. In terms of taxation on labour, in 1996 the percentage tax take under the Rainbow Coalition was 36.6 per cent. The figures available to me at short notice indicate it stood at 30.9 per cent in 2002. What does this confirm? It confirms that the economic model we should be discussing is whether we want to go back to a failed policy of high taxation rates, high corporation tax rates and fewer jobs or whether we accept the current taxation system.'

So Cowen certainly had his core beliefs. Various issues would affect his term, though in October 2004 we see the first of these, as Fine Gael, who had long been critics of benchmarking due to what they saw as poor value for private sector taxpayers, raised the issue of the next round of awards.

In answer to a question by Richard Bruton on whether he planned to institute changes in the benchmarking exercise proposed for assessing increases in public pay, Cowen replied: 'In the public service pay agreement under *Sustaining Progress*, the parties committed to engage in consultation on the terms of reference and *modus operandi* and the establishment and timescale of further benchmarking exercise. … The parties agreed to review the operation of the first benchmarking exercise and consider ways in which, having regard to the experience gained, the process can be improved and streamlined. The parties also stated that the body should seek to ensure the optimum level of transparency consistent with the efficient and effective operation of the benchmarking process …

'The body should seek to ensure the optimum level of transparency consistent with the efficient and effective operation of the bench-marking process. As it is independent, how the body reflects this in its report is a matter for itself. In the last exercise, the body felt constrained in the amount of information it could provide due to assurances of confidentiality it gave when researching the data underlying its examination. In any event, to avoid endless debate and nit-picking in the context of an exercise of this type, all information cannot be released. Some degree of selectivity must enter into the matter … The establishment in *Sustaining Progress* of monitoring of real change by independent performance verification groups was a significant departure. For the first time, real change and modernisation have been linked to pay increases. It is a welcome development. I will seek to ensure in future that under *Sustaining Progress* all pay increases, whether general round or benchmarking, will be tied to an ongoing programme of public service modernisation. Such modernisation is a far better criterion than the previous relativity considerations.'

Benchmarking was a thorny issue. It is obvious that Cowen certainly believed in it as an approach to dealing with public sector pay. But reforms of the system were clearly necessary. Some contested that the pay awards to the public service were excessive, others that it did not put enough onus on reforms and performance, and others that it benchmarked public sector jobs against equivalents in the private sector and could recommend pay increases on this basis, but the private sector is controlled by the market and there was no provision for the public sector to take pay cuts if private sector salaries fell. For Cowen even at this early stage it would appear that he was happy that there was an independent body to decide such issues and his respect for the public sector prevented him from proposing any sweeping changes to the system.

On 14 October Cowen faced questions on the upcoming budget. Richard Bruton in particular had some serious issues to raise: 'Does the minister agree with me that much of the buoyancy in tax receipts for the past two years has arisen from income tax largely on the backs of contributions made by PAYE workers for whom tax bands and tax credits have been frozen? As a consequence, these workers are looking to the minister for tax justice in the forthcoming budget.'

It is safe to assume from this question that in 2004 Fine Gael was clearly of the belief that taxes needed to be cut. Cowen outlined measures already taken and laid out his stall: 'The role of this government will be to ensure that those on low pay receive the best benefits. I will not accept the contention that this government has not been according tax justice to more taxpayers. Not alone has it done so, it has reduced rates. The net tax take from those on the average industrial wage, including PAYE, PRSI and the health levy, has been reduced by 10 per cent from 27 per cent under the Rainbow Coalition to 17 per cent under this administration.'

Cowen also faced questions about the most serious issue facing him at the time – value for money. While the government was undoubtedly spending huge amounts, there were still reports of waste and a failure to deliver improvements commensurate with the level of investment: 'While much has been achieved as a result of the increased investment by government, I accept that there have been issues in regard to value for money and cost overruns on major capital projects raised by, among others, the ESRI [Economic and Social Research Institute] in the mid-term evaluation of the National Development Plan.

'The onus is on departments and implementing agencies to appraise and manage properly capital projects and programmes under their aegis. My department's capital appraisal guidelines provide a framework for this. The government has taken a number of initiatives which are designed to secure better value from public expenditure and to improve project appraisal and evaluation. The new rolling five-year multi-annual capital envelopes announced in last year's budget will enable departments to plan, implement and manage their capital programmes and projects more effectively and efficiently and to secure better value for money from their capital expenditure ... departments are required to comply with the capital appraisal guidelines of my department in all cases, to report regularly to their management advisory committee on the evaluation of capital projects prior to approval and to report progress on the management of capital programmes and projects. Departments are also required to put in place appropriate contractual arrangements for all significant grants of public funding to private companies and individuals or community groups to protect the state's interest in the asset created by the funding.

'My department is in the process of updating and revising its 1994 guidelines for the appraisal and management of capital expenditure.

Revised draft guidelines have been circulated to line departments for their comments and I envisage that the revised guidelines will be published before the end of this year.'

Cowen's revision of the capital appraisal guidelines would have a significant impact upon government spending. As we will see, he instituted many reforms in this area. However, it often took far too long for the effects of such measures to be felt. Cowen displayed an understanding of problems and an appreciation of how to deal with them in the long term; however, he rarely displayed any willingness to introduce short-term or radical measures. His approach was ponderous and cautious, and generally aimed at the longer term.

On 23 November the issue of value for money is still on the agenda. Richard Bruton asked Cowen if he was satisfied that the extra tax collected in the past seven years was delivering value for money through the spending increases they were used to finance. Cowen replied: 'The government has more than doubled total spending on public services between 1997 and 2004 to over €41 billion. As provided for in the Abridged Estimates Volume published last week, the government will add a further €2.5 billion to this in 2005 on a pre-budget basis to fund day-to-day spending on public services. Priority has been given to expenditure on social welfare, health, education and investment. Gross current spending on health has increased by 176 per cent to €9.6 billion in 2004, spending on social welfare has increased by 97 per cent to €11.3 billion while expenditure on education has increased by 103 per cent to €6.1 billion. Capital spending to address the country's infrastructural deficit has increased by 178 per cent. The general government debt ratio has decreased from 65 per cent of gross domestic product, GDP, in 1997 to an expected ratio of less than 32 per cent by the end of this year. In addition almost €10.5 billion has been set aside for long-term pension and social security costs by investing in the National Pensions Reserve Fund.'

There were of course other issues, some of which might not have a major impact on finances, but certainly had popular support. One such issue was the number of wealthy individuals who seemed to pay little or no tax: 'There has been much comment in recent weeks on these figures and the fact that a very small number of high earners have managed to pay little or no tax through the use of tax incentives. Therefore, I take this opportunity to put the figures in their correct context. Of the 270 PAYE income earners on €500,000 or more per annum, 263 were liable to tax at the 42 per cent rate, one was liable at the 20 per cent rate and nine had a nil net income tax liability. Of the 590 self-employed income earners on €500,000 or more per annum, 552 were liable to tax at the 42 per cent rate, six were liable at the 20 per cent tax rate, and 32 had a nil net income tax liability …

'It is worth noting that the ten most costly reliefs cover items such as pension contributions, stamp duty and capital gains tax exemptions on one's home, mortgage interest relief, non-taxation of child benefit, medical insurance relief and SSIAs. These reliefs are widely used by all classes of society and the cost pertaining thereto amounts to more than €5 billion. They are not tax reliefs that should be characterised or referred to as reliefs for the rich.'

The housing market was another area of crucial importance to the Irish economy and Cowen took questions on this also. Paul McGrath asked Cowen if he was satisfied with the tax treatment of the housing sector. Cowen replied: 'Government policy in the housing market has focused, among other things, on improving supply, assisting home ownership particularly for first-time buyers, facilitating the expansion of the private rented sector and promoting the regeneration of certain areas. In this context, a range of tax incentives exist in regard to the housing market in the case of first-time buyers and other owner-occupiers, for tenants and investors. I can detail these for the deputy if he desires.

'The years 2002 and 2003 were the eighth and ninth successive years of record housing output with 57,695 and 68,819 completions, respectively. This positive trend in supply has continued into 2004, with statistics for the six months to June showing that overall house completions at 35,957 were up 21.4 per cent on the same period last year. The rate of house building is now more than double that in 1996. We have had some success in our tax policy but we do not claim all the credit.

'Like all other goods and services, the state finds it necessary to raise taxes from this area. However, there has been some badly informed commentary recently in regard to the tax take from new homes. Figures in excess of 40 per cent have been attributed to the amount the government raises in tax from each new home. However, this figure is wrong. The cost of a new home that accrues directly to the exchequer through taxation is more like 28 per cent, based on both Dublin and national prices. This is broadly in line with the tax take on the overall economy.

'The housing market is a complex and dynamic one and demands continuous monitoring and adjustment to address changing circumstances.'

On 25 November Cowen discussed the estimates for the public services in the Dáil. The economy was in a healthy state: 'I am acutely conscious that what we are talking about today is the expenditure of €43.5 billion of taxpayers' money. The individuals and businesses that pay the taxes to make this level of expenditure possible require that the government takes account of their priorities in deciding on how the resources are allocated ...

'Taxpayers also rightly expect that they will get value for money for the expenditure of their taxes ... there has been impressive improvement in public services in recent years and the 2005 estimates will build on this development. I am, however, determined that departments and offices will intensify their efforts to ensure the best possible value for money from the very significant funds being provided in the estimates …

'As a result of the international downturn that began in 2001, the government had to keep a tight rein on public spending in recent years. We have reduced the gap between revenue and public spending growth and managed to consolidate our fiscal position. Managing public spending growth in line with the growth in resources and in a manner sustainable in the medium term remains essential. The government intends continuing with this general approach so as not to undermine the hard work of recent years, which ensured that we are now better placed than most to take advantage of the current international economic upturn.'

The government had reigned-in public spending to a certain extent. Considering the problems that the economy would run into four years later, the controls might have been better, but it was clear that the government trod a fine line between delivering the level of services the public demanded and the threat of causing a shock to the economy by drastically cutting spending in the absence of a solid argument proving the need for such measures.

Cowen did outline the possible threats, but the world and domestic outlook was increasingly positive: 'While the world economic outlook is now improving and we are experiencing an economic upturn, our economy will not return to the very high growth rates we saw in the period up to 2001. The consensus among most commentators is that economic growth in 2004 will be about 5 per cent. This is a continuation of last year's positive trend. There are, however, a number of risks to our economic performance next year. These include oil prices, the dollar and a possible weakening of the US economy. A combination of these events could lead to a slow-down in domestic economic activity. However, despite these risks I would say that the economic prospects for 2005 and beyond facing into my first budget as minister for finance are fairly positive.'

Cowen made the case for prudence based on the experience of 2002. He clearly believed that spending had to be monitored to allow for a downturn. He was to take the government far more in the direction of the social agenda and equality than had been the case up to now. ICT in schools was to receive a boost in the estimates: 'In addition to the promotion of the knowledge society the estimates provide significant additional funding for research at third level. In this context, the roll-out of broadband ICT facilities in our schools is also a key component of the government's strategy. A total of €145 million, current and capital funding, has been invested in the schools ICT programme since 1998. Next year will see an increase of 28 per cent in current funding for this programme.'

Child benefit was also identified as a key target of government: 'The provision of child benefit expenditure, which has been identified as a key mechanism for reducing consistent poverty in Ireland has been supported hugely by the government. Expenditure on child benefit has increased from under €500 million in 1996 to a pre-budget allocation of €1.8 billion this year.'

But with the benefit of hindsight there was a clear problem for government with regard to the cost of the public service: 'The gross provision for exchequer-funded public service pay and pensions is €15.3 billion, an increase of €1 billion or 7 per cent on 2004. The increase makes full provision for the carry-over of the first phase of *Sustaining Progress*, the payment of the final tranche of benchmarking and the increases due in 2005 under the mid-term review of *Sustaining Progress*.

'In Budget 2003, in order to control public service numbers, the government decided to cap numbers at the existing authorised level and to reduce numbers by 5,000 by the end of 2005. As part of our commitment to address priority areas of service we subsequently agreed some adjustments to the figures for health, education and the garda síochána in respect of front-line staff. Outside the health and education sectors, the numbers serving in 2004 indicate that the 2004 targets for a reduction in public service numbers will be met.'

It is also clear that while the position with regard to health, education and the gardaí was understandable, these are also the three biggest areas of staff expenditure. Any plan to cut the cost of the public service pay bill would always be a rearguard action in the absence of any cuts in these sectors which were the major drivers.

Richard Bruton had the job of attacking the estimates. At this stage his main concern was not market volatility, overspending in the public sector, or overspending generally, but the value for money element. Fine Gael did not object to the money the government was spending on services, but did object to potential waste: 'Let us not underestimate the importance of this challenge. Ireland is a small open economy dependent on foreign investment and international trade. A recent assessment of our public capital infrastructure ranked us second last of twelve countries studied. In critical areas vital to competitiveness we lag behind. We are fifteenth of fifteen in respect of ports; eleventh of twelve in respect of motorways; eighth of eight in respect of speed of delivery in the capital city; fourteenth of fifteen in respect of broadband access; fifteenth of sixteen in respect of energy infrastructure and eleventh of fifteen in respect of investment in telecommunications. We expect that we will continue to attract strong foreign direct investment and build a strong indigenous sector but such infrastructure cannot support that.'

Cowen could reasonably argue that he did deliver reform in regard to value for money issues over the course of his term. But it was certainly clear that in the winter of 2004 there was little talk of recessions or their possibility. Value for money was a concern, but in terms of the overall amount of money being spent this was a fixable problem.

That was the environment in which Cowen introduced his first budget. His view of the budget was outlined as follows: 'This is a budget for the people as a whole. It is a budget that will protect and increase jobs in a more competitive business environment; build up and modernise our economy through major capital programmes; distribute the fruits of growth to all our people through better services and a fairer sharing of resources; and redouble our efforts to help those most in need, particularly those with disabilities.

'Good government and sound policies created these opportunities and good government will ensure we succeed in addressing the needs of all our people in the future. Good government does not mean responding blindly to headlines or being pressured into half-responses. It means sensible policies, soundly based, with realistic, achievable and prioritised targets.

'A single budget cannot achieve all that we desire, nor should it try to do so. There are always risks to the economic outlook, especially in a small and open economy such as ours. Therefore, it is important to take into account the unpredictable nature of our economic environment. Ordinary taxpayers know that this makes sense. I hope they will recognise the firm resolve of the government to secure their welfare now and for the future.'

So Cowen clearly felt that he was taking account of risks and providing for them at this point: 'The prospects for the economy are fairly positive for the next few years. If international growth holds up and we do the right things, we have the potential to grow at around 5 per cent per year in real terms and to keep inflation in the 2 per cent to 3 per cent range. Of course, our economic situation also contains risks. The main question mark arises from the international economic situation where answers to some questions are not so easy. For example, how will oil prices fare? Last December few would have predicted that oil prices would reach $50 per barrel during the course of this year. How will international exchange rates evolve? What will be the international policy response in terms of interest rates? The answers to these questions and the response of the world economy will have a significant influence on our prospects.'

Of course, a few years later, $50 per barrel would be a bargain for oil. In his budget Cowen made infrastructure a key priority: 'I am providing €334 million in additional exchequer capital for 2005. This will bring the total exchequer cash available for capital spending next year to almost €6,300 million, 20 per cent ahead of the 2004 cash outturn. This means that for 2005–09 we will maintain our high level of investment in infrastructure at nearly twice the European average.'

He introduced a ten-year capital envelope for transport: 'I have agreed in principle with the minister for transport that an extended capital envelope of ten years is more appropriate in the case of investment in transport. Proposals for such a ten-year investment will be submitted shortly for consideration by government. This is a necessary development in forward budgeting. It will afford the government greater flexibility and clarity in planning and, most importantly, in delivering a twenty-first-century transport infrastructure for a twenty-first-century economy. This is a new initiative we must put in place if we are to position the economy to continue to grow and compete over the medium term.'

He brought minimum-wage workers outside of the tax net for the first time: 'I am increasing the employee tax credit by €230 to bring it to €1,270 per year. I am also increasing the personal tax credits by €60 for a single person and €120 for a married couple to bring those to €1,580 and €3,160 per year, respectively. This will benefit all workers and will ensure that all those on the minimum wage are fully outside the tax net.'

A range of taxation reliefs was announced, including a measure to take 47,000 elderly persons out of the tax net. But Cowen also announced that he was commencing a full review of all tax-relief schemes and incentives in the system: 'The time is now right to conduct a full review of these incentive reliefs and to evaluate in detail their impact and how they are operating in practice. My preference is for a complete and comprehensive reform of the system rather than a piecemeal approach. For this reason, I have directed my department, together with the Revenue Commissioners, to undertake a thorough evaluation of the effect of all relevant incentive reliefs and exemptions and to bring forward proposals which would achieve the balance to which I have referred.'

It was a clear effort to deal with the argument against high earners avoiding tax. In answer to complaints that first-time buyers could not afford a house, changes were made to stamp duty: 'I am aware of the difficulties that many first-time buyers face in their efforts to get onto the property ladder. To assist first-time buyers of secondhand houses, I am providing for a significant reduction in stamp duty for them. Full details are set out in the budget summary …

'As a result of this, there will be no stamp duty on first-time purchasers of secondhand houses up to €317,500 in value and reduced rates on such purchases up to €635,000.'

He continued the government's firm commitment to improving the lot of old-age pensioners through a series of significant pension increases: 'This government has a proud record of improving income support for pensioners. It is an area which we have concentrated on since our return to office. I am increasing the full personal rate of old age and related pensions by €12 per week which is an increase of over 7 per cent. This will bring the old age contributory pension to €179.30 per week and means we will be well on the way to achieving the programme for government commitment to increase the state pension to €200 per week by 2007.'

It was certainly a positive budget and one that showed little fear of problems in the economy. The opposition clearly saw no immediate problems either and the criticisms were mainly due to the fact that not enough was spent or that it was spent in the wrong areas. Richard Bruton, for example, raised issues over child poverty and young families: 'Many looked to this budget to see something real done for child poverty. The last minister made a solemn commitment that he would increase child benefit by €17.60 by 2003. Almost two years later, only €10 of that has been delivered. That is not good enough. The government is not willing to deliver on the promises made to the children. There is unanimity that the child dependant allowance needs to be addressed. Nothing has been done to help those on this allowance. I am glad to see there is some improvement in private rented accommodation in the way of tax relief. Is 88 cent a week going to make any significant difference to many people struggling on low incomes in private rented accommodation? …

'Many families could have expected to see something in today's budget. There are young families struggling with the unaffordable cost of childcare which has now reached a rate of €150 per week in Dublin. There is chaos in our traffic policy and people are struggling to make ends meet. Those seeking help for children with special needs are frustrated by the failure of the government to deliver on its promises. People are worried they cannot afford health care. Many older family members must shoulder responsibilities they never thought they would have to face. They are raising second mortgages to help their children step onto the first rung of the home ownership ladder and acting as unpaid childminders for their grandchildren. People face growing uncertainty as to whether they will be able to obtain emergency care for grandparents …'

It is interesting that over this period there was so much talk of first-time buyers. While on one hand it was argued that the government should not interfere in a market, on the other it was argued that they had to help first-time buyers. However, with hindsight it is clear to see that each measure brought in to assist first-time buyers was an artificial intervention to try and make houses more affordable, thereby fuelling the housing boom. The government has often been criticised as having been complicit in creating the boom through the revenue it gained, but it is clear that in those years it faced tough choices. Cowen could try to halt the housing boom, and cause market turmoil and perhaps precipitate a recession. If he did not take taxes from the property sector he would have been failing to get a fair cut for the taxpayer. If he helps first-time buyers he fuels the market and if he doesn't, young people become priced out of the market. Some years later as the market began to collapse, first-time buyers became the winners, clearly illustrating that the only measure that could rectify the situation was the market itself.

Cowen was not at ease in this situation, but there was nothing in his speech to suggest that he was deliberately trying to fuel a property boom at the time. On 1 February 2005 he was back to discussing his action with regard to value for money, still the big issue of the day. Mr Bruton asked him if he had satisfied himself with the progress under the expenditure review initiative; and if he would make a statement on the matter. Cowen replied: 'The first formal report from the Expenditure Review Central Steering Committee on Progress, under the expenditure review initiative for the period June 2002 to June 2004, was submitted to me on 3 November 2004 . This report found that progress had been made by departments and offices in undertaking systematic evaluation both within and outside the expenditure review initiative and in building an evaluation culture. However, it also highlighted some deficiencies in the process and made a number of recommendations designed to improve it.'

We can see from this that Cowen believed that real progress was being made. However, it was also slow progress. He also had the opportunity to expand on the other big issue of the day, tax avoidance: 'In Budget 2005 I announced that my department, in conjunction with the Revenue Commissioners, would undertake this year a detailed review of certain tax incentive schemes and tax exemptions.

'There are a number of elements to the review which is already underway. It will evaluate the impact and operation of certain incentive schemes and exemptions including their economic and social benefits for the different locations and sectors involved and to the wider community, including external consultancy work on the evaluation of property-based tax incentive schemes. It will examine the degree to which these schemes allow high-income individuals to reduce their tax liabilities.'

Richard Bruton did seem to believe that the process would lead to a result: 'I know the minister does not have a reputation for conducting reviews and then doing nothing about an issue, so will he indicate his intention for next year's budget? Will he have ready for that budget a comprehensive response, a set of measures as a result of this review?'

Mr Cowen: 'That is my honest intention. Rather than considering this matter piecemeal and reacting to whatever issue is more fashionable in any given week or day, I intend to consider the entire issue. It would be helpful for the ordinary taxpayer to see what role these schemes play and to see their wider benefits.

'Successive governments devised these schemes. They were changed and modified and they evolved through circumstances including judgments justified in their own way and time. A wider community benefit derives from these schemes. Too often, critics like to portray them in terms of being some sort of sop or concession to high earners. Their purpose is rather to gain a wider community benefit, which has taken place.'

Dan Boyle of the Green Party raised the issue of a danger of a reliance on property speculation. He also criticised that reliefs were still in place for property developments which, in his view, were fuelling speculation: 'Does the minister accept that before the review examines any individual reliefs, the central question must be asked as to why property-based tax reliefs exist in respect of a sector of the economy that is already responsible – before one breaks down the effects of the individual reliefs – for 12 per cent of gross national product? I put it to him that his lack of clarity regarding whether some schemes will continue is causing a corresponding lack of development in certain areas. I cite here the example of Cork city where there has been no development in the docklands areas because of an expectation among developers that either tax reliefs will be continued or that a special tax designation will be made. As a result, there is an onus on the minister to put this issue beyond doubt once and for all.'

Mr Cowen: 'The deputy stated that the industry is already responsible for 12 per cent of GNP. That is a high percentage and I am delighted the domestic construction industry is responsible for it.'

Mr Boyle: 'It is also a result of property speculation.'

Mr Cowen: 'No, it is because there are over 200,000 people working in the industry. These people are all working here whereas when there were downturns in the industry in the past, they were obliged to go elsewhere. I am delighted we have a buoyant construction sector and that we have twice the capital budget, in terms of a percentage of GNP, of any of our European counterparts. The latter would love to be in the same position as Ireland.

'Let us not decry the fact that we have a buoyant construction sector. One of the important things we must do in the coming years is to ensure that if demand is not maintained at its current level – housing output now is 80,000 units compared with 30,000 six or seven years ago – a way to make a soft landing is found. We must ensure the construction sector continues to make a positive contribution, without there being any adverse economic impact in terms of reduced demand.

That is one of the issues the economy and the government and its successors must face. Assertions to the effect that we have had some tax incentive schemes and that the latter is a reason we should not have had them because we would still have had the same level of activity do not stand up to scrutiny.'

Dan Boyle elaborated on his fears during a debate on the finance bill on the 8 February 2005: 'We are, in many respects, a satellite economy of the United States, an economy that has the highest trade deficit and the highest budget deficit in the world ... It is likely that the type of dependence and economic impetus by which it is fuelled in terms of our reliance on oil will come back to haunt us, maybe not in the short term but certainly in the medium term. If there is an oil price shock and it affects interest rates, we can all envisage what is likely to happen in an economy that has a gross national product with 12 per cent reliance on property.'

This warning was timely and true. However, it offered little suggestion as to what Cowen should actually have done. Property reliefs were already under serious review at this stage, but in themselves they were not a major factor. The fact was that while everyone was aware of the dangers, no one seemed able to suggest where spending should be cut or how to stop the housing market appreciating at pace.

On 3 March other threats were among the issues to be discussed, especially ones that the government did have real control over, in particular benchmarking. According to Mr Bruton: 'On the last occasion, benchmarking cost the taxpayer €1.3 billion. Surely somebody representing the taxpayers' interests should have a role in deciding the membership of the benchmarking body. Should there not be a member of that body who is watching out for issues such as value for money and public service reform? I am not satisfied at the way this is being structured because benchmarking was charged with problems over non-transparency before and it looks as if this will happen again.'

Mr Cowen: 'To answer that specific supplementary question, as stated in the national pay agreement, the parties considered in its request that the body should seek to ensure the optimum level of transparency consistent with the efficient and effective operations of the benchmarking process. How this is reflected in the report is a matter for the benchmarking body as it is independent. ... It would be desirable for the body to give a greater amount of information this time around. However, that is a matter for the body to decide and the government represents the taxpayer in these matters.'

Bruton and Cowen were at polar opposites on this argument. Bruton saw it as an inefficient and costly system hanging over the taxpayer, particularly the private sector taxpayer. Cowen felt it was a good system and that the taxpayer was well served; he leaned more in the direction of public-sector opinion on the issue and Bruton to the private sector.

Cowen had always been a champion of sticking to budgets and attaining value. He seems beset on all sides, however, by departments that do not adhere to such strict ideas. He had set about rectifying the problem, but in the meantime damage was being inflicted on the government and on his own reputation in terms of the ability to deliver value.

On 17 May the Labour Party attempted to up the ante in this regard by tabling a motion on public expenditure. Joan Burton laid out the case, making reference by way of example to the approach taken to the introduction of the medical card scheme for the over seventies. Given Cowen's opposition to such a move while minister for health and his agreement to withdraw the universal benefit in 2008, she may have unknowingly hit a chord that Cowen might not have disagreed with in private: 'The examples of government waste are too numerous to go into great detail, although my colleagues will refer to many of them, but I want to elaborate on three examples.

'The medical cards for over seventies scheme was announced to great applause from government benches in the budget of 2001 and welcomed on all sides of this House. What deputies did not know, however, was the secretive and ham-fisted planning behind the proposal. It was politically motivated to win votes at the expected election a few months later. There were no negotiations with the doctors, no proper costings and not even a proper study of the number of recipients. The cost of the medical card bonanza jumped from an estimated €19 million to an estimated additional annual cost of €51 million.'

In the debate Cowen laid out his argument in defence of government policy, but never mentioned medical cards: 'As investment projects proceed from initial concept to final tender price, the estimates change as more information comes to light and changes in the scope and specifications are made. Often it can be many years before a project moves from concept to tender stage and it is ridiculous to compare estimates at both these stages. The key benchmark for comparison purposes of cost overruns is the tender price. When a person is in a position to do the job, is it done for the price in the tender? That is the issue. To suggest otherwise is to suggest that costing can be based on doing everything the same day in the same way. It is ridiculous. If we are to have an intelligent discussion that does not suggest everything is all right or is a waste of time, we must have an honest debate about the issues before us.

'The comptroller and auditor general's report of April 2004 detailed the reasons for the increase in the cost of the NDP roads programme. He identified construction and land inflation as contributing 40 per cent of the cost increase. He further said that less than 20 per cent was due to initial cost underestimation, which he put down to a systematic failure to cost certain elements of the schemes at the planning stage ...

'The establishment of the cost estimation function and the expertise that has come with it are showing results. The committee further acknowledged that contracting procedures had improved since my predecessor announced different ways of contracting. Many road construction projects are being completed on or within schedule and within budget, but that was not mentioned in the motion. Recent examples include the N2 Carrickmacross bypass – three months ahead of schedule – the Monasterevin bypass – one year ahead of schedule – and the Cashel bypass – seven months ahead of schedule. We must also acknowledge that in the transport area in particular delays have arisen as a result of planning and environmental objections and legal challenges, many of them supported by those on the other side of the House …

'With effect from the end of 2005, public sector construction projects will be tendered competitively on the basis of a fixed-price lump sum contract in which appropriate construction risks are identified and transferred to contractors. Under this system the amount of variation, or extras, will be limited to the greatest extent possible.

'The government is also modernising the system for employing consultants, such as engineers and architects, to decouple professional fees from project costs …

'The ESRI, in its mid-term evaluation of the National Development Plan, concluded the GNP level will be approximately 3 per cent higher than it would have been in the absence of the plan's infrastructural investment.'

Cowen had a strong case, but in terms of perception he was always on the back foot on this issue; however, it is clear that upon his appointment he did go about making headway at reducing waste. Unfortunately Cowen does not appear to subscribe to the idea of perception being important, and even though he was introducing measures, the government were still being hammered publicly on the issue.

Another issue cropped up to cause controversy, namely government plans to privatise Aer Lingus. Sinn Féin had tabled a motion on the issue on 24 May. Many people were ideologically opposed to privatisation. Brian Cowen who had shown himself such an admirer of the semi-state sector put the case for the government's approach: 'A key part of the decision is the mandate to the board of Aer Lingus to prepare and submit a plan for future profitable growth as soon as possible on the basis that additional equity capital will be available within a reasonable timescale. This decision allows Aer Lingus to secure funding for new aircraft and in turn to open and compete on new, particularly long-haul, routes …

'Over its history Aer Lingus has had its share of crises and has come close to failure. That this did not happen is a testimony to the efforts of successive management and dedicated staff. However, the minister for transport wants to end these crisis cycles where every few years a crisis is followed by survival followed by stagnation and back to crisis again. The government decision means that for the first time, there can be investment for growth and not just a short-term response to a crisis …

'Regarding suggestions of a wider, all-Ireland, strategy on aviation, deputies will appreciate that, since the full liberalisation of the European aviation market in the 1990s, there have no longer been any government or EU controls in the Irish aviation market. That obviously influences the overall approach to that market. Liberalisation of the European air transport sector has ensured that fares, routes and frequency of services operated by carriers at all airports on the island of Ireland are entirely commercial decisions for each airline in consultation with the relevant airport authorities. That basic fact has not been incorporated into the rationale or argument I have heard from the opposition benches regarding the motion they are proposing to the House.'

Cowen then made clear that the government had moved to save Aer Lingus once before and could not do so again – the challenges faced by the airline meant that it needed the freedom to compete with other airlines on an equal footing: 'I was minister for transport in 1993 and 1994. I recall when Aer Lingus was in very serious difficulties and the future of the company was at risk. When the government obtained a once-off state investment for the company in compliance with EU rules, dealing with Commissioner van Meert at the time, many continued to say that the company could not flourish. In recent years, when one sees what has happened to long-standing brands in international aviation on both sides of the Atlantic and in Asia, one must recognise that the company is operating in a totally new environment. None of us is here to argue for the demise of a company that has served us well.

'People quite rightly spoke of the vision of the pioneers who founded these companies when there were no capital formation markets in this country – a development with which my party was particularly associated – but it is incumbent on us, given contemporary realities, not to allow policy to be driven by sentimentality or emotion. If we allow that to happen, we put at risk those very jobs that we argue we must protect and expand. We must ensure that Aer Lingus can get out in that more liberalised aviation environment in which it now operates, with dog-eat-dog competition on short-haul routes ...

'Swissair is no longer in a position to serve Switzerland well. Sabena is no longer in a position to serve Belgium well. We allowed ourselves to be blinkered in our approach and we did not see what was happening in the market. If we do not take cognisance of the market, we will put at risk the great contribution that has been made thus far and we will deprive workers of jobs. Those workers are as good at their job in the company as any other that I know, and I flew with quite a few airlines in my role as minister for foreign affairs. We can give the direction for people to work together co-operatively.'

On 1 June debate still raged about the ability of a small portion of millionaires avoiding tax. Joan Burton pulled no punches in accusing Cowen of protecting his friends; Cowen took extreme offence to the allegation made in a statement by Ms Burton: 'Will the minister confirm whether, under the Cinderella rule, it is possible to leave the state at one minute to midnight and return to the state at perhaps 1.10 a.m., an hour and ten minutes later, and satisfy the rules on exit from the state? Compliant taxpayers are greatly concerned that a single person earning €30,000 will pay some of their tax at 42 per cent while, as the Revenue Commissioners have said, very wealthy individuals who are non-resident for tax purposes but who attend every charity function, ball and race meeting appear, as the programme indicated, to live here full-time. Will the minister clarify the exit rule under the Cinderella rule?'

Mr Cowen: 'Non-residence for tax purposes does not mean that people are exempt from paying tax in Ireland. It means that they only pay tax on their Irish sourced income. Non-residency enables them not to be subject to tax on worldwide income.'

Ms Burton: 'Almost none of them have Irish-sourced income, and the minister knows that. He is protecting his rich friends again.'

An leas-cheann comhairle: 'We must proceed to Question No. 19.'

Mr Cowen: 'Every time I come into this House there is a theme from the Labour Party spokesperson, based on her acute sense of conspiracy, that I am knowledgeable about the income tax affairs of individuals other than myself. I certainly am not and if she is, she is a better woman than I am. I understand that everyone's tax affairs are confidential between the individual and the Revenue Commissioners. The purpose of question time is to give accurate information to the public.'

Ms Burton: 'Can the minister clarify the Cinderella rule?'

Mr Cowen: 'I want to make this clarification.'

Ms Burton: 'Be prince charming and clarify it for us.'

An leas-cheann comhairle: 'We must proceed to Question No. 19.'

Mr Cowen: 'A serious charge has been made. I must insist on replying.'

Ms Burton: 'Did the minister watch the *Prime Time Investigates* programme?'

Mr Cowen: 'I am not prepared to allow such unnecessary charges to go unchallenged. They are unnecessary and have no basis in fact.'

Ms Burton: 'The minister should clarify the rule and give the House the information.'

Mr Cowen: 'It would be far better if the deputy were to be so gracious as to withdraw such charges. I would never make such misleading charges against a deputy in this House. It does not become Deputy Burton. If she thinks she can make such charges and that people whose job it is to report to the wider public will publish these charges unchallenged, it suggests there is some foundation to what she alleges. However, what she has said is a total untruth.'

Ms Burton: 'The eminent minister is at every race meeting in this country where people who are non-resident for tax purposes are walking around.'

Mr Cowen: 'On a point of order –'

An leas-cheann comhairle: 'The minister is in possession.'

Mr Cowen: 'The non-residency rules that apply in this country were agreed under a Fianna Fáil-Labour coalition government in 1994.'

Ms Burton: 'We are asking the minister to review them.'

Mr Cowen: 'It has been suggested that I am seeking to help or protect people. That is not the situation. I am here to provide factual information. The Cinderella rule means that only if one is resident in the state at midnight is one deemed to have been resident in the state for that day. The deputy can conjure up any number of possibilities, however realistic or precedent-setting, that meet that rule. I cannot verify where the regulation has been used. I can confirm that the Revenue Commissioners, in whom I have full confidence, monitor this situation very closely. In so far as matters stand, they are satisfied that there have been no deviations from the regulations and they will continue to monitor and will report to me in due course. Perhaps Deputy Burton will, upon reflection, withdraw the charge she made, which I find ungracious and unnecessary but not untypical of her style.'

An leas-cheann comhairle: 'We must proceed to Question No. 19.'

Ms Burton: 'On a point of order, the minister is supposed to answer my questions. He earlier said that there was an ongoing review.'

An leas-cheann comhairle: 'That is not a point of order. The chair has called Question No. 19. We have spent fourteen minutes on a question that should have been limited to six minutes.'

Mr Cowen: 'It is unfortunate, but some things cannot be allowed to pass.'

Ms Burton: 'The minister should give us the answer.'

Mr Cowen: 'My integrity is not going to be challenged under privilege. If the deputy wants to challenge it outside the House, she should do so. I will gladly sue her.'

The impression of the Dáil record in relation to the new minister for finance thus far was that while he had a significant amount of good news to tell and things were going particularly well, he was bogged down by other issues that would not go away. Even though he had taken steps to move on these, he was still struggling to get a good news story onto the record against the opposition. Again we can see that while Cowen's approach to doing things right and planning for the long term may be admirable, the failure to accompany it with any immediate measures was costing him.

Cowen may have hoped that the summer recess would have provided some relief on this and allowed him to re-focus debate. On 5 October we get some interesting figures in reply to a parliamentary question. It does perhaps answer the often-asked question 'where did the boom go?'

Mr Cowen: 'The published finance accounts show that the exchequer current account surpluses for the years 1998 to 2004 inclusive were as follows: 1998, €2,649 million; 1999, €4,367 million; 2000, €6,971 million; 2001, €4,724 million; 2002, €5,400 million; 2003, €4,410 million; and 2004, €5,619 million.

'The general government balance is a broader measure of the fiscal performance of government. In addition to the exchequer, it includes local authorities, non-commercial state-sponsored bodies, the National Pensions Reserve Fund and the Social Insurance Fund. It also includes elements of accrual accounting while the exchequer balance is a cash-based measure. On a general government basis, the current account surplus for each of the years in question was: 1998, €3,471 million; 1999, €6,039 million; 2000, €8,011 million; 2001, €5,828 million; 2002, €4,272 million; 2003, €4,975 million; and 2004, €6,713 million.

'The current surpluses on exchequer account have been used to meet existing and future needs. For example, investment in capital infrastructure has been increased in recent years to around 5 per cent of GNP per annum, twice the EU average. Capital expenditure is funded, in whole or in part, by current surpluses.

'The National Pensions Reserve Fund, established in 2001, requires the statutory investment of 1 per cent of GNP annually, to meet part of the escalating costs of social welfare and public service pensions. The current surpluses meet the cost of the 1 per cent contribution. The surpluses are used to reduce the national debt, thereby freeing resources to fund other priority areas. Debt as a percentage of GDP has fallen to below 30 per cent.'

In short, all that money went on paying off the national debt, contributing to the pension reserve fund, and investing in capital infrastructure (roads, social housing, hospital and school buildings etc.). It is worth remembering that there was a significant body of opinion during this period and before that Ireland should, like a lot of other countries, borrow to pay for capital infrastructure and keep current surpluses for reinvestment on the current side. While there is merit in this argument, with hindsight in this much at least, Cowen and his predecessor were indeed prudent, and saved Ireland from an unimaginable crisis in 2008.

By October 2005 Cowen was able to report the economy as being in good shape and still performing ahead of expectations, but a significant cloud had emerged as regard oil and exports: 'As is usual my department published the annual economic review and outlook, ERO, in mid-August. The economic forecasts for 2005 contained in the ERO were based on data to the end of July. The ERO forecast was broadly unchanged in overall terms from that published on budget day, with growth in real GDP again forecast at 5.1 per cent and growth in GNP revised upwards slightly from 4.7 per cent to 5 per cent.

'The composition of the two forecasts, however, was different. The forecasts for domestic demand were significantly strengthened in the economic review and outlook. In particular, the forecasts for personal consumption and investment were increased as lead domestic demand indicators such as retail sales, tax revenues, etc. indicated the domestic economy was growing more strongly than anticipated on budget day. In addition, the projected increase in employment in 2005 was revised upwards on foot of strong data for the first quarter of the year. However, weaker than expected trade data and higher oil prices prompted a significant reduction in the forecast contribution from net exports. The forecast for growth in exports of goods and services was reduced from 7 per cent to 3.9 per cent. My department will update the ERO view on budget day in December. Account will be taken of all published data since July when framing the budget day forecasts.'

Dangers were also evident in relation to corporation tax and the international economy: 'There are more downside factors coming into the equation on the international economic scene than would have been the case six months ago. The energy issue is certainly one of which people would be much aware. It is against a background of world trade growth, which is still strong when one looks at the emerging economies such as India, China and other Asian economies. The American economy continues to defy some of the odds, despite some downsides in terms of its imbalances, both fiscal and budgetary.

'The point we would make is that this situation must be managed. This country is achieving growth rates much higher than our European counterparts. Officially, there is recession in Italy. There are the difficulties of high unemployment in Germany and France. Compared to some of these European economies, one aspect that is different in Ireland is the strong domestic demand and that is a stronger component in our growth than would have been the case previously. It is good that we have that domestic demand. Indeed, the Achilles' heel of the European economy is that they cannot generate any and that is having its effect on them in terms of higher unemployment – double our unemployment rate ...

'On corporation tax the trend evident all year has been one of just about meeting the profile. In some cases, it is down. On exports, we are seeing a reduction in the profile in terms of an increase, from 7 per cent down to 3.9 per cent. These are competitiveness issues of which we must be mindful and we must make sure, in the context of our social partnership talks and our policy responses to some of the higher energy environment issues arising, that we make the right choices. Unless we concentrate on increasing productivity and making sure we maintain our position in the international marketplace, we put at risk the volume of goods and services that we can provide which is the means by which we have generated the activity, created the revenues and created the jobs.'

So there is no sign of Cowen being caught unawares at this stage. Ireland did indeed have a strong domestic economy, but the reduction in the exports suggested that there was now an over-reliance on the property sector to drive the economy. However, there was still little suggestion as to how Cowen could tackle this. It would have been economic suicide to do anything to harm the property sector at this point, while any move by the government to suggest it would cut its tax take would only fuel the market further; and of course services still needed to be provided and money had to be found to pay for them. Global problems left Ireland particularly exposed, but Cowen later pointed out that the only solution to these kinds of problems lay with Europe, and Europe needed a better decision-making process: 'Globalisation is a major issue for Europe. Driven by lower communication costs, reduced barriers to trade and the emergence of China and India, this process is likely to intensify further. This will create many benefits for the European Union. However, it will also entail significant challenges and therefore the European Union must improve the flexibility of its markets and enhance the incentives for enterprise and innovation if it is to respond to globalisation and achieve its objectives regarding jobs and growth.

'Europe can no longer afford to wait because what is different five years on is the added sense of urgency. On the policy responses for the European economy, ensuring macro-economic stability is a key requirement in reducing uncertainty and providing the basis for future prosperity.'

But if international concerns were going to have an impact, there is little sign of anyone panicking about it as late as November 2005.

Joan Burton is pressing Cowen to deliver on promises in relation to tax reform. She asked him about the number and percentage of income earners who are paying tax at the higher rate and the standard rate for 2005, what the comparative figures for each year since 1998 were and when the government would honour the commitment given in *An Agreed Programme for Government* that 80 per cent of all earners would pay tax only at the standard rate.

Mr Cowen: 'I refer the deputy to tabular data provided in reply to parliamentary Question No. 531 on 28 September 2005. This remains the most up-to-date information available. The data indicates that for 2005 only one third of earners will be on the higher rate of tax, while almost 31 per cent are on the standard rate and almost 36 per cent are exempt.

'The 80 per cent target in *An Agreed Programme for Government* was set in the context of a broader economic and budgetary strategy which provides, among other things, that the public finances will be kept in a healthy condition and that personal and business taxes will be kept down in order to strengthen and maintain the competitive position of the economy. Further progress in this area will be a matter for consideration in the context of the annual budgets over the coming years consistent with the government's overall economic and budgetary strategy.'

There was still a confidence that Ireland was going to be alright for the foreseeable future. Dan Boyle did raise the issue of personal indebtedness, however, and Cowen makes a strong case as to why this is a concern but not an issue of crisis. Boyle asked about the measures he had taken since taking office to protect vulnerable borrowers and the economy more generally from excessive levels of indebtedness. Cowen replied: 'The role of government on credit growth and associated indebtedness has a number of distinct dimensions. First, it is important to note that, as far as overall economic and financial stability are concerned, the relevant measure of credit encompasses both public and private sector credit and debt levels ... the growth of private sector credit and indebtedness needs to be assessed in an appropriate context. In evaluating the financial position of the private sector, it is too narrow an approach to consider the level of indebtedness in isolation from the asset side of the private sector's balance sheet. A high proportion of household indebtedness in Ireland relates to borrowing for house purchases which, in turn, creates an asset for the households. In the same way, borrowing by the business sector underpins high investment levels and the creation of business assets yielding future income.

'Account must also be taken of private sector savings levels. The government has been actively promoting saving by individuals in the recent past, notably through the SSIA scheme. Comparatively high household savings rates by international standards in Ireland support the sustainability of household debt overall.

'As far as looking after the interests of the individual borrower and the individual investor is concerned, the function of government is to provide an appropriate legislative framework for regulation of the financial services sector, one that is both comprehensive and robust. I am satisfied that on foot of the progress made in recent years, especially in establishing the financial regulator with a particular focus on the interests of the consumer, we have such a framework in place.'

Cowen had provided a framework for consumer protection and in this instance he clearly did not believe in a nanny state. Consumers were old enough to look after themselves. Rather than a government issue it was something that borrowers and lenders needed to consider. He believed the Central Bank backed him up on this: 'The Central Bank's recently published *Financial Stability Report* concludes that a range of fundamental factors, such as growing employment and incomes, falling inflation and low interest rates, have supported the pattern of mortgage growth and associated debt levels in the economy. The report, however, emphasises the importance of responsible behaviour by both borrowers and lenders to factor into their financial decision-making the prospective impact of potential changes in any future economic environment. I share the Central Bank's assessment of the importance of maintaining financial and economic stability.'

As Cowen debated the estimates, threats were recognised and were being taken into account: 'Our public finances are extremely sound. We will comfortably achieve our budget targets for 2005. I expect the economy to grow close to its potential rate of 4.5 per cent to 5 per cent over the medium term. While these rates of growth will be lower than in the previous decade they are strong by international standards. We have, by any standards, made remarkable economic and social progress since 1997. We have achieved an average economic growth rate of 7 per cent, more than twice the EU average. Our debt GDP ratio will be approximately 29 per cent at year end, compared with 65 per cent when we took office. With a record high of nearly two million in work, approximately 500,000 more are employed compared to when we took office.

'The risks ahead include oil prices, interest rates, increased international competition for investment and in product markets. We will continue with prudent fiscal policies to ensure we have the flexibility required to deal with economic shocks, to promote sustainable economic and employment growth and competitiveness and to tackle social inequalities.

'This year gross public expenditure is expected to be approximately €45.5 billion. A small underspend on current expenditure of approximately €75 million is expected. Capital spending in 2005 in cash terms will be approximately €6 billion capital, including carryover of approximately €137 million from 2004. This represents 15 per cent more than the equivalent spend in 2004. The multi-annual system for managing capital, which we now operate, with its 10 per cent carryover arrangement facilitates better management of capital programmes and projects.'

By any assessment the economy was still performing well. Cowen returned to the burning issue of the day – value for money: 'I am absolutely determined that the principle that every euro of the taxpayers' money must be well spent should apply. We must in particular ensure that best practice is employed in the appraisal and management of ICT and capital programmes and projects. We must also be prepared to learn lessons and address shortcomings which may come to light.

'Building on reforms such as the five year multi-annual capital envelopes, revised capital appraisal guidelines and planned improvements in construction and construction-related contracts, we recently announced two initiatives to further improve the approach to securing value for money. These were an initiative on management of ICT projects and consultancies and additional measures on value for money that I announced on 20 October 2005. Departments have been asked to give effect to the measures that can be implemented immediately and work is under way on updating the necessary guidelines and other necessary steps to implement all these measures.'

Once again, however, in the estimates we can see just the size of the public service bill which is still increasing. Also Cowen pointed out that numbers in all areas other than health, education and security had been kept at below 2002 levels, but we can still see the draw on resources these big three were having: 'The gross provision for 2006 to fund public service pay and pensions is €16.4 billion, an increase of €1.1 billion or 7 per cent. It makes full provision for the final phase of *Sustaining Progress* and includes some €430 million for service improvements and extra numbers. The extra numbers are primarily employed in a frontline capacity in areas of health, education and the garda síochána. Despite the contrary perception created in some quarters there has not been an increase in the share of overall current expenditure attributable to pay and pensions. In 1997, this was around 40 per cent of gross current spending and in 2006 on a pre-budget basis it is nearly 39 per cent.'

On 7 December 2005 Cowen introduced his second budget: 'We are living in the midst of the longest and strongest era of sustained prosperity in our history. This did not happen by chance. It involved careful planning. It involved investment in infrastructure development where we had considerable ground to make up. It involved a commitment to educate our children so they could be a match for their peers across every discipline. It involved careful fiscal management and the creation of an economic environment that attracts investment. Furthermore, it represents the hard work of the Irish people themselves …

'It is a new Ireland – prosperous, but not without challenges. This budget is largely about two key objectives: the facilitation of sustained economic growth and improved equality and opportunity for all in society. We have made our choices in the light of a simple, but powerful principle: we cannot take prosperity for granted. We will not put at risk the prosperity the Irish people have achieved.'

The department of finance was pleased with performance and confident of the future: 'Economic growth this year is projected by the department of finance at 4.6 per cent in GDP terms, that is the value of all goods and services produced in the state. Growth of 4.8 per cent is predicted in GNP terms, that is the income we earn from producing goods and services. The success story of 2005 has been the very strong growth in employment, which has resulted from to the correct policies which have been followed by the government. The latest labour force data show that employment grew by 96,200, or 5 per cent, in the past twelve months. Almost 71,000 of that increase represents additional full-time jobs. The number of people on the live register – 150,000 – is 14,500 lower than two years ago. Ireland's employment record, which is far ahead of the rest of the EU, is a testimony to the enterprise and effort of our workforce.'

The issue of public spending was something that concerned Cowen in this budget, but there were no drastic measures taken to reduce it: 'Of the €43.8 billion in gross voted current spending, more than one in every four euro, or €12.2 billion, is spent on health. Expenditure on health amounts to €3,000 for every citizen in the state, or over €9,000 for every taxpayer. The other major current spending departments are the departments of education and science and social and family affairs. Education expenditure accounts for one in every six euro spent. Expenditure on social and family affairs accounts for one in every three euro spent. Taken together, the departments of health and children, education and science and social and family affairs account for three in every four euro required to fund total day-to-day voted spending next year. It is a question not only of the quantity of spending, but also of the quality of expenditure. We need to consider whether expenditure meets current needs and provides for the future. We should determine whether we are getting full value for it and whether we could achieve the same for less.'

The simple fact was that while spending was high there was no effective way of reducing this figure considerably without hitting health and education, where the majority of spending went on salary costs, and there was little appetite for this. As with staff numbers, anything else would just be tinkering around the edges.

In the budget itself, education received a boost in a number of areas: 'As it is a major plank of the government's policy, I am announcing the allocation of €300 million to the strategic innovation fund for higher education over the next five years …

'In addition, it is essential that investment in modern facilities is maintained in university and institute of technology campuses around the country. As a result, we are committing €900 million to the third level sector over the next five years as part of the department of education and science capital envelope. Of this, €630 million will be exchequer capital funding and €270 million PPP funding. The physical development will need to reflect the changed approach where there must be greater co-operation between the institutions involved to give maximum benefit for the taxpayer.'

Cowen also hinted that it was important that the public service remain well motivated: 'To support this level of activity we need a professional and well-motivated public service. The numbers employed reflect that many of these services are labour intensive, particularly in areas such as health, education and the security forces. Some 40 per cent of public spending goes in the form of pay. We have an obligation to ensure that value for money is central to how we reward our public officials. The provision for 2006 to fund public service pay and pensions is €16.4 billion, an increase of €1.1 billion or 7 per cent. It makes full provision for the final phase of *Sustaining Progress* and includes €430 million for improvements in services and extra staff to deliver those services. I do not intend to prejudge the outcome of negotiations on a further public service pay agreement so I am not making any special provisions in the estimates for public service pay in 2006 other than what is provided for in the current agreement.'

The difficulty for the government was that they had created a situation where they had managed to ensure industrial peace, but budgeting was not easy as there were effectively two pay processes. Public servants received increases as negotiated under national wage agreements but also from the benchmarking process.

The pensioners would again receive a significant increase: 'The government has a proud record of improving income support for pensioners. I am increasing the full personal rate of old age and related pensions by €14 per week, an increase of almost 8 per cent …

'We recognise that many non-contributory pensioners want to work beyond retirement age but the means test system stops them doing so. We intend changing the non-contributory pension system so that earnings from employment up to €100 per week … will be disregarded for means test purposes.'

Other improvements were made for social welfare recipients, but it was clear from reaction that plenty of people still felt that the government was not doing enough.

Mr Cowen: 'Social welfare recipients would like to hear the details of the budget and we should respect that. The budget summary contains a wide range of other social welfare improvements the full details of which will be announced by the minister for social and family affairs. In the light of my opening remarks on the social welfare package, I would like to highlight the following planned improvements: an increase in the rate of the national fuel scheme from €9 to €14 per week …'

Deputies: 'Hear, hear.'

Mr S. Ryan: 'Shame. It would not buy a bag of coal.'

Mr Cowen: '… and I will also announce cuts in home heating oil taxes later in my statement to address fuel deficits on a broader basis; an increase in the rate of respite care grant to €1,200; an enhanced carer's allowance rate of €200 per week for people aged sixty-six or over and €180 for those under the age of sixty-six …'

Deputies: 'Hear, hear.'

Mr Stagg: 'They will be rich.'

Mr Cowen: '… and improvements in the terms of the disability allowance, back to work allowance and back to education allowance schemes to assist participation in the labour force. In addition, in line with commitments under *Sustaining Progress*, the rate of maternity benefit will be increased from 75 per cent to 80 per cent of reckonable earnings.'

One of the major developments in Budget 2006 was a new measure to assist in childcare: 'The government is very conscious of the difficulties faced by many parents and families in securing affordable childcare. Our task is to assist all parents in the early years of child rearing by widening the options they have. Some parents like to use family care or informal arrangements while others prefer the formal childcare setting. In addressing this issue, I have tried to take account of the following considerations. Where are the greatest pressure points for parents? How can I be fair to everyone, to both lower and middle income groups and to working parents, to those who are in the tax net and those who are not, to working parents as well as those who make their contribution to society through their work in the home? What is the administratively simplest and most user-friendly system? What is sustainable for the exchequer?

'Having carefully considered all the complex issues involved, the government has developed a five-year strategy to tackle the problem … The government is also very conscious of the importance of the first year in the life of a child and the strategy provides for a significant extension of maternity leave. The strategy also seeks to address the immediate cost pressures facing parents of young children by providing a new childcare supplement for all children under the age of six years.'

Mr Quinn: 'Chicken feed.'

Mr Cowen: 'I am making a significant start in implementing the programme today by providing €317 million in the 2006 budget for this purpose. The cost will increase to more than €600 million a year by 2008.

'I am providing for a number of measures which will increase the supply of childcare places. As part of the overall childcare strategy I am today announcing a major new five-year national childcare investment programme which will run from 2006 to 2010 and will support the creation of an extra 50,000 childcare places. This will be achieved through enhanced capital grant aid to private providers, the limit for which will double to €100,000 ...'

Mr Stagg: 'Is that all that is in it?'

Mr Cowen: '... and continued support to community providers of up to €1 million per facility subject to a maximum grant per place of €20,000.'

It was a considerable commitment on behalf of the government in this respect. Cowen certainly made the first serious effort to tackle problems in this area. He also delivered on promises with regard to tax reform with nearly €1 billion in tax reduction measures and other tax-relief schemes were reviewed as promised: 'This winding down of property-based tax reliefs is consistent with the greater capacity of particular economic sectors nowadays to fund such investment from their own resources, and the sizable capital investment which the government itself is making through the major new investments I referred to earlier.

'In line with the recommendations of the consultants, I propose to continue the tax reliefs for nursing homes, childcare facilities and private hospitals. Special arrangements will apply for park and ride facilities and the living-over-the-shop scheme as indicated in the summary of budget measures.

'The reviews also proposed that any new reliefs should be time-limited and should, where relevant, be subject to an assessment of costs and benefits prior to their introduction. They also proposed that recipients of these kinds of tax reliefs be required to supply full data to Revenue to assist in the costing and assessment of reliefs. I will be following this advice as far as appropriate ... It is necessary not only to eliminate some incentive reliefs but also to regulate the use that can be made of those that remain. We cannot stand over a situation in which some high-earning tax residents, through the use of incentive reliefs, can reduce their taxable income to nil.'

Mr Stagg: 'Hear, hear.'

Mr Cowen: 'This is simply not fair, although I should point out that high-earning non-payers are in a very small minority. Accordingly, I propose now to place an annual overall cap on the extent to which specific incentive reliefs can be availed of. The cap will apply to those with incomes over €250,000 per year.'

Mr F. McGrath: 'Hats off to the artists.'

Mr Cowen: 'It will operate by reducing by half the amount of income that can be relieved from tax by certain specified tax reliefs. This measure will help eliminate the phenomenon of tax-free millionaires and increase the effective rate of tax on those with high income towards a minimum of 20 per cent.'

From an opposition point of view there were no major cries to reduce spending or to make provision for a rainy day, but we can see in the budget that value for money was still being identified by the opposition as the government's Achilles heel:

Mr Bruton: 'The government has become spendthrift – spending money, not delivering value and overlooking waste, which is not acceptable. It is remarkable that after eight-and-a-half years in office and now facing the judgment of voters, the government seems to have suddenly woken up to problems people encounter in trying to work and look after their children and the problems older people experience seeking suitable support so that they can stay in their homes. Is it not remarkable that it takes the arrival of a general election to launch plans to address these needs? We have grown tired of hearing of plans from government. We want results. The minister for transport, Deputy Cullen, produced beautifully colour-coded maps and lovely tables but it was a sham, another five-year plan.'

Clearly Bruton also believed that the government should still be reducing taxes: 'The minister for finance announced he will reduce the amount people will pay in tax by €20 per week. That is the sum total of his boast. Let us not forget where this came from. Compared with this time last year, the minister will collect €3,750 more from every household in the country …

'The government has reneged on its commitment. Far from reducing the number of people paying tax at the top rate the number is increasing every year and the minister knows that because it is in his own tables today.'

Bruton did identify that the construction sector was masking an underlying problem that had not been addressed – namely Ireland's high costs and loss of competitiveness: 'The problem is that while the construction sector can absorb people and conceal problems in underlying trading sectors, that cannot go on forever. As a small, open economy, we need to survive on the basis of competitive businesses and that is not happening. Ireland's enterprise strategy was once the envy of emerging countries but it is feeling the strain and the cracks are showing.'

On 13 December there were fears emerging about the effects of a rise in interest rates. Bruton asked the minister for finance if he had estimated the impact of a one per cent increase in interest rates on business and on personal repayments and if this would fall disproportionately on recently formed families. Cowen replied: 'As the deputy will be aware, there is a broad range of factors that determine the effect of changes in interest rates on individual loan repayments. These include, for example, the outstanding loan amount, whether the lending rate is fixed or variable, the length of time over which the increase takes place, the pass-through of interest rate changes to lending rates, the repayment term and the specific nature of the financial product involved. My department, having consulted the Central Bank, has concluded that, as detailed information relating to all these factors is not available, an accurate estimate of the figure requested by the deputy cannot be constructed ...

'As far as the position of recently formed families is concerned, the Central Bank's recently published *Financial Stability Report* concludes that fundamental factors, such as increasing employment and incomes, low inflation and interest rates, have underpinned the pattern of mortgage growth and associated debt levels in the economy. The maintenance of Ireland's strong economic performance and, in particular, its strong income and employment growth, provides a positive and supportive economic environment within which households can successfully manage their finances.'

The strategy was that the government had to try and maintain economic growth, and increased income levels were the best protection against interest rate rises. Cowen continued to clarify the advice he was receiving in relation to banks and the levels of debt: 'It is important to remember that while personal liabilities have increased these are backed by real assets. In this context a major element of outstanding indebtedness is accounted for by residential mortgages. ... Insofar as the banking sector is concerned, the Central Bank in its recent *Financial Stability Review* concluded that the Irish banking system is in a good state of health and is reasonably well placed to cope with any adverse short or medium-term developments.'

Cowen referred regularly to the Central Bank report in the months to come. He relied heavily on the advice of the Central Bank and IFSRA [Irish Financial Services Regulatory Agency] that the Irish banking sector was in good health and could withstand any crisis as a result of the credit crunch. Cowen had an approach that had served him well in the past. He believed a minister had to take advice and act on it and be decisive; but that a minister was a facilitator rather than a strict manager. This idea was sound enough – politicians are rarely experts in the fields to which they are appointed, and that is one of the main reasons behind democracy. Therefore, politicians who interfere in day-to-day tasks or refuse to take advice often cause more problems than they solve. It had always been a positive approach. However, with the banking sector, the advice would let him down and questions would be asked as to why banks were not challenged. Cowen had no reason to change his approach or to assume that the advice he was getting was incorrect; the banks simply did not see the crisis that was coming.

At this stage Cowen still saw the economy having a very positive outlook: 'There is broad consensus among commentators that the Irish economy is set to continue to perform strongly, expanding close to its growth potential both this year and next. Over the medium term, the economy is expected to grow at almost double the rate forecast for the euro zone overall. The pace at which new housing output adjusts downwards to long-term, sustainable levels is an important risk for the economy, and new housing completions are projected to decline by 2.5 per cent next year and 5 per cent in 2007 and 2008. That will be offset by investment in other building and construction, including a significant increase in spending on the public capital programme. That is the level of economic activity that we predict, and we therefore anticipate a soft landing. We envisage that the issue will be dealt with in a planned way over a period owing to demographic, employment and other factors that differ greatly from those in other European economies and this means that housing output is justified.'

The much-famed soft landing was something that the government was actively trying to arrange. As regards a housing boom, Cowen was quite clear as to the reasons: demand was still high for homes. Once the government managed to get housing output to a level where there was a sufficient number of houses to meet demand, then the market would stabilise. It is true that at this point the main concerns among the public were that there were not enough houses, getting on the property ladder was too difficult, and the government was not able to build social housing in fast enough numbers to meet the demand for them.

In February 2006, during a debate on the finance bill, Cowen was eager to discuss the idea of individuals avoiding tax and the real impact of this on the exchequer: 'I wish to make it clear in this context that I am committed to having an *ex-ante* cost-benefit assessment of any new schemes and I am also in favour of time limits on schemes, as recommended in the reviews. However, I do not believe it is necessary to provide in the legislation on any particular scheme that there must be a cost-benefit analysis for that scheme. Indeed, the consultants recommended a continuation of the existing tax reliefs for private hospitals, nursing homes and childcare facilities without suggesting a time limit for these particular schemes. As I said, I agree with cost-benefit analysis of, and time limits on, new schemes, but they are a matter for government practice rather than statutory provision.

'A picture has been painted by some commentators and certain opposition spokespersons of a tax system which has resulted in the emergence of a substantial body of high-income individuals who pay little or no tax. That is a distortion of the position. Despite assertions to the contrary, the position is that those who earn more contribute more to the income tax yield than was the case in 1997, when we took office. It is estimated that in 2006, the top 1 per cent of income earners will pay approximately 20 per cent of all income tax collected. In the 1997-98 tax year, the top 1 per cent paid less than 15 per cent of all income tax collected.'

Interestingly, Cowen also pointed out that by raising money from a reduced corporation tax and by capitalising on other areas such as stamp duty, it had enabled the government to deal with an over-reliance on high income taxes: 'Under this government's management, we have given money back to the taxpayer. We have become less reliant on taxes on labour to fund government expenditure. In 1997, income tax represented 37 per cent of total exchequer tax revenue while taxes of a capital nature represented less than 5 per cent. In 2005, income tax as a proportion of total tax revenue was less than 29 per cent while the tax take from capital taxes and stamp duties increased to approximately 13 per cent of total tax take.'

In effect government always needs to raise tax, but for Cowen it was a question of where this was raised from, and he did not believe that it was fair that such a high proportion of tax should be based on income. He therefore favoured taking tax in other sectors to relieve pressure on income taxpayers.

One of the interesting things that is often overlooked in these years is that the government was running a surplus in the budget and tax take often exceeded expectations. Therefore in its estimates the department of finance was being conservative. This would suggest an inbuilt insurance against a downturn in the property sector. It is clear that the government did not rely on or expect windfalls from the property sector and had under-budgeted the amounts that would be brought in.

But the opposition were clear that if the government was bringing in more money than was expected time and time again, then this conservatism in estimates was causing the taxpayer to pay more tax than was required to keep the country on budget. Any fears about the economy were still not, therefore, dominating the debate with regard to cutbacks or money being put aside from either a government or opposition point of view. Richard Bruton raised the issue: 'Does the minister believe that the forecasts, which were 7,440 per cent wrong, could conceivably be treated as best practice? Is there not a need for the department's officials to go back to the various experts and re-examine how these yields are being estimated? It is putting a huge extra burden – a sum of €3,000 million over three years – on ordinary taxpayers.'

Mr Cowen: 'It is not putting a burden on ordinary taxpayers but is ensuring that capital taxes, given that there are low rates of income tax, are making a far better contribution than we expected. Sustained buoyancy in the property market in 2005, which is behind the excess yields in stamp duties, and capital gains taxes defied expectations. The department of finance, in common with most other commentators, including the Central Bank and the ESRI, had expected a cooling off in the property market in 2005, but it did not occur. In the circumstances, there was no real basis in December 2004 for projecting increases of more than 30 per cent in these taxes, which took place in 2005.

'The big four taxes – VAT, income tax, corporation tax and excise duties – represented close to 90 per cent of all targeted tax revenues in 2005 and accounted for 87 per cent of tax revenues collected. Excluding the excess from the Revenue Commissioners' main special investigations, these tax headings together came within less than 1 per cent of target and accounted for approximately 13 per cent of the total excess in tax revenues in 2005.'

Economies are always a delicate balance. They depend largely on consumer confidence to create and drive growth. One of the first major threats to the Irish economy was becoming very real in March 2006, as inflation started to rise. Cowen reported that: 'On budget day, inflation as measured by the consumer price index was forecast to average 2.7 per cent in 2006. Part of the pick-up in the annual inflation rate in February reflects the rise in interest rates by the European Central Bank. In addition, the price of oil rose throughout most of last year, which had an impact on the annual rate of inflation in February. We have no control over these external factors. My department will publish updated forecasts in the autumn.'

This could arguably mark the beginning of problems with regard to the economy in the Dáil record. It was a slow process, but here we can see the seeds of the future problems begin, although at this time they do not appear overly serious. But oil prices, and the ECB's policy of increasing interest rates were to have a direct impact upon Ireland. The ECB raised rates to try and combat inflation in the euro zone. At the time it was accepted best practice; in hindsight and in the aftermath of a banking crisis it was not so wise. Interest rates would significantly hit Irish borrowers and directly impacted upon the Irish property market. It is perhaps a blunt tool used to combat inflation by making loans and mortgages so expensive that people have no more money to spend. In time, perhaps alternative ways will be found to combat inflation, in the wreckage of the banking crisis.

On 23 May the problem of rising inflation is still an indicator of a serious risk in the economy and Cowen addresses this: 'Inflation, as measured by annual changes in the consumer price index, CPI, was 3.8 per cent in April. A large part of the recent pick-up in the annual inflation rate is owing to external factors such as higher oil prices and interest rate increases by the European Central Bank …

'Maintaining a moderate rate of inflation remains a key priority of economic policy because of its importance to competitiveness. The government is doing its bit to contain inflation by implementing responsible fiscal policies. In addition, we have not increased excise duties for the last two years, and we are promoting greater price competition by removing the 1987 groceries order. We are also seeking a reasonable wage deal to maintain and improve our international competitiveness. We are investing in public infrastructure that will enhance our ability to produce more goods and services and keep inflation down in the process.'

Cowen could be criticised for not being alert to the fact that international factors were changing. There seemed to be a policy that Ireland had no control over international factors – therefore all the government could do was manage domestic issues. However, one could argue that as these international issues arose the government should have looked at putting more aside by cutting spending to meet any possible challenge. But even from the opposition the debate centred around domestic issues and what the government had done, rather than on the dangers of continued high spending in future years against this background. What is patently apparent is that at this stage no-one was looking to the international picture and predicting crisis. No one was tackling the government on its plans to deal with a significant downturn from factors outside of its control. The truth was that it was probably because it was an unwinnable argument. It would have meant that either the government or the opposition would have had to take a serious popularity hit by suggesting that in order to provide for a possible risk spending may have to be scaled back.

We can see from later questions that there was a feeling that there was no end in sight to escalating house prices. Politically the main concern was whether or not people could afford to buy a home. Mr Connolly asked Brian Cowen if he intended to introduce a more equitable stamp duty regime on house purchase. Cowen replied: 'Any proposals concerning the rates, structure and impact of stamp duty are a matter for the budget. I have acted already in several respects to reduce the burden of stamp duty on low value properties and on first-time buyers. New houses are generally exempt from stamp duty. Considerations of equity within the stamp duty code must be balanced by requirements for equity in the overall tax system. It is a question of ensuring that a fair share of taxation is paid all round …

'There is currently a broad consensus among commentators such as the OECD and the IMF that the most likely outcome for the housing market is for what is termed a soft landing. However, we cannot be complacent by assuming this is inevitable. As I said on a number of occasions and acknowledged in the stability programme update published with the 2006 budget, the fact that the construction sector now accounts for a historically high share of economic activity and employment implies that the economy is vulnerable to any shock affecting this sector.

'For its part, the government continues to run a prudent, stability-oriented budgetary policy which gives it room for manoeuvre in the event of an economic downturn, whatever the cause. Its planned infrastructural investment programme is largely being funded out of current revenues rather than borrowing, while the careful choice of appropriate projects enhances the overall productive capacity of the economy and thus should underpin future growth.'

The main challenge that was facing the government was finding a way to address this problem and allow greater access to the market and assist people in purchasing a house. The problem was only twelve months away from being rectified, however, when the market would collapse. A major reason in this collapse was the amount of pressure the government was under to reform stamp duty to benefit first-time buyers. The continual debate around stamp-duty reform would lead to buyers beginning to hold off from making a purchase while they awaited changes in budgets and elections. Cowen failed to convince people that there was nothing to be gained by waiting. This debate, therefore, played a significant part in the beginnings of a downturn in the property sector when set against rising interest rates. But in mid-2005 there was no reason to believe this was about to happen, and Cowen outlined some interesting thoughts on the market: 'It is extraordinary in some respects looking back over the past decade, that the affordability of housing is still sustainable ... repayments of up to €1,500 are commonplace. Given that average industrial wage earners now have on average a take-home pay of €11,400 more than eight years ago, that helps to put in context why, perhaps, it is now more affordable for people to make those types of repayment as a percentage of total disposable income. Wages growth has well outstripped inflation and there has also been tax reform which has made the difference between the net and gross disposable income in Ireland the narrowest in any OECD country ... People in the construction industry and commentators in general, including economists, have been forecasting a cooling off in the requirements for increased output in the housing sector for at least four or five years, yet housing output is again at record levels this year, compared with 2005.'

On 28 June we find that continual interest rate increases were starting to cause serious problems. Joan Burton asked Cowen for his views on the fact that monthly mortgage repayments had increased over the past year by approximately €120 per month on an average €300,000 mortgage and by approximately €200 per month on an average €500,000 mortgage. She questioned whether he intended to implement measures to provide clear information for mortgage holders on the effect of projected future interest rate increases on their monthly payments, and if his attention had been drawn to the fact that the European Central Bank had indicated the likelihood of further interest rate rises.

Mr Cowen: 'As the deputy will be aware, there is a broad range of factors that determine the effect of changes in interest rates on individual loan repayments. These include, for example, the outstanding loan amount, whether the lending rate is fixed or variable, the length of time over which the increase takes place, the pass-through of interest rate changes to lending rates, the repayment term and the specific nature of the financial product involved. In reviewing the broad impact of projected increases in interest rates on households, account must also be taken of such factors as private sector savings levels as any increase in interest rates will obviously have beneficial effects for savers, as well as the broader macro-economic climate comprising strong employment and incomes growth and continuing robust performance of the economy overall.

'As far as the provision of information by mortgage lenders is concerned, mortgage providers are specifically obliged under the Consumer Credit Act 1995, to inform borrowers of the effect on the amount of their repayment instalments of a one percentage point increase in interest rates in the first year of their mortgages. This is intended to ensure that consumers, when making such a significant borrowing decision, are properly informed regarding the impact that changes in the cost of servicing the loan will have on the household budget over time.'

Cowen felt that all the possible protections had been put in place for consumers but that he had no control over the issue. However, it was a serious threat, as continual rate rises began to hit consumer confidence and people began to plan to cut back their spending. Interestingly Cowen later shows his reliance on the advice from the Central Bank in this regard: 'I share the Central Bank's assessment of the importance of maintaining financial and economic stability.

'The stability report to which I referred, which was published last autumn, showed the trend for mortgage repayments for first-time buyers over the past fifteen years within a range of approximately 23 per cent to 33 per cent of household disposable income on a national basis. Irish house buyers benefit from a range of supporting factors, including healthy income growth, low income tax rates and relatively low level of interest rates by historical standards. Affordability is also supported by the strength of the economy, record employment levels and relatively high savings rates. The expected shift in the interest rate environment will impact on affordability which, together with the large increase in new housing supply, should support equilibrium in the market. It is important we present the results in that context.

'Banks are required to stress-test at a rate above existing rates. It is also in the interests of financial institutions to have good loan books as that determines profitability in the longer term. The growth in credit is a matter for the Central Bank, particularly through its participation in the European Central Bank where interest rates are set.'

It is clear that rising interest rates were viewed as a problem but one that the economy could manage as it progressed. The higher interest rates may even help the hoped-for soft landing as the property market might stop accelerating and this would solve one of Cowen's headaches.

But the economy was far from in crisis. The main debate in October focused still on government spending and rather than criticise the level, it was they way in which money was spent that the opposition focused on. Joan Burton again hit a weak point in government policy – the extension of the medical card scheme to over seventies and its excessive costs: 'The medical cards case is not acceptable. This was driven by a budget day announcement – one of these rabbits that was produced out of the hat, providing medical cards for everyone over seventy. We know that project was not costed and the number of people and the cost were incorrectly estimated.

'They put themselves in an impossible negotiating position whereby they had to pay a huge amount for it. Then they used a trailing issue of the new discretionary cards. It is unclear where the information came from, but they came up with a figure that 75,000 of these cards were provided because of exceptional medical circumstances. They paid away merrily on the basis of those 75,000 but we now find in an audit that the database only shows 36,000 such cards. Not even all of those cards were supposed to be compensated because they did not all come within the criteria for compensation. Once again, we see the taxpayer being treated like a patsy or fall-guy who must take up all the slack and carry the cost of ministers making announcements they did not think through in the first place.'

Cowen was convinced that real value for money was being delivered: 'It is important the record is set straight with regard to achievements for the expenditure applied by this government. It is very easy for the opposition to play politics with this area in an attempt to undermine government achievements by singling out individual instances of waste for mention or by making exaggerated claims that expenditure on programmes is wasted if any part of it showed waste, or that the failure to solve every problem means there has been no progress on delivering services. The vast bulk of all public expenditure provides real value for money and delivers essential services and a good return for the taxpayer. Every day this expenditure is effectively delivering significantly important services to our citizens. Over €50 billion will be spent this year and social welfare, health, education and capital investment will account for almost 80 per cent of that expenditure, bringing significant improvements.'

The management of the economy was the central task for Cowen and keeping the finances on track was of primary importance. On 21 November Cowen was presenting the estimates for 2007: 'We are spending €6,700 more on public services for every man, woman and child in the country than we did in 1997. This extra expenditure has led to real improvements in our public services. On the capital side, as a result of the increased spending, great advances have been made in the provision of new roads, radically improved public transport, new and improved schools and hospitals, more social housing and other essential infrastructure that has improved prosperity and enhanced quality of life.'

The levels of spending were enormous. Debate would centre on whether the results of the spending were good enough, but there is little doubt that the government could point to a long list of achievements. Current spending was still reaching astounding levels if threats were actually being considered: 'On the current side the 2007 estimate is

€47 billion or a 7.4 per cent increase on the 2006 forecast outturn. Over €2.4 billion, or 75 per cent of the additional €3.2 billion, is being allocated to the three priority areas of health, education and social welfare.

'The total current spending allocation for health next year is almost €14 billion, an increase of €1.4 billion or 11.3 per cent on the 2006 outturn of €12.5 billion. The 2007 pre-budget provision for health will fund service improvements in key areas and will include €75 million to commission and open in 2007 eight new units in acute hospitals. A further €40 million is being provided in 2007 on top of the substantial increase in 2006 to meet a commitment to expand services for the elderly and there will be an expansion of primary care teams and of education and training for health professionals.'

Equally, the public-sector pay bill showed no sign of reform or impact: 'The gross provision for 2007 to fund public service pay and pensions is some €18 billion, an increase of €1.2 billion or 7 per cent. This represents 38 per cent of the total gross current expenditure provision for 2007. The pay terms of the *Towards 2016* social partnership agreement accounts for just over €740 million of this.

'The 2007 pay and pensions bill of €18 billion is a significant commitment of resources. Of this amount, some €14.9 billion or 83 per cent is in respect of the frontline services of health, education and security. The government has permitted increases in the number of staff in these areas in recent years and I make no apology for this. These are labour-intensive services and if we wish to get maximum benefit from enhanced capital expenditure in the areas of health and education we must adequately staff the resultant new or enhanced facilities and see a contribution from other parts of the service, which is happening.

'Nonetheless, the taxpayer is entitled to full value for money in respect of this significant outlay. Accordingly, payment of the pay increases under *Towards 2016* will be dependent, in the case of each sector, organisation and grade, on independent verification of co-operation with flexibility and ongoing change, including co-operation with satisfactory implementation of the agenda for modernisation set out in the agreement.'

Richard Bruton was critical of the spending: 'The minister said an extra €6,700 was being spent for every man, woman and child in the country. That is true. The government has spent an extraordinary amount of money in the last few years. In the seven years 2000 to 2007, current spending by the government has increased by an astonishing 120 per cent. That is €19,000 more in that period for every family in the country. Consumer prices in that period have increased by 28 per cent so the government has been commanding a significant extra dollop of resources.'

However, Bruton's argument would centre on what Cowen had done with the money rather than any suggestion of cutting spending. To be fair it is still evident from the Dáil debate that on all sides opinion held that while international threats might hold back or slow the economy they were not likely to result in a major reversal of fortunes in the near future.

Indeed Bruton argued that the government was still taking in too much money from the public: 'An additional €1,000 million in motor tax, social insurance and health and training levies will be raised from families and businesses in 2007. Families will struggle to find this extra money at a time when they are already tightly strapped from meeting the costs of rising interest rates, mortgage payments and energy bills. There is no evidence of sensitivity in this government to the fact that it should cut its cloth, in terms of raising tax, to the measure of what people can afford. The estimates also conceal increases in local authority commercial rates and planning development charges because the minister is only making provision for a 2 per cent increase in local government spending. I do not know how he will square that with the extra 7.4 per cent he has allotted for the government's general services.'

On 22 November the annual stability report from the Central Bank caused much discussion. But it is clear that Cowen was still relying heavily on the Central Bank's advice that the Irish banking system was safe and robust despite the dangers in the air: 'I welcome the publication by the Central Bank of its *Financial Stability Report 2006* which reflects the Bank's mandate to contribute to the stability of the financial system in Ireland. I note the report's main conclusion that Ireland's financial system continues to be in a good state of health. This is based on a detailed assessment of the risks facing borrowers, the financial position of the banking sector as well as recent stress testing of the system.

'The Bank's central expectation, based on an assessment of the risks facing borrowers, the financial position of the banking sector as well as the results of recent stress testing of the system, is that the current shock absorption capacity of the banking system leaves it well placed to withstand possible pressures. The report also highlights that the strength of the economy continues to support the stability of the financial sector.

'The Bank's report identifies vulnerabilities facing the financial system, including those arising from credit growth and house price inflation. Within the implementation of the overall legislative framework, private sector credit growth and debt levels are, in the first instance, a matter for the Central Bank and Financial Services Authority of Ireland. While the strong increase in borrowing is a sign of a healthy economy and a positive economic outlook on the part of borrowers, I fully support the vigilance of the Central Bank and the financial regulator on the issue of personal credit and mortgage debt and in reminding both borrowers and lenders of the need for responsible behaviour. The government, for its part, will continue to contribute to economic and financial stability by pursuing a prudent fiscal policy.'

One gets the impression the Cowen agreed with much of the financial advice of the time. He felt that Ireland was exposed and it was quite possible that the economy could face a property collapse. However, he was confident that the government had the resources to deal with any such crisis and there was enough revenue from other sources to compensate. Times might get tougher but the economy was well placed to take corrective action and survive without much difficulty. Clearly he was shown nothing to suggest that there was a chance, however small, for all factors to hit at the same time and form a 'perfect storm': 'Of course one keeps a close eye on these matters, as one must and should. Interest rate policy, as a result of our euro membership, is a matter for the ECB in the first instance. Ireland is represented on the ECB by the governor of the Central Bank. Mr Trichet, President of the European Central Bank, when addressing the European Parliament's economic and monetary affairs committee – his comments were not confined to Ireland but related to a number of European countries – said that the housing market in a number of European countries has been considerably buoyant, but monetary policy decisions are taken with regard to the euro area as a whole and cannot be taken with regard to individual conditions in specific countries.

'The Central Bank has been consistently pointing to the requirement for prudence on the part of both borrowers and lenders in the housing market here …

'A soft landing is being encouraged by the continuing supply of houses to a market which continues to have strong fundamentals. Anecdotal evidence suggests the market is softening but we will not be able to ascertain until spring of next year whether interest rate increases are contributing to that situation. The important point is that we should not be predicting a hard landing when the Central Bank and all the evidence of continuing high income growth and low unemployment rates indicate otherwise. When people saw problems in the housing market across the water, it was against a background of rising unemployment and much higher interest rates. Taking nominal inflation into account, real interest rates are significantly lower at present.'

We also find in later questions an innocuous enough question that would contain a term that would enter household use in later years, 'sub-prime' lending. Deputy Tommy Broughan asked Cowen if his attention had been drawn to reports that more lenders planned to launch sub-prime mortgages in 2007 in addition to the existing packages offered and if the financial regulator was in discussion with these banks to ensure that charges such as arrangement fees and rates are set at reasonable levels and remain at reasonable levels. Cowen stated: 'I am aware of the reports referred to by the deputy. The sub-prime market exists to provide finance to those who have difficulty accessing mainstream credit, usually owing to an adverse credit history or difficulties proving income. Consequently, interest on such loans is normally higher than in the case of mainstream credit, as the lender must allow for a greater degree of credit risk. As the deputy may be aware, the level of lending in the sub-prime market is currently extremely small.

'Sub-prime lenders are regulated in Ireland in respect of their lending activities under the Consumer Credit Act 1995. The Act makes detailed provision for the form and content of the various loan agreements and advertising of consumer credit. The financial regulator has powers of investigation, review and enforcement regarding matters covered by the act. ... In view of my role as minister for finance, I will give full consideration to any recommendation from the financial regulator that may require a legislative response.'

So we can see that sub-prime was not considered an issue in Ireland and also that Cowen views his position as acting on advice from IFSRA on this issue.

But although such threats existed, the economic situation was reasonably strong and it was against this backdrop that Cowen introduced his third budget in 2006: 'Growth is running at 5 per cent, its ideal, sustainable level, and more than 2 million people are at work. We are making unprecedented investment in our infrastructure and this will enhance our competitiveness and improve our quality of life for years to come.

'In 2007, our country will extend its record of outstanding economic progress. The economy will grow by 5.25 per cent; we estimate that 72,000 new jobs will be created next year, representing a 3.5 per cent increase in the numbers at work; unemployment will remain low at 4.4 per cent, among the lowest in the EU; and inflation, as measured on the harmonised EU basis, will moderate from 2.7 per cent on average in 2006, to 2.6 per cent in 2007.

'Of course these projections are subject to some degree of risk from international factors. These include a possible sharper than expected downturn in the US economy; a slower growth rate than is currently forecast in Europe; further ECB interest rate increases; and the ever-present unpredictability of oil prices and exchange rates. There are also domestic risks of losing competitiveness and from unbalanced economic growth. This budget addresses those risks by taking a long-term, sustainable approach to our economic management.'

There was certainly no evidence of a significant downturn in the outlook. But Cowen did feel that he was providing for the future: 'I am not proposing that because we have extra resources we should spend it all now. That would be irresponsible and short-sighted. Responsible government involves finding the balance between meeting immediate priorities and making provision for future uncertainties. Of the additional resources at my disposal this year, I am returning some to the taxpayer and committing some to additional support in the social welfare and health areas, in care of the elderly and in improving services for the disabled. I am also using some of the additional revenue to run a very substantial budget surplus. In the event of a global slowdown, we will be able to use some of this flexibility generated during the good times to protect jobs and public services at home.'

Focus was again on a more social agenda. Provision was made for senior citizens earning income: 'The income tax exemption limits for senior citizens aged sixty-five and over are being raised from €17,000 and €34,000 to €19,000 and €38,000 per year respectively for single and married persons, removing a further 9,000 from the tax net. This means our senior citizens will be exempt from income tax if they earn less than €19,000 single or €38,000 married per year.

'I propose to increase a number of other tax credits which affect certain people because of their particular circumstances. Widowed persons currently receive an additional tax credit of €500 per year. I am increasing it by 10 per cent to €550 in 2007. A special tax credit is also given to widowed parents in each of the five years following the year of bereavement. I believe that widowed parents deserve greater support during these difficult years and I am increasing the credit by €650 in each of the five years after the year of bereavement. The increased tax credit will range from €1,750 in year five to €3,750 in year one.'

Cowen also delivered tax cuts and credit improvements across the board but of particular note was a move on a promise to cut the top rate of tax: 'We believe that the economic circumstances are sufficiently buoyant now to enable me to reduce the top rate of tax from 42 per cent to 41 per cent today.'

Deputies: 'Hear, hear.'

Mr Cowen: 'This rate cut will cost a net €125 million in 2007 and a net €186 million in a full year. If this government is returned to office, and is honoured with a further term, then on the basis of our current economic strength being maintained, it is our shared intention to complete the commitment to cut the top income tax rate to 40 per cent in next year's budget …

'I propose to increase the health levy from 2 per cent to 2.5 per cent on income exceeding €1,925 per week or just over €100,000 per year. This extra money will help fund services such as long-term care initiatives for the elderly. We need to act now to secure such funds and I believe it is only right that those best able to afford it make an increased contribution. This will raise €34 million in a full year.'

Some commentators have pointed out that Cowen may have brought about a reforming social agenda to Irish budgetary policy, but that this in turn weakened the pro-business approach taken by his predecessor that had significantly contributed to economic success. This argument depends largely on a view of left or right wing policies, but Cowen certainly did introduce measures to assist business also: 'On foot of this review and the suggestions of groups such as the Small Business Forum, I am announcing an extension of these schemes for a further seven years and I am raising the ceiling per company on total BES investment from €1 million to €2 million. The annual limit on BES investment per investor, which has not been increased since 1984, is being raised from €31,750 to €150,000 …

'It is often pointed out that much of the dynamism of an economy comes from small firms and there is a real need for small companies to make use of innovation and modern technology to maintain competitiveness. To help bring that about, the minister for enterprise, trade and employment has announced a provision of €5 million in 2007 for innovation vouchers, knowledge acquisition grants and ICT audits, all of which were recommended by the Small Business Forum.

'Small businesses are a major source of employment and growth in this country. Small businesses are big business. There are approximately

250,000 small businesses in Ireland today, employing almost 800,000 people, or 40 per cent of the workforce. Recognising their important contribution and their development potential, I am pleased to announce the following package of measures aimed at reducing the administrative burden on this important sector. Small companies whose corporation tax liability is currently less than €50,000 can pay preliminary tax based on their previous year's final tax liability. This removes the need for small businesses to forecast their projected full-year performance prior to the end of their accounting year. To alleviate further the burden on small business, I am increasing the small company liability threshold from €50,000 to €150,000.'

Deputies: 'Hear, hear.'

Mr Cowen: 'Over 97 per cent of Irish companies will have the benefit of this simpler and more straightforward system. It will help them to get on with their business without putting the state's cash flow at risk. I am also introducing measures proposed by Revenue whereby new start-up companies will not have to pay preliminary tax in respect of their first accounting period. In addition, I have asked Revenue to explore further opportunities to reduce the tax compliance burden on all firms, large and small.

'The annual VAT cash accounting threshold for small firms is being raised from €635,000 to €1 million from 1 March 2007 to simplify administration and reduce working capital requirements. This allows smaller firms to pay VAT on receipt of payment rather than at the time a sale is made. The small business VAT registration turnover thresholds are being increased from €27,500 per year for services and €55,000 per year for goods to €35,000 and €70,000, respectively, from 1 March 2007. This measure could take up to 8,000 businesses out of the VAT system and will considerably reduce their administrative burden. The frequency of VAT payments for smaller firms is being reduced from six VAT returns to three each year in some cases and to two each year in other cases. This will provide a cash flow boost to firms and significantly reduce compliance costs. The transaction threshold which triggers the requirement for a tax clearance certificate is being increased from the current €6,500 to €10,000 …

'I am also enhancing the existing research and development tax credit for firms so as to promote research and development spending in our manufacturing sector.'

Cowen also pursued environmental aims particularly in relation to cars: 'I would like to mention a number of measures in the fiscal area which I am bringing forward.

'In the case of Vehicle Registration Tax, I intend to change the current rating system to relate it more closely to environmental policy objectives, in this case reducing carbon dioxide emissions. I intend that there should be some reward in the VRT system for choosing lower-emission vehicles, and that those choosing higher-emission vehicles should pay more.'

Mr Cuffe: 'What about the Lexus?'

Mr Cowen: 'For that reason, I am setting out a range of options in the budget booklet for making such a move. My department will carry out a public consultation process on these proposals before coming back to government. Any changes will have effect from a target date of 1 January 2008 …

'The greener homes scheme has had a very positive response from the public. The scheme provides grants for the installation of new energy technologies such as bio-mass burners, heat pumps and solar panels. There have been about 10,000 applications so far. I am increasing the planned spend in this area by €20 million between now and the end of 2009.'

Deputies: 'Hear, hear.'

Mr Cowen: 'In the commercial area, we introduced a bio-heat scheme for grant-aiding, for example, wood pellet burners. I am extending this scheme to cover the installation of other technologies such as solar panels. I am also extending it to buildings in the non-commercial sector such as community centres, and sports facilities so that they will also be able to avail of the grants. The planned additional spending for the next year is €4 million, partly funded by a reallocation of resources within the department of communications, marine and natural resources.'

To help inflation excise was abolished on home heating oil: 'As I announced in last year's budget statement, I am abolishing the excise on Kerosene and LPG used for home heating from 1 January 2007.'

And Cowen ensured pensioners were looked after again: 'In the good times we enjoy, we owe it to them to make their lives a little more comfortable. We had a headline commitment to raise the old-age pension to at least €200 per week during our term of office. I wish to confirm today, that by raising the contributory old-age pension by €16 per week and the non-contributory pension by €18 per week, we have fulfilled this commitment. The new rates will be €209.30 per week for the contributory old-age pension and €200 per week …'

Carer's allowance, the respite grant and fuel allowance measures were also aimed at the elderly: 'I am also increasing the annual respite care grant by €300 to €1,500. We are increasing the back-to-school clothing and footwear allowance to €180 and €285. We are increasing the free fuel allowance to €18 per week and increasing the income threshold for eligibility to €100 per week. This means we will have doubled this allowance in the past two years.'

Cowen held fast to his principle of making those who could afford to pay do so with regard to health, as he imposed a large increase on the cost of private beds in public hospitals: 'These improvements will be part financed by a 25 per cent increase in the charge for private beds in public teaching hospitals.'

Earlier in the year Progressive Democrat leader Michael McDowell had said that he favoured major reform in stamp duty, and the market took a hit as buyers held off until the budget. Cowen's announcement was a disappointment for many: 'In 2007, I want to see additional support going to those who have bought, or are trying to buy, a home for the first time.

'In the current market situation, any stamp duty cuts would, more likely than not, be incorporated into the sale price and so end up in the pocket of the seller ...

'The government therefore proposes to double the ceiling on mortgage interest relief for first-time buyers from €4,000 per year for single people and €8,000 per year for married or widowed people to €8,000 and €16,000, respectively.'

For Cowen the crucial point was to convince buyers to keep buying as there was no reason to hold off hoping for change. He failed to convince buyers, however, as debate then moved on to changes that might come in the 2007 election, and the market as a result began to stagnate.

Budget 2006 was certainly a big spending budget. Cowen introduced many welcome reforms and reliefs. However, they were based upon an economy continuing to stay on course. Inflation was rising, interest rate rises have posed a threat, oil prices had added to this, and now a fourth element was entering the equation as consumers held off buying houses in the hope that stamp duty might be reformed or even abolished.

Richard Bruton pointed out the dangers of an over-reliance on property but still fell short of suggesting another course of action in the short term: 'The government has doubled its dependence on the construction sector to support its revenue. A total of 25 per cent of every tax euro spent by the government comes from the construction sector. We are not in a strong position; we are, in fact, in a vulnerable position.

'The real question is whether the government has done enough to build the capability of the economy to withstand the real pressures under which it is about to come. Those pressures do not merely revolve around the possible slowdown in the housing market; they relate to the relentless march of competition that is coming our way. Our competitiveness has declined in each of the past five years. In the same period, our share of export markets and the level of manufacturing employment have fallen. Some 50 per cent of the jobs that existed in IDA Ireland and Enterprise Ireland industries five years ago have disappeared.'

On 7 February there seemed no let-up on inflation despite the interest rate increases and Cowen felt inflation was actually on the up as a result of the rate increases. Joan Burton asked if Cowen's attention has been drawn to a recent warning by the Central Bank of the risk posed to the Irish economy and its competitiveness by continued high inflation and the Bank's prediction that annual inflation was set to rise to 4.5 per cent in 2007. Cowen responded positively: 'I am aware of the report by the Central Bank and welcome its broadly positive assessment of the Irish economy. The best measure of underlying inflation is the EU comparable measure of inflation, known as the Harmonised Index of Consumer Prices. Average HICP inflation in Ireland was 2.7 per cent in 2006 and my department is forecasting HICP inflation averaging 2.6 per cent in 2007.

'The annual rate of inflation as measured by the consumer price index was 4.0 per cent in 2006 and is forecast to be 4.1 per cent in 2007. The CPI differs from the HICP in terms of coverage. The main difference between the CPI and the HICP is the inclusion of mortgage interest repayments in the CPI. Recent CPI inflation has been impacted by six interest rate increases since December 2005, each of 0.25 per cent. I agree with the point expressed by the Central

Bank in its bulletin that the outlook for CPI inflation will depend in large part on the future path of interest rates.'

There were concerns about speculation in the housing market, but Cowen did not believe that this was as easy to deal with as people thought without creating harm elsewhere. Joan Burton asked: 'Can the minister do something about the manner in which builders engage in land speculation?'

Mr Cowen: 'I do not know who else the deputy expects to build houses. The capacity of the construction industry has expanded in recent years, thankfully, so it is now able to meet demand by providing up to 80,000 houses per annum. That contrasts with an annual average of between 30,000 and 35,000 houses when Deputy Burton's party was last in office.'

Ms Burton: 'A nurse could afford to buy a house at that time.'

Mr Cowen: 'These are all indications of increased capacity.'

Ms Burton: 'Nurses could afford to live in the Dublin area.'

Mr Cowen: 'Annual house price inflation has decreased to approximately 5 per cent over the last six months.'

This figure for a deceleration in the housing market seemed to point to a possibility of a soft landing still being on the cards. Despite this and the growing risks to the sector there was still pressure in early 2007 for some form of intervention to make house prices more affordable, as people did not seem to think the prices were going to come down. Deputy Kehoe asked whether Cowen had assessed the affordability of house purchase for young families in view of the 40 per cent increase in the cost of mortgages in the past twelve months and questioned the implications of this increase for government policy. Cowen replied: 'As the deputy will be aware, housing policy is primarily a matter for the minister for the environment, heritage and local government. From an economic perspective, house buyers benefit from a range of supporting factors, including healthy income growth, low income tax rates and relatively low levels of interest rates by historical standards. Affordability is also supported by the strength of the economy, record employment levels and relatively high savings rates. Recent indicators point to continued moderation in house price inflation in line with increased housing supply and higher European Central Bank interest rates.

'The consensus among commentators is for this trend to continue, resulting in a gradual cooling and soft landing for property prices in Ireland. The Central Bank's *Financial Stability Report 2006* shares the view that this is the most likely outcome, while noting that increases both in house prices and interest rates are contributing to reduced house price affordability. House prices rose at a markedly reduced rate of only 0.1 per cent in December 2006 and, according to economic commentators, this signalled the beginning of a slowdown and expected soft landing in the property market.'

While hopes existed of a soft landing clearly the primary worry of politicians was for first-time buyers. The simple fact was that in the course of the next year first-time buyers would be in a better position than they had for many years as house prices tumbled.

In February there was definitely no sign of a future concern over the economy as the government launched one of the most ambitious National Development Plans in history. Cowen announced: 'I am pleased to open this debate on the new National Development Plan. The plan sets out a vision of how Ireland can be transformed over the next seven years and how we can provide a better quality of life for all. It is an ambitious, fully costed, multi-annual blueprint for sustainable development. It encompasses a broad and comprehensive approach to our economic priorities but also to regional development, social inclusion and environmental sustainability.

'The objective of a better quality of life for our people informs the National Development Plan. This objective will be delivered in particular by the following measures and strategies in the Plan: an investment of some €88 billion in our economic and social infrastructure; a major programme of social inclusion measures costing some €50 billion over the period, including services for children, the elderly and the disabled; a major focus on environmental sustainability backed up by total investment of €25 billion in key areas, including a quadrupling of investment in public transport over the levels in the last plan; a model for regional development that, through the framework of investment and complementary land use policy, can assist all regions to achieve their potential and promote a better environment and quality of life; and strong and tangible all-island co-operation implemented in a co-operative way to the benefit of all citizens on the island …

'The plan will involve an estimated expenditure of €184 billion over seven years. This investment will be rolled out within a framework of economic and budgetary stability and in full compliance with the requirements of the EU Stability and Growth Pact. The economic framework underpinning the plan assumes annual average economic growth over the period of 4-4.5 per cent and it is affordable on that basis.'

That last line alone sounds ominous in today's world. While the government has continued to commit resources to the NDP it would seem on the basis of its calculations that the Plan will have to lose some elements in the short and medium term unless Ireland has a dramatic recovery.

By March 2007 the general election was looming. The housing market was almost at a standstill as the debate about possible reforms in stamp duty raged. Politicians of all shades must shoulder the responsibility for stalling consumer confidence and damaging the market at this time. It was an example of how talk at a political level can do serious damage. Cowen originally led the fight against change, but under pressure from

Bertie Ahern he would eventually agree to reforms in the Fianna Fáil election manifesto. But in the Dáil, well in advance of that situation, Cowen was clear on his position: 'The government is very aware of the importance of the construction sector to the economy, as evidenced by the large numbers working in the area and the sums that come from it in taxation. With the sector directly responsible for 13.5 per cent of total employment, government policy should be aimed at supporting an important driver of economic activity.

'The provision of adequate numbers of new houses has been a key policy priority in recent years. We have seen numbers of house completions increase to over 93,000 in 2006, up from 52,000 in 2001. We are now at a stage where housing demand is beginning to match housing supply, and that is reflected in the market, with a significant slowdown in property inflation. That is clear evidence that our housing policy is working well.

'The stamp duty code applies a single rate to the full value of the property, where the rate applicable depends on the value of the property concerned. Given the growing market of recent years, it is not surprising that the yield from stamp duty has increased. ... Consideration of ways to improve the structure of the tax would have to have regard, among other things, to simplicity and cost. For example, the estimated cost of introducing a system whereby stamp duty would be applied on a marginal basis for houses priced above the current exemption thresholds, based on the full year 2006 yield, is €553 million – that is, more than 42 per cent of the yield on residential property ...

'Stamp duty is a significant contributor to the exchequer, which helps fund public services such as health and education, while keeping the direct tax burden low, thereby facilitating continued economic success which is of benefit to all taxpayers. It has helped us to reduce taxes on work and enterprise with clear benefits for the economy as a whole ...

'While there have been increases in the yield of this tax in recent years as a result of increased property prices, that is not something we can factor into future revenue yields either from that tax or the general revenue take. Nor can we expect that market conditions, which have softened in recent times, will be renewed with the increased price inflation that would result.'

There is an underlying argument here which was in favour of the government raising resources on behalf of the taxpayer from the buoyant property sector. One also gets the impression that Cowen and the department of finance in no way believed that this would last forever or that the money would not dry up. However, there is a tone of confidence that suggests they had calculated that when the problem arose they could deal with it on the strength of other sectors even if construction had been the main driver of the economy.

Some of Cowen's plans were hinted at in reply to a question on inflation on 20 March: 'The prospects for the economy are favourable. Strong growth is expected this year with both GDP and GNP forecast to increase by 5.3 per cent. With more than two million people now employed in the state and unemployment forecast to be under 4.5 per cent this year, we are effectively at full employment. However, we recognise that clear challenges remain, which must be addressed if living standards are to continue to improve as they have done over the past ten years.

'The government is keenly aware of the importance of Ireland's competitiveness position concerning investment, exports and, hence, jobs. Inflation is one of the factors impacting on competitiveness. Competitiveness is also influenced by exchange rates, wage inflation, public spending growth and capital spending on infrastructure.

'The annual rate of consumer price index, CPI, inflation was 4.8 per cent in February, down from 5.2 per cent in January. ... We all recognise that the Irish economy cannot compete on the same basis as in the past. To maintain and enhance competitiveness in the context of a higher-cost economy, a greater focus on productivity across all sectors of the economy is essential because in the long run, in a small economy like Ireland's, economic prosperity ultimately depends on our ability to sell goods and services abroad. Recognising this challenge, the government has developed policies which are designed to help Ireland's competitiveness. Important policy issues in the medium term include developing our innovation potential, improving the regulatory environment, enhancing the human capital of the country, and developing our economic and technological infrastructure.'

The problems caused by interest rates would not go away. If inflation, interest rates, rising oil prices and a stagnant house market had spelt serious threats, then we can begin to see the rise of the fifth element coming into play. This would take another year to be felt fully, but the problems in the US sub-prime market were the trigger that led to a credit crunch and eventually a global banking crisis that would cripple economies. The five elements of the perfect storm were now coming together, but very slowly, and no one had identified the risk as yet: 'The sub-prime mortgage market in Ireland is small and exists to serve a need for mortgage finance by borrowers who experience difficulty in accessing finance from mainstream lenders owing to an adverse credit record or difficulties in verifying income. Sub-prime borrowers tend to refinance their mortgage in the standard mortgage market once they have restored their credit record. The Consumer Credit Act 1995 requires information on key aspects of mortgage lending to be provided to borrowers on a mandatory basis. This includes, in particular, information on the impact of an increase of 1 per cent in interest rates in the first year of the mortgage.'

It was Joan Burton who raised the term 'toxic debt' for the first time – this would soon become another household term: 'Has the minister heard of the phrase "toxic debt", which is used widely in the United States in reference to the sub-prime market? It refers to the situation of a family that has borrowed heavily, usually initially for housing purposes, before proceeding to refinance its borrowing, perhaps to take in other short-term borrowings such as car loans and so on. With continuous increases in the rate of interest, the net result for such families is a growing unaffordability of the debt they have accumulated.'

Cowen was confident no such problem existed in Ireland: 'I have heard the term "toxic debt" in regard to sub-prime lending. It is a feature of the liberalised market in the United States where some companies have got into serious difficulties as a result of the sub-prime lending policies they have pursued. There is no evidence from the financial regulator that a similar situation exists here. The sub-prime mortgage market is relatively small. There is evidence that where people have regained credit with regard to how they are viewed as borrowers, they have moved from the sub-prime market back into the mainstream mortgage market.'

The June 2007 election had seemed to start positively for the opposition. However, Brian Cowen's performance helped to turn the tide and he was rewarded with the position of tánaiste. Ironically it was in large part due to Cowen's tough talking on the economy where he said that Ireland now faced very serious threats and challenges. Rather than had been anticipated by all the early manifestos that the election would be decided by giveaways and promises, the deciding factor in the 2007 election turned out to be a fear of a serious threat to the economy and a decision not to opt to change government as a result. The election did mean however that the Green Party joined Fianna Fáil in government, which was an interesting departure, especially in terms of policy on Europe.

By 26 June serious problems were now emerging in relation to the amount of tax coming in. However, while it was disappointing, Cowen was confident it could be dealt with, as there was still no hint of the impending storm gathering worldwide that would completely destroy both consumer spending power and confidence: 'Exchequer tax receipts to the end of May were, at €18.603 million, just €19 million or 0.1 per cent below profile. They were 9.6 per cent up on the same period last year. This compares with a budget day target of an increase of 7.8 per cent for 2007 as a whole.

'While overall tax receipts were almost exactly on target at the end of May, there are some variations under particular tax heads: corporation tax receipts are €221 million or 17.5 per cent above profile; customs receipts are €4 million or 3.6 per cent above profile; VAT receipts were €28 million or 0.4 per cent below profile; income tax receipts are €56 million or 1.1 per cent below profile; excise duties were €120 million or 4.7 per cent below profile; stamp duties were €16 million or 1.1 per cent below profile; and capital taxes were €71 million or 5.8 per cent below profile. Of these, capital gains tax was €79 million or 7.2 per cent below profile and capital acquisitions tax was €8 million or 5.1 per cent above profile.

'Given the significance of tax payments in the latter part of the year, it would be unwise to attempt to draw conclusions about the performance of the economy based on tax receipts at this early stage. The latest available economic estimates show that the economy continues to perform well. Preliminary CSO data for 2006 as a whole indicates that GDP growth was 6 per cent, while, in GNP terms, the growth rate in 2006 was estimated at 7.4 per cent.

'In the circumstances, I do not see a need to revise our forecast at this stage. However, my department monitors tax receipts on an ongoing basis and, as more data become available, any significant changes to the expected end of year receipts will be signalled once the position becomes clear.'

Mr Richard Bruton: 'Is the tánaiste aware that the data relating to housing starts suggest that they are 30 per cent down on their peak? Commentators for Davy have indicated that this could lead to housing completions falling from 95,000 to 65,000. Do I infer from the tánaiste's reply that he sees such a fall-off in housing activity as having no impact on tax revenue? Has he considered the likely impact of such a fall in housing construction on employment in the sector? Davy suggests that as many as 28,000 jobs could be lost in the construction sector as a result of the decline in activity. Does the tánaiste believe that exchequer revenue will be immune to this decline or is he of the view that the data relating to housing starts are wrong?'

Mr Cowen: 'Housing market activity impacts primarily on VAT, stamp duty and capital gains tax. It also impacts on income tax and PRSI receipts and corporation tax from construction sector company profits. While revenue from housing market activity, such as that relating to stamp duty and capital gains tax, has made an increasing contribution to the exchequer in recent years, we are not overly reliant on receipts from this source. Taken together, for example, the stamp duty and capital gains tax heads are forecast to contribute approximately 15 per cent of total targeted tax revenues in 2007 …

'It is worth noting that a significant proportion of receipts from these tax heads comes from sources other than residential property.

'On housing starts, a correction has been taking place in the market since last autumn. This has resulted in an easing in house price inflation. The latter is a welcome development because continuing double digit house price inflation would not be sustainable. There is also the question of trying to ensure that we achieve a soft landing for the housing sector, particularly in view of the fact that the Central Bank and Financial Services Authority of Ireland, the ESRI and others forecast over a period that there would be a reduction in housing starts and completions to a level of approximately 65,000 to 70,000 per annum in the next few years.'

If Brian Cowen was guilty of one thing at this point it would appear to be an obsession with the domestic. All plans seemed to revolve around how Ireland would cope with a property crash, there was little thought about what would happen if other areas collapsed due to international problems. Ireland and Cowen were caught up in a debate on how to deal with problems in housing to the exclusion of everything else.

The one element of the storm that might have been expected to abate at this stage was inflation, but it showed no sign of doing so and says much about the ECB policy. Cowen stated: 'On budget day, 6 December 2006, the department of finance forecast that consumer price index inflation would be 4.1 per cent this year. That forecast was based on the normal technical assumption of unchanged interest rates. The budget day forecast for the Harmonised Index of Consumer Prices inflation – the EU inflation measure – was 2.6 per cent this year. As usual, the department will publish updated inflation forecasts in the pre-budget outlook, which is due in the autumn. There have been three interest rate increases of 0.25 per cent since budget day, the latest of which was earlier this month. CPI inflation has averaged 5 per cent, year-on-year, in the first five months of this year, during which two of the three increases took place. As interest rates are a matter for the governing council of the European Central Bank, they are outside the control of the government.

'Mortgage interest accounts for approximately half of Ireland's rate of inflation. If the effect of mortgage interest is excluded, the year-on-year CPI average is 2.6 per cent so far this year. The CPI excluding tobacco has averaged 0.2 per cent lower than the full CPI so far this year ... it is important that we do not seek to compensate ourselves for such rises in interest rates, as that would lead to a wage-inflation spiral and would reduce our competitiveness and, ultimately, our real standard of living.'

On 2 October Cowen was introducing the Markets in Financial Instruments Bill. This was an EU directive, but some of the comments are interesting with regard to how oblivious Cowen was in regard to what 2008 would bring: 'The MiFID [Markets in Financial Instruments Directive] is one of the most significant items of EU financial services legislation agreed in recent times and applies to both investment firms and credit institutions when providing investment services. The aim of the MiFID is to create a pan-European market in investment products by replacing a patchwork of national rules with harmonised EU-wide regulation and investor protection so as to allow investment firms to sell investment products and services outside their home markets, across the Union, based on a single licence from their home country regulator.

'The MiFID also aims to increase transparency and to reduce costs for users of financial instruments such as equities and shares, bonds and derivatives, for example, credit or commodity derivatives or financial contracts for differences. This is being achieved through standardised rules on the dissemination of quotes and on pre- and post-trade transparency, as well as best execution practices …

'This directive is a further element of the comprehensive and detailed EU-wide framework for regulation of financial services which is implemented in Ireland by the financial regulator. Arising from developments in global financial markets in recent weeks, I wish to reiterate briefly a number of key points which I have previously highlighted regarding the quality of Ireland's financial system and its regulatory regime.

'The single most important point to be made in the national context is that Ireland's banking system is well-capitalised, profitable, liquid and soundly regulated. This is confirmed by the conclusions of the recently published IMF report which also noted that the Central Bank is satisfied that major lenders here have a solid financial base. As far as the effectiveness of the Irish regulatory system is concerned, the IMF report explicitly acknowledged the strengthening of the financial regulatory and supervisory system in Ireland over recent years which conforms to international best practice standards.

'It is important to highlight the Central Bank and Financial Services Authority of Ireland, CBFSAI, integrates within a single institutional structure both the supervision of individual financial firms by the financial regulator and the monitoring of overall financial stability, which is the responsibility of the governor of the Central Bank. This structure yields significant advantages in terms of the appropriate co-ordination of these two activities under the current legislative framework. In addition, the Central Bank and Financial Services Authority of Ireland operates within the overall context of the euro system and the European Central Bank which has ensured a consistent and coherent approach across the euro area to addressing current uncertainty in financial markets.

'In contributing to the further development of financial services regulation at EU level, important lessons are to be learned from recent developments in global financial markets. This process of review and examination is already under way. A key issue following recent events in the UK is the effectiveness of deposit protection arrangements across the EU. The European Commission has recently concluded a review of the Deposit Protection Schemes Directive which sets the framework for national schemes in the EU. It is necessary to look again at this work and in the light of recent developments to make sure that deposit guarantees strike the right balance between protecting depositors and making sure banks are not encouraged to take inappropriate risks.'

It is plain to see that on the advice given to him, Cowen had complete faith in the Irish banking sector and its strength. He was very much aware of the difficulties being experienced worldwide but there is no hint that he felt there was a threat of Armageddon proportions waiting in the wings for Irish banking. Many plans were made on this basis and neither he, nor anybody else for that matter, predicted or suggested any possibility of what would eventually transpire.

By October 2007 the storm had gathered and Irish tax receipts were being heavily hit. Cowen stated: 'At €31,462 million, exchequer tax receipts to end-September were €490 million or 1.5 per cent below profile. They were up 6.1 per cent on the same period last year. Corporation tax and income tax both performed well, coming in at €296 million and €56 million above profile respectively, reflecting the health of the economy generally. Receipts from each of the other main tax heads were below profile. Stamp duties were €401 million below profile, excise duties were €225 million below, VAT was €132 million below and capital gains tax was €107 million below. A significant amount of tax revenue is due for collection in the last quarter of the year, especially in November when a particularly large share of tax is collected annually from corporation tax, capital gains tax and income tax of the self-employed.

'The performance of tax revenue in the coming months, particularly in November, will inform the position for the year as a whole. As of now, a shortfall of up to €1 billion in taxes this year is the current estimate. However, this shortfall will be offset to some extent by positive developments on other elements of the exchequer account and an overall exchequer deficit of up to €1 billion now seems likely at year-end. The budget day estimate was for a deficit of €546 million this year.'

Mr Richard Bruton: 'What are the other revenue sources that will mean that an apparent deficit of €1 billion will only be off by €500 million at the end of the year? Has the minister had cause to revise what his economists call elasticities concerning various taxes, in other words the relationship between growth in income tax and growth in incomes?'

Mr Cowen: 'Last year's points were made on the basis of maintaining current economic strength. In the first six months of this year the economy improved by 6.4 per cent, but there has been a different story in the second half. We will have to make decisions closer to budget time, when we know the outcome of revenue trends, where we stand on future expenditure levels, and how we will try to maintain a capital investment programme. There will be a moderation in day-to-day current expenditure next year compared to recent years.'

However, the moderation may have been coming too late, as all factors were coinciding in a way not predicted and the government's fall-back position of having other sectors and taxes to rely on if the property market crashed, evaporated. Cowen had planned that if he lost property he would have cuts and tough times, but probably along similar lines to those in 2002; he never envisaged what was to come: 'We had projected that tax receipts in 2007 would increase by 7.8 per cent over last year's record levels. They were at a figure of 6.1 per cent in the first six months but there will be a further drag going into the final three months. Even allowing for significant tax income in the last couple of months, on tax heads which are still holding up, we expect the total increase in tax revenue this year over last year to culminate at a figure of approximately 5.5 per cent based on the information we have available to us after nine months. We will have a more accurate assessment as we get close to the budget.

'Having left a surplus position moving into a year such as this in which receipts, for example, from the residential property market have reduced, we expect to come in with a surplus this year. We can still provide for maintaining the existing level of services this year, already at a record high, and look to the unified budget proposal on 5 December, where we will take taxes and expenditures together, to see how we can maintain the level of output and keep unemployment levels as low as possible.'

On 16 October Cowen answered questions on financial regulation: 'The information available suggests that the level of lending in the sub-prime market is currently extremely small. For instance it is estimated that sub-prime loans make up roughly 2.5 per cent of the overall mortgage market. The sub-prime market exists to provide finance to those who have difficulty accessing mainstream credit, usually due to an adverse credit history or difficulties proving income. Consequently, interest on such loans is normally higher than in the case of mainstream credit, as the lender must allow for a greater degree of credit risk. In practice, various credit providers offer loans where the interest rate or conditions differ from those generally available in the market. These interest rates and conditions depend on a number of factors, including risk …

'I have already announced my intention to propose an amendment to the Markets in Financial Instruments and Miscellaneous Provisions Bill 2007, at committee stage this week, with a view to regulating the non-deposit taking lending sector, including sub-prime lenders. The text of the amendment has already been circulated. The main aim of the proposed measures is to ensure that borrowers from sub-prime lenders, or from other lenders in that sector, will be able to benefit from the additional safeguards which the financial regulator's Consumer Protection Code provides.'

There is still no hint of a threat to banking in Ireland or a risk for the taxpayer: 'A comprehensive system of banking supervision is in place under both EU and domestic law to ensure that credit institutions do not put customers' deposits at risk through imprudent lending practices. Banking supervision encompasses the authorisation of banks and building societies, their prudential supervision on an ongoing basis and the development of supervisory guidance and requirements for their operation. Prudential supervision involves monitoring the business of banks and building societies and how it is planned, managed, and controlled and checking compliance with statutory and non-statutory requirements.'

The unfortunate problem was that Europe was equally unprepared. Cowen dismissed any idea of a problem in Irish regulation on 17 October: 'I am concerned about people giving publicity to suggesting there was some problem for the Irish regulatory regime. There was not. Yesterday, I answered this question by way of a parliamentary question put by Deputy Costello and my response explained the factual situation on that matter. The fact is that structured investment vehicles, SIVs, and conduits are not regulated. However, as a result of recent market turbulence the EU, ECOFIN [Economic and Financial Affairs Council], the European Economic and Financial Centre, EEFC, central banks and experts in the area are examining what lessons can be learned for the future and how we can ensure we have regulation where required. We are also trying to ensure we have functioning markets that are at the forefront of innovation and which will acquire business and ensure business is conducted. Ireland has been able to achieve that ...

'The financial framework of this country is strong and liquid if one listens to what the Central Bank governor has to say. I am glad we have an influential governor who is held in high esteem by the industry generally, here, internationally and within the corridors of the ECB.

'It is not a question of being complacent, dismissive or conservative, but of facts. The last thing we want is to have fictional information in the public domain suggesting we are at risk. Of course, we are not immune from the turbulence which has taken place, but we are in a good position. If the Central Bank governor can state this, I should also be able to do so.'

Cowen was sticking to the policy of listening to people 'far more expert that I'. On 23 October Cowen discussed the pre-budget outlook: 'When I commented last week on this year's economic developments, I indicated that this year represents a turning point for the Irish economy. While the economy performed well in the first half of the year, the current indications are that the short- to medium-term outlook has changed from that envisaged on budget day last year. At that time, growth for this year was forecast at 5.3 per cent in GDP terms, whereas GDP growth of 4 per cent is now anticipated. Like other commentators, the department has had to consider the national and international developments that are likely to affect activity this year.

'The main reason for the more modest growth this year is the firm prospect of lower new housing output. While a small decline was assumed on budget day, in line with the prevailing consensus at the time, later data now confirm that output will be considerably lower. Interest rates have risen by 75 basis points since budget day and this, and other factors, have weighed on consumer confidence and also have impacted on the inflation performance this year. The current level of oil prices and the appreciation of the euro-dollar exchange rate also impact on the outlook.

'As against this, it must be recognised that the decline in housing output is occurring at a time when other parts of the economy, such as the exporting sector, are performing well and this is partly offsetting these negative influences.

'My department's GDP growth forecast for this year is of the order of 4.75 per cent. The current market consensus for growth in 2007 is around 5 per cent. However, it should be noted that more recent forecasts, which take into account the less favourable new house developments over the summer, tend to be closer to my forecast.

'In terms of the outlook over the next few years, I now find myself being criticised as being too pessimistic. At the time of publication, I indicated the forecasts being published were just that – forecasts based on the latest information to hand. If later information shows more favourable factors, then my department will obviously take such new information on board. However, at present it would seem to me that it would be unwise to ignore the signs that are there for all to see …

'GDP growth is expected to be 3.25 per cent next year, which is not out of line with others that have published forecasts since the summer. This forecast is based on a considered view of economic prospects and is not slanted to achieve a purpose, political or otherwise, as some have mistakenly claimed.

'Looking at the overall period 2008–10, GDP growth is forecast to average 3.5 per cent. This level of growth is lower than we have experienced in recent years and it will have implications for us all. For instance, lower levels of activity are assumed to result in some employment losses in the construction sector. As a result, the rate of employment growth is expected to slow to 1.25 per cent next year from an estimated 3.5 per cent this year. Consequently, unemployment is forecast to rise from 4.5 per cent this year to 5.5 per cent next year. In this regard, a provision for an increase of 10,000 in the live register has been made in the pre-budget estimates for 2008 …

'The tax shortfall of €1 billion that now seems likely for 2007, along with the reduced economic forecasts for the period 2008-10, means that tax revenue over the period will be lower than previously envisaged. Fewer resources will mean that choices will have to be made and actions prioritised.'

Problems were certainly foreseen, but it was the scale of these that seemed to defy the logic of the day and as a result public spending would not slow very much in the budget: 'Approximately 4,500 additional front line staff have been deployed since 2005, made up of medical and dental personnel, nurses and other health professionals such as speech and language therapists, physiotherapists, social care and social workers, psychologists and environmental health officers. The service provided by these front line staff has a real impact on the quality of health care being experienced by people across the country. Today, the number of people holding a medical card stands at more than 1.25 million, an increase of approximately 108,000 since 2005. The number of persons holding a GP visit card is more than 73,600.

'The pre-budget estimates provide for €8.4 billion in gross current spending on education. This is an increase of approximately €500 million on the 2007 allocation and brings the total increase over the past three years to more than €1.75 billion or 27 per cent. This has enabled us to reduce the staffing schedule at primary level from 29:1 to 27:1 since 2005, thereby reducing average class sizes.'

Richard Bruton was quick to pick up on the missed opportunity of reform in the public sector during better times: 'It was being funded for a number of years by the golden goose laying eggs in the form of stamp duties, housing taxes, VAT and so on from the property boom. That golden goose has stopped laying and funding for those services will have to come from ordinary taxation. The tragedy is that we did not squeeze out the efficiency. Those golden years when money was available were not used to reform to provide a strong, well-functioning system. There are creaking systems in crucial areas such as health. We will rue the day we did not have a government more alert and more hungry to deliver change and public service reform when it was needed.'

Public sector reform is always a touchy subject for governments, however. There is little doubt that to have had any real impact on this area, significant measures would have had to be taken in health, education and justice. This was never popular and the threat of industrial action in any of the big three would spell disaster for a government.

Perhaps with renewed confidence in his position, Bruton does begin to pose serious questions and alternatives: 'I welcome the output statements. However, we have been down this road before with the strategy statements. The departments of education and science, and transport are the worst in this regard. What they regard as output statements are input statements. The department of education and science will state we are to have more teachers. However, it does not outline what this will deliver. Output statements should address what will happen to literacy and dropout rates, and what will happen to children with special needs. That is what an output statement is. Outcomes and outputs are different from inputs, which are teachers and, in the transport area, buses and tracks. Output statements on transport relate to what happens to passenger numbers and the modal split. This is what we ought to see if we want our output statements to trigger meaningful debate about spending choices and how well departments are doing.'

Cowen robustly defended his actions, however, and made clear that all his policies were in line with the very best of advice that was available: 'Several points were made during the course of the debate about forecasts for the economy and how they have changed. Before reminding the House of the forecasts contained in the pre-budget outlook, it is no harm to focus on the changes in the economic environment this year.

'Last December on budget day, I set out the department's three-year growth forecasts for 2007 to 2009. At that stage GDP growth was forecast to grow on average by 4.7 per cent with growth of 5.3 per cent for 2007. I also forecast taxes would grow by 7.8 per cent in 2007 and that on a cash basis the exchequer would have a deficit of €546 million. The general government balance was forecast to remain in surplus at 1.2 per cent of GDP.

'At the time, others took the view that my tax forecasts were somewhat prudent. The ESRI in its winter quarterly economic commentary forecast an exchequer surplus of over €1 billion and a general government balance of 2 per cent of GDP. At the time its view for growth in GDP at 5.4 per cent was no different from mine. Likewise, the Central Bank forecast GDP growth of 5.5 per cent in its January 2007 quarterly bulletin. This general consensus lasted through the first six months of the year, but circumstances have now changed.

'The pre-budget outlook is my updated forecast, but others such as the ESRI and the Central Bank produce quarterly forecasts. The ESRI still expected GDP growth of 5.4 per cent for this year in its spring quarterly forecast but by its summer quarterly forecast it had revised growth down to 4.9 per cent for this year. Most institutions that produce regular forecasts for the economy revised down their outlook over the summer and autumn. The economic environment has changed and the forecasts published in the pre-budget outlook reflect this …

'Deputy Bruton referred to the debt-driven property boom which completely misses the point. First, the level of new housing output has been ramped up in recent years in order to achieve greater balance between housing demand and supply. Had this large increase in house completions not occurred, first-time buyers and others would have been excluded from the market.

'Second, while all Members are aware of the rise in personal indebtedness, less attention is given to developments on the asset side of the household balance sheet. Between 2001 and 2005, the ratio of net household assets to GDP has been on a rising trend. It is also worthwhile to note the age structure of the population, being younger than most other EU countries, is such that a relatively large proportion of the population is at the life-cycle stage of borrowing to acquire real assets.

'Deputy Bruton suggested the government had become overly dependent on revenues from the property market, squandering the extra tax receipts from that area. While we undoubtedly benefited from the extra resources arising from the buoyancy in the property market, we have not staked all on them. We prudently used these receipts as a bonus to reduce debt levels while new services were not based on them.

'Care has been taken not to plan the public finances around the assumption that tax receipts from the property and wider construction sector would continue to grow as they did in the recent past. It is important to put the increased contribution from stamp duty and capital gains tax in context. The budget forecast of the yields from stamp duty and capital gains tax combined, in 2007, represents about 15 per cent of tax revenues overall. In contrast the big four taxes – VAT, income tax, corporation tax and excise duty – were expected to account for close to 85 per cent of total tax revenues this year.

'As in previous years, the department adopted a cautionary approach and factored in an easing in property market activity this year when making its budget day economic and fiscal projections.'

By 20 November a less generous approach to benchmarking was evident. Cowen stated: 'The public service pay bill is the biggest single element in public expenditure, accounting for approximately half of all current expenditure. Every 1 per cent increase in the public service pay bill costs approximately €180 million. The total cost of meeting the public service pay commitments arising from the current pay agreement under *Towards 2016* will come to approximately €1.7 billion. … In preparing for any forthcoming negotiations on arrangements to follow the current pay agreement under *Towards 2016*, it is important that expectations are kept in line with the economic realities we face. In particular, regard must be had [*sic*] to the need to maintain and improve our competitiveness and, in the case of the public service, of the need to maintain budgetary discipline.'

Part of the problem was that much of the accepted sources of advice would get predictions wrong. There was also an assumption that stamp duty reform in the budget would re-ignite the housing market. This ignored the fact that consumer confidence in this sector was falling fast and that people had quite simply got out of the habit of buying. Reform had been promised, but there was a danger that it could be an experiment that would cost the exchequer returns while not delivering any impetus to the market: 'The question of equity in the treatment of housing, of which the stamp duty code is a part, must be seen in the context of the overall tax treatment of property owners. The OECD has reported that Ireland 'has some of the most generous tax provisions for owner-occupied housing'. Ireland is the only country to allow tax relief on rent, mortgage interest payments, capital gains and capital acquisitions, while not applying an annual property tax. Furthermore, stamp duty helps fund public services such as health and education, while keeping the direct tax burden low. This facilitates continued economic success which benefits all taxpayers and their families and has allowed us to reduce taxes on work and enterprise with clear benefits for the economy as a whole.'

Politics was still at play, as Richard Bruton applied pressure on Fianna Fáil for not meeting manifesto promises: 'In the manifesto set out by Fianna Fáil, tax revenue for 2010 was projected at €61.4 billion. This manifesto, which committed to major improvements, will have a black hole of €4.9 billion by that year. The total for the improvements committed to is €5.2 billion if the commitment to have a surplus that year is included. Given that the minister will have less than 10 per cent of the revenue he thought he would for these improvements, what is going to give? Will he revise these commitments or will we pretend the minister will be able to fund 4,000 extra gardaí, 2,000 extra consultants and 4,000 extra teachers? Will he have a medium-term prospect of what is realistic given the resources available?'

Mr Cowen: 'In our manifesto we set out what we expected from a 4.5 per cent rise in growth per year and the spending priorities we would outline. Since then, we had the election and a programme for government in which we set out the stall of the government. In the second half of this year we saw a further slow down. The entire programme for government and all manifesto commitments based on the assumptions set out are based on prudent and efficient management of the economy. If the suggestion is that I am obligated to proceed regardless of present economic circumstances or forecasts and proceeding with spending plans based on 4.5 per cent growth which will not be achieved next year, I do not believe this is a responsible fiscal position to take.

'During the course of the election campaign, I outlined what my priorities would be in the event of a slowdown and I note Fine Gael's attempt to continue to run it. Fianna Fáil documentation on jobs and employment which is available on the website confirm the priorities to maintain capital spending under the development plan and to target tax changes towards those most in need. This has always been my position.'

It was clear that if Cowen attempted to deliver on many of these issues he would have been reckless on a level that would exceed the mistakes of all politicians and governments prior to 1987: 'Deputy Bruton's critique is that I will not reduce current spending quickly enough. I do not know where this will leave his figures. I seek to accommodate all day-to-day expenditure in the context of a responsible fiscal policy which will not compromise capital investment, because this was the mistake made by past successive governments when faced with the same dilemma.'

Cowen was also still confident in the strength of the Irish banks: 'The *Financial Stability Report 2007* published last week by the Central Bank and Financial Services Authority of Ireland, CBFSAI, is a comprehensive and detailed assessment of the impact of international financial market conditions on the Irish financial services sector and on financial conditions in the economy generally. I welcome the CBFSAI's conclusion that the financial system is well placed to withstand any adverse economic and sectoral developments in the short to medium term. The report highlights that based on key indicators such as asset quality, profitability, solvency and liquidity the Irish banking system is strong and robust and is clear that domestic banks have no significant direct or indirect exposure to US sub-prime mortgages.

'The Central Bank's report draws attention to a number of welcome improvements in the overall financial environment over the past year, in particular to the moderation in growth in house prices and private sector credit growth. The report also finds that underlying fundamentals of the residential property market continue to appear reasonably strong.'

Other warnings were coming to the fore, however: 'The governor of the Central Bank … noted that while much depends on the possible evolution and duration of the current market turbulence, there are concerns that a prolonged period of market disruption could affect economic activity by increasing the cost of credit to firms and individuals and reducing the volume of credit banks are willing to extend to borrowers.'

Budget 2008 was seen as a major challenge. Brian Cowen did take decisive action based on his views and advice up to this point. The Irish economy was showing signs of a significant decline. However, that did not mean its underlying strengths had disappeared overnight. If other areas of taxation could be improved again by a boost in consumer confidence and perhaps some positive move in housing as a result of stamp duty changes, then the economy could start to recover. Cowen had two choices: with falling taxes he could slash spending and cut services drastically to save the exchequer. The danger with this was that it would depress consumer confidence further and almost certainly cause a recession, even if it saved on a borrowing requirement at the end of it. On the other hand he could try to kick-start the economy, try to appeal to its own strengths, spend reasonably but not wildly with the hope of stimulating activity, and boost consumer confidence. If this worked, Ireland could retain its solid growth. The danger was that consumers were not ready to spend, that it would fail to ignite activity and that the economy would be exposing itself in the year ahead. It also took no account of the fact that the fifth element of the perfect storm, the banking crisis, was about to reach full force in 2008: 'Today, I present my fourth budget and this government's first one against a challenging economic backdrop.

'Our economy has experienced extraordinary growth for more than a decade. At home and abroad our success has been lauded. That success is down to the commitment and drive of our people. Recent governments have succeeded in managing the growth of the economy so that it has been sustained for much longer than anticipated.

'The global economy is beset by uncertainties, financial markets are highly volatile and the construction sector domestically is experiencing a slowdown. However, we must not lose sight of the fact that the fundamentals of the economy are still good – a point often lost by some. Next year will see our economy growing at a relatively modest pace. In this changed environment of more moderate growth, this government will manage the resources available so that growth will be sustained into the future. Today's budget is important in that context.

'As minister for finance, I must place one economic objective ahead of any other – that we do things now that will position our country for sustainable development over the years ahead. This objective does not conflict with our commitment to make Ireland more environmentally friendly …

'By making spending and revenue decisions in a more transparent manner within the overall economic and budgetary parameters, we will ensure that Ireland maintains a sound and sensible fiscal policy, fully in line with the provisions of the EU's Stability and Growth Pact.

'What this means is that the rate of increase on public current expenditure in 2008 has to moderate to take account of the resources available but, even so, I am still providing almost €53 billion, which is a net increase of more than €1.7 billion.'

The outlook on this occasion looked a lot riskier: 'For 2007 as a whole my department expects GDP growth of around 4.75 per cent is now likely. This is a very good performance in the circumstances. We estimate that an additional 72,000 jobs will have been created this year and that unemployment will be among the lowest in the European Union.

'This budget is being framed against the background of significant uncertainty in the international economic environment. Since the summer, global financial markets have experienced considerable volatility and while the impact of such developments on the world economy appears to have been contained so far, we must acknowledge that downside risks remain.

'Another issue is the significant appreciation of the euro against the dollar. This partly reflects financial market developments as well as growing concerns regarding the outlook for the US economy. This is of particular concern to us given the importance of the US both as an export destination and a source of inward foreign direct investment …

'The main factor weighing on overall growth is the prospect of somewhat lower output in the new house building sector. Against this background, my department is forecasting that GDP will increase by 3 per cent in real terms, 24,000 new jobs will be created with the total number at work increasing by a little over 1 per cent and unemployment at 5.5 per cent by the end of next year, inflation will ease and the Harmonised Index of Consumer Prices will average 2.4 per cent ...

'Responsible management of the public finances has been one of the prime drivers of our economic success. Our national debt is now around 25 per cent of GDP, one of the smallest in the developed world. It is right and appropriate that we should run budget surpluses when the economy is performing very well. It is equally right and appropriate that we borrow when the growth outlook is less favourable. However, the move into deficit must involve productive borrowing, which will strengthen our economy for the long term.

'Accordingly, I have set the following fiscal targets for next year: growth in total spending of 8.6 per cent to maintain and improve the provision of services and to invest in the future; gross current spending growth of 8.2 per cent; capital spending growth of the order of 12 per cent; a general government deficit of 0.9 per cent of GDP, which is fully consistent with our EU obligations; and a debt to GDP ratio of just under 26 per cent. These targets are realistic and achievable and a reflection of the underlying health and strength of our economy.'

Cowen banked on sticking to the National Development Plan as a route through the difficulties: '... my determination to maintain capital investment as set out in the National Development Plan. A measured deceleration is required, not a sudden slamming of brakes, especially when we are entering a period of below trend growth by Irish standards.'

One of the more interesting features in the budget was Cowen's moves in the environmental area: 'As I announced in last year's budget statement, a public consultation process was carried out by my department in relation to rebalancing Vehicle Registration Tax to take greater account of CO_2 emission levels. There has been broad support for a fundamental reorientation and rebalancing of that tax. I am bringing forward today a series of changes that constitute the most fundamental reform of VRT since its inception in 1993.

'The revised VRT system will be enacted in the finance bill and will be introduced with effect from 1 July 2008. The main features of the new scheme are: the VRT rate applicable to cars registered on or after 1 July 2008 will be determined by the CO_2 emission rating of the car and will no longer be related to engine size; a seven band CO_2 emissions system – A to G – will apply. It will be underpinned by a new CO_2 emissions labelling system for cars, on the lines of the energy efficiency labels for white goods, to be introduced by the department of the environment, heritage and local government and seven VRT rates, ranging from 14 per cent to 36 per cent, depending on the car's CO_2 emission level, will continue to be applied to the open market selling price of the car …

'In an effort to foster the use of electric cars and electric mopeds I am also introducing an exemption from VRT. This exemption will apply from 1 January 2008. Further information on the new VRT system and related changes to the car capital allowances scheme are set out in the summary of budget measures and in Annex D.'

Times might be getting tougher but Cowen still believed in delivering for pensioners: 'Today, the government will further build on these achievements by increasing the full personal rate of the state contributory pension by €14 per week and the state non-contributory pension by €12 per week.'

Carers too were to receive a boost: 'The government also recognises the huge contribution to society made by carers and will increase carer's allowance and carer's benefit by €14 per week. I will also raise the income disregard for carers by €25 for a couple to €665. I increased the respite care grant last year from €1,200 to €1,500. This year, I am increasing it by a further €200 to €1,700.'

There were clearly no cutbacks in health: 'Despite budgetary constraints, the government is providing nearly €16.2 billion for health next year, an increase of over €1.1 billion on this year's provision.'

And even in such times increases were made to development aid: 'In addition to our commitments to the vulnerable here in Ireland, the government recognises our responsibilities as a rich country to the poorest of the poor in developing countries. I am providing for an additional €84 million in the Vote for International Co-operation in 2008. This will bring our total ODA [Official Development Assistance] allocation for next year to €914 million, up to 0.54 per cent of GNP. This amount is three times that spent in 2000.'

There were a range of measures in taxation including: 'With the needs of certain more vulnerable groups in society in mind, I propose to provide further increases in the value of a number of other personal tax credits. The tax credit for an incapacitated child will be raised by 22 per cent, or €660 per year, to €3,660. The level of the married personal credit and the home carer tax credit is being increased by almost 17 per cent to €900 per year.

'The age credit will be increased by €50 to €325 for a single person and by €100 to €650 for a married couple, with the age exemption limits also being increased by €1,000 and €2,000 to €20,000 and €40,000 respectively. I am also providing for significant real increases in the credits for widowed persons and widowed parents. These are targeted and concrete measures that underline the government's resolve to look after the needs and welfare of those most deserving of our support. I also intend to increase the allowance for trade union subscriptions from €300 to €350 per annum.'

Small business was targeted as a potential driver in a renewed economy: 'In terms of supporting small and medium enterprises I will introduce the following measures: the small company tax liability threshold for the payment of preliminary tax on the simpler prior-year basis is to be increased from €150,000 to €200,000; the tax liability threshold for new start-up companies at or below which they do not have to pay preliminary tax in their first accounting period will be increased from €150,000 to €200,000; the small business VAT registration thresholds will be further increased from €35,000 per annum for services and €70,000 per annum for goods to €37,500 and €75,000, respectively, from 1 May 2008 – this measure will take about 2,700 businesses out of the VAT system. These measures will support business and enterprise and will cost €16.5 million in 2008 and €27 million in a full year.'

Mortgage interest relief was also a feature: 'In the Programme for Government we signalled that the first-time buyer, and recent purchasers, would benefit from further increases in the ceiling on mortgage interest relief. Today, I will honour the government's pledge by increasing the ceiling on mortgage interest relief for first-time buyers by €2,000 for a single person and €4,000 for a married couple or widowed person to €10,000 and €20,000 respectively.'

But the main event was changes to stamp duty: 'Over recent months, the dynamics of the housing market have changed fundamentally. A natural and welcome slowdown in property price inflation has been compounded by higher interest rates, tighter credit control and changing consumer sentiment as well as uncertainty about the global economic outlook and turmoil in international credit markets. I have made it clear on many occasions that any stamp duty reform which I would contemplate would have to be affordable and would have to support, rather than potentially destabilise, the market ...

'Purchases of residences with a value of less than €1 million will be charged to stamp duty on the basis that no tax will be payable on the first €125,000 of the consideration, and the balance will be charged at 7 per cent. Only those houses valued in excess of €1 million will pay at a higher rate of 9 per cent on the portion of the price which is in excess of that figure. There will be no losers and no anomalies will be created by this banding system.'

Mr Michael Creed: 'There will be no winners either.'

Mr Cowen: 'It will be extremely simple and considerably less expensive for both buyers and sellers. More importantly, this regime will also provide for a highly progressive stamp duty system whereby those buying the more expensive houses will always pay a higher effective rate than those buying the average house. That is equity at work.'

Cowen believed he had delivered a budget that would show Ireland was open for business and could give an impetus to new sectors to take up the challenge of renewing the economy: 'Growth is moderating, the international financial markets have been turbulent and the global outlook is uncertain. Rather than adopt a conservative, cautious stance, I believe we must respond to the challenge by taking determined action and pushing ahead with renewed vigour.'

Deputies: 'Hear, hear.'

Mr Cowen: 'Today's budget meets the challenge head on. It supports the incomes of the vulnerable. It keeps taxes low for working people and it helps home buyers and the housing market. It protects our environment for the future. It keeps the National Development Plan on track and it borrows modestly to invest ambitiously. It will sustain our development as an economy, a society and a nation. I commend the budget to the House.'

Unsurprisingly Richard Bruton was sceptical: 'They say that if one gets the reputation for being an early riser, one can lie in bed all day. That could be said of this government. In the early years, it was alert and ready to face changes. It felt the throb of the economy and it moved to deal with issues and real challenges, but that day is long gone.'

Mr James Bannon: 'They are jaded.'

Mr Richard Bruton: 'They have got used to lying in in the morning, bingeing on junk food and not exercising. The result is what we see today. At the slightest hint of deterioration in the economy, we see the public finances plunge from a €4 billion surplus to a €2 billion deficit. That is some achievement for a minister – to have squandered all that money and to have so little to show for it. It is shoddy spending habits.

'Under the guise of this debt-fuelled tax bonanza, the government has thrived. We have seen government spending grow by an alarming six percentage points of GNP. That is three percentage points extra on income tax and three percentage points extra on VAT. That is the reality of the extra costs this government has loaded on in the space of seven years. Now the property boom bonanza is gone, those realities will come home to roost. … Today's budget presents us with €3.9 billion extra in spending and €1.6 billion extra in tax. In any man's language that is spending more than double the revenue coming in. That is not sustainable. One cannot go on plugging the hole by borrowing, as the government plans to do this year. This time last year we were told we would have a surplus of €1.8 billion in 2008 and yet the minister told us today we would have a deficit of that amount.'

But Bruton's wise warning was tempered by the fact that he was also critical of a lack of spending in certain areas and there was no talk of cuts in his contribution: 'We were told there would be a major increase in the supplement in respect of children and that it would be indexed in accordance with the industrial wage. A family with two children is deemed by the minister to be too wealthy to receive a medical card if the parents are on the minimum wage. At €17,800 they will be deemed too wealthy to receive a medical card. What sort of planning for the future is that if low-income families cannot be permitted receive care for their children from a doctor when needed? It is so shortsighted and such an abandonment of the sense of equity that the minister said would inspire his budget that I cannot understand the thinking.

'Children will be affected by the decision to provide no extra psychological assessment services in the coming year.'

At least by 30 January everything seemed to be on track for Cowen's plan: 'Last month in my budget, I indicated that the outlook is for a moderation in the rate of economic expansion this year. At the time, my department forecast GDP and GNP to rise by 3 per cent and 2.8 per cent, respectively. These forecasts reflected the transition to a more sustainable level of output in the new housing sector and a more moderate rate of growth in some of our major trading partners was assumed.

'In my budget, I indicated risks to this outlook, including a less benign international economic climate. However, the general consensus is that once these adverse influences begin to fade, the pace of economic growth in Ireland will return to our potential growth rate of between 4 per cent and 4.5 per cent because our medium-term prospects remain favourable and the economy's underlying fundamentals are strong ...

'My recent budget provided a significant stimulus, with current spending rising by 8 per cent while revenues are projected to rise by approximately 3.5 per cent this year. I announced an increase of approximately 12 per cent in capital spending, confirming again that the implementation of the National Development Plan would be a key priority of the government. The consensus approach to policy formulation through social partnership will help us to address any short-term economic slowdown by ensuring that all stakeholders in our economy have a shared sense of the emerging issues.'

A new approach was emerging in relation to benchmarking however. Cowen said: 'Public service pay must develop in a manner consistent with competitiveness, price stability and budgetary policy. Government policy on public service pay is that the public service should be in a position to attract and retain its fair share of good quality staff at all levels. It should neither lead the market nor trail it …

'Benchmarking has been accepted by employers and unions as a significant improvement on the old pay determination system. That was based on relativities whereby if one grade or group of public sector workers received an increase, it led to leap-frogging and catch-up claims across the public service. Experience, particularly during the 1990s, showed the demands for pay increases by reference to relativities were not sustainable.

'The benchmarking body produced a report in accordance with its terms of reference. It is agreed between the government and the trade unions that the best approach to ensuring that individual public service grades are paid appropriately is to compare all aspects of public sector jobs with their private sector equivalents.

'While the current benchmarking exercise may yield little for most public servants, they have benefited significantly in recent years from the first benchmarking exercise and the general round increases under successive national agreements. The framework in place of assurances of regular benchmarking reviews of public service pay against the market, conditionality of pay increases on the basis of co-operation with change and industrial relations stability and verification mechanisms is a balanced and sensible approach to the management of public service pay.

'In more difficult international economic conditions, maintaining and enhancing the competitiveness of our economy is critical, particularly for a small open economy.'

By February Cowen commented in the finance bill on the first signs that things may not go to plan: 'Yesterday's figures showing taxes for January down 2.9 per cent compared to January 2007 must be seen in the context of one month's data in twelve months. While it is too early to draw any firm conclusions, the weakness in January was due primarily to the continuing weakness in the property market, which has been factored in to the projections. In addition, it is also fair to say that most other taxes, particularly income tax, performed well in the circumstances. Thus, the January figures are in line with the budget forecasts …

'As I stated, while the outlook for growth over the short to medium term has deteriorated somewhat, we expect the economy to pick up again once housing output stabilises at more sustainable levels. However, this relatively benign outlook is of course subject to risks, both external and domestic. There are several downside risks on the external side, including oil prices, the euro-dollar bilateral exchange rate and the changing conditions in the US economy. Sterling's recent falls against the euro could cause difficulties for exporters to the UK. In addition, it is too early to gauge the full extent to which recent conditions in financial markets internationally have affected global economic trends.'

But by the end of February the department of finance was still sticking to the forecasts and Cowen was defending the actions he took on the basis of the department's calculations: 'It is a new line of attack from the Labour Party to suggest that I should have a tighter fiscal policy and no deficits. Perhaps the party would outline, in the course of the next weeks and months, what areas of current and capital expenditure it wishes to cut so we can accommodate its new fiscal stance. I will be glad to hear that. Comparing the challenges currently facing the economy as equivalent to those that faced the economy in 1980 is not only specious but absurd. The fundamentals of the Irish economy are far stronger now and we are in a far better position to withstand international pressures. When global conditions change and currency, financial and equity markets take the tumble they have taken since last autumn, which was after the election and was not predicted by the deputy or anybody else, we must accommodate those changes as an open economy.

'With regard to the growth rate, Davy Stockbrokers are in the lower band of predictions at 2.1 per cent GNP. The predictions are: Central Bank – 3 per cent, the ESRI – 2.3 per cent, EU Commission – 3.5 per cent, OECD – 2.9 per cent, the IMF – 3 per cent, AIB – 2.5 per cent, Bank of Ireland – 4 per cent, Friends First – 3 per cent, Bloxham Stockbrokers – 3 per cent, Goodbody Stockbrokers – 2.3 per cent, National Irish Bank – 3.9 per cent and Ulster Bank – 2.1 per cent. Basically, these are predictions based on certain assumptions such as whether downside risks are realised, to what extent the current problem in the United States deteriorates, for how long that will happen and its impact. It is not correct to suggest that everybody is on the button in this matter. I predicted in my budget statement, despite setting out downside risks, a GDP growth rate of 3 per cent for this year and GNP growth of 2.8 per cent. Those predictions are broadly in line with the market consensus. They are not exactly what Davy Stockbrokers predict but there are other predictions that are even more optimistic. We took the median position, which was fair. Who will be right at the end of the day will depend on many things between now and next December.'

Cowen did have one crucial political argument on his side. Few people had argued to cut spending and among those who did no one offered a suggestion as to exactly what should be cut and how much money could be saved: 'The budgetary stance I took, taking into account all of the downside risks, was to provide an impetus into the economy of approximately 1.5 per cent of GNP. I have increased the capital programme by 12 per cent but the deputy [Joan Burton] obviously believes that is too much. I await the list of the deputy's proposals for cutting it and day-to-day spending. Otherwise, she does not have credibility.'

Cowen was still confident the economy could recover, however: 'The European Commission recently published its annual assessment of the Irish stability programme update. The assessment highlighted the overall strong position of the public finances and pointed out that the fundamentals of the Irish economy remain sound. It referred to challenges in the transition to lower growth, mainly linked to a return to more sustainable output in the housing sector. This assessment is consistent with the view outlined in my recent budget.

'The latest IMF forecast for Ireland was published in September last year, when it forecast GDP growth of 3 per cent for 2008. Recently, the IMF published a paper entitled *Spillovers to Ireland*, which referred to Ireland's exposure to developments in the US economy. In this working paper, the IMF postulated that a 1 per cent decline in US GDP growth would negatively impact by 1.75 per cent on Irish growth. This analysis, which others dispute, does not take into account other factors such as lower import growth and, as such, I do not share its view of the severity of the impact on Ireland of any downturn in the US economy. However, as a small trading nation we are vulnerable to downturns elsewhere and as I have already outlined, slower growth in our trading partners has been factored into the budget day economic projections.'

Cowen saw the risks to be in line with those suggested by Europe: 'The European Commission gave a very balanced view of where the Irish economy is going and the downside risks mentioned in my budget were replicated in its assessment. Regarding the building industry, it is clear we are adjusting to a more sustainable rate of growth having sought to meet an economic demand that exceeded supply. In the adjustment process, we have been able to put in place plans for a significant capital investment programme, which will assist our competitiveness greatly, and to ensure a competitive workforce through capital programmes and investments envisaged for science, technology, innovation, reskilling and upskilling. If we manage our position in the coming years, we can come out the other side with renewed growth in the economy. For these reasons, the European Commission's assessment is not one with which I am in fundamental disagreement.'

Debate on the issue of the budget and the approach was still heated: 'The fiscal and budgetary stance I adopted relates to trying to manage our way through the issue. We are putting in place a capital programme and decelerating the increase of current expenditure this year, which will be a progressive measure.'

Mr Richard Bruton: 'Each of the tánaiste's measures is expansionist. He should not need to ...'

Mr Cowen: 'The criticism I am receiving from the left and the deputy is that the budget is too expansionist.'

Mr Bruton: 'That is not what I stated.'

Mr Cowen: 'In every constituency, all of the deputy's colleagues decry the fact we are not expanding services fast enough.'

Also in February Cowen gave another vote of confidence to the financial regulator: 'A comprehensive system of banking supervision is in place under both EU and domestic law to ensure that credit institutions do not put customers' deposits at risk through imprudent lending practices. Banking supervision encompasses the authorisation of banks and building societies, their prudential supervision on an ongoing basis and the development of supervisory guidance and requirements for their operation. Prudential supervision involves monitoring the business of banks and building societies and how it is planned, managed and controlled, and checking compliance with statutory and non-statutory requirements. This system of prudential regulation is administered in Ireland by the financial regulator, which has extensive powers of inspection, review and enforcement under the relevant legislation …

'My function, as minister for finance, is to provide an appropriate and robust framework for regulation of the financial services sector with a particular focus on the consumer. I am satisfied that, since the establishment of the financial regulator and the Financial Services Ombudsman, and on the basis of enhancements, such as the introduction of the financial regulator's Consumer Protection Code, we have such a framework in place.'

But that confidence would be shaken in the months ahead, eventually culminating in the state having to guarantee Irish banks, assist in recapitalisation and nationalise Anglo Irish Bank. However, Brian Cowen did prove himself to be a reforming minister for finance. He was certainly responsible for many positive and welcome measures with regard to taxation. He was also responsible for delivering significant new measures with regard to providing value for money and delivering projects on budget. He did fail, however, to deliver significant reform in the public sector; he would appear to have been too close to the opinion of the public sector to ensure radical and speedy reform. He was happy to let this develop at a pace dictated by the public sector. In hindsight, he also failed to curb spending sufficiently, although that could be considered a harsh criticism. Certainly there are few politicians who would face down issues on current spending, knowing that for real impact it would have to hit health, education and security. Ray McSharry is probably the only man to claim such an accolade, but it most certainly did not make him popular at the time and politicians must be aware that their route is that of compromise. Cowen's trust in advice let him down, but then every country in the western world suffered the same fate and he can hardly be blamed for this. Had the perfect storm not occurred then perhaps Cowen could have dealt with the property market, and perhaps his final budget could have ignited the economy again. If that had happened he would have been hailed as a visionary. Those are the breaks. What we can say is that Brian Cowen operated in accordance with the best advice available and does not appear to have deliberately tried to mislead the Dáil in relation to the economy; he acted in what he believed were the best interests of the country at the time. It could be argued that he was wrong, but it could probably be said that we can generally ask for no more from a politician.

Bertie Ahern had originally intended to stay on as taoiseach until after the 2009 local and European elections. Ahern and Cowen were a formidable team in ensuring Fianna Fáil party loyalty and in inspiring confidence in the people. Ahern's appreciation of what people wanted and Cowen's tough stance complemented each other perfectly. One can only guess if the situation might have been different for Budget 2009 had problems at the Tribunal not caused Bertie Ahern to pack in his position as taoiseach one year early. It is an intriguing thought that perhaps the real sting in the tail of all the matters before the Tribunal is that maybe, and it's a big maybe, things could have been different for the country and a more comprehensive and sound budget introduced for 2009.

COWEN THE LEADER

When Brian Cowen achieved his ultimate ambition of becoming taoiseach, it was the fulfilment of a lifelong dream. He was the unanimous choice of the parliamentary party. Even Bertie Ahern faced more doubts upon his accession than Cowen did. He was phenomenally popular within Fianna Fáil. He was popular among the public too. He had an image of a tough man for a tough task and held the confidence of the people. There was nothing to suggest that Cowen was going to face any immediate difficulties as taoiseach in terms of support.

For many he also had the potential to rejuvenate Fianna Fáil, which having enjoyed electoral success faced many challenges as regards an aging membership and the level of involvement. No one would predict that before the year would be out he would be on the receiving end of Fianna Fáil's worst opinion poll rating in its history. The task ahead of Cowen would be immense before 2008 was out, but he still relished the challenge despite the bad news.

In his nomination speech Bertie Ahern made clear the esteem in which Cowen was held, as did his seconder John Gormley of the Green Party. Mr Ahern stated: 'Deputy Brian Cowen is immensely well qualified to undertake the duties of the office of taoiseach. First elected to Dáil Éireann in 1984, he has been re-elected in every election since. In addition to his having extensive experience of local government, he has been a member of the British-Irish Interparliamentary Body and an opposition spokesperson on agriculture, food and forestry. He has shown ability and leadership in a succession of demanding ministerial positions, as minister for labour, minister for transport, energy and communications, minister for health and children and minister for foreign affairs, including a critically important role during our successful presidency of the European Union ... Deputy Brian Cowen's extensive experience across his ministerial career, his deep involvement with Northern Ireland and the peace process and his skilled and widely admired engagement in Europe on behalf of the European Union during our presidency all equip him to undertake the obligations of office of taoiseach with flair and capacity ... Throughout his career, Deputy Brian Cowen has been a fair-minded and straight-talking participant in the social partnership process and has all the necessary skills to lead the process towards the next stage of development in line with the needs of our economy and society. In short, I consider him to be a uniquely well-qualified candidate to succeed me in the position of taoiseach and to lead the country towards the realisation of our shared objectives and through the challenge we face in the period ahead.'

Mr John Gormley: 'During the protracted and sometimes tense negotiations that led to the formation of the government, I got to know Brian Cowen the politician and the private man. The Brian Cowen I know is tough but fair-minded and gregarious but thoughtful. He is relaxed but always focused on the task in hand. He knows the task he now faces as taoiseach is onerous. He knows that, to complete this task successfully, there must be a strong and unified government – a lesson he has learned so well from former taoiseach Bertie Ahern, a man to whom this country owes a great debt of gratitude ...

'We now enter uncertain times, with rising oil and food prices, the credit crunch and climate change all posing major challenges to governments all over the world. The minister for finance, Deputy Brian Cowen, is ideally placed to tackle these challenges and to turn them into real opportunities for this country. He has the ability to harness the energy and innovation of the Irish people to embrace this transformational agenda. The decisions we take now will have profound consequences, not just for five or ten years, but for twenty-five years and for future generations.'

His old enemy Joan Burton was not so complimentary, however: 'I know that the tánaiste, Deputy Brian Cowen, has the confidence of his party, which is well and good. He will have a fair wind from the country for a while to see if he can get to grips with current problems in a fresh and imaginative way, but, frankly, I doubt it. Everything suggests that the people of Ireland will need to look elsewhere for the kind of leadership that can offer honest government in turbulent times as an alternative to one that is tied hand and foot, as this one is, to the vested interests of speculators, developers and reckless bankers.

'Time and again the tánaiste, Deputy Cowen, waved away warning messages that flashed as brightly as neon signs. Every time, however, vested interests won the argument. The casual reaction of Deputy Cowen to the decline in the public finances is ominous ... Is this minister for finance the person to guide the country as taoiseach through the more difficult times ahead?'

Once elected taoiseach, Cowen made his maiden speech, which was generally well received and laid out his plans for Ireland: 'I am deeply honoured by my nomination for the position of taoiseach. A number of weeks ago, my parliamentary colleagues chose me to lead Fianna Fáil – that was a great honour in itself – and today this House has elected me as taoiseach. I am the twelfth person to have bestowed on him the honour of being nominated leader of the executive since the foundation of the state and I accept the honour with a genuine sense of humility. That sense is engendered in large part from a love of Ireland. This is a wonderful country and we are a fortunate people ...

'Tomorrow I will have the privilege of addressing the investment conference for Northern Ireland with the Prime Minister of the United Kingdom, Gordon Brown. It is appropriate that, on my first working day as taoiseach, I will have the opportunity to advance relationships and deepen engagement, on a north-south and an east-west basis. Consolidating the peace through economic development and mutual understanding will have my full engagement and wholehearted support. Tomorrow's conference is a timely reminder that our destiny on this island cannot be secured in isolation from the rest of the world.

'We share too much history and culture with our neighbouring island not to work for the deepest friendship and the most fruitful engagement. Our economic success on this island owes much to the strength and depth of our relationship with the United States, through the very many investors who have found here a successful partner for investment and through the scale of the trading relationship between the two economies.

'However, it is in the context of our European identity and membership of the European Union that our place in the international arena and our relationships with other nations, near and far, find their proper perspective and most potent context. As a member of the European Council, I will strive to ensure that our European vocation is a live, engaged and creative thing, not a passive recipient of the fruits of the labours of others. In the same spirit, I look forward to leading a campaign in the coming weeks to assure the Irish people that ratification of the EU Reform Treaty is in our interest. Far from damaging our interests, the Treaty will enhance our capacity to shape developments in line with our perspectives and principles. There is no more urgent or important task ahead of me in the immediate future.

'In considering my role as taoiseach, I have thought a great deal about Ireland's place in the world today. Where does Ireland stand as we approach the closing years of the first decade of the twenty-first century? We know it is very different from what it was ten years ago when we were heading towards the millennium.

'Our economic success, which was in its early years a decade ago, has been sustained. We have settled our relationships on this island and reached accommodations that had been inconceivable for generations. With our increased confidence we explore and exploit new opportunities overseas. The movement of our people is now by choice; in the past, it was by force of circumstance. Perhaps most strikingly of all, we have accommodated tens of thousands of migrants who have come to our shores to help us sustain our economic success.

'All this represents considerable change in a short period. It would be challenging for any society, but it is particularly challenging for us given our location and history. We have adapted well and established many common values with the rest of Europe. They are largely positive values. We have matured through the process and learned from our new experiences how to right some of our failures of the past …

'In the first budget I presented to this House, I talked of economic activity as a servant of society. The statistics speak volumes for what has been achieved in the past fifteen years. They also might receive too much attention. Some might ask what year-on-year growth amounts to if it does not improve some people's lives. However, Ireland in 2008 is a much better place to live for more of our people than ever before. Far fewer of our people are struggling on the margins of our society. We have moved from a Third World infrastructure to one that is progressing well and will be the match of many of our European peers in the years ahead.

'One of the challenges we face today is to temper a rising tendency towards individualism within Irish society. We rightly have encouraged a culture of the individual taking personal responsibility for his or her well-being. We have reaped benefits from the more confident Ireland as presented by its most successful people forging new opportunities at home and abroad. Overdone, however, this carries risks. Not correctly harnessed, this can sap the energy of our sense of community, which still is strong and visible in many ways. We must prioritise turning the benefits of individual flair to the benefit of the community as a whole …

'Our particular charge is to represent the interests of our young. The character of the generations that will build this century still is being formed. These generations will decide the shape of the future. It is the job of the government and of parliamentarians to take the steps that will make it clearer for that generation to help shape this republic in a way that realises its greater potential …

'Our job as legislators is to provide leadership to society at this time of change. However, society must engage with us in this process. Change of this nature cannot simply be driven by the government. The common good is enshrined in the constitution and should have special relevance in Ireland at the beginning of the twenty-first century. The ultimate test of our progress will be the extent to which we can mobilise all of the people to think and behave in a manner that puts the interests of society as a whole ahead of our own private interests. As Seán Lemass observed, all 'national progress … depends … on an upsurge of patriotism' among the people. It is the job of government to lead on this issue, but that of society as a whole to address …

'I wish to reflect on what this means to me. On assuming the position of leader-elect of Fianna Fáil, I stated that I was excited if not a little daunted. I have assumed the position of taoiseach with an even greater sense of responsibility. I have been overwhelmed by the good wishes I have received from people the length and breadth of the country, as well as from abroad, of all political persuasions and none. In particular, I thank my family. I received my grounding in politics from my father Ber, who in turn received it from his father, Christy, a founding member of the Fianna Fáil party. Politics is about public service above all else …

'I thank the men and women of this House for the generosity of their support and good wishes. I look forward to them extending that blanket of goodwill for many months to come. All of these greetings from within this House and without are most welcome, although in some respects they add to the sense of expectation. I will commit myself completely to meeting those expectations. I sincerely hope I can do so in full.'

There is little doubt that any failures that may occur under Brian Cowen will never be for want of effort, conviction or desire. Cowen did surprise a lot of people in his appointments to cabinet. Widespread change was not expected; he had taken over in very different circumstances to his mentor Albert Reynolds. But he did spring some upsets. Noel Dempsey, Dermot Ahern and Michael Martin were three of the most experienced politicians in the country; he also had other big hitters to choose from, such as Mary Hanafin. However, the two most central and vital roles in cabinet – tánaiste, who takes leaders' questions in the taoiseach's absence, and the all-important minister for finance – went to two of the lesser experienced cabinet ministers in the form of Mary Coughlan and Brian Lenihan respectively. They were to become his kitchen cabinet. It was a surprise that other ministers were overlooked for these roles, but Lenihan in particular was regarded as a highly able and intelligent politician, and people eagerly awaited his approach to finance. Coughlan was also popular, not well known in the heat of debate in the House, but few doubted her being capable at the time.

In announcing the cabinet Cowen outlined the challenge they faced: 'In putting forward these names for the approval of the House for their appointment by the president, I should like to indicate my thinking about the priorities which my government will observe.

'We meet at a time of considerable global uncertainty. This applies to international economic conditions, reflecting the impact of turbulence in financial markets, inflationary pressures associated with the market for commodities, especially oil and food and the economic consequences of significant realignments in the geopolitical order. We face the more strategic challenges of climate change and the appropriate response to be made across all sectors of the economy, both domestically and internationally. We face the reality of international migration flows, and the human disaster of under-development which gives rise to them.

'More immediately, at home we have the reality of an economy in transition to lower levels of growth: from an unsustainable level of activity in the housing market to a more balanced provision for a mature but growing population, with housing needs which will continue to require levels of housing output that are relatively high by European standards. That has had a direct impact on employment and tax revenue. However, the pace of activity across the economy is otherwise very resilient. Significant investment decisions are being announced which reflect the reality that Ireland is a good place to do business, and to make and renew investment.'

Cowen went on to refer to the first and most pressing challenge – the Lisbon Treaty referendum: 'The first lesson I draw from that is the need to secure our place at the heart of Europe, as a shaper and influencer of policies that will benefit our people. Failing to ratify the European Reform Treaty because of some misguided attempt to send a message about issues, which have nothing whatever to do with the Treaty, can only weaken our position of influence. For that reason, my first priority and that of the government will be the ratification of the Treaty on 12 June.'

Reform of the public service was now clearly on the agenda also: 'One important dimension of the partnership process has been its application in the public service. The recent report from the OECD shows clearly that the Irish public service performs strongly across a range of dimensions of both efficiency and effectiveness. However, it must be acknowledged that there are problems that need to be addressed. There is, overall, insufficient focus on performance that delivers outcomes in line with the needs of citizens. Even our public service reform process has correctly been categorised by the OECD as too inward-facing without sufficient engagement with the complex and diverse needs of citizens in an integrated and flexible manner.'

But getting down to real business, on 20 May Cowen outlined for the first time as taoiseach his stance on public sector reform in light of an OECD report: 'I welcome the opportunity to commence this debate on the OECD's report on its review of the public service. The report, *Towards an Integrated Public Service*, marks the culmination of sixteen months of work by the OECD, which involved intensive analysis and extensive consultation. Members of the Oireachtas were consulted in their roles as chairs of a number of committees, members of such committees and party spokespersons. This substantive report is widely recognised as an authoritative assessment of the current state of the public service. It has been accepted as such by the government ...

'It acknowledges that there is an insufficient focus on performance that delivers outcomes in line with the needs of citizens. It correctly categorises our public service reform process as being inward-facing and overly focused on processes and procedures, without sufficiently demonstrating that it is driven by the complex and diverse needs of citizens or focused on making a difference to the quality of their lives.

'The report recognises the value of the extensive reform efforts which have been undertaken to date in areas like customer service, e-government, human resources, financial management and better regulation. The positive results of the change and reform programme in the quality customer service area can be seen by citizens. Management and organisational reforms introduced via the performance management development system have resulted in better functioning individual organisations. The OECD recognises that the dividend from many of these reforms will be fully harvested as they become increasingly embedded. Having said that, the OECD clearly believes we can and should do better. Despite the significant improvements and reforms which have been introduced, many challenges remain. The past decade has seen increases in public service expenditure and employee numbers. Expectations for improved service delivery, greater efficiency and better performance from our public service have increased. The OECD has indicated that if we can sequence future reforms in a better way, we can improve performance and service delivery and achieve greater efficiencies. Many of the reform initiatives which have been introduced to date have focused largely on the civil service, which comprises just one tenth of the public sector, as opposed to the broader public service.'

For the first time Cowen seems to point to the fact that public sector reform cannot be simply limited to the civil service who, in overall terms, only form a small proportion of the public service. But Cowen was clearly not intending a dramatic gesture with regard to the public service; however, he set about bringing together another task force to examine implementation: 'I am pleased to inform this House that today I am appointing a task force to develop an action plan for the public service to report to government before the end of the summer.

'The task force is also being asked to outline a set of criteria to inform the way in which the business of government is structured and organised, with a strategy to enable necessary changes to be planned and implemented successfully; and the benefits of greater use of shared services across all sectors of the public service …

'Change and transformation has become a way of life in the private and public sector. The key skill is no longer managing a steady state, it is about managing and sustaining change. These skills need to be embedded into the service at all levels.'

Pressure was mounting on a number of fronts, however, and on 21 May we find Cowen far from calm while trying to make his point in a debate on health. It was apparent that the opposition were determined that they could rile Cowen and Cowen was quick to say he would not accept this kind of treatment: 'Every morning, the problem with the leader of the opposition is that his party has not yet supported one initiative in regard to health service reform.'

Mr Richard Bruton: 'Play the man, not the ball.'

Mr Brian Hayes: 'Answer the question.'

Mr James Reilly: 'The taoiseach keeps accusing people of playing the man and not the ball. He should play the ball himself.'

The taoiseach: 'For Deputy Reilly's attention, I can organise it so that every time his man completes a sentence, I can have people roaring and shouting on this side if he wants.'

Mr James Reilly: 'His ministers keep coming out to say people are playing the man, not the ball.'

An ceann comhairle: 'Deputy Reilly …'

Mr James Reilly: 'He will not answer the question.'

The taoiseach: 'Every time I open my mouth, I hear something from the deputy.'

Mr Brian Hayes: 'Answer the question.'

The taoiseach: 'I want to answer the question.'

Mr Pádraic McCormack: 'You are in government.'

Mr James Reilly: 'Stop playing the man and start playing the ball.'

The taoiseach: 'The deputy's problem is that he is not the leader of the opposition.'

Mr James Reilly: 'The taoiseach's problems are myriad.'

An ceann comhairle: 'Deputy Reilly, this is leaders' questions.'

Mr Enda Kenny: 'Answer the question.'

The taoiseach: 'Listen to me, I want to answer the question but I will make one point. If you keep that tactic up, I will make sure he will not be heard in this House.'

(Interruptions).

The taoiseach: 'It can be organised.'

Mr Michael Ring: 'The new statesman.'

Mr Enda Kenny: 'The taoiseach will not silence the people on this side of the House.'

An ceann comhairle: 'The taoiseach without interruption.'

Mr Enda Kenny: 'I am not going to take that from any Member of this House. The taoiseach will not silence the Fine Gael Party or any of its members.'

The taoiseach: 'I will not be shouted down by the orchestrated tactic engaged in by the opposition for months. That will not work with me.'

Mr Brian Hayes: 'What is the answer?'

Mr Pádraic McCormack: 'He is filibustering.'

The taoiseach: 'I want to answer the questions but if leaders' questions ...'

Mr Enda Kenny: 'You will not silence the people in this House.'

The taoiseach: '... is about you organising a shouting match, then you will not get answers.'

Mr Tom Hayes: 'The taoiseach might treat Fianna Fáil backbenchers like that but he will not do the same to the House.'

Mr Brian Hayes: 'Will the taoiseach just answer the question?'

The taoiseach: 'I will answer the question but I will not listen to that sort of nonsense.'

Mr Brian Hayes: 'Let us have it.'

Mr Tom Hayes: 'He will not control us.'

An ceann comhairle: 'The taoiseach without interruption.'

The taoiseach: 'If Deputy Kenny cannot control his own party, that is his problem. Leaders' questions involve the leader of the opposition asking questions and me answering them.'

Mr David Stanton: 'What is the answer?'

The taoiseach: 'If I may reply without interruption, I will do so.'

Mr Pádraic McCormack: 'He has no answer and that is why he is filibustering.'

The taoiseach: 'The problem with Fine Gael is it wants it every way.'

Mr Paul Connaughton: 'Blame everyone else.'

Mr Richard Bruton: 'Can the taoiseach answer the question?'

The taoiseach: 'Let me answer the question.'

Mr James Reilly: 'He cannot answer the question.'

The taoiseach: 'I am able to answer the question.'

Mr Richard Bruton: 'He is dodging.'

The taoiseach: 'I have Deputy Bruton coming in …'

An ceann comhairle: 'I have to interrupt. We must understand each other. This is leaders' questions.'

Mr Tom Hayes: 'He is making a joke of it.'

An ceann comhairle: 'Deputy Kenny asked his question legitimately and the taoiseach is entitled to reply.'

Mr Brian Hayes: 'Let us have it.'

An ceann comhairle: 'Allow him to speak.'

The taoiseach: 'Without interruption.'

Mr Tom Hayes: 'He is unable to reply.'

The taoiseach: 'The leader of the opposition is complaining that insufficient money is being spent in the community on mental health and palliative care services. He made the point that we are making cutbacks to front line services. That is not correct.'

Mr Emmet Stagg: 'It is correct.'

Mr Pádraic McCormack: 'Those are the facts.'

The taoiseach: 'If deputies want to hear the facts, an additional 3,500 front line staff are working in the health service this year compared to last year.'

Mr Emmet Stagg: 'The home help service has been cut everywhere.'

The taoiseach: 'The suggestion that there is a reduction in front line staff is incorrect.'

On 27 May Cowen also walked into a problem. While all parties were campaigning for a 'Yes' vote on the referendum, Fine Gael took offence at a suggestion by Cowen that there was perhaps more they could do. Enda Kenny stated: 'This is not a comment which the taoiseach should take personally, but I was disappointed at the tenor and import of his remarks at the weekend in regard to both Fine Gael and the Labour Party – for whom I do not speak on this matter – about the effort that good people all over the country are putting into the campaign. People who are supporting the "Yes" campaign but are not supporters of Fianna Fáil have felt the antagonism. It is necessary that the taoiseach clarifies this matter. I ask him to withdraw that remark and to say he encourages everybody who is supporting the "Yes" campaign to continue to do so. We do need co-operation among those supporting the "Yes" campaign to have everybody properly informed about what is in this treaty and how it can equip Europe to meet the challenges that lie ahead. From that perspective, the taoiseach's remarks at the weekend, as reported, have caused a great deal of antagonism and difficulty for people supporting the "Yes" campaign who are not supporters of Fianna Fáil. In the interests of harmony and running a cohesive "Yes" campaign by all parties that support the Treaty, I ask the taoiseach to withdraw those remarks and clear this matter up.'

The taoiseach: 'I do not understand what the issue is for the leader of the opposition.'

Mr Pádraic McCormack: 'He knows nothing. He does not understand.'

The taoiseach: 'In response to a question I was asked about the opinion poll, I indicated that all the parties that support the referendum intend continuing to ramp up and intensify our campaign over the coming two-and-a-half weeks. If people want to seek out offence I suppose they can take it. I would not offer any offence to anybody – quite the contrary.'

But the first disaster of Brian Cowen's term as taoiseach was about to strike, when a large turnout in a referendum voted down the Lisbon Treaty. It was a huge blow to Cowen's popularity and image of being in control and trusted. In the current economic environment it was also a setback in Cowen's plans. There is little doubt but that Cowen felt that the "No" vote had damaged Ireland significantly and made the long-term picture for economic recovery more difficult, as he believed we needed a decisive Europe. It was also a disappointing culmination to what had been years of negotiations and what had been a deal particularly associated with Ireland and the ability of the Irish presidency to get agreement. Cowen stated: 'I will formally advise my European Council colleagues that the Irish people have rejected the proposal to amend our constitution to enable ratification of the Lisbon Treaty.

'The members of the Council, who negotiated and agreed the draft treaty, and who agreed to a number of specific provisions to address Irish concerns in that process, will wish to understand the reasons this rejection has occurred. In my discussions with my colleagues, I will be stressing that the people have spoken and that the government accepts the result.

'I also will emphasise the need for all of the EU and its member states, not just Ireland, to reflect on what such a vote means and to play their part in working together to examine the possible ways forward …

'What is clear is that we are now in an uncertain situation about our future relationship with Europe, where the European Union wants to go and our place in it. My job is to try to ensure that Ireland remains very much engaged with the Union, that the decision made is respected and that we consult with others as it is a treaty between twenty-seven countries. I want to hear their concerns now that this has occurred in Ireland and to see if there is a way forward. The political implications are not simply for Ireland, but there are wider legal and political implications for the Union as a whole in terms of the direction in which it wants to go.'

The new taoiseach's response to assessing the vote was remarkably similar to his response on the first Nice Treaty, but then again the referendum debate had been remarkably similar: 'I do not know whether we can address those concerns, some of which are contradictory. People voted against the Treaty for a range of reasons. Different people had different perceptions and a different view of what the Treaty involved, which may or may not have been objectively based on the Treaty provisions. To what extent the government or the Irish people can be assisted in addressing some of those concerns remains to be seen. We must assess and take stock of last week's result. I intend to start a process that will garner as accurate a picture as possible for the motivation and reasons behind the votes on all sides. That does not take away from the fact that a majority voted "No" last Thursday and that fact of life must be dealt with.'

What was different was that now he was taoiseach we certainly find Cowen in a much less combative approach than when he was minister for foreign affairs. After Nice 1 there was little doubt Cowen was determined to carry on the debate and start the fight-back straightaway. After Lisbon, as taoiseach, Cowen endeavoured to be more diplomatic: 'EU law is implemented in Ireland in compliance with legal requirements. We do all we can to make it as simple and proper as possible. It also must meet the principles of accountability and must be fair and proportionate. The whole idea behind the Lisbon Treaty was to delineate more clearly those areas of competence that were exclusive to the institutions, those that were mixed and those that could be dealt with at national level. There was an explicit Treaty provision regarding the question of proportionality and subsidiarity being a fundamental part of how the European Union would work in the context of the Treaty being ratified, but we are not now in that position as we rejected it in a referendum last Thursday. It remains a continuing issue, however.'

After questions on Lisbon the hits kept coming, as questions were raised on rising oil prices and Cowen assured Enda Kenny that the government was certainly not making any windfall from petrol sales: 'The fact is that oil prices are higher due to rising commodity prices in general. If we use the taxation system as a means of assistance, we will provide benefit to the producers and not to the consumers. The benefit will go to those who are already getting a higher price for their product. The deputy is making the point that there is a windfall available to the government, but that is not the case. The overall reason for that is very simple. If people have a set disposable income, while they must pay more of that on petrol than before, they still have only the same income to spend. The fact that more of it is being spent on petrol does not mean that there is a windfall available to the government, as the overall consumer spend is the same. A greater amount is spent on petrol and that is what is causing hardship in certain sectors. That is why there has been a meeting between ministers and their representative bodies.'

Fine Gael did seem to suggest that perhaps the government should look at reducing their take in an effort to ease the price pressures. Luckily Cowen did not agree in this instance as the country's finances were already rapidly declining. In a short time the need to increase the tax take from the petrol pumps would be evident.

Eamon Gilmore laid out the scale of the task that was emerging for the new taoiseach: 'This country is now facing some very big problems. We were in here earlier this afternoon talking about the aftermath of the rejection of the Lisbon Treaty. We are now probably facing the biggest diplomatic challenge since the Second World War. Last week the live register went above the 200,000 mark. We have seen the biggest increase in unemployment over the last year in forty years. Jobs are being lost in our economy at a rate of 235 a day, or 1,600 a week. On top of that, there has been a great change in our public finances. There was a €5 billion surplus two years ago, but there is a €1.5 billion deficit already this year. Our economy is heading for a recession.'

The bad news was that things were about to get much much worse. But on 18 June Cowen defended his budgetary policies: 'The downside scenario and risks that were outlined in the budget statement have materialised in practically all cases. Ireland is not immune from those international developments. The government will seek to ensure that it works within the budgetary parameters it has set itself, which will involve budgetary discipline. The leader of the opposition will have to make a choice as to whether he believes this is the approach or whether he wishes to continue to spend.'

Indeed all the risks had indeed materialised and Ireland seemed caught in the headlights. Cowen by now certainly realised that all back-up plans were out the window as Ireland was battered on all sides.

The Labour Party suggested that perhaps the answer was to save the construction sector by implementing a major schools building programme. Cowen discussed this at length: 'There are 850,000 pupils in first- and second-level education and 4,000 schools. The deputy is correct about the unprecedented capital investment programme for school building over the past ten years, something of which this administration is very proud. In an effort to deal with historic problems, there has also been a need to provide extra teachers quickly – particularly resource teachers for students with specials needs. These were in their tens and hundreds when we came into office and I am glad to say they are now in their thousands. We are providing 8,000 special needs assistants alone and 7,000 resource and learning support teachers. That is an indication of the effort to deal with this issue …

'I do not suggest for a moment that there are not continuing challenges or that one can be complacent about their nature. However, I defend the government's record in terms of what has been achieved under successive ministers as a result of successful policies. I recognise that, in reducing class sizes, providing thousands of resource teachers and more special assistances, there will be cases – as there always have been – where temporary accommodation is required. I acknowledge that in some instances this has been going on too long and I respect that some people have grievances in this regard, but do not portray the education system as being totally bereft of development or modernisation because that is not a true reflection of the situation.'

As one crisis melded with another, later in the day Cowen had the opportunity to return to the Lisbon Treaty defeat and give his full assessment: 'We must be honest with ourselves now that our country has taken its decision. Today is about contemplating not just the events of last week, but what they might mean for our nation in the years and decades to come. It is many decades since Ireland took a decision to turn outwards to face the world in an effort to improve the welfare of her people. I have acknowledged previously the significance of that shift and the wisdom of those who had the courage to bring it about …

'It is appropriate today for me to give this House my initial reaction and my assessment of the referendum outcome which has given rise to that uncertainty. I will begin by repeating that the will of the people is sovereign in our democracy and in Europe democracy is no less sacrosanct. The principles of democracy are the threads that weave the fabric of the European Union.

'The debate that has taken place in Ireland in recent months saw many disparate views, and in some cases contradictory positions, put forward by those advocating a rejection of the treaty. That makes it particularly difficult to analyse the key messages underlying the outcome of the referendum. I recognise the considerable unease expressed about an apparent diminution in Ireland's representation and influence in the institutions of the Union. I note in particular that the fact that for five out of every fifteen years, there would not be an Irish commissioner was an issue which weighed with people. This is despite the fact that under the Nice Treaty, which the Irish people accepted and which Ireland ratified, a reduction in the number of commissioners will occur next year and not in 2014 as proposed in the Lisbon Treaty which was rejected and without a settled basis for the equal rotation between the member states as provided for in the Lisbon Treaty.

'Arguments were repeatedly advanced about a threat to our right to maintain our tax system and tax rates, even though the Lisbon Treaty provided for a continuation of the legal arrangements that currently apply under existing treaties. This was in part due to continued references to the Commission bringing forward a proposal on a common consolidated corporation tax base, despite the maintenance of the unanimity requirement in the Lisbon Treaty.'

The fact that so much debate had taken place within the Dáil on these issues in the previous years – yet the public still did not understand or even pay heed to it – presented a real problem for the body politic. Cowen felt the core message of the 'Yes' side was simply lost: 'For those of us who supported the referendum, the core message of the need for the European Union to function more efficiently, democratically and effectively in the international arena did not register sufficiently with the public. In contrast, many were more comfortable citing examples where they felt the EU was not sufficiently in touch with the concerns and needs of people at local level.'

One of the problems was, however, that there was no one to fill Cowen's boots as attacker in chief, still ready to carry the fight. Cowen did manage to point out that despite any claims of it being a good result for Europe, the only parties rejoicing were devoted euro sceptics: 'I should acknowledge though, openly and honestly, that my assessment of the rejection of the Treaty in Ireland will have to be viewed alongside its approval in the majority of member states. This is the difficulty which faces Ireland and the Union. There is no doubt in my mind that our partners tomorrow will express their strong preference to find a shared solution, something very much in the tradition of the European Union. I believe, too, that they will accord us the time we need to play our part in understanding last week's vote. For my part, I will impress upon them the need to avoid prejudicing the process which we must now undertake in Ireland …

'Many of our partners have already expressed their disappointment at the outcome of our referendum and their difficulty in interpreting the signals that it may send. However, their disappointment is not entirely universal. On the contrary, there are some individuals and groups across Europe who now wish to claim the Irish people as their new friends. They are headed by the likes of Jean-Marie Le Pen and Nigel Farage. No proud Irish man or woman could but be uneasy that they rejoice in our decision.'

On 24 June leaders' questions was another torrid affair for Cowen, shrouded in depressing news. The budget was ineffective in igniting the economy in the prevailing circumstances. By now that much was evident. The ESRI had announced the dreaded recession. Cowen reported: 'The ESRI believes there will be negative growth of 0.4 per cent this year. That would be the most negative forecast we have heard in recent times. The consensus is that we will have some growth. Obviously, we will be providing our half yearly figures from the department of finance next week and will make an assessment based on the most up-to-date data we have. By their nature, forecasts are essentially just that – forecasts.

'Six months ago, I set out the possibility of 3 per cent growth in the economy, but I also set out various downsides and risks that will affect that forecast, all of which have now materialised. Twelve months ago, Deputy Kenny suggested the economy might grow by 4 per cent. Forecasts are forecasts based on various assumptions. Since then, we have had a change in the global economic environment that affects Ireland in the same way as it affects everyone else. Allied to that has been a correction in the domestic housing market in addition to an increase in commodity and oil prices. All of this has an effect and drag on growth. The ESRI has made its prediction that there may be negative growth this year ...'

The hope was still very much alive that Ireland could return to growth. Indeed the argument still remains that if the government can deal with its problems and cut spending, that that underlying economic strength may still re-emerge; but it will probably be a five-year plan at this stage at the very least.

On 25 June Cowen explained his belief that Irish banks were still in solid shape: 'In my previous capacity as minister for finance, I was obviously in constant contact with the sector through the Central Bank mechanism and other mechanisms. This was to ensure that, in dealing with the situation that has arisen with regard to international financial market turbulence, our banking system was able to operate appropriately and properly despite the fact that an international credit squeeze was taking place, for which I was to take some responsibility, according to the deputy yesterday. With regard to the question of the banks providing finance, while there is this international situation of which we are all aware, I agree it is important that banks continue to provide prudent risk to business and that the performance of Irish business during the good times should stand as a strong criterion for continued support for those businesses which continue to invest and to require access to finance.

'It is true there has been difficulty with regard to inter-bank lending. The provision of money supply has been an issue in international banking circles for over nine months and the provision of money beyond thirty, sixty and ninety days has not been as plentiful as would have been the case in the past. This is as a result of the lack of trust that has emerged due to the outcome in the United States of the developments in the sub-prime market there and the ripple effect this has had on wider banking circles.

'It is important to point out, however, that, as the Central Bank has confirmed, the Irish banking system is well capitalised and is in a healthy state in terms of its own financial situation. I would agree it is important that while we recognise there has been a change in the international environment, and indeed the domestic environment, the banking system remains an important access point for capital for the development of markets and companies, and their ability to continue to trade. This is a point that will be continually made both by me and my successor in the department of finance.'

Cowen later explained that the department of finance only depend on their own figures and this level of downturn could not be predicted: 'We do not deal with strategies based on the publication of any finance house, however reputable. We base them on our own official data, which will be becoming available to the department of finance in terms of its mid-year ...'

Ms Joan Burton: 'The data were pretty wrong at budget time.'

The taoiseach: 'The budget day statement outlined the downside risks, all of which have materialised. If the deputy knows of anybody who predicted the downturn in the international economy that we have seen in the past eight months, I ask her to give me a shout because I do not know of anyone who did.'

Ms Joan Burton: 'There were many people who did.'

The taoiseach: 'It certainly was not in any of the policy positions put forward by Deputy Burton's party during the election.'

The Lisbon Treaty was still the big news of the day, however, and Cowen explained what happened at the European Council meeting: 'The main focus of the meeting from an Irish perspective was the issue of the Lisbon Treaty following the rejection the previous week by the people of a proposal to amend our constitution to allow the government ratify the Treaty. I am pleased that the Council conclusions reflect the views and concerns I brought to the meeting, including the need to respect fully the Irish "No" vote in the referendum. I made clear in the run up to and during the Council that our ratification procedure and vote would need to be respected, just as we would respect the procedures and decisions of others. The central focus of our efforts over the two days was to try to manage the situation which arises as a result of the referendum outcome. The referendum was an Irish vote, but it has serious implications for all of our European partners.

'Over dinner, I gave my European colleagues my initial assessment of what had happened in Ireland and explained that we now need time to analyse the result and its full implications. Only then could we turn to what possible ways forward there might be for Ireland and the Union. What I said to my colleagues at the Council reflected closely the comments I made to this House last Wednesday during our debate on the referendum. At the outset, I laid considerable emphasis on my view that the vote was not in any way a rejection of Europe and the good that it delivers. In addition to the more tangible economic developments which were widely accepted, I stressed the broad recognition in Ireland of the Union's achievements in securing peace, providing economic stability, reinforcing cultural, social and environmental development and promoting European values of democracy, tolerance and equality. I explained that, against that positive background, it is clear that the debate reflected anxieties about potential future developments and the potential future direction of the Union …

'The Council members listened carefully to my comments. They accepted the outcome of the referendum. They were aware that this is not the first time the EU has found itself in this type of situation. I am sure they were conscious of the fact that such a vote reflects broader concerns over how the Union manages its business and its relationship with the citizens of the member states. They were certainly very concerned at what the outcome means. They highlighted the dilemma of trying to respond to the concerns of the Irish people while still trying to advance a process which they consider to be vital and which has been in preparation for many years.

'Many of them were perplexed. Some found it hard to understand how Ireland could reject a Treaty which they see as improving the functioning of the Union and redressing perceived difficulties of democratic accountability. … I made it clear that, however frustrating for them, it is simply too early to know how to move forward at this point. I was straightforward and honest and said that I did not have answers at this time. I stressed that the views and concerns expressed in the campaign were varied and complex. There is no quick fix or easy solution at this stage … Working closely with the incoming presidency will be central to the consultation with partners. During the meeting, President Sarkozy and I agreed that he would come to Dublin at the start of the French presidency on 11 July for intensive discussions. I am pleased that, following discussion, the Council accepted that deeper analysis and consultation is needed before any conclusions can be drawn.'

Returning to questions on the economy, Cowen made clear that in light of the deterioration in the public finances he believed now more than ever that Budget 2008 had been the right course of action: 'The point is this, a budgetary strategy this year which provided a fiscal stimulus of 1.5 per cent into this economy was the right stance given the outcome that we have now seen. We can take corrective action which is proportionate and allows this economy to withstand the challenges that are in front of us, but we will not do so …'

Mr Pádraic McCormack: 'It is called cutbacks.'

The taoiseach: 'The ESRI has not suggested that we should take such corrective action, as it would totally disrupt the provision of services for remainder of this year.'

Mr Paul Kehoe: 'The government blew the boom.'

Mr Enda Kenny: 'It was wasted.'

The taoiseach: 'I make that point because there is a contention by the opposition that this is what the ESRI is saying, but in fact it is not saying that. What we will do …'

Mr Tom Sheahan: 'Has the taoiseach not been listening to George Lee?'

The taoiseach: 'We freely acknowledge that tax revenues will be down this year and the exchequer returns for the first six months show this. We will work within the approved spending limits that we have set ourselves and we will ensure that we devise a budgetary strategy and carry out the estimates process and the next budget in a way that will see this economy recover as soon as possible.'

Mr Paul Kehoe: 'What about the cutbacks?'

The taoiseach: 'We will not defer the corrective action that is necessary now because we know from bitter experience under administrations of which Deputy Kenny was a member that deferring corrective action only exacerbates the problem. The position of the opposition is that it has a finance spokesman who says I spent too much, yet Deputy Kenny and everyone else say I spent too little. Fine Gael has policies that are meant to exacerbate the problem, not correct it.'

Cowen was determined that his government would meet the challenges head on and reacted quickly by announcing a series of spending cuts for the remainder of the year: 'I point out to Deputy Kenny that 80 per cent of day-to-day expenditure is in the areas of health, education and social welfare. However, economies have to be made and moneys must be reallocated, while keeping the overall spending limit for this year at what we intended. Because of the deteriorating economic situation, where we have increased allocations to provide in areas over and above what was projected, money must be reallocated from within the overall government spend …

'This our initial reaction to the situation. We are saying that in the context of the estimates for 2009 further decisions may be required to make sure that we have a sustainable public finance position going forward. That would be determined by information as it emerges during the course of the year. It is necessary for the government to do whatever is required to make sure we work within the Stability and Growth Pact principles that have been set out, which is the basis of our membership of the euro currency. We have seen a deterioration of €3 billion in our tax revenues this year. That means we must work within the spending limits we have set ourselves to underline confidence in ourselves going forward and to devise a strategy next year that will be sufficient to be sustainable going forward. That is the position.

'I made it clear yesterday that this is a process by which the government is tailoring its response in an effort to meet the requirements of the situation as it emerges … We are also examining the position for 2009. We are putting out the information as we have it on what we are trying to do. We are not suggesting that this process is now *finito*, that this is the end and that all members can sit back until next February. We have to manage this serious situation, and we intend to do that. We intend to discharge our duties in government and bring to the attention of the House, as I have done, through the course of the debate on this issue today and tomorrow, whatever information ministers are required to bring forward; that will be brought forward and detailed to the House.'

There was no two ways about it – these were cutbacks, but they were necessary in order to put a brake on spending in an attempt to rectify the situation. Cowen stated: 'We will outline to the House in full all the issues making up the figure of €440 million. We have no problem doing that. That is the purpose of the debate from the government's point of view. Any suggestion to the contrary by the opposition is ridiculous. We will set out our position during the course of this debate. I have explained to the deputies that the figure of €440 million includes €140 million in deferred capital expenditure, there is also €300 million on the current side, €240 million of which relates to efficiency savings, and there is another €60 million from other savings, administrative and otherwise.'

Mr Eamon Gilmore: 'The taoiseach has now given us three different figures.'

The taoiseach: 'No, that is the €440 million, they are not different figures.'

Mr Eamon Gilmore: 'They are.'

The taoiseach: 'Deputy Gilmore has been trying to suggest that they are different figures, it is the same figure, €440 million, divided as I have outlined, and the ministers will set this out in detail during the course of the debate.'

The question was, however, whether this measure – welcome though it was – went far enough, despite the fact that the government were being severely criticised for the move. The most striking thing about it was the speed at which the government could implement it when there was no other option available.

By 24 September the situation was spiralling into chaos; the government decided to move to calm fears by bringing forward the budget. This was an attempt to show control and leadership and to try to stabilise consumer confidence. In a speech Cowen said: 'The government is acting on this matter by bringing forward the date of the budget to 14 October, which is the most important decision that has been made. It is an indication of the seriousness of the intent of government to take whatever decisions are necessary to meet, as Deputy Kenny has said, the new economic situation we now face. While I do not intend getting involved in a debate during leaders' questions this morning on the record of the government, which we can defend, it is a question of facing up to the situation with which we are confronted … The downturn is taking place in every economy. What we must do and are intent on doing is to bring to the Dáil within three weeks a budget proposal that will set out clearly what the expenditure issues must be. With less revenue coming in it is clear economies must be made. What we must contend with are what our priorities will be as they relate to the capital programme and what the issues will be regarding the protection of tax breaks …

'We must also help those who are in work by ensuring that we run the finances of the state in such a way that the economy is more sustainable than would be the case if we operated on a no policy change basis. We will not have such a policy in the coming twelve months and beyond and must take account of the changed circumstances. Luckily we are working off a lower unemployment rate than was the case when we faced challenges such as this in the past. The economy is in a stronger position. I know that is no comfort for anyone who has lost his or her job, at any time, during good times or bad. The issue for us is to continue to work with the state agencies and to have an overall responsible budgetary position that will uphold confidence in the economy and ensure that those who are at work have the prospect of continuing in their jobs, with people trying to obtain more market share.'

One crisis was followed by another, and on 30 September the government announced that it was introducing a scheme to provide a state guarantee for Irish banks. The move was quick and decisive. There was a risk for the taxpayer, but if it worked it meant it did not cost the taxpayer anything, as taking an equity share would have. Considering the government were strapped for cash it was an ideal solution. While it showed that the Irish banking sector was not as strong as had been thought, Cowen and Minister for Finance Brian Lenihan could feel happy with the work in that it was generally greeted as a strong and determined response. Fine Gael had many questions, but agreed to facilitate the government in bringing in the measure.

The taoiseach: 'I thank Deputy Kenny for his offer of co-operation on this important matter and I also thank all Members who have been briefed about the situation which has arisen. The action taken by the government last night was necessary based on the advice available to us from the Central Bank and regulatory authorities. This action was to ensure we maintain the stability of the Irish financial system and has been taken in response to the severe dislocation in the international credit markets which has impacted both in the United States and in the European Union. Throughout the current period of turmoil, the government has stressed its commitment to the stability of the Irish financial system and in particular to ensuring that money placed with an Irish credit institution would not be put at risk. This government action is first and foremost in the interest of the stability of the Irish economy and the long-term interests of the taxpayer. A secure and stable financial sector is essential for the Irish economy and is obviously in the best interests of the Irish people.

'With regard to the guarantee there have been what I regard as misleading indications as to the exposure being placed on the taxpayer. We are providing a guarantee as a means of dealing with the basic problem for the banks which has occurred over some time, the question of accessing liquidity in the form of cash in order to conduct their business. The banking system in Ireland has assets which exceed its liabilities. The assets of the Irish banking system amount to approximately €500 billion and the guarantee liabilities are approximately €400 billion. The first call on the funds of a bank will be on shareholders, on their assets, capital and funds. The Irish banking sector has very well-secured loans and loans which are underwritten by the European Central Bank. It is important to make the point that in the event of any further call, it is my intention to ensure the Irish taxpayer will not be held liable in any way for any deficit that might occur in the event of there being a problem in the future. I intend that the sector will have to discharge any liability that may arise …

'The state guarantee is provided at a price. It is not for free. The state guarantee will have a mechanism whereby a fee reflecting commercial realities will have to be paid by those banks which may access the liquidity provided by the Central Bank.'

Cowen was conscious that the taxpayer would need to be protected: 'Regarding protections to be put in place for taxpayers and the regulatory situation, I stress this guarantee was not given lightly. It was informed by the strong advice of the Central Bank and the financial regulator that, on account of unprecedented disruption in international financial markets, a system-wide state guarantee was required to ensure Irish financial institutions have access to the normal liquidity and funding to effectively operate their day-to-day business. It will also provide confidence to depositors and wholesale lenders that they can continue to transact their business as usual with the institutions concerned …

'How far back do people think the country would be if we awoke this morning, in the absence of the state guarantee that has been offered in the way it has been offered, to find a failed banking system on our hands? What would be the situation then for Irish people or Irish workers? There are corporate organisations which must get access to funds, as well as employers and businesses which must get access to funds on an ongoing basis to conduct their business …

'The second point is that no money has been handed over by the state to the banks in relation to the provision of this guarantee. The state guarantee we have devised enables the banks to get access to funds. Deputy Gilmore's argument about the taking of equity completely misses the point. The taking of equity would not provide the liquidity necessary to maintain a stable financial system in this country in the short, medium or long term. The issue here is that solvent banks, which have assets in excess of their liabilities, are faced with an unprecedented situation whereby there is a credit crunch and they have an inability to access credit and liquidity in order to conduct business. That is a problem not only from the banks' point of view but from the point of view of everybody who deals with banks, including every citizen of this country.'

Cowen was also certain that now was not a time for indecision: 'I could not absolve myself from the responsibility of making the decisions. On the advice of the relevant people who have the competent authority in this area, I had to make that decision. Government made that decision with the impact that it has since had. That was the situation.'

This had inspired confidence in many quarters that Cowen's government did indeed know what it was doing and would and could manage the situation. On budget day, 14 October, the country braced itself for very heavy cuts, but there was a feeling that the people might rally to the cause for the sake of the country. The questions would be tough, however, and Cowen entered the battle in leaders' questions that morning: 'The particular issues affecting us now with regard to the downside risks that have come to pass, such as higher commodity prices and a global financial crisis, probably the worst we have seen since the 1930s, means an open economy such as ours cannot be immune from these developments.

'A particular issue on the domestic front also affects our performance, that is the reduction in residential housing output, which has a drag of approximately 4 per cent on growth this year alone. That in itself is a particular reason beyond what one can look to in other countries as being a reason for the present performance of our economy. During that period, this economy also provided itself with the ability to reduce its debt considerably. The National Pensions Reserve Fund represents another 14 per cent of GNP, which is an asset to the country.

'While this year and next year we will face into a far more difficult set of circumstances, the purpose of the budget today will be to frame an objective where we seek to restore stability to our public finances and create a pathway back to current budget balance in time, recognising – I would not regard this as wanton waste – that we have had an unprecedented capital investment programme, practically all provided for from cash from surpluses in the past.

'We are talking about continuing with a very significant public capital programme for which we will borrow. The return on the investment we saw from the last National Development Plan was in the region of 18 per cent. Borrowing for capital purposes is absolutely above board as far as I am concerned, despite the fact that in previous years we funded the investment from surpluses.

'Where we have an issue is with regard to the current budget deficit and the need to stabilise that situation and work back without cutting back unnecessarily on public services … To find a balance will require further reforms and policy changes, the beginnings of which will be announced today.'

After Cowen had outlined the position he faced tough questioning, but seemed up to the task: 'Last December, the ESRI suggested the growth in the economy this year would be 2.7 per cent. They were the most pessimistic.'

Mr Bernard J. Durkan: 'So were they right?'

The taoiseach: 'The Central Bank said it would be 3.5 per cent.'

Mr Durkan: 'But they were wrong.'

The taoiseach: 'I brought in a budget that put out a growth profile of 3 per cent, which was the median. So there was nobody, including Deputy Quinn, who suggested – obviously no one could predict – the outcome we have seen during the course of this year as regards the international climate that has developed.'

Mr Leo Varadkar: 'Alan Ahern of NUIG.'

The taoiseach: 'Nobody saw it, but that is not to suggest in any way that I avoid my responsibilities – quite the contrary. However, I will not accept the contention from the parties opposite that there were people at the end of last year, coming in to frame a budget, who suggested that we would not have growth rates of at least 2.7 per cent this year.'

Mr Durkan: 'That is not true.'

Mr Dermot Ahern: 'They will get it right eventually.'

The taoiseach: 'That was in the aftermath of the sub-prime issue that arose in the United States the previous August. Let us be fair and honest in getting the facts out on the floor.'

Mr Durkan: 'The taoiseach is in denial.'

The taoiseach: 'The situation now is that, as a result of the hard landing that has come to the residential property market, it is imposing a fiscal drag of 4 per cent on what would otherwise be a growing economy. We have to deal with that situation now. When people talk about the need for more housing, they have a lot to say about those who are involved in property markets, but that industry employed 250,000 people. It grew from an industry of 120,000 people ...

'There will be challenges facing us in the months and years ahead and there will be a requirement for everybody in the system to pay more than was the case previously. That is true. However, in relative terms after this budget and the next couple of budgets, as we face into this situation in the next year or two, we will ensure that we are still in a far better position than we were five or ten years ago. The relative position, therefore, having increased the level of economic activity from one point to another, and even if it does not proceed in an incremental positive line now and even flatlines, is that we are still in a far better position now or in the year ahead than we were five or ten years ago when 600,000 fewer houses were built and one million fewer people were working in our country.'

But after the introduction of the budget, things started to unravel for the government. In 1987 Ray McSharry took uncompromising decisions; the key to his success, however, was that McSharry maintained support and would not revisit decisions despite public opinion. The golden rule is that if a tough decision must be made, ensure that there truly are no other options and you can gather support; also, if it was necessary to make the decision, don't go back on it. After the budget, backbenchers seemed happy; even Independent TDs like Finian McGrath expressed no difficulties. However, after a few days of opposition pressure and media attention combined with a few protests, the government consensus started to crumble. This would be the first major question of Cowen's ability to lead people especially where they might rather not go. It will take Cowen some time to re-establish his credentials after this. The problems were evident as soon as the day after the budget. Eamon Gilmore raised the contentious issue of the medical card: 'Specifically, in respect of the withdrawal of the medical card from pensioners, I received a call this morning from a pensioner who was on VHI but qualified for the medical card when he turned seventy and stopped paying VHI. Can that pensioner get back into VHI now and, if so, what will it cost? What type of cover will the VHI provide to such a pensioner if he does manage to get back into it?'

The taoiseach: 'It is not a question of my being embarrassed by any of these measures, which are necessary in the interests …'

Ms Róisín Shortall: 'The taoiseach should be embarrassed.'

The taoiseach: 'These measures are necessary in the interests of trying to provide a sustainable public finance position for the country.'

Mr Bernard Allen: 'It is a nice mess the taoiseach has got us into.'

Ms Olivia Mitchell: 'The government made a bad deal with the doctors and it is making the public pay.'

Mr Dermot Ahern: 'The deputies speak out of both sides of their mouths.'

The taoiseach: 'If it is Deputy Gilmore's contention – it was certainly Deputy Bruton's contention last night – that there should not have been any tax-raising revenue provisions in the budget, what part of the expenditure programme would he cut by another €2 billion? That is what is required.'

Deputies: 'Hear, hear.'

The taoiseach: 'If it was also the case that he did not believe there were discretionary spends in the capital programme that should not have been deferred, what further €1 billion in cuts – making a total of €3 billion – would he estimate we could find in the public expenditure programme? If we were to move, as Deputy Bruton said, to a 5.5 per cent deficit instead of the 6.5 per cent deficit and if we were not to raise taxes, this would require another €2 billion of expenditure cuts.'

Mr Enda Kenny: 'There is no plan, none.'

The taoiseach: 'If the Fine Gael budget which has been outlined by its finance spokesperson is that we would have a 5.5 per cent deficit and not raise any taxes …'

(Interruptions).

Mr Ahern: 'The deputies are speaking out of both sides of their mouths.'

The taoiseach: 'I want to make it clear …'

Mr Emmet Stagg: 'The government should tax the fat cats who caused this.'

An ceann comhairle: 'Let the taoiseach finish.'

The taoiseach: 'I want to make it clear that if this is the Fine Gael position – it was their stated public position on the *Prime Time* programme last night – they are required to find another €5 billion in expenditure cuts to make that budget stick. That is the reality.'

Mr Richard Bruton: 'The taoiseach can read out policy statements, but why does he not look for something from the banks?'

An ceann comhairle: 'Let the taoiseach finish.'

The taoiseach: 'Those are the facts. Whether one is on the opposition benches or the government benches, two plus two is four, and you add the zeros later.'

(Interruptions).

Mr Enda Kenny: 'An ceann comhairle, the taoiseach is …'

A deputy: 'He is on his own.'

Mr Conor Lenihan: 'Enda cannot even get the people behind him to calm down. He has no leadership skills whatsoever.'

An ceann comhairle: 'The taoiseach should be allowed to finish.'

Mr Bruton: 'The minister of state, Deputy Conor Lenihan, should not shout down his taoiseach.'

The taoiseach: 'Deputy Gilmore decries all the methods of raising tax revenue. I do not believe it is the view of the Labour Party that we should cut expenditure further – I do not think that is its position. I have heard what Deputy Gilmore had to say in regard to some tax expenditures. We will debate those in the House and assess their impact, and at least we can have a debate that might make sense. However, the debate I am trying to have with the opposition here does not make any sense because it is €5 billion out before it starts.'

Mr James Reilly: 'It will make a lot of sense to those whose medical cards will be cut. Health cuts hurt the old, the sick and the disabled. Is that right? Where did we hear it before?'

The taoiseach: 'With regard to the specific point raised by Deputy Gilmore, the medical card is available for GP services.'

Mr Bernard Allen: 'Willie will have an army with no barracks.'

The taoiseach: 'The VHI does not provide cover for GP services.'

Ms Joan Burton: 'Some plans do.'

Mr Emmet Stagg: 'It covers far more than GP services.'

The taoiseach: 'Let us be clear. That is not the situation.'

Mr Emmet Stagg: 'It also covers accident and emergency and hospital charges.'

Ms Olivia Mitchell: 'It covers a lot more.'

The taoiseach: 'Excuse me …'

An ceann comhairle: 'Let the taoiseach finish, please.'

Mr Emmet Stagg: 'That is wrong.'

The taoiseach: 'The position is …'

(Interruptions).

The taoiseach: 'I am making the point and shouting me down will not change it.'

An ceann comhairle: 'This is leaders' questions.'

Mr Emmet Stagg: 'He is wrong.'

The taoiseach: 'Shouting me down will not change it.'

Mr Emmet Stagg: 'He is wrong.'

An ceann comhairle: 'It does not matter. The deputy has no input to make on this.'

The taoiseach: 'With respect, I am not wrong. VHI does not cover

GP services and the medical card does cover those services. Let me make it very clear, I very much regret the fact …'

Mr James Reilly: 'VHI covers €25 …'

Mr Dermot Ahern: 'Deputy Reilly should keep quiet. I will show him what he said in 2001.'

Mr James Reilly: 'Do that, by all means.'

(Interruptions).

Mr Dermot Ahern: 'Deputy Reilly fought this. He is a hypocrite. He threatened to strike.'

An ceann comhairle: 'Order, please. Let the taoiseach finish.'

The taoiseach: 'Just so we get the full flavour of consistency, as I wish to deal with Deputy Gilmore's substantive point …'

(Interruptions).

An ceann comhairle: 'Excuse me, I wish to make one thing clear. This is leaders' questions and the taoiseach must be allowed to finish.'

The taoiseach: 'Deputy James Reilly, when he was chairman of the IMO's GP committee, condemned the government's decision to offer medical cards to all pensioners over seventy. His position was that it was not acceptable. Now, of course, he decries the fact that we have changed that arrangement.'

Mr James Reilly: 'That was without means testing. Since that time, for seven years …'

The taoiseach: 'I presume the deputy is proud of the fact that, when he was chairman of that GP committee, he negotiated four times the charge for people in less disadvantaged areas than in disadvantaged areas. He effectively got a payment …'

Mr James Reilly: 'For seven years people have had these cards. Now, the government takes them away from pensioners and wants to tax them.'

The taoiseach: 'He effectively achieved a payment of €641 for every such person who was on the GP list …

'On Deputy Gilmore's point, I very much regret that this was a necessary decision. I would like to have been in a position to say the present situation could have continued, but it was not possible in the context of all the decisions that had to be taken …'

Mr James Bannon: 'Why?'

The taoiseach: '… because we have €6.5 billion less in revenue than was anticipated.'

Mr Bernard J. Durkan: 'Why is that?'

The taoiseach: 'In that regard, a very balanced approach was taken which sees expenditure cuts of over €2 billion …'

Mr Bernard Allen: 'It is a nice mess the taoiseach got us into.'

The taoiseach: '… tax revenue raising of €2 billion and …'

Mr Ruairí Quinn: 'The taoiseach should at least apologise for his mismanagement.'

The taoiseach: 'One moment, please. In addition, there is €1 billion in regard to the capital programme.'

'I regret that is the situation, but we have sought to achieve that seven of every ten people over seventy will be eligible for that medical card on the means test grounds, based on the data that are available for those who were in receipt of medical card between the age of sixty-six and seventy and who got the card when they came to the age of seventy.'

On 21 October, Cowen outlined the changing nature and importance of social partnership: 'On Friday, 5 September, I held a series of discussions with the social partners during which I underlined the changed context in which the pay talks were taking place in terms of the evolving economic situation. The parties affirmed to me their commitment to engaging in further discussions aimed at establishing if an agreement on a new pay deal would be possible.

'An intensive round of negotiations resumed on Monday, 8 September, within a tight deadline. Throughout this process I monitored developments closely and in the course of the final overnight session of negotiations I held a series of meetings with the parties with a view to facilitating a meeting of minds on the key issues on the agenda. As deputies will be aware, negotiations reached a successful conclusion on the morning of Wednesday, 17 September, when an agreement was reached on a successor to the first module of *Towards 2016*.

'The agreement provides for pay increases to be paid to workers over a period of twenty-one months, with pay pauses of three months and eleven months agreed for the private and public sectors, respectively. The agreement reached between the parties also covers a range of non-pay and employment law-related initiatives, including those related to agency workers, employee representation and victimisation, pensions, procurement, managing change and innovation, upskilling and public sector modernisation.'

As Cowen battled to keep his government together and still address the problem a compromise was reached on the medical cards row where a means test was still introduced, but at a much higher level than anticipated. The government had also introduced a 1 per cent income levy, but during partnership talks they were forced to exempt those on the minimum wage from this: 'Regarding the first question, it is out of our respect for and in view of the importance of assisting the social partnership process that the government is indicating that it is prepared to provide that the levy will not apply to incomes up to the level of the national minimum wage. I do not have the figures in front of me but approximately 850,000 workers are outside the tax net, some 36 per cent of the workforce. In the context of the finance bill, the minister for finance will be ensuring that revenue is in line with the contribution this would make towards the social partnership process.'

Cowen later returned to the issue of public sector reform. While other issues grabbed the short-term headlines, it is perhaps this issue that in the long term may define Cowen's leadership abilities: '… the minister for finance outlined in the budget statement his intention to move on public sector reform. As I said, there is a task force which will provide the implementation plan in coming weeks. This will implement and sequence the OECD report on reform of the public service and how to integrate public services in order that we can improve those services. The plan will improve opportunities for those who work in our public services to provide an integrated, co-ordinated and citizen-centred approach. It will seek to ensure that the very considerable resources provided by taxpayers are used to the best possible effect in terms of the administrative structures we devise and that there is ability to move beyond departmental and agency boundaries and to work in a co-ordinated fashion to get the best possible output for taxpayers.'

The taoiseach then elaborated on changes to the medical card scheme: 'The announcement made this morning was for the purpose of allaying the concerns of the people involved in this situation. As I stated, approximately 95 per cent of people who had cards in the past will retain them under the new arrangements. The core decision and the requirement for a core budget arithmetic to be respected is incorporated in the revised scheme brought forward in the interests of providing a sustainable way forward … we are now extending medical card eligibility, as I have stated, right up to those who have income of €700 per week for a single person or €1,400 for a couple. For those reasons, this is a comprehensive response by government in the face of such concern to allay it, dispel it and deal with it …

'From next week there will be an agreed common single capitation rate for those over seventies on the medical card scheme, which will provide savings. Of course, the committee, chaired by the person we have obtained, for the purpose of dealing with drug usage will provide the significant and substantial savings which we believe, on the basis of consultation with GP representative bodies, are available given that total drug spend at the moment is approximately €1.95 billion. That has almost doubled since 2003.'

Cowen was always fighting a rearguard action, however: 'There are many deputies on the other side of the House, who at the time of this scheme's introduction and since, are on the record as saying they were not in favour of that universality being provided.'

Mr Enda Kenny: 'Yes, but it was brought in.'

The taoiseach: 'So therefore it clearly was not a principle then. Perhaps it is a principle now because the deputy sees a political opportunity.'

Mr Bernard J. Durkan: 'It was introduced.'

The taoiseach: 'Be that as it may, it is the deputy's version of leadership.'

Mr Enda Kenny: 'I will not take that nonsense from the taoiseach.'

The taoiseach: 'I will not take barracking from the deputy either.'

There was a serious threat that another climb-down would be forced on education; however, the government simply could not afford this without a risk that the entire budget would have to be re-introduced. The government finally held fast: 'As the leader of the opposition has already pointed out, a private members' motion has been tabled and a debate will take place this evening and tomorrow, during which all of these issues can be addressed in some detail. The government has had to allocate scarce resources and the department of education and science has been given increased resources this year, unlike many other departments. One of the unfortunate issues is that 80 per cent, or four-fifths, of moneys in education relate to payroll and pension costs. On the question of finding savings, we are going back to the teaching schedule of September 2007. This is what is required in order to ensure we maintain the budgetary parameters we have set ourselves. That is what has been proposed by the minister for education and science and adopted and agreed by the government. Obviously, we must implement these decisions in the interests of recognising that there are certain unavoidable additional costs coming on stream in that budget in 2009 which also have to be accommodated.

'All of this is against the background of an increase of 300 per cent in funding for education since 1997. Capital investment in the sector has been unprecedented, as has the increase in the number of teachers and teaching assistants. However, we are in a new economic situation now and budgetary decisions must be taken in that context. Given that approximately three quarters of total day-to-day spending is on health, education and social welfare, to suggest that one could deal with the difficulties without impacting on those areas is to underestimate and fundamentally misunderstand the size of the problem we face ...

'Last week, Deputy Brian Hayes indicated that implementing a pay freeze for teachers who earn over €50,000 would save €128 million a year. The proposal Deputy Kenny is now making is that such a pay freeze should apply to all public servants, but we work in partnership with public service unions. In fact, we want to work in partnership on this issue as well. Social partnership is not just about working together in good times, but also in bad times. It is also about implementing difficult decisions, some of which one would prefer were not necessary, but by reason of the economic circumstances in which we find ourselves are necessary.

'The minister of education and science has contended, and it is true, that there have been great improvements in the education system over many years in terms of both capital and current spending. Improvements have been made in the pupil-teacher ratio and in the numbers assisting teachers, who are there in their thousands as opposed to their hundreds, as was the case when we took office more than ten years ago.

'One of the accommodations we must make relates to the pupil-teacher ratio, which will be increased by one at primary and post-primary level. The minister has pointed out that, in net terms, he expects that to equate to 200 teachers at each level and he outlined to the House the basis for that expectation. In terms of the overall number of teaching posts, we are talking about less than 1 per cent whereas other departments have been asked to make payroll savings of 4 per cent in order to deal with the situation …'

Mr Eamon Gilmore: 'Before we debate the Labour Party private members' motion on the education cuts and the government's scandalous and short-sighted decision to increase class sizes, I seek clarification from the taoiseach as to where the government stands on these issues. We have had two different messages from the government in recent days. From the taoiseach and the minister for education and science we have had the message that there will be no change; that the government is hanging tight and standing firm; and that there will be no change in the education measures, including the decision to increase class sizes, which was made in the context of the budget.

'We heard a different message from the Green Party yesterday. Following its meeting the Green Party issued a statement saying it was seeking changes in education funding on an ongoing basis, especially in the short term. The Green Party has apparently decided to send Deputy Paul Gogarty to negotiate with the minister for education and science. It must be the first time that a party in government has sent a backbencher to re-negotiate measures already agreed by its ministers in government.'

Mr P. J. Sheehan: 'They have gone underground.'

Ms Kathleen Lynch: 'A letter from St Paul to the Thessalonians.'

Mr Eamon Gilmore: 'When it comes to this exchange, my money is on the minister, Deputy Batt O'Keeffe. Will the taoiseach answer specifically …'

Mr Pat Rabbitte: 'My concern is with Deputy Gogarty.'

Other hits would come some weeks later when Mary Harney announced that plans to implement a cervical cancer vaccine would not proceed. Cowen stated that the resources were instead being allocated to screening programmes, but it cost him the support of one of his own TDs, Dr Jim McDaid. This increased the pressure on the government, but Cowen managed to hold it together and ride out the initial storm despite some appalling opinion poll results. Brian Cowen could be forgiven for thinking that the gods were conspiring against him when feed used in pork products was found to be contaminated and the government, acting in accordance with the advice it received, withdrew all pork products from shop shelves. This did much damage to the pork industry but, similar to earlier CJD scares, Cowen again showed that he did not believe in taking any risks with public health.

Cowen has not been leader long enough to give a fair assessment of his capabilities in the role. His first six months were disastrous, from the point of view that he lost a major vote on a vital European treaty. He had severe economic problems, some of which he showed real leadership on. But with regard to the budget, things went wrong; he lost two TDs from Fianna Fáil in the process and the support of Independent Finian McGrath. He was also forced to row back on major decisions. His opinion poll ratings were the worst ever recorded for Fianna Fáil.

The crisis in banking proved one of the most difficult issues facing the government. The bank guarantee scheme proved to be only a first step, and the government later devised plans for recapitalising the banks. But the biggest disaster involved Anglo Irish Bank, where Cowen and Lenihan were forced to take a step they had done everything to avoid – full nationalisation of the bank. Cowen still believed in the strength of Irish banking, especially of the two major banks. However, only time will tell if Cowen is right on this and whether the banks can weather the storm of the international crisis long enough to survive. Much depends on the international situation and how quickly both the USA and Europe can find a way to begin to restore consumer confidence.

Cowen's views on the economy were made clear on 28 January 2009 in a statement to the Dáil. He said: 'We are facing the most difficult global economic conditions in seventy years. The most severe financial crisis since the Great Depression is taking its toll, for example, on the US economy, now in the middle of recession that began in December 2007 and which may prove to be the longest and most severe of the post-war period.

'The International Monetary Fund is expected to make further significant downward revisions to its global forecasts, beyond those already made in November. Most of the world's advanced economies are in recession. Global output is expected to decline for the first time in recent memory. International trade is also declining sharply, with the World Bank expecting global export volumes to be down for the first time since 1982.

'As a regional economy accounting for around 1.8 per cent of euro zone output, Ireland is particularly exposed to these developments. The combined value of our imports and exports is equivalent to approximately 150 per cent of national output which is among the highest shares in the developed world. Exports of goods and services represent approximately 80 per cent of our national output, which is over double the EU average, and means our fortunes are inextricably linked with those of global and European markets.

'The scale of the economic challenge which we in Ireland face is clear. It is evident in the distressing rise in the number of people becoming unemployed. It is evident in the downturn in economic activity and the associated sharp reduction in exchequer revenue. It is clear from the crisis in the banking sector and the associated difficulties in securing access to credit on a consistent basis and at competitive rates. It is also evident from the global spread of the crisis, and the uncertainty about its likely depth and duration.'

Cowen goes on to elaborate on the areas of potential that he sees for Ireland going forward: 'Our people need to have confidence that the difficult decisions taken now are part of a coherent approach to return the economy to sustainable growth. That approach is articulated in the framework for sustainable economic renewal, which was published by the government in December. That framework, based on the development of a smart economy, reflects the government's determination not only to meet the severe short-term challenge we face, but also to make the structural reforms which ensure that Ireland emerges from the global downturn in pole position to benefit from the international recovery when it comes. We have set out clearly the measures we are taking to support a return to sustainable growth and jobs over the medium term, with specific actions in the following areas: maximising the potential for growth by building on our strengths in innovation and research and development; addressing the huge market for environmental- and energy-related products, services and innovation; investing in critical infrastructure, while favouring more employment-intensive activity in the short term; and driving our reform agenda for a more efficient and effective public service supported by smart regulation.'

However by 3 February the government's attempts to gain an agreement with the social partners had failed. For Cowen who, as we have seen, was a major supporter and believer in social partnership this was a disappointment. But the unions were unwilling to support the cuts that the government felt necessary and the introduction of a pension levy for the public sector. Cowen moved to take decisive action in the absence of an agreement: 'The inability of the Irish Congress of Trade Unions to agree to the government's proposals does not mean that the partnership process has failed. The overall framework remains in place and will be built on. Congress has indicated that it is available to continue discussions on the implementation of the overall framework, as have the other social partners. The government will continue to engage with it over coming weeks as it implements the strategy agreed in the framework document regarding support for enterprises, refining price regulation in the energy sector, stabilising the financial and banking sector to meet the needs of the Irish economy and society, implementing a pro-active labour market approach appropriate to Irish conditions to support vulnerable employment and those who lose their jobs, developing a new national pensions framework, and completing the reform and economic renewal agenda to which we are committed.

'The decisions taken by government lay the foundations for the next phase of our development. Despite the budgetary constraints, the government is maintaining proportionately the largest capital investment programme in Europe at over 5 per cent of GNP. We will continue to commit considerable expenditure on roads, schools and housing. We are investing significantly in important infrastructure and research and development to drive competitiveness, growth and jobs in the future. We have proportionately the largest investment programme in the EU. This is an investment in the future as well as being our own stimulus package for the Irish economy. We have also decided today to reprioritise €150 million of capital expenditure to employment-intensive activities in the areas of school building and energy efficiency improvements.'

But while the pension levy would mean a significant saving for the Irish taxpayer, it took considerable time to get to the point of implementation and the failure to stick to a very hard budget the previous October was now causing problems. Strike action was threatened by several public sector unions, but this threat paled in comparison to the gaping hole that was already opening in the 2009 figures where the government was now over €4 billion off target by the beginning of March. The government needed to take action quickly and a date was set for a supplementary budget in April. On 4 March during leaders' questions the taoiseach outlined his fears and his hope for recovery: 'First, I take full responsibility for all decisions I have taken throughout my career as a minister and as taoiseach. I want to make that point very clear. Second, at the time much of the critique that was coming from that side of the House related to the failure by government to invest even greater amounts of money into public services ... The important point to make regarding that matter is that basically the country has a strong balance sheet in terms of the relative low debt we have – although rising – but we have a very weak profit and loss account because our day-to-day expenditures well exceed our revenues. That is the issue we face. In the past increased public services were required as was increased capital investment, which was required to deal with the infrastructure deficit, a source of complaint by many on all sides of the House in terms of the growth that was being achieved in the economy. Employment creation was also high, some of which we are losing now. Even so, with more than 350,000 unemployed – every one of whom is too many as far as all of us are concerned – it represents 10 per cent of the work force when ten or fifteen years ago it would have represented an unemployment rate of 20 per cent and more. Our policies at that time were working for the economy. We are in a totally new situation now, as is every economy and country.'

Cowen later went on to elaborate on the need for a budget: 'The government made a decision yesterday that by the end of the month we will make whatever decisions are necessary to ensure we, to the greatest extent possible, can provide a deficit position for this year of 9.5 per cent, which does not exceed the figure the markets have factored in as part of our correction process over the coming years to bring order back to our public finances. It is a huge challenge, as has been said, and one that will require the full efforts of everyone in the

House. I look forward to everyone constructively contributing to that debate. We will also have the social partners brought in to be briefed tomorrow to bring them up to date as to the impact of the February figures, and we look forward to hearing what they have to say.

'The government obviously has the bounden duty to address this issue quickly and to do so after giving full consideration not only to the impact of the figures, as best as one can gauge them in month two when facing into a situation this year which is difficult in any case, but we also have a duty to consider the impact the various policy initiatives being considered would have and how we come forward with an overall approach which, to the greatest extent possible, while it will not be able to eliminate further casualties on the jobs front during the course of this year, will seek to maximise that position.

'Finally, the figures that were mentioned in regard to unemployment were somewhere in the region of 400,000. It appears clear that if the present rate of job loss were to continue, we are looking well beyond that, certainly in the region of 450,000 and more. We have to be cognisant of that as well.'

Cowen's government is under increasing strain, the Green Party has had a baptism of fire in government and only time will tell if the party truly was ready for government, as they maintained, or whether their own grass roots are still too deeply embedded in protest politics to take tough decisions on behalf of the country. Keeping the government together will be a major task for Cowen in this regard. The economic situation is likely to get worse, with commentators ranging from predictions of dramatic recessions that will turn around in the next few years, to those who see a coming depression or, indeed, another few who seem to envisage Armageddon. But Cowen may believe that his own position probably can't deteriorate. Most people expect a huge defeat at the local and European elections, so in 2009 Cowen knows the task ahead. If he can limit losses and ensure the country accepts

Lisbon at the second chance then he may be well placed to begin a political recovery in 2010. If he fails in either of these tasks he may find himself consigned to the history books. He has never been the type of politician to give up or give in. Based on the evidence so far, however, we have certainly not seen the best of Cowen as taoiseach and he does not take the role lightly nor does he accept defeat. Cowen will fight, that much is for sure.

WIT, WISDOM AND JUST PLAIN FUNNY

Sometimes its those bitter comments, the sharp words, thrown in an exchange that tell us more about someone's views than all the statements in the world. Here are some gems from Cowen's time in the Dáil.

While in government Cowen wonders how farmers managed under Fine Gael:

Mr Sheehan: 'I call on the minister for finance to wake up before it is too late and to give our farmers, business people and workers an opportunity to live in decent conditions. A nation's wealth is its people. Preserve them before it is too late.'

Mr Cowen: 'How did they survive in your time?'

Mr Sheehan: 'We are still there and we will be back to ensure their survival.'

Mr Cowen: 'The Lord help us.'

In November 1992 Cowen makes his assessment of Fine Gael's aims for Ireland: 'Deputy O'Keeffe's party would have us part of the UK if they had their way.'

In the same debate Cowen lets Dick Spring know he is happy with his local roads:

Dick Spring: 'Indeed, there is a new illness in this country and it is described as "pothole nervosa". Unfortunately, many people are suffering from it due to the condition of our roads in all counties. We face a housing shortage worse than any since the sixties.'

Mr Cowen: 'We have great roads and good councillors in County Offaly.'

Cowen crosses swords with McDowell and Rabbitte:

Mr Rabbitte: 'Is it not the case that one cannot devise a National Development Plan on the basis of lopping 15 per cent off specific projects, constructing buildings without a roof ...'

Mr Molloy: 'Or windows.'

Mr Rabbitte: '... or roads without an end?'

Mr Cowen: 'That was true of the deputy's friends in Eastern Europe.'

Mr Rabbitte: 'Bart Simpson is off again.'

Mr M. McDowell: 'The minister for graciousness is speaking again.'

Mr Cowen: 'The minister for self-righteousness is appearing again.'

Brian Cowen gives his assessment on Trevor Sargent during a debate on the Beef Tribunal: 'The Green McCarthyite on hallucinatory drugs.'

Cowen wonders just who Trevor Sargent is addressing:

Mr Sargent: 'I wish to address my final comments in this debate not to the ceann comhairle ... nor to those who form the government of this beautiful country. I do not even wish to use the occasion directly to address the taoiseach whose judgment and political priorities did so much to make the Tribunal necessary.'

Mr Cowen: 'Will the deputy address ET?'

Cowen is glad Fianna Fáil meets some of Sargent's requirements:

Mr Sargent: 'Fianna Fáil has had its day and in this debate we have glimpsed how that was forged and executed. It is a dying party and that is a good thing. Change and growth in human development is as necessary for the well-being of a healthy, organic democracy as it is in the intimacy of each of our lives.'

Mr Cowen: 'At least we are organic.'

As John Bruton attacks fellow Meath TD, Noel Dempsey, Cowen steps in:

Mr J. Bruton: 'The main point is that the minister has a good job and wants to keep it; that is about the sum of it.'

Mr Cowen: 'That is what the people in Meath say as well; they dealt with you at the polls.'

Cowen reckons Pat Rabbitte will be owed some expenses by the Beef Tribunal:

Mr Dempsey: 'We have had ...'

Mr Rabbitte: 'A total of 226 days.'

Mr Dempsey: '... a total of 231 days of a Tribunal. The deputy must have missed the five most important days, four when the taoiseach was present and one other.'

Mr Rabbitte: 'They were the only days I missed.'

Mr Dempsey: 'That is why his allegations did not stand up and why he has a distorted view of it.'

Mr Cowen: 'Deputy Rabbitte will have to increase his claim.'

Charlie Flanagan suggests ministers might be busy selling passports. Cowen is in no doubt what Flanagan's friends might be doing:

Mr Flanagan: 'He could be selling a passport.'

Mr Connolly: 'I resent that remark.'

Mr Cowen: 'If he was one of the deputy's colleagues he could be bankrupting the country.'

Cowen is disappointed that they didn't get the joke:

Mr Harte: 'For the information of the younger generation, as a student John Bruton identified himself with a movement aptly named by the late James Dillon, former leader of the Fine Gael Party, as the Fine Gael Young Tigers. John Bruton in his student days wanted to change Fine Gael.'

Mr Cowen: 'For dentistry reasons.'

Mr Harte: 'Perhaps Deputy Cowen would show some respect.'

Mr Cowen: 'Where is Deputy Harte's sense of humour?'

Cowen notes a move in a national institution:

Mr Ring: 'I wish the outgoing taoiseach well because his son also travelled to Westport to meet his wife. We are accustomed to having the taoiseach of the day visit Westport and I look forward to seeing John and Finola make regular visits, like the former taoiseach, to the capital of the west, Westport.'

Mr Cowen: 'Knock Marriage Bureau has now moved to Westport.'

Cowen is not impressed by the condition of the opposition seats:

Mr McCormack: 'I am glad to be here on this historic and unique occasion when a new government has been elected without the need for an election. Even when I entered the House for a second time today I almost sat beside my constituency colleague, Deputy Geoghegan-Quinn.'

Mrs O'Rourke: 'She would be delighted.'

Mr McCormack: 'While it will take some time to get used to our new seating positions, they are not much different from where we sat for the past four-and-a-half years.'

Mr N. Treacy: 'Not yet.'

Mr Cowen: 'There is a lot of dust on them.'

Cowen is impressed by his opponents poetic skills:

Mr McCormack: 'I am willing and able to learn those lessons. I made up a limerick about Deputy Cowen when minister.'

Mr Cowen: 'And it rhymed.'

In 1995 Cowen questions who the real leader is: 'To avoid future confusion in the taoiseach's question time and, given the importance of the prime minister taking responsibility for Northern Ireland, has he given any consideration to changing his name, by deed poll, to Richard Spring?'

Cowen suggests a name for John Bruton's new book:

The taoiseach (John Bruton): 'I will have to publish an edition of my collected speeches.'

Mr Cowen: 'I can give you a title: *Death in the Afternoon.*'

Cowen points out a hole in government policy:

Mr B. Ahern: 'I think I have gone far enough back to make the point that Democratic Left and its leader are totally exposed by bringing in the lowest social welfare increases in thirty years. It is not an answer to say the payments are being brought forward six weeks. That should certainly be done as well, but not at the expense of lowering the rate increase to its lowest level in thirty years.'

Mrs Geoghegan-Quinn: 'Tell that to the old-age pensioner.'

Mr Rabbitte: 'We have given a £7 increase in child benefit.'

Mr Cowen: 'What if you do not have children?'

Cowen is not sure of Pat Rabbitte's true standing in government as a super-junior minister: 'On a point of order and to ensure protocol is observed, I want to know if the hyphenated hybrid across the floor is a member of the government?'

Cowen reckons John Bruton won't be missed:

The taoiseach: 'I will be in the United States and at most four Cabinet ministers will be abroad ...'

Mr Cowen: 'That will not make any difference.'

The taoiseach: 'I ask Members of the opposition to remain quiet.'

Cowen finalises the procedures for the government in 1997:

Mr B. Ahern: 'Will the legislation to break up RTÉ be introduced shortly?'

The taoiseach (John Bruton): 'The Green Paper will be followed by a White Paper, which will be followed eventually by legislation.'

Mr Cowen: 'And then by a general election.'

Cowen points out a difficulty to John Bruton:

The taoiseach: 'This is the second time today the leader of Fianna Fáil attempted to put words in my mouth. He should not do so. I am more than adequately able to speak for myself ...'

Mr Cowen: 'If the taoiseach took his foot out of it we might be able to put words in it.'

Cowen pays credit where its due:

The taoiseach: 'The legislation is being prepared by the department of agriculture, food and forestry and is at an early stage of preparation. I am not in a position to give any information about when precisely it will be introduced. However, I understand it is being actively dealt with and that a meeting of officials is taking place today on the matter.'

Mr Cowen: 'That is dynamism – a meeting of officials.'

Cowen won't be depending on John Bruton for survival:

The taoiseach: 'The deputy is becoming an object of charity.'

Mr Cowen: 'I will be waiting a long time for £1 from the taoiseach.'

It's amazing what is allowed and what is not in Dáil debates, but Cowen tells it like it is:

An ceann comhairle (Seán Treacy): 'Perhaps Deputy Byrne will allow the business to proceed. I have called Deputy Harney.'

Mr E. Byrne: 'Hypocrisy is alive and well …'

Mr D. Ahern: 'You are the hypocrites.'

Mr Cowen: 'Political scumbag.'

An ceann comhairle: 'Let us be careful of the words we use. The word "hypocrite" is not in order.'

Mr B. Allen: 'Deputy Cowen used outrageous language and should withdraw the remark.'

Mr Cowen: 'It is accurate.'

Mr B. Allen: 'There should be some standards in the House.'

Ms O'Donnell: 'Yes, and the deputy should sit down.'

Mr B. Allen: 'Calling another deputy a scumbag is not helpful and the remark should be withdrawn.'

An ceann comhairle: 'The minister of state is not helping the chair to bring order or decorum to the House. If Deputy Harney does not proceed now I will call another deputy.'

Mr Cowen: 'Accuracy is an offence.'

Brian Cowen's assessment of minister Michael Lowry: 'I would not believe one word from the minister.'

Both sides make their feelings known:

Mr Cowen: 'On promised legislation, will the taoiseach indicate when the proposed bill on the reform of the greyhound industry will be introduced in view of the number of dead rabbits ministers have been pulling out of the hat recently?'

Mr Barrett: 'We will be putting a muzzle on the deputy shortly.'

The taoiseach: 'I believe there is a wolf loose in County Fermanagh and I suggest that the deputy go in pursuit of that animal.'

Mr Cowen: 'When will the promised legislation be introduced?'

(Interruptions.)

The taoiseach (John Bruton): 'I am aware of the deputy's interest in this and it is one that he, like myself, has acquired from his family. I am glad to be able to tell him that we believe this important legislation will be submitted early next year. It is designed to restructure the industry generally.'

Mr Cowen: 'We will have to pickle the rabbits.'

The taoiseach: 'The rabbits are well stuffed.'

Mr Cowen: 'The minister has been stuffed.'

Mr D. Ahern: 'The deputies opposite already have a stuffed rabbit in the form of the minister.'

The taoiseach: 'The stuffing is coming out of the deputy in various places.'

Brian Cowen gives an analysis of his interaction with Ivan Yates: 'He refused to answer anything. He cooed at me as if he were a lark.'

Cowen questions the Rainbow Coalition's use of resources: 'Is it good utilisation of resources to set up a task force to find out how to give tax relief to old-age pensioners, who are not in the tax net, to buy a burglar alarm?'

John Bruton had said his government would operate as if behind a pane of glass, such would be the transparency. As problems mounted for the Rainbow Coalition, Cowen makes an observation: 'The silence through the pane of glass is deafening.'

We can only wonder what Deputy Cowen was doing:

Mr B. Ahern: 'There is only one true group of founders of the state. Can I get the taoiseach's attention?'

The taoiseach (John Bruton): 'I am being distracted by Deputy Cowen.'

Mr Cowen: 'The taoiseach is easily distracted.'

Cowen picks up on a comment by Dick Spring after his constituency colleague in Offaly has finished trying to raise a constituency issue, Cowen reinforces the point before asking his question: 'When my colleague, Deputy Connolly, concluded, the tánaiste remarked, "now for something serious". That comment will be remembered by the people of Portarlington. Will the taoiseach indicate when it is intended to introduce the Bord na gCon bill?'

There was clearly no love lost between Pat Rabbitte and Brian Cowen:

Mr Cowen: 'Must we listen to the minister of state, Deputy Rabbitte, the so-called defender of agribusiness, when his irresponsible approach over the years undermined confidence in it at all times?'

An ceann comhairle: 'If Members wish to pursue this matter they must do so in accordance with the procedures of the House.'

Mr Cowen: 'Deputy Rabbitte is a disgrace. He has some neck to come into this House to defend it.'

(Interruptions.)

Mr Rabbitte: 'You are one of Albert's pups.'

Mr Cowen: 'And what are you but a rogue pig, like a few more?'

Cowen assesses where leaders' questions is going wrong to John Bruton's annoyance:

The taoiseach (John Bruton): 'Much less time is allocated to questions to the prime minister in the House of Commons and, to give credit to the opposition here, is a noisier and less informative procedure than question time to the taoiseach in this House. Much of the credit for that is due to the extensive questions asked by Deputy Harney.'

Mr Cowen: 'Better questions but worse answers.'

The taoiseach: 'The deputy should not be churlish.'

The Dáil poses as a classroom during the Rainbow government:

The taoiseach (John Bruton): 'Furthermore, since this government took office many of the workers have received a 45 per cent increase in child benefit. Also, the university fees employees with sons or daughters attending college previously had to pay have been abolished. That constitutes a benefit for the average family of approximately £2,000. In addition, the average mortgage payment by employees …'

Mr Cowen: 'Is the taoiseach responsible for that?'

An ceann comhairle: 'Deputy Cowen must restrain himself.'

The taoiseach: '… receiving payments under the Programme for Competitiveness and Work is £100 to £130 per month less than they were when Deputy Cowen's party was in office.'

Mr Cowen: 'The taoiseach is a joke.'

An ceann comhairle: 'If Deputy Cowen continues, I shall have to ask him to leave the House.'

Mr Cowen: 'The taoiseach is a joke.'

An ceann comhairle: 'The deputy heard what I said and I mean what I say here.'

Mr Cowen: 'It is on the record.'

Mr Rabbitte: 'I hope we get the créche.'

An ceann comhairle: 'If Deputy Cowen persists I must ask him to leave the House.'

Mr Cowen: 'The saviour of Packard is on the other side of the House; the defender of the working class.'

An ceann comhairle: 'Deputy Cowen, leave the House.'

Mr Rabbitte: 'That will put up the IQ.'

Mr Cowen: 'It says a lot for Minister Rabbitte's IQ.'

An ceann comhairle: 'Deputy Cowen, leave the House.'

Deputy Cowen withdrew from the Chamber.

Cowen and Rabbite are at it again in 1996:

Mr Cowen: 'The Einstein of the Left has spoken.'

Mr Rabbitte: 'Deputy Cowen is back with us again.'

Mr Cowen: 'Deputy Rabbitte used to warm up for Proinsias at one time.'

Cowen assesses John Bruton: 'The taoiseach is the "Manuel" of Irish politics – he knows nothing.'

Cowen gets a lesson in animal anatomy from Sinn Féin:

Mr Ferris: 'I do not know if this simple bill will address the problems of the industry but it will give representation to consumers on the board of An Bord Bia. I am sorry Deputy Doherty left the chamber because when I entered he said my presence reassured him we had an interest in the industry. I would like to have reminded him in his presence that I know as much if not more than he will ever learn about the industry because I have been involved in agriculture since I left school. I served on the animal health council and participated in disease eradication schemes before Deputy Doherty knew from which end of a cow milk came.'

Mr Cowen: 'I did not know it came from either orifice.'

Cowen gives his view on Labour:

The taoiseach (John Bruton): 'That is not the reason Fianna Fáil is in opposition today. It is in opposition because its partners did not trust it.'

Mr Cowen: 'The feeling was mutual.'

Cowen does not trust Nora Owen's competencies:

Mrs Owen: 'Has the deputy a good knowledge of the Greek alphabet? I did not study Greek.'

Mr Cowen: 'The minister cannot read English either.'

Cowen suggests a new record for John Bruton and his best friend Michael Lowry:

Dr Woods: 'Why is the government and the taoiseach ignoring this matter?'

An leas-cheann comhairle (Joe Jacob): 'We cannot debate this on the Order of Business.'

Mr Cowen: 'He is too busy making records on LM-FM – Charlie Landsborough, my forever friend.'

Pat Rabbitte gives his assessment of Brian Cowen's appointment as minister for health and children: 'I commend the taoiseach on his choice of somebody with the sensitive touch of Deputy Cowen to bear responsibility for the children of the nation. With his deft touch, no doubt they will be in safe hands.'

Brian Cowen is worried for John Bruton's health:

Mr J. Bruton: 'I will not detain the House further. May I ask the taoiseach ...'

Mr M. Ahern: 'We will be detained all day.'

Mr J. Bruton: 'Did I hear a voice?'

Mr Cowen: 'In your head.'

Brian Cowen is impressed that Louis Belton has learned off one of his lines:

Proinsias De Rossa: 'One of the parties currently in government introduced a private members' bill to abolish ground rents.'

Mr Belton: 'When in doubt leave them out.'

Mr Cowen: 'How long did it take Deputy Belton to learn that line?'

Brian Cowen is sarcastic about Trevor Sargent's contribution to legislation:

Mr Sargent: 'I welcome the interim decision by the minister for the environment and local government to limit the floor space of giant retail units, following my call for this in the Adjournment debate last week.'

Mr Cowen: 'Only for the deputy, it would not have happened at all.'

Brian Cowen ponders the future for Pat Rabbitte: 'If Deputy Rabbitte's party changes its name again it will become known as the "Democratic Leftovers".'

Cowen points out where Socialist Joe Higgins heart is:

Mr Higgins: 'By way of clarification, as far as I am concerned, there is no leader of the opposition in this Dáil. Deputy Bruton is not my leader.'

Mrs Owen: 'Are you it?'

Mr Higgins: 'No.'

Mr Cowen: 'Trotsky never believed in having an opposition.'

At the height of the O'Flaherty affair, Cowen expresses shock that radio might actually have people talking on it:

Mr J. Bruton: 'There are suggestions that more people will appear on radio shows.'

Mr Cowen: 'That is outrageous, more people on radio shows. How many more?'

In 2001 Cowen hits out at Pat Rabbitte again:

Mr Rabbitte: 'Will the taoiseach clarify for the social partners whether reports that the government is planning to do a U-turn on the changes to the PRSI ceiling are true?'

The taoiseach (Bertie Ahern): 'No changes are proposed in respect of employers.'

Mr Rabbitte: 'There will be no U-turn in the finance bill on this issue?'

The taoiseach: 'The rumour has not even got to me.'

Mr Rabbitte: 'What if the rumour had got to the taoiseach?'

The taoiseach: 'I would have said no because I met IBEC [Irish Business and Employees Confederation] prior to Christmas and said no.'

Mr Cowen: 'The deputy is both a creator and conveyor of rumour.'

In June 2002 Brian Cowen questions Michael Ring's loyalty to his constituency colleague to the annoyance of his opponent:

Mr Ring: 'We have been sent here today by the people. My colleague, Deputy Kenny, has been proposed as taoiseach. I make a plea to all deputies from the west and the Independents. This is their opportunity. Those in the west have been giving out for fifty years that they have been controlled by Dublin 3, Dublin 4 and Dublin 5. Deputies have an opportunity today if they want a Fine Gael taoiseach, a west of Ireland taoiseach and a Mayo taoiseach … If Members elect Deputy Kenny as taoiseach, we will reverse that.'

Mr Cowen: 'Is it Deputy Ring's contention that, like him, we should all vote for Deputy Kenny for the first time?'

Mr Ring: 'The deputy was always a nasty piece of work and he has proved it again today. He spends more time in the air than Aer Lingus.'

Mr Cowen: 'Like the Mayo forward line.'

Brian Cowen asks why Joe Higgins doesn't build a house:

An ceann comhairle: 'No legislation is promised. I call Deputy Ring.'

Mr J. Higgins: 'This is most unfair. There is legislation.'

An ceann comhairle: 'The deputy is in the House long enough to know the Standing Order. The tánaiste says legislation has not been promised.'

Mr J. Higgins: 'But how can we prevent speculators from …'

An ceann comhairle: 'The deputy should table a parliamentary question to the minister for the environment, heritage and local government.'

Mr Cowen: 'The deputy's problem is that he builds no houses at all.'

Mr J. Higgins: 'This is most unfair.'

Mr Cowen: 'That is the deputy's problem. Is he building a house at all?'

Mr D. Ahern: 'He would not pay for it.'

Mr O'Donoghue: 'Or for the bin outside the house.'

Mr Timmins: 'The government housed Deputy Higgins for a few weeks.'

In 2004 Brian Cowen gives some comedy advice free of charge to Richard Bruton:

Mr R. Bruton: 'I am sure on this important morning the taoiseach has had his breakfast of nutty gizzards ...'

An ceann comhairle: 'The deputy should raise a question on legislation. Several colleagues wish to ask questions and we have a lot to cover.'

Mr Cowen: 'Not another Bruton attempt at humour.'

Mr R. Bruton: 'The great silent one has emerged from the darkness.'

An ceann comhairle: 'Allow Deputy Bruton to continue.'

Mr Cowen: 'The deputy need not redden when he is telling a joke. He should relax, let it out and let it flow.'

An ceann comhairle: 'I ask Deputy Cowen to allow Deputy Bruton ask a question appropriate to the Order of Business.'

Mr Cowen: 'He should be a stand-up comedian for once in his life.'

Mr R. Bruton: 'On the deputy's side, comic acts seem to be the order of the day. There is little substance anyhow.'

Mr Cullen: 'The deputy should put his red nose back in his pocket.'

Mr R. Bruton: 'I wish to ask about No. 60 on the government legislative agenda where I see the tánaiste proposes protected cells.'

Mr Cowen: 'That is far better from the deputy. He is far better at that.'

Mr R. Bruton: 'Are those proposed for some of her colleagues she now wishes to get on with on the implementation of the government programme?'

Mr Durkan: 'It is a very good idea.'

Mr Cowen: 'Deputy Bruton has done well. One cannot beat gravitas.'

In February 2006 Brian Cowen reckons its time to go:

Mr Sargent: 'Did the taoiseach hear President George Bush's state of the union address in which he stated the following?

'"Keeping America competitive requires affordable energy and here we have a serious problem. America is addicted to oil which is often imported from unstable parts of the world."

'The US president used the term "addicted to oil". Now that the tánaiste has banned magic mushrooms, will the taoiseach agree that he is an oil addict and energy obese?'

Mr Cowen: 'Will someone sound the bugle and get us out of here? It is time to leave.'

Brian Cowen doubts John Gormley's word:

Mr Ring: 'May I share time with Deputy Gormley?'

Mr Kitt: 'Take a deep breath.'

Mr Gormley: 'I will be brief.'

Mr Cowen: 'Another first.'

On 28 January 2009 Cowen was not impressed by the humour on offer: 'I do not know who writes Deputy Kenny's quips, but I hope he can get somebody to improve them.'

Index